KIM,

EXTREME SUCCESS
TO YOU IN ALL YOUR
VENTURES.

"All projects I meet today fit Doug's description of eXtreme. This book is something that we all need to face the current environment with a realistic mind-set and real tools to be successful."

    —K. C. Yelin, Yelin Associates

"Perfect for the project manager looking for alternatives to process-heavy, bureaucratic management. Doug opens the door for new management strategies to deal with the rapid-fire complexity of projects in a constant state of flux."

    —Carl Pritchard, principal, Pritchard Management Associates

"Drawing on his unique combination of project management experience, technical/scientific training, and esoteric studies, Doug has given us a profoundly thoughtful and useful approach to managing the chaotic projects of our time. Easy reading on a complex topic for project executives and managers."

    —Ed Mahler, PMP, president, Project Administration Institute; and president, PMI Westchester, New York, chapter

"Our medical center has greatly benefited from the application of the concepts and principles described in this book in organizing, managing, and successfully completing our most complex and extreme projects. I highly recommend this book to anyone facing similarly challenging projects!"

    —Zed Day, CIO, University of Kentucky Medical Center

"Finally, a project management philosophy that actually supports true teamwork! This is an extremely useful book—a quantum leap forward for project teams that want their planning tools to match how they really work!"

    —Christopher M. Avery, author, *Teamwork Is An Individual Skill: Getting Your Work Done When Sharing Responsibility*

"At last! Doug has provided us with a way to break from the 'normal' waterfall world and given us a look at projects as they really are today. The book is an easy read and a necessary companion for anyone who must tackle today's fast-paced delivery cycles."

    —Donald Gardner, Gardner Project Integration Group, Ltd.

"The unpredictable is the project manager's playing field. Doug changes the rules to achieve success in the extreme! He captures the extreme need for forward and creative thinking in project management. It's an educational quantum leap in the field of project management."

—Frank P. Saladis, PMP, president, Project Imaginers Inc.

"Project managers and business owners will benefit from the eXtreme project management approach described in Doug DeCarlo's book. Moving beyond the traditional IT project management approach to an approach that acknowledges the complexity and fluid nature of business change programs—in most cases 'uncertain journeys to uncertain destinations'—will greatly increase their chances of successfully delivering business value."

—John Thorp, president, The Thorp Network Inc.;
and author, *The Information Paradox*

"'Drive along the freeway for exactly one hour, then hang a left . . .' Instructions like that court disaster, so why do we stubbornly stick to prescriptive project management that does little better? Humankind is exquisitely competent at dealing with complexity, responding to emergent information, and adapting to current reality. So why not just describe the destination and let the competent driver figure out a successful journey? General Patton famously said, 'Never tell people how to do things. Tell them what to do, and they will surprise you with their ingenuity.' Doug DeCarlo has captured that vision in this excellent volume: absorb and practice the principles and you will achieve mastery in eXtreme project management."

—Ralph White, Ph.D., MRPharmS; and director, PPMLD Ltd

"A must-read for all levels of practitioners of project management. Doug provides new insights on the most important success factor for projects: the people and how to manage the relationships."

—Theresa Kane Musser, senior director, project management,
Rigel Pharmaceuticals, Inc.

"It's refreshing to read a book by a real practitioner of non-traditional project management. Traditional project management often falls short in projects containing a great deal of uncertainty. Doug's approach, exemplified by the eXtreme methods of iteration and adaptation, fits the world of high-technology, new-product development."

—Martin Wartenberg, senior consultant, Engineering and
Information Technology, University of California

eXtreme Project Management

Using Leadership, Principles,
and Tools to Deliver Value
in the Face of Volatility

Doug DeCarlo

Foreword by James P. Lewis

Afterword by Robert K. Wysocki

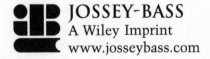

JOSSEY-BASS
A Wiley Imprint
www.josseybass.com

Published by Jossey-Bass
A Wiley Imprint
989 Market Street, San Francisco, CA 94103-1741   www.josseybass.com

Jossey-Bass books and products are available through most bookstores. To contact Jossey-Bass directly call our Customer Care Department within the U.S. at 800-956-7739, outside the U.S. at 317-572-3986 or fax 317-572-4002.

Jossey-Bass also publishes its books in a variety of electronic formats. Some content that appears in print may not be available in electronic books.

Library of Congress Cataloging-in-Publication Data
DeCarlo, Doug, 1942-
    eXtreme project management: using leadership, principles, and tools to deliver value in the face of volatility/by Doug DeCarlo; foreword by James P. Lewis; afterword by Robert K. Wysocki.—1st ed.
        p. cm.—(The Jossey-Bass business & management series)
    Includes bibliographical references and index.
    ISBN 0-7879-7409-9 (alk. paper)
  1. Project management. 2. Leadership. 3. Teams in the workplace—Management.
I. Title. II. Series.
    HD69.P75D43   2004
    658.4'04—dc22

                                                                    2004015788

Printed in the United States of America
FIRST EDITION
HB Printing   10 9 8 7 6 5 4 3 2

The Jossey-Bass
Business & Management Series

Contents

To unleashing the power within
each of us to make a difference

Foreword

It has been asserted that there are only two things of which we can be certain: death and taxes.

It isn't true.

The only thing of which we can be certain is that *certainty is impossible.*

Some quantum physicists have concluded that reality is much stranger than the strangest of science fiction. Fred Alan Wolf, one of Doug DeCarlo's favorite physicists and authors, says in his book *Mind into Matter* (2000) that atoms are believed to come into being only when we observe "them"—whatever "them" is.

And it has been known for a very long time that the process of observing atomic particles affects what takes place. If you treat a photon as a particle, it behaves like one. If you treat it as a wave, it behaves like one.

Strange.

But this applies only to those pesky little things at the quantum level, doesn't it?

No.

The same phenomenon has been found in observing interactions in groups. The observer's presence, even when the observer is behind a one-way mirror so that the group members are not aware of his or her presence, affects group behavior. Maybe the only reality is quantum, whether it be micro or macro in nature.

The reason this is important is that our worldview determines how we approach things. Human beings would like the world to be a nice, tidy place where everything is deterministic and predictable. We all know this is not the reality, but we behave as if it were, and thereby we get into trouble. In project management, for example, we guess at how long a task will take, then plug these guesses into a scheduling software program, and out comes a critical path schedule that we then treat as deterministic! It is utter nonsense, because the software creates the illusion in the minds of senior managers that we have a precision that does not exist, and these false expectations lead to trouble for all of us in the long run. No matter how you look at it, activity durations are all probabilistic, not deterministic. This is another way of saying that we are living in a quantum project world, one where change and uncertainty are the norm. What is project management like under those circumstances?

There is another thing of which I am certain. Robert Wysocki writes in the Afterword to this book that this is not your father's project management. In fact, it isn't even your father's projects. What I am certain of is that this book will either create huge excitement in the world of project management, or it will be branded heretical. After all, it may well be a paradigm shift, and as Thomas Kuhn has so convincingly shown in his book *The Structure of Scientific Revolutions* (1996), new paradigms are usually ridiculed, resisted, and suppressed. Such may be the case with *eXtreme Project Management*. Not only does DeCarlo open a new paradigm, he provides the model and road map in the form of principles, values, and tools that make it work. For projects that have a high uncertainty factor, he gives a real-world solution to the question: How do I keep the project in control and provide value in the face of volatility?

Whatever the case, you will never be the same after you read this book. No longer can you take solace in your deterministic critical path schedule, so elegant in its illusion of certainty. No longer will you be able to conclude that you know the status of the project because earned value analysis tells you the current state. No longer will you believe that a project can be managed in the sense of your being able to control it so that you can say with certainty that certain milestones will occur on certain dates.

Nope. It all depends on those little quantum gremlins—fuzzy things like information, communication, fields of influence, and other things that go bump in the night and can't be seen, heard, tasted, touched, or smelled.

In a way that's reminiscent of Margaret Wheatley's classic business management book, *Leadership and the New Science,* this book dispels many of the commonly held myths about what it takes to succeed on today's change-ridden, volatile projects.

Ilya Prigogine (1997) wrote a book entitled *The End of Certainty*. Maybe this book should be titled *The Death of Project Certainty*—but, then, was there ever any certainty in the first place? Or perhaps we should call it *The Death of Project Management As We Know It*.

Vinton, Virginia   James P. Lewis
August 2004   President
                                                           The Lewis Institute

Preface: Out of the Darkness

This is a book about a new way to understand and manage the kind of projects that the world is throwing at us today. It is the result of an eight-year journey through frustration, failure, and discovery. Until 1996, I had been preaching the gospel according to TPM (traditional project management) as I knew it, and it wasn't working. I had been so busy teaching and consulting that it had not dawned on me that the world of projects had changed and I hadn't kept up.

A New Breed of Project

At the time, I was running into more and more projects that didn't fit the mold I was brought up in. These new projects were chaotic. They featured high change, high speed, and high stress. They were expected to adjust continually to sudden competitive threats, new technologies, changes in government regulations, or late-breaking information about customer needs. Sometimes the project sponsor simply had a provocative idea that would require going back to the drawing boards (but wouldn't allow the schedule to change).

The stakes were high for many of these projects. They would have an important impact on how the organization did business—for instance, moving a line of financial products into a Web environment in order to give customers and prospects direct access.

Many of these new breed projects were also politically charged: jobs would change or be eliminated, or sacred cows would be slain. They tended to create winners and losers. Not only were such projects organizationally complex, they were often technically complex as well, being built around new technologies.

On top of all this, more and more projects I encountered were dependent on geographically dispersed teams, making communication difficult and loyalty to the project a major challenge. Within this setting, I was confronted with client organizations that practiced project du jour, launching more projects than could ever be staffed. People were spread thin, and project managers were left in the lurch.

Adding fuel to the fire, many projects did not have a strong business rationale behind them or a strong business sponsor who would champion the project and eliminate barriers. It is no wonder I saw project managers leading lives that vacillated between quiet and frantic desperation. The impact of all this was high risk, high failure rates, chronic crunch time, and poor quality of life both on and off the job.

Why would anybody want to live this way?

More of the Same Doesn't Work

Under these circumstances, how does one succeed? I thought the answer was to promote more and better planning, so that's what I preached and taught. Yet, no matter how well thought out the plan, it would be obsolete as soon as the client hit the Print key. I learned that Microsoft Project and other such packages were excellent scheduling tools for writing fiction.

In a desperate attempt to control the uncontrollable, I had jumped on the bandwagon and became a big proponent of putting in place more robust project management methodology. I advocated the use of more templates, more control procedures and policies, and conformance to strict standards, all in the hopes of getting a grip on these difficult projects. But as I found out, all this bureaucracy backfired. It simply added more documentation and paperwork and effectively put an already energy-starved project in a straitjacket, if not a coma.

I wasn't alone in this lunacy. I witnessed project offices that would, with the best of intentions, bring in new methods, templates, and software tools in their effort to bring order to chaos. Bureaucracy and monumental methodologies abounded in a futile attempt to gain control over chaos, but they served only to stifle innovation and adaptability. Things were getting worse instead of better.

Organizations realized something still wasn't working. The answer that they came up with usually turned out to be project management training. People would be sent off en masse to training and certificate programs in the hopes of teaching them how to corral these renegade projects. This made little impact as far as I could see.

Despite the chaos and uncertainty surrounding these projects, management wanted to be able to turn on a dime and at the same time demanded that project managers provide accurate projections. While all this was happening, everybody was losing sight of the bottom line. Projects that were brought in by the due date either missed the intended customer need or if they did meet it, there was no way the project would give a satisfactory return on the investment. In the panic to deliver something, people had lost sight of the main idea: the purpose of a project is to make money.

In the process, people were working fifty- to sixty-hour weeks, burning out. A better quality of life seemed inconceivable.

I had been conditioned by traditional project management dogma and therefore kept looking at the world through the wrong lens: I was trying to force-fit projects and the world into my passé paradigm. It was an insurmountable task. Looking back, I can see the face of reality watching in amusement and at times even laughing hysterically at our futile attempts to get it to obey our grandiose plans and elaborate control procedures.

I had failed to notice that a new breed of projects had been born: eXtreme projects. These eXtreme projects disobeyed the classical TPM model whether I liked it or not.

Searching for New Answers

I began to discuss my observations with clients and colleagues. The breakthrough came when I finished reading Ralph Stacey's book, *Managing the Unknowable* (1992). A week later, I had a series of catalytic insights, revelations that would change everything:

1. Traditional project management is about managing the known, but eXtreme project management is about managing the unknown.
2. You don't manage the unknown the same way you manage the known.
3. No matter what I did, I wasn't going to change the circumstances surrounding the new breed of projects. Nobody was going to. Reality rules.
4. To succeed, *I* had to adapt.

As my eyes opened, I began to see reality for what it was. I soon found that I wasn't alone. I just *thought* I was. I learned that reality was also whispering in the ears of many others, and they too were beginning to awaken. I used my workshops and keynote speeches in the United States and Canada to search out project managers who were looking for new answers. Here and there I found project managers who were gaining the courage to start throwing out the old rules and tools. They worked in a wide variety of industries (pharmaceutical, biotech, manufacturing, federal and state government, insurance, finance, health care, food and beverage, construction, entertainment) and were applying eXtreme project management principles to many types of projects (software development, e-commerce, process reengineering, new product development, business mergers, information technology rollouts, telecommunications installations, sales generation and organizational change initiatives).

Reality was also whispering to members of the project management establishment, gurus such as Jim Lewis and Bob Wysocki, who were beginning to question the effectiveness of traditional methods applied to new breed projects. Harvey Levine, a renowned expert in the use of project management tools and former president of the Project Management Institute, sent me an e-mail in which he admitted to throwing up his hands. "I'm engaged in mental gymnastics about what to do about project environments that do not allow for the highly structured approaches of traditional project management." Levine then went on to address this quandary in his recent book: *Practical Project Management: Tactics, Tips, and Tools* (2002), where he describes methods of applying traditional project management concepts in simplified ways that cut to the chase and do not require a full-blown project management culture and infrastructure.

No, I wasn't alone. The Cutter Consortium, a prestigious information and consulting firm for information technology professionals, invited me to join what is now known as their Agile Project Management practice. The practice consists of luminaries in software development who, under the leadership of Jim Highsmith, have joined together to reinvent project management practices to meet the challenges of today's change-driven, fast-paced information systems projects.

Even the construction industry, the bastion of traditional project management, was getting the word. In "Reforming Project

Management: The Role of Lean Construction," authors Gregory Howell and Lauri Koskela hold nothing back. They open their paper with these words: "Project management as taught by professional societies and applied in current practice must be reformed because it is inadequate today and its performance will continue to decline as projects become more uncertain, complex and pressed for speed. Project management is failing because of flawed assumptions and idealized theory. . ."

Encouraged by the turning of the tide, if not a sea change, I turned my journey to reinvent project management into a problem to be solved: keeping an eXtreme project in control and delivering bottom-line results in the face of volatility *and* maintain an acceptable quality of life on and off the job. This book shows you how to do this.

In solving the problem, my workshops and clients became my laboratory. Both venues enabled me to test new approaches and get instant feedback. I fine-tuned the lessons learned from one engagement for the next one and introduced them into my workshops as well. Like an eXtreme project, my model, set out in this book, was undergoing constant change. It still is. After all, in the world of extreme projects, nothing stands still.

What You Can Expect

In this book you will find proven approaches for succeeding with the new breed of eXtreme projects. These are projects that feature two or more of these dynamics:

- High stakes: failure is not an option.
- Deadlines are short.
- Innovation is paramount.
- Success is to be measured in bottom-line results.
- Bureaucracy can't be tolerated.
- Quality of life is important.

This book is not about another panacea methodology and flowchart. Rather, it presents a holistic framework built on an integrated set of principles and shared values and practices. It includes tools that accelerate performance on all three levels essential for success on very demanding projects: self-leadership, project leadership, and organizational agility. The holistic model, people centered, reality based, and business focused, takes the form of the following overall framework:

- The 4 Accelerators (principles for unleashing motivation and innovation)
- The 10 Shared Values (for building trust and confidence)
- The 4 Business Questions (for ensuring that customers receive value early and often)
- The 5 Critical Success Factors (that provide the practices, tools, and infrastructure to succeed)

eXtreme project management encompasses both hard and soft skills. Project management can no longer separate people from projects. The book combines the essential soft (interpersonal) skills with the critical eXtreme project management hard skills.

eXtreme project management is adaptable. To use it successfully, it is important that you apply the overall framework I outlined above. Then, take the element as far as it makes sense.

The Audience for This Book

eXtreme project management is for everyone. Its principles and practices can be used on any project because it strips away all nonessential project management ceremony. I have been gratified to learn that more and more people have been applying the principles and tools covered in this book to manage traditional projects that have been overburdened with excess methodology and documentation.

eXtreme projects level the playing field. This book is written for everyone who touches an eXtreme project. Everyday-business managers are now finding themselves leading, sponsoring, or participating on eXtreme projects. Projects are becoming part of their real job. And project management is becoming a survival skill. That's why I've written *eXtreme Project Management* in plain English and not in project management technobabble. Besides, those terms wouldn't apply to eXtreme project management anyway. It's a new game.

Both beginners in project management and seasoned practitioners attend my eXtreme Project Management workshops: all are looking for a better way. These include core team members as well as other stakeholders from business functions whose livelihood and departmental objectives depend on successful projects. All of them want to become more project savvy.

There is much in this book for project sponsors who will use it to gain a new understanding of their special role when sponsoring an eXtreme project and how they can best contribute to success. Program managers and heads of project offices will find material they can use to expand their project management offerings to their customer community. And the final chapter is written in the form of a briefing for senior management. As it outlines practices for becoming an agile organization, it addresses one of management's most burning questions: How can we accommodate high change and still have predictability? Senior managers who are ready to eliminate counterproductive organizational practices and replace them with a project environment that is change tolerant and adaptable to all types of projects, from traditional to extreme, will find the final chapter particularly compelling.

If you decide that eXtreme project management is for you, then this book will become your guide. A lot of it will remind you of what you already know. It will enable you to express and extend your natural talents and skills in a way that will have an even greater impact on the lives and projects of those around you. It will help you make heroes and heroines of yourself and others.

In a large sense, this book is intuitive. It is organized common sense, and that's why it works. Unlike traditional project management, eXtreme project management is built around how people are naturally motivated to work instead of being built around a sterile methodology and then trying to force people to conform.

What's Ahead

This book has four parts. Part One describes the reality we face today and explains in greater detail why this reality requires a new mind-set based on the premise that radical change and uncertainty are the norm, not the exception. Part Two focuses on the leadership skills that are critical to success on eXtreme projects, including self-leadership. The job of the eXtreme project manager is to gain and sustain the commitment of others. The successful project manager is able to unleash motivation and innovation, establish the trust and confidence to succeed, and ensure that the customer receives value each step of the way. All of these critical outcomes call for leadership. When eXtreme projects fail, it is most often due to a lack of leadership or poor leadership skills.

Part Three provides a thorough grounding in the flexible project model for eXtreme projects, covering project start-up to project turnover. The model provides just enough discipline to allow people the freedom to innovate and to get work done. The model is iterative and consists of four cycles: Visionate, Speculate, Innovate, Reevaluate, and one final element, Disseminate.

Part Four provides practical guidance on managing the project environment. Communication is critical on eXtreme projects, which require that information be available at any time to anyone who needs it. eXtreme projects also require an agile organization, that is, a change-tolerant, project-friendly culture that recognizes and supports the special needs of different projects from traditional to eXtreme.

The eXtreme Tools and Techniques section at the end of the book is a collection of tools and techniques for use with eXtreme projects. Most of them focus on the essential soft skills of eXtreme project management for improving self-mastery, interpersonal skills, and team leadership and facilitation skills.

No Excuses Project Management

To succeed on today's extreme projects, you can't wait for the organization to get sane, become project friendly, and make your life easer. That would be insane to think so. If you don't believe me, try explaining to your sponsor or customer that the project failed because they doubled the scope, cut the time line in half, and continually made changes to the plan.

This book will help you succeed under any circumstances, even if it means that you decide you have to walk away from an impossible project. What greater success than to be true to yourself?

If there's one thing I've learned after being around projects for thirty-five years, and in particular the past eight years, eXtreme project management boils down to just one word: courage. Courage to do *things right*. And courage to do the *right things*.

The principles and tools in this book will get you up to speed. But only you can get up the courage to use them. You don't need permission from anybody to begin to apply this approach and to make a difference.

Burnsville, North Carolina   Doug DeCarlo
August 2004

Acknowledgments

Many people contributed to this book both directly and indirectly. A handful of people influenced me at the most fundamental level through their writings or in our conversations. They were willing to question current dogma and provided a forum that enabled me to open my mind to new possibilities. My heartfelt thanks go to friends Tobi and Bruce Andrews and my late great friend and business partner, Bob Forest. I'm indebted to Byron Katie for teaching me to cooperate with reality and to "love what is"; Meg Wheatley for her groundbreaking book, *Leadership and the New Science;* Ralph Stacey for his provocative book, *Managing the Unknowable;* Goleman, Boyatzis, and McKee for writing *Primal Leadership*, which helped me to further understand the profound importance of the leader's role in managing the emotional well-being of the organization; Gerald Weinberg for his relentlessly insightful writings; Marianne Williamson's book, *A Return to Love*, which taught me that the real meaning of a miracle is a change in one's perception of any situation; and Viktor Frankel for his book, *Man's Search for Meaning*, for reminding me that the ultimate freedom is our ability to choose our attitude in any situation.

I thank KC Yelin, founder of ICS Group, and Ron Yelin for hiring me into their project management consulting and training firm, giving me my first job in the profession. KC turned out to be my de facto mentor and role model and brought me to the realization that good project management is organized common sense.

There is a cadre of thought leaders to whom I am indebted. At the top is Jim Highsmith, who carries high the banner of agile project management and is an endless font of ideas and insights. As one of the founders of the Agile Alliance and as director of the Cutter Consortium's practice in agile project management, Jim is a thought leader who has played a leading role in reshaping how the world practices project management—not only in the arena of software development but for just about any kind of project. Jim is also the prime mover behind the Agile Project Management Group, which is dedicated to supporting and promoting the agile project management movement. His work has influenced me from the inside out.

I am indebted to the Cutter Consortium for providing a forum for leading-edge thinkers and practitioners of agile project management. Those whose philosophy and work have especially filtered into my bloodstream include Kent Beck, Tim Lister, Tom DeMarco, Ken Schwaber, Rob Thomsett, and Ed Yourdon.

I am indebted to Jim Lewis and Bob Wysocki for encouraging me to write this book. Both are leaders in the world of traditional project management, yet willing to question current practices and foster new thinking.

I'm very grateful for those who have stepped out of the box and had the courage to provide me with an audience for my writings, conference presentations, and keynote speeches on the subject of eXtreme project management: Eric Welsh and Carina Kuhl of ProjectWorld USA; David Barrett of ProjectWorld Canada along with AITP (Association of Information Technology Professionals); the many PMI (Project Management Institute) chapters as well their e-project management and information systems special interest groups; DIA (Drug Information Association); HIMSS (Healthcare Information Management and Systems Society); and ProjectConnections.com, Villanova University, through Chuck Arnao.

Special thanks to friends, clients, and colleagues who encouraged me, provided feedback, and helped me refine my ideas: Mike Aucoin, Wes Balakian, DeAnna Burghart, Omer Bakkalbasi, Victoria Bradley, Zed Day, Randy Englund, Gary Heerkens, Bill Jacobson, Michael Kaplan, Joan Knutson, Mignon Lawless, Harvey Levine, Jim McDonough, Sara McKenzie, Sharon MacLaughlin, Ravi Mohan, Theresa Musser, Marina Spence, Frank Saladis, John Turanin, Witold Urbanowicz, Cinda Voegtli, Marty Wartenberg, Ralph White, and Steve Weidner.

Several people collaborated directly with me by contributing content for this book. I thank Avon D'Cunha, Deborah Duarte and Carl Pritchard for their expert contributions on the vital subjects of virtual teams and real-time communication. Scott Edgett's help was invaluable in reviewing my early drafts on calculating return on investment, as were John Thorp's comments regarding how to map project benefits.

In preparing the final manuscript, I was blessed to have been assigned a very talented editor, Alan Shrader. Alan made significant improvements to the organization and flow of the material I first drafted, and was relentless in getting me to question, refine, and fill in the blanks in my eXtreme project management model so that readers could get the full picture and be better able to understand and apply the principles, values, and tools that make up this book. Mary Garrett and Beverly H. Miller deserve a round of thanks for their attention to quality and detail and for keeping this project on track, never letting it turn into one of those eXtreme projects.

Last and far from least, I thank my life partner, Radavie Riom, for encouraging me every step of the way down to the finish line, for acting as a sounding board day and night, and for willingly giving up weekend after weekend after weekend as I wrote this book. Her presence has helped me to explore and expand in all directions.

The Author

Doug DeCarlo is principal of the Doug DeCarlo Group (www.doug decarlo.com). He works with organizations that undertake projects in demanding environments: settings that feature high speed, high change, and high uncertainty, where the mind-set and bureaucratic approaches of traditional project management often stifle performance and morale.

His work has earned him international recognition as a consultant, keynote speaker, trainer, coach, facilitator, and columnist. He helps clients to produce immediate and sustainable results by applying proven practices in self-mastery, project management, team leadership, and grassroots organizational change. His approach to project management and self-mastery is set out in Chapter Seven in the landmark *The World Class Project Manager: A Professional Development Guide,* by James Lewis and Robert Wysocki.

DeCarlo is also a senior consultant on agile project management for the Cutter Consortium and an advisory board member and columnist for projectconnections.com, and he has served on the advisory board of ProjectWorld as well as being a member of the project management advisory group for George Washington University.

DeCarlo is noted for his innovative, motivational, and entertaining keynote speeches in which he plays live percussion instruments to illustrate the dynamics of today's eXtreme projects.

eXtreme Project Management

Introduction
Into the Light

The world of project management has changed radically, totally, and irreversibly. It is not just that today's projects don't share even a family resemblance with yesterday's. It is that the world in which projects are managed has changed irrevocably. To explain what I mean, let's consider two brief examples of projects: a traditional project and what I call an eXtreme project.

Here is an example of a traditional project. As it happens, it was completed over the course of several months in 2002, but it would have looked pretty much the same in 1982 or 1972.

> The food technology department of a consumer snack food company had just concluded its annual survey of its manufacturing plants. Based on the survey, senior management determined that the Miami facility would need to replace one of its manufacturing lines in order to meet capacity requirements for the Asian market and accommodate two new consumer products. This was to be the third major upgrade that the plant experienced in five years. The two previous upgrades had required an average of four months from start to full production.
>
> The Miami plant manager appointed Harry Galt as the project manager responsible for installing the new line and gave him the blueprint for the new system. Galt had participated in the two previous projects and quickly assembled a team. Since there was little turnover of personnel at the plant, he was able to recruit six people who had participated on the two previous projects to join his eight-person team. Galt was also pleased that five members of the project team would be available full time since the project would take place

1

during the slow season. In the kickoff meetings, which went smoothly, the team realized that the current project was similar to the earlier projects and they could use most of the documentation from the earlier projects, which included a project plan broken into phases and with three levels of detail. The team was also confident about the technology and the vendor, which were tried and true from the two earlier projects. The contract was for a fixed price and was basically a boilerplate of the previous two, requiring no negotiation. The third installation was scheduled for a six-month start-to-finish time frame, even though the earlier projects took four months to complete.

As the project progressed, Galt's team received a request to improve throughput by 20 percent to accommodate that latest sales forecast. The request came well in advance of installation and was easily accommodated with no impact on the schedule, which had a two-month buffer built in.

This is the kind of project that traditional project management (TPM) evolved to deal with. The project manager received a clear statement from the customer as to what was wanted, when it was wanted, and how much the customer was willing to pay for it. The i's were all dotted and the t's were all crossed. All the correct forms were filed and all the boxes filled with the information requested. Moreover, the customer did not change his mind halfway through the process. And the methods for achieving the results were proven and well understood. No new technology was involved. And the world it was dealing with experienced change as incremental—not always smooth and not always predictable, but taking small baby steps.

Now let's look at a recent project that was characterized by speed, uncertainty, rapidly changing requirements, and high stakes:

A large financial services company was steadily losing its position among upscale customers: individuals with a high net worth of $1 million and above. The organization had slipped from third to fifth place in market share in two years and would drop to number six within months at the current rate. The *Wall Street Journal* had even run a feature story on the organization's plight.

Senior management decided to revamp the entire portfolio of financial offerings for the high-net-worth market. A critical project in the new program was to upgrade the company's e-commerce capability in order to improve the customer experience, reported to be significantly below par according to third-party research. Sarah

Niebel, an experienced manager in the information technology department, was appointed to head a project to upgrade the organization's e-commerce capability. Her assignment was to create a revamped Web site to improve the customer experience in four months, about half the time it would normally take. (Marketing was already starting to promote the new portfolio and the new customer-friendly e-commerce site.)

Realizing she had been handed a fuzzy goal—What exactly did "improve the customer experience" mean?—Niebel tried to get clarification. As she worked to set up meetings and get clear guidelines, she realized that the project had no clear-cut sponsor. Marketing, sales, and information technology all wanted a voice in the project but didn't seem to want responsibility. As a result, Niebel was left at the mercy of conflicting interests. She had no one to go to for funding or needed staff resources, or to prioritize and sign off on requirements for the new e-commerce capability. She also realized that to get the revamped site up and running would represent a quantum leap in new technology. She managed to assemble a team, but the project seemed to rank low on everyone's list of priorities. (Her team members were spread among several projects and working upwards of fifty to sixty hours per week.)

As she worked to push the project forward, the requirements came under constant change and debate in response to newly discovered customer needs, new competitive offerings, and the latest government regulations. Management needed a win, but marketing, sales, and finance couldn't agree on the product mix. After sixty days, nearly half of the project team had either been assigned to other projects or had left the organization. The four-month deadline came and went as the project limped along, with each week's delay costing the organization an estimated $1.5 million in lost business in addition to possible bad press.

This is a clear example of an eXtreme project:

- Requirements changed overnight.
- The project involved new technology and new methods that no one had tried before.
- The deadline was half the normal time.
- Quality of life during the project was likely to be nonexistent.
- Halfway through the project, the customer suddenly decided he wants something else.
- The environment surrounding the project was chaotic and unpredictable, and it was changing discontinuously.

Under these conditions, innovation is at a premium. And this environment is becoming the norm. Sara J. McKenzie, senior program director at Sepracor, says, "This is the kind of project management reality that I am engaged in, and the very reason that I have drifted away from Project Management Institute with their base in traditional approaches."

How eXtreme Projects Are Different

TPM is about managing the known. eXtreme project management is about managing the unknown. Traditional projects are slow and stable and lend themselves to orderly planning. eXtreme projects are chaotic, messy, and unpredictable; speed and innovation are critical, and planning is chaotic and just-in-time.

eXtreme Projects Require Managing the Unknown

A major difference between a traditional project and an eXtreme project has to do with the level of predictability surrounding the undertaking. Since eXtreme projects live in turbulent environments that feature high change and high uncertainty, the project requirements are constantly shifting throughout the venture in response to internal as well as external factors, such as competitive moves, new technology, shifts in customer needs, changes in regulatory requirements, and general economic and political conditions. Not only is change the norm, change *is* the project.

Heed the words of Frank Saladis, former president of the New York City chapter of the Project Management Institute (PMI®). Frank and I were doing a joint presentation on the subject of extreme projects at ProjectWorld, a leading conference and trade show for project managers and their teams. Frank stood up to speak and boiled it down to the essence: "Extreme projects are about planning, deplanning, and replanning."

eXtreme Projects Are Chaotic and Messy

An eXtreme project is messy. That's reality. Reality happens while plans are being made, and it can't be changed. It has a mind of its own. Reality rules. All we can change is how we respond to it. This is so fundamental and essential to remember that if you are in charge of an eXtreme project, I strongly suggest that you tattoo the phrase "Reality Rules" on your forehead and do so in reverse letters. That way in the morning, when you are shaving or putting on your makeup, you have an indelible reminder of this lifesaving, guiding principle for eXtreme project managers.

eXtreme Projects Require Speed and Innovation

With constantly changing requirements, rapidly evolving technology, and a competitive landscape that shifts daily, eXtreme projects move forward at high speed. They typically involve time lines that seem impossible to meet. If you take the time to plan each step of the way carefully, the project will usually be irrelevant by the time you are done. The problem or opportunity it addressed will have morphed into a new, perhaps unrecognizable, shape. For an eXtreme project, since change is constant (and stability is the exception), yesterday's plan is about as fresh as last month's tunafish sandwich. An eXtreme project is like a car with the throttle stuck down and no brakes.

Innovation is critical in eXtreme projects. In fact, it is more than critical; innovation is what eXtreme projects are all about. In the extreme sense of the word, innovation means more than coming up with new or breakthrough products and services. It also includes coming up with innovative processes and methods to manage the projects that turn out those winning products and services. You can't cut a twelve-month time line in half by working twice as hard. That's the outmoded worldview. In eXtreme project management, innovation is both the means and the end.

eXtreme Projects Require Just-In-Time Planning

An eXtreme project is a process of discovering what is truly wanted through trial and error. It's not unlike a heat-seeking missile in search of a moving target. The eXtreme project is self-correcting because you don't have time to run every decision up the hierarchy. And even if you did, the people upstairs are not often in touch. Team members need to make frequent and on-the-spot decisions and in the light of rapidly changing requirements or circumstances.

In contrast, the goal of traditional projects is to produce the planned result and do so with efficiency by minimizing variances to the original plan. Optimization and efficiency are the goal. The project team drives toward the planned result by following prescribed procedures and policies. Elaborate control measures are often put in place so that the project does not deviate excessively from the approved baseline of cost, quality, or schedule. Rigorous change management practices are enforced in order to achieve efficiency and be true to the original baseline. When applied to an eXtreme project, the traditional approach is the equivalent of attempting to drive full speed ahead on an expressway by navigating through the rear-view mirror.

In the case of an eXtreme project, which by nature is messy, we are focused not on efficiency but on effectiveness. We want to produce the desired result, which may bear little resemblance to the original target. The iron triangle of traditional project management—bring it in on time, on quality, and on budget—is not relevant under extreme conditions. Why? Because the definition of on-time, quality, and budget typically change many times throughout the project.

Ready, Fire, Aim

A traditional project looks like a waterfall, representing neatly cascading, sequentially flowing Gantt charts with eight levels of detail (Figure I.1). Waterfall project management works well under conditions of relatively low speed and low uncertainty. It is well suited for traditional construction and engineering projects and others that have a well-defined, concrete goal and a proven path to get there. The shutdown process for a nuclear power plant and the project to put up a new McDonald's restaurant are well represented by the waterfall model (Figure I.1).

In contrast, eXtreme projects, characterized by changing requirements, dead ends, unpredictability, messiness, speed, and innovation, do not fit the waterfall model. An extreme project looks more like a despondent strand of overcooked spaghetti (Figure I.2).

Figure I.1. Traditional Project Mental Model

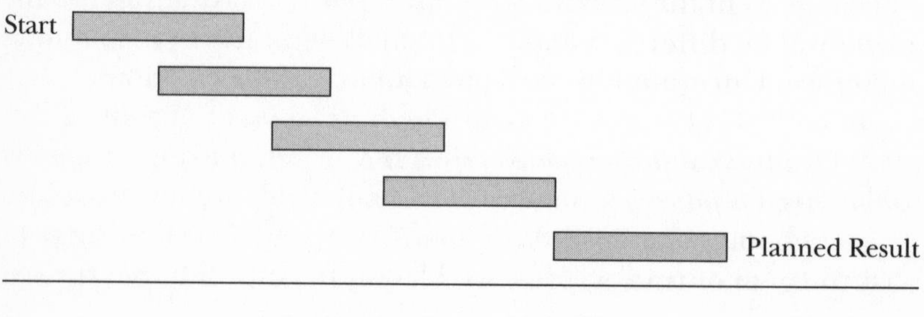

Start

Planned Result

Figure I.2. eXtreme Project Mental Model

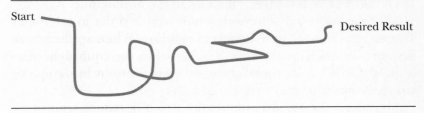

Start

Desired Result

If you want a definition of an extreme project, here's the one I use with clients.

> An extreme project is a complex, high-speed,
> self-correcting venture during which people interact
> in search of a desirable result under conditions of
> high uncertainty, high change, and high stress.

Traditional projects follow the classic model of ready, aim, fire. In contrast, on eXtreme projects, we shoot the gun and then attempt to redirect the bullet. This is the reality that business managers, project managers, and their teams of professionals face. The bureaucracy, rules, and mechanistic practices that are characteristic of traditional projects backfire on eXtreme projects, where uncertainty, improvisation, and spontaneity replace predictability, command, and control. This suggests that we apply a different approach to planning and managing an eXtreme project, one that is change tolerant and adaptable, or, as some pundits like to say, agile.

How eXtreme Project Management Is Different

In eXtreme project management, we recognize that the plan has to change to fit the world as we know it right now. Chances are the world will be different tomorrow, and so will the plan. Change is the norm. Uncertainty is certain. Stability is an aberration.

- *Traditional project management is past oriented. eXtreme project management is future oriented.* Jim Highsmith sums it up in his award-winning book, *Adaptive Software Development* (2000). He points out that the goal of traditional project management is to get it right the first time; the goal of agile or adaptive project management is to get it right the last time. That's when it counts.

The ready-fire-aim approach is indicative of a fast-paced, highly volatile experience. The focus is always on the customers, whose active involvement is essential. They are the primary stakeholders and, with the project manager, are constantly redirecting the project toward a goal that is both changing and coming into clearer focus as each iteration is completed. To survive in this dynamic environment, the team must anticipate change by using a minimalist approach to planning the next iteration. If you don't know the future, why waste time planning it! The eXtreme project management approach does not. At the same time, eXtreme project management is designed to deliver the expected business value for the time and money invested. All of this is ensured because the eXtreme project is under the watchful eye of the customer in collaboration with the extreme project manager.

• *Traditional project management makes people the servants of the process. eXtreme project management makes the process the servant of people.* Traditional project management is a set of practices, procedures, and policies where people become servants of the process. Gantt charts, issues logs, status reports, and other processes are used to control the activities of people. eXtreme project management is based on the premise that people are crucial to the success of the project: thoughts, emotions, and human interactions are the wellspring of creativity. If the team is demoralized, the project will suffer in terms of schedule, quality, and budget. Thus, eXtreme project management focuses seriously on quality of life and puts people in control of the process rather than the other way around.

• *Traditional project management is about centralizing control of people, processes and tools. eXtreme project management is about distributing control.* Traditional project management tries to minimize change and tends to keep tight control over policies and procedures. eXtreme project management recognizes that you don't manage the unknown and unpredictable the same way you manage the known and predictable. You are wasting your time trying to change reality to fit a project plan. On an eXtreme project properly run, no one is in control. Instead, everyone is in control.

• *Traditional project management tries to take charge of the world (things, people, schedule). eXtreme project management is about taking charge of yourself, your attitudes, your approach to the world.* Traditional project management focuses on making, people, budgets, and schedules conform to the plan. eXtreme project management anticipates change by using a just-enough minimalist approach to planning and distributing control. This requires that project managers first focus on themselves by adopting a mind-set that is compatible with, even thrives on, constant change and innovation.

- *Traditional project management is about managing. eXtreme project management is about leading.* The hallmarks of traditional project management—working to plan, minimizing change, keeping tight control—are essentially managerial tasks. Traditional project managers are taskmasters, a style that is more appropriate for stable projects. On eXtreme projects, where planning is minimal and change is constant and unpredictable, the key tasks are those of leadership. As we will see, good process leadership on an eXtreme project will enable people to discover the best solution and to continually self-correct.

Changing the Paradigm

For today's high-speed, change-driven projects, the traditional world of project management belongs to the past. The paradigm must shift. Any company that doesn't make that shift is sure to be lost in the rush. Consider the realities of today's business environment and where eXtreme project management fits into the picture (Figure I.3).

The two quadrants on the left of the figure represent the world of traditional project management, a discipline that was born out of the construction and engineering industries. Here, the approach to project management was closely aligned with the Newtonian world of science and physics. The Newtonian worldview is based on determinism and reductionism, a paradigm that says the world can be dissected into a predictable set of cause-and-effect relationships among the parts. It's left brain, linear, logical thinking at its best. It's analytical. This mechanistic view has led to the conclusion that we can plan with confidence. It gave rise to what continues to be called waterfall project management. On the other side is the right brain, which works in a nonlinear way. Its process is relational and random and solves problems using systems thinking.

In the land of eXtreme projects, the plan is not a prediction. And unlike in the Newtonian world, eXtreme projects obey the laws

Figure I.3. Business as Unusual

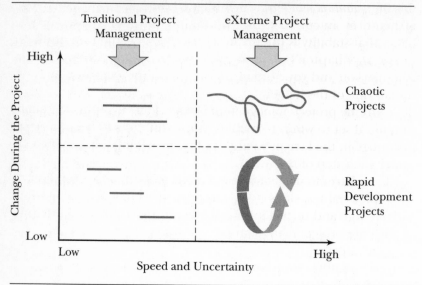

of the new science: the world of quantum physics, self-organizing systems, and chaos theory.

Many businesses have only recently realized the pain of not having a project management process in place and are struggling to adopt the traditional practices represented by the Software Engineering Institute (SEI), the PMI®, and others. Unfortunately, these businesses are most likely wasting their time. According to Bob Kulin, PMP® (Project Management Professional), a program manager of pension implementation, "I always believed that the project management profession is doing itself a disservice if it doesn't recognize that many, if not most, projects don't follow the guidelines set forth by the Project Management Institute's Project Management Body of Knowledge." It's time to awaken to the realities of today's business environment and discover the way to survive and thrive under the new circumstances:

- Failure is not an option.
- Speed, innovation, and profitability count.
- Bureaucracy is to be avoided.
- Quality of life is important.

A new mind-set is needed to succeed on extreme projects. I call this the *quantum mind-set,* which is based on the reality that change is the norm. In contrast, the Newtonian mind-set is based on the belief that stability is the norm. I describe the quantum mind-set in full in Chapter One and give you an opportunity to assess whether you and your organization fall on the quantum or Newtonian side of the ledger.

eXtreme project management is the vehicle that puts the quantum mind-set to work. It enables its practitioners to keep projects in control in the face of volatility, while providing value to the customer each step of the way.

The eXtreme project management model consists of a set of principles, values, skills, tools, and practices that are compatible with change and uncertainty and form the soft and the hard glue of extreme project management:

- 4 Accelerators—principles that unleash motivation and innovation
- 10 Shared Values—A set of values that establish trust and confidence among stakeholders
- 4 Business Questions—questions that, when addressed, ensure that customers receive value early and often
- 5 Critical Success Factors—the skills and tools and organizational support essential for success

The eXtreme project management model loads the deck in favor of success because it is holistic, people centered, humanistic, business focused, and reality based. It is new, it is exciting, and it works.

This is definitely not your father's or mother's project management. It is a radical shift in thinking about projects and their management. In the typical eXtreme project, there is a rough idea about the goal and little or no idea about how to achieve that goal. Obviously the traditional linear approach to project management just won't work. For one thing, the standard tools, templates, and processes of traditional project management are almost useless to the eXtreme project manager. Rather, the eXtreme project manager, with the help of the customer, chooses one or more directions that seem probable, learns from what happens, and recalibrates for the next cycle. This constant recalibration occurs several times as the customer and the project manager look for convergence toward the stated goal, which in all likelihood has changed as a result of learning and discovery that took place in earlier iterations.

Managing an eXtreme project can be a dynamic and exhilarating challenge for the team when it means being first to market, unseating the number one competitor, winning back a large customer, or turning around a dying product line all while working decent hours with time and energy left for personal life. Managing an eXtreme project does not have to be a soul-destroying slog against reality—if you abandon traditional project management and adopt the quantum mind-set. This is the subject of the next chapter.

The New Reality

In the Introduction, I described the need for changing the paradigm of project management for today's high-speed, change-driven world. This paradigm shift needs to happen on two levels. On one level, we need to change the model of what project management is all about. On a deeper, more fundamental level, we need to change our own perceptions of reality and our relationship to it. The two chapters in Part One address both levels.

Chapter One examines the paradigm shift at the deeper level, in ourselves. Virtually all management theory and practice, whether related to project management or not, is based on the mind-set that reality is stable, predictable, and knowable. The quantum mind-set, in contrast, is based on the reality that change is normal and unpredictable.

Coping with an eXtreme world requires us to start at the beginning by changing our own mind-sets. I describe the quantum mind-set in full and provide an opportunity to assess how well your own beliefs and practices, and those of your organization, align with the quantum mind-set.

In an eXtreme world where change is normal and unpredictable, the standard tools, templates, and processes of traditional project management are almost useless. Chapter Two offers a set of principles, values, and practices that are compatible with change and uncertainty—a paradigm shift concerning what projects are all about. The eXtreme model for success takes the focus away from templates and tools and places it squarely on leadership, the only thing that can keep us on course in the face of rapid, unpredictable change.

Developing a Quantum Mind-Set for an eXtreme Reality

We are facilitators of disorder.
MARGARET WHEATLEY,
LEADERSHIP AND THE NEW SCIENCE

Just like a software package, our brains come with default settings—
a mind-set. By *mind-set,* I mean a set of beliefs and assumptions
about how the world works. This is our internal programming. In
this chapter I take a closer look at the eXtreme, or quantum, mind-
set, contrast it sharply with the Newtonian worldview, and highlight
the absurd project management behavior that results when one attempts to apply Newtonian thinking in a quantum world.

Here is a quick review of the key ideas to keep in mind:

- By quantum mind-set, I mean a worldview that is compatible
  with change and unpredictability. The quantum mind-set
  assumes that change is the norm.
- The Newtonian or linear mind-set assumes that stability is
  the norm.
- eXtreme projects need to be managed with a predominantly
  quantum mind-set.
- Applying a quantum mind-set to a traditional project will
  ensure a poor result.
- Applying a Newtonian mind-set to an eXtreme project will
  wreak havoc.

Unlike the Newtonian cause-and-effect mind-set and related principles, eXtreme project management recognizes that although goals are achievable, how we get there is unpredictable. Hence, adaptability is more important than predictability. And since outcomes are not predicable, this paradigm shift in mind-set opens the door to applying the right-brained principles of quantum mechanics to project management. Quantum mechanics is the study of motion in the subatomic realm. This domain deals with unpredictability and the forces and laws that lie beneath and beyond the physical world. The Newtonian world is about predictability and how the physical world works. The quantum world is about patterns and probability and how the subatomic world of particles and energy works.

Adaptability is more important than predictability.

A critical component of the quantum world is Heisenberg's uncertainty principle, which says that with subatomic particles such as electrons, we cannot know both the particle's precise position and its momentum (or velocity). The more precisely we measure its position, the less we can know about its momentum, and vice versa. The uncertainty principle does not state that it is hard to measure both simultaneously or that we don't have good enough instruments. It states that we cannot do so in principle because the act of measurement affects what we measure.

In the Newtonian world, we can measure these two quantities as precisely as we please (more or less). In other words, a traffic officer can point a radar gun at your car and tell exactly where the car is and its precise speed, simultaneously. Imagine a traffic officer who lived in a subatomic world. He could never issue a speeding ticket. If he measured a car's speed, he wouldn't know where it was (and so couldn't know it's in a 35 mph zone). If he pinpointed exactly where a car was (in the 35 mph zone), he couldn't measure its speed. When dealing with eXtreme projects, we have to realize that a similar uncertainty principle applies. The more we try to control one aspect of a project, the less control we will have over others.

Is There a Method to Your Madness?

The importance of adopting a quantum mind-set to eXtreme projects is illustrated by a story.

While having lunch in the serene and sylvan setting of the Sterling Farms Golf and Country Club in Stamford, Connecticut, my stomach started to knot up. On this sweltering summer day, my chicken caesar salad ended up mostly untouched. It wasn't the warm creamy dressing and the soggy croutons that were getting to me. It was the scenario being described by my luncheon guest, Tammy. Tammy (not her real name) was the head of software application development for a high-flying and very visible dot.com company. We were talking about project management when I asked her to tell me about the major challenges in running projects in a dot.com environment. She described a "typical" project environment, one that would make chaos seem like a snooze under the umbrella on a quiet beach.

Marketing, sales, finance, application development, customer support, network services, database management, senior management, and eight outside vendors were all interacting with one another, she told me, and mostly in an ad hoc way. On top of that, the information technologies they were working with were also in a state of flux. Moreover, this dot.com wasn't the only game on the net. So on top of it all, Tammy's application development group had to react to what the competition was up to. Change was frequent and relentless. Time frames and budget didn't mean anything. And management wanted accurate forecasts. The impact of these dynamics made for a stress-filled workplace and an unfulfilled workforce.

I was sure that all this frustration had to overflow into everyone's family life as well. A toxic scenario.

Six months later I again had lunch with Tammy. This time there was no time to enjoy a sylvan setting, so we ate in the employee cafeteria. Since the day of our first lunch together, the company had gone public, and there was heightened pressure for accountability and predictability. To help get things under control and to establish some project management standards, a new software tool had been brought in, along with a time reporting system. Tammy related that the training on the software tool was thorough and that the vendor provided a support person who had been on site for the past three months. An experienced project manager was also recruited to head the project office and establish best practices.

Yet this was not a happy place. There was little dot.calm at this dot.com. In fact, the increased project reporting structure was alienating people and beginning to cause some to leave the company.

Why was the new software and new methodology not producing results? The new scheduling tool was based on the old Newtonian mind-set and model of the world, which assumes a linear (cause-and-effect-like) relationship among tasks and events. We recognize this as the waterfall model, which reflects the time-honored plan-and-control approach to getting results. As we have seen, this model is a useful tool for certain kinds of projects—those that have a well-defined, concrete goal and a proven path to get there. But the waterfall model was not well suited to Tammy's dot.com project endeavors, which feature high velocity, high change, and high uncertainty. Tom Tarnow, former vice president and head of project management organization at Morgan Stanley Dean Witter, says, "Standardized project management approaches will likely fail in an entrepreneurial and individual-oriented business setting." Those cascading, sequentially flowing Gantt charts with eight levels of detail fail to capture the dynamics of the dot.com world of projects.

Linear Lunacy

To apply the linear and classical (plan and control) approach to an eXtreme project is lunacy, which is why people in Tammy's organization were so unhappy. The good news is that organizations that do this sooner or later recognize that it's not working. But the bad news is that they typically pick the wrong cure. Usually this process begins with the observation that not everyone is on board with the newly released software tools and the requisite project methodology. At this point, Newtonian-minded management leaps to the conclusion that if everybody were following the same rules, then there would finally be consistent and predictable results, as if cranking out projects was like stamping out cookies in a factory. "We need to bring in more discipline" is the cry. In other words, the prevailing management philosophy is, "If it's not working, let's do more of it."

Remember Heisenberg's uncertainty principle: it's not that measurement of a subatomic particle's position and momentum requires lots and lots of high-tech measurement equipment and rigorous training to use it. It states that such measurement is physically impossible. So it is with eXtreme projects and the quantum mind-set. If we adopt a quantum mind-set, we can see that eXtreme projects by their very nature cannot be forced into the Newtonian straitjacket of project schedules and Gantt charts. So millions of dollars are misspent on training programs that teach and certify people in traditional project management approaches, which backfire on eXtreme projects. I refer to this as linear lunacy, an advanced form of project management insecurity that ultimately leads to what I call *totoolitarinanism* (pronounced *tow-tool-ah-tarian-ism*).

> *Millions of dollars are misspent on training programs that teach and certify people in traditional project management approaches, which backfire on eXtreme projects.*

Totoolitarianism manifests itself in the form of heightened project governance through which tools and rules from above are substituted for spontaneity and decision making from below. Totoolitarianism often manifests itself as the project office, which sets project policy. As Margaret Wheatley, renowned author of *Leadership and the New Science* (1992), pointed out in a speech, "The only difference between the word 'policy' and 'police' is just one letter of the alphabet." People intuitively know this. As a result, the term *project office*, which smacks of bureaucracy, is being replaced in some circles by the more project-friendly name of *project support group,* or the innocuous-sounding *Project Management Organization* (PMO).

PMOs can be a valuable asset to an organization when they encourage and support a suite of approaches that can be matched to the type of project at hand. Unfortunately, most try to enforce adherence to a single set of tools, and these tools do not work with eXtreme projects.

Newtonian Neurosis and the eXtreme Project Manager

Psychologist Carl Rogers uses the term *cognitive dissonance* to refer to the discrepancy between our mental model of how we see or want the world to be versus the reality of the situation. For example, the reality is that an eXtreme project is a squiggly line. It looks

like the strand of despondent spaghetti I mentioned earlier. But
most classically trained project managers have quite a different
mental model, albeit unconscious, of what a project should look
like. They want it to look like this:

Start ————————➤ End

This is solid, left-brained linear thinking at its best and is the
underlying cause of Newtonian neurosis: the compulsive need to
make an eXtreme project into a straight line. Tim Lister, senior
consultant and fellow of the Cutter Consortium, refers to project
managers who think this way as "flatliners." Flatliners relentlessly
attempt to bludgeon every squiggly line project into submission
through the excessive use of project management tools, rules, templates, policies, and procedures.

Sooner or later, flatliners realize it's not working. They typically
complain that the organization is not properly supporting them
and does not believe in project management. They also admit their
own shortcomings. If you were to peek into the head of a despondent project manager, the self-talk you hear might go something
like this: "The world is not conforming to my plan. I must not be
a good planner or project manager after all. I'd better take more
project management courses and get more PDUs [professional development units]. I will do better and promise to use more templates and tools."

The world is not conforming to my plan. Let that sink in. Is the
world supposed to conform to our project plan? How arrogant can
we get? Newtonian neurosis leads to the futile practice of attempting to change the world to fit your plan, which is fiction in
the first place. Why would anyone want to change reality to conform to fiction? Newtonian neurosis, that's why.

Newtonian neurosis leads to the futile practice of
attempting to change the world to fit your plan,
which is fiction in the first place.

Traditional project management concepts are inappropriate
for eXtreme projects. Percentage complete, for example, is the
most basic measure of progress, but it is a silly measure for an

eXtreme project because the plan for an eXtreme project is not a prediction. That means the end date, given our best estimate, is only fiction. So if we are four months into a so-called ten-month project, are we really 40 percent complete? Percent complete (4/10, as someone pointed out to me) is merely Fantasy divided by Fiction.

Don't misunderstand me. I believe that certification in project management is a good thing for job mobility, and it beefs up the resumé. So do proudly display your PMP® (Project Management Professional designation) on your business card. Even get a tattoo. But don't think that the tools and concepts you learned apply all the time, everywhere. On eXtreme projects, many of them don't.

Newtonian neurosis is by no means limited to managers of eXtreme projects. It's common to run into this insidious affliction among project sponsors, customers, and senior managers who insist that linear and Newtonian approaches be applied in an effort to stabilize an increasingly unpredictable world.

Self-Diagnostic Tool

Which of the two mind-sets, Newtonian or quantum, represents your predominant worldview? Let's take a look at how you're wired. Does your brain default to Newtonian or to quantonian?

Your Belief System

Your belief system represents your view of how the world works. For each row, check the phrase that best describes you:

Newtonian Mind-Set: *Stability is the norm*	*Quantum Mind-Set:* *Chaos is the norm*
The world is linear and predictable.	Uncertainty reigns.
It's controllable.	Murphy's law rules.
We can minimize change.	We should welcome change.
Add rigor to the process to increase the feeling of security.	Relax controls to increase the feeling of security.

If most of the items you circled fall under the Newtonian mind-set, you may have trouble coping with eXtreme projects. For your own sanity and quality of life, you may want to find a work situation that offers a more predictable and stable environment. But do keep reading, as I hope to show you that living in an eXtreme world can be satisfying and rewarding. Being aware of your own mind-set is the first step on the way of taking control of it and possibly changing it. If you came down in the quantum mind-set, then you are already a step further than many other people on coming to grips with eXtreme projects. Be careful though: the items you circled may not really reflect your underlying assumptions about life and the world. As I discuss below, some people espouse a quantum mind-set but really don't act as if they believe it.

Some people espouse a quantum mind-set but really don't act as if they believe it.

By temperament and preference, some people are simply not cut out for managing or participating in these high-stress, demanding adventures. If this is true about you, there is nothing wrong with you. Instead you are getting a strong signal that you have another calling. Congratulations! Answer the phone. Head for Chapter Three, Leadership Begins with Self Mastery, which covers Critical Success Factor 1. It will help you reinvent your life.

Your Management Style

Your management style reflects how your belief system translates into how you do your job. As a project manager running an eXtreme project (or if you are a project customer, sponsor, or senior manager), which of the two hats do you wear most of the time? For each question, decide whether you wear hat A or hat B:

Newtonian Hat	*Quantum Hat*
My job as a project manager is to:	
A. Deliver on the planned result	B. Discover the desired result
The best way to do this is to:	
A. Use the plan to drive results.	B. Use results to drive planning

My preferred approach is to:

A. Aim, aim, fire

B. Fire. Then, redirect the bullet

I always try to:

A. Keep tight control on the process

B. Keep the process loose

When things start to slip out of control, I try to:

A. Establish stronger procedures and policies

B. Agree on guidelines, principles and values

When the project goes off course, I:

A. Correct to the original baseline

B. Correct to what's possible

I see my role as a:

A. Taskmaster

B. Relationship manager

A successful project:

A. Gets its right the first time

B. Gets it right the last time

If you are wearing a Newtonian hat and using a Newtonian compass to navigate your way through a quantum world, you are likely to feel frustrated and under stress most of the time. You will not be at ease. You will suffer from dis-ease, namely, Newtonian neurosis.

Now, what about your organization? If you were applying the above diagnostic tool to assess your organization, what is its predominant mind-set? Even if you personally have a quantum belief system and wear a quantum management hat, it is likely that your organization is thoroughly Newtonian in its belief system and management approach. Is this a cause for despair? Does this mean that your eXtreme project is dead out of the starting gate? Not at all. As we discussed above, reality happens. eXtreme project management does not try to change reality; rather, it works to deal with it. The eXtreme project management model presented in this book is specifically designed to help you deal with all the Newtonian land mines that litter typical organizations.

*eXtreme project management does not try to change
reality; rather, it works to deal with it.*

Do You Walk Your Talk?

I run into a fair number of project managers who espouse a quantum belief system yet act in a Newtonian way. Their behavior is not congruent with their beliefs, even though their intentions are noble. This phenomenon, unconscious Newtonianism, is at the heart of Newtonian neurosis and is the root cause of totoolitarianism, which is the institutionalization of what doesn't work. Unconscious Newtonianism accounts for the promulgation of inappropriate and monumental project management methodologies and explains why organizations develop elaborate systems, procedures, and policies in a futile attempt to get a grip on eXtreme projects. They unwittingly legislate, reward, and lock in dysfunction.

eXtreme projects call for a predominantly quantum mind-set *and* quantum hat. Traditional construction and engineering projects and other waterfall-like, predictable endeavors do very well with the Newtonian approach. But you can't manage the unknown in the same way that you manage the known. To be successful in managing the apparent chaos of eXtreme projects, it is fundamental that one's belief system and management style be consistent with the quantum reality. If your system and style are not, you need to fake it until you make it. Act as if. Subsequent chapters in this book will show you how. Your ability to succeed on an eXtreme project that is organizationally complex requires it.

It's Jazz, Not Classical Music

eXtreme projects are like jazz. To the unaccustomed ear, jazz might appear to be random and chaotic, but it is not. There is a framework, and the jazz musician has a lot of room to improvise within it. Jazz is not ad hoc. Nor is eXtreme project management, as many mistakenly believe.

Traditional projects are more like classical music. They are well orchestrated and directed. You stick to the score, or the conductor will tap his baton at you. Some organizations are beginning to see the light. They recognize that ultrademanding projects get bogged down with heavy-duty methods and too many templates, best practices, and policies. Their response, though, is to take a traditional, heavyweight methodology and scale it down. But that doesn't work. eXtreme project management is not traditional project management on a crash diet. Moving back to the music metaphor, if you left out the percussion section and violins from a classical music performance, the piece would remain classical music because the mind-set and the rigor remain intact (just on a smaller scale). It's still Newtonian neurosis.

---

eXtreme project management is not traditional project management on a crash diet.

Toward Peaceful Coexistence

I'm not saying that there is no place for the rigor of traditional or Newtonian principles on an eXtreme project. There are parts of eXtreme projects that absolutely require rigor, such as software testing procedures or the execution of a scientific experiment. Both the Newtonian and quantum worldviews are necessary. But to succeed on an eXtreme project, the venture is far better served when the predominant mind-set is quantum. This means that you need to use both the left and right sides of the brain and know when to use each. eXtreme projects are primarily quantum, right brain endeavors. (Think of it this way. Your right hand may be your dominant hand, but that doesn't mean you tie your left hand behind your back. Don't park your right brain at the door either.)

There is nothing inherently wrong or right with either Newtonian or quantum principles. Which to use depends on the circumstances. The same knife that can be used in surgery to save a life can also be used by a thug to take a life.

At its best, the Newtonian mind-set provides the needed predictability and control when predictability and control are possible. At its worst, the Newtonian mind-set is ego driven, arrogant, and warlike. It's fear based: fear of change, fear of failure. The mentality is to keep bad from happening. It seeks to change reality to fit someone's notion of how things should be. It seeks to win through domination. Applying this traditional approach in unpredictable environments can be hazardous to projects and to your personal health and well-being.

At its worst, the quantum mind-set will relax all controls when controls are vitally needed. Imagine New York City with no traffic regulations. (You'd get Rome.) At its best, eXtreme project management is reality based, on the offensive, change embracing, and future oriented. The mentality is to make good happen. It's peaceful yet proactive. Applying eXtreme project management means to look at the world the way it is, as it presents itself, and not fight it each step of the way. After all, by the time it has presented itself, it is already a reality. Attempting to change reality is an attempt to change history. It's futile. Instead, we forgive the past, join hands with reality, and change the plan to fit reality, not the other way around. There's no Undo button on your computer for reality.

Using eXtreme project management means to take responsibility and respond with ability. Under conditions of high speed, high change, high uncertainty, and high complexity, applying the traditional approach is to respond with disability.

In his masterful book *The Dancing Wu Li Masters: An Overview of the New Physics* (1979), Gary Zukav sums it up: "The Wu Li Masters perceive in both ways, the rational and the irrational, the assertive and the receptive, the masculine and the feminine. They reject neither one nor the other. They only dance" (p. 44). (*Wu Li* is Chinese for physics.)

Conclusion

Both traditional and eXtreme project management start out with a set of requirements and a path. But the requirements and the path are merely speculation when managing eXtreme projects. Both are being constructed as the project goes along. It's jazz. The prevailing mind-set is that we will discover the desired result as time goes by. This means recurring trial and error. Tom Peters, the management guru, calls this approach "fast failures." In eXtreme project management, the team and sponsor are wed to the future, to what's possible, and not to sticking to the original baseline.

In the next chapter, I provide an overview of the eXtreme project management model. In the meantime, the serenity prayer can work wonders. It's the secret for inner peace. I recommend you say it at the beginning of each day and put it on a sign for your desk. Read it early and often:

> Grant me the serenity to accept the things I cannot change
> The courage to change the things I can,
> And the wisdom to know the difference.
>
> Reinhold Niebuhr (1892–1971)

Chapter Two

The eXtreme Model for Success

Simple clear purpose and principles give rise to complex intelligent behaviors.

Complex rules and regulations give rise to simple, stupid behaviors.
DEE HOCK, "INSTITUTIONS IN THE AGE OF MARKETING"

The fundamental task of leaders is to prime good feelings in those they lead.
DANIEL GOLEMAN, RICHARD BOYATZIS, AND ANNIE MCKEE, *PRIMAL LEADERSHIP*

eXtreme project management is a new way of thinking and acting that's appropriate to projects that live under the special conditions of high turbulence, high change, and high uncertainty. It is about maintaining control and delivering value in the face of volatility. What it takes to succeed on an eXtreme project is the central focus for this chapter.

Two Keys to Success

Success requires adopting a quantum view of the world, a mind-set that is compatible with and thrives on constant change and innovation. By choosing a change-tolerant mind-set, you are choosing a worldview that is in sync with chaos and unpredictability and one that puts the emphasis on people and interactions more so than on processes and tools. By choosing the quantum mind-set, the first key, you have taken the first big step to succeed.

Figure 2.1. The Path to Success

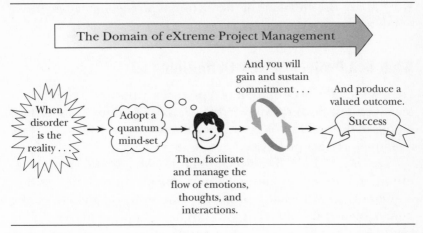

The other key success factor is to be able to gain and sustain commitment to the project mission under conditions that are turbulent and complex—those that feature high speed, high change, and high uncertainty.

And how are these two challenging feats accomplished? In the previous chapter, Margaret Wheatley gave us a hint: she said that managers and leaders are "facilitators of disorder." How do we facilitate disorder? Dee Hock and Daniel Goleman, Richard Boyatzis, and Annie McKee provide the two secrets to success:

Secret 1: Give people the latitude to put their intelligence to work.

Secret 2: Focus on managing the emotional well-being of the endeavor.

For the project manager, this means facilitating the flow of emotions, thoughts, and interactions in a way that produces a valued outcome (Figure 2.1). How does eXtreme project management get you there? In this chapter, I will address these specific questions:

- What is a project?
- What is project management?
- What is an eXtreme project?
- What is eXtreme project management?
- How is success measured on an eXtreme project?

- Who holds a stake in success?
- What are the elements of the eXtreme project management model for success?

What Is a Project? A New Definition

Here is the official definition of a project as appears in the Project Management Body of Knowledge (PMBOK® Guide), a standard espoused by the PMI: "A project is a temporary endeavor to create a unique product or service."

This is a technically correct, but it is a lifeless and sterile definition of a project. It fails to capture the dynamics—the motion and emotion—of what a project is all about. It's devoid of the human element. Contrast it with this new people-centered definition: "A project is a localized energy field comprising a set of thoughts, emotions, and interactions continually expressing themselves in physical form." Let's look at what this means.

Energy is the capacity for doing work. This means the higher the quality of thoughts, emotions, and interactions, the greater is the capacity for doing work. When the energy field is toxic, that is, filled with negative emotions, people's capacity to do work is compromised and reflects itself in project deliverables (physical forms) that miss the mark entirely or are eschewed by customers.

By *localized,* I mean that a project has a beginning and end point. This is nothing new and lines up with the PMBOK definition. What is new is that I'm suggesting that a project is a living thing that is organic and fluid. The noted author of several project management books, Jim Lewis, is fond of saying, "Projects are people." And how do people spend their time all day? Having thoughts and emotions and interacting. eXtreme project management is centered on and built around how people think, feel, and interact.

> *I'm suggesting that a project is a living thing that is organic and fluid.*

Thoughts express themselves in the form of ideas, decisions, facts, data, and breakthroughs. When thoughts and emotions converge, they manifest in meetings on flip charts and in bar conversations as diagrams on napkins. They spring to life in the form of physical prototypes, pictures, memos, PowerPoint presentations, project plans, and project documents, and the final project deliverable.

Emotions continually express themselves in physical and bodily form when people get angry or smile or when they whip off a sharp e-mail or when they go wild and celebrate victory the first time their experiment finally works. In contrast, traditional project management dwells on the mechanical (read Newtonian) side of things and pays lip-service to the human side. Its body of knowledge is built on practices, procedures, and policies where people become servants of the process. Can we afford to dehumanize projects? Not in a quantum world.

Interactions refer to the intricate web of communication that takes place as information, including thoughts and emotions, is exchanged among project stakeholders. When you look at a project's output, you are seeing the sum total of people's thoughts, emotions, and interactions embodied in physical form.

A project, in sum, is a process throughout which thoughts and emotions take form. You can think of a project deliverable as being that which is in formation, that is, being formed. And as more and more thoughts and emotions are exchanged, the project's end result takes on an increasingly concrete form. In this sense, a project can be thought of as being information; that is, the product of thoughts and emotions taking form. A project's physical outputs live two lives: first as thoughts or ideas and then as a tangible reality. An important goal of eXtreme project management is to collapse the time it takes for thoughts, emotions, and interactions to manifest in physical form.

A project, in sum, is a process throughout which thoughts and emotions take form.

Traditional project management has appended the human element to its body of knowledge. In contrast, eXtreme project management is based on the human element.

What Is Project Management? A New Definition

Project management, eXtreme or otherwise, involves much more than the act of designing and building the thing or putting in place a new service capability that the customer has asked for. It is not merely about the production of artifacts (Gantt charts, issues logs, status reports and other myriad documents). Rather, it is much more: *project management is the art and science of facilitating and managing the flow of thoughts, emotions, and interactions in a way that produces valued outcomes.*

The fundamental question in eXtreme project management is not how to build a better mousetrap. Rather, it is how to create an environment that will give birth to the best solution for catching mice.

As an energy field, a project consists of much more than its physical outputs and supporting documents, just as an actual vacation is much more than a travel brochure. Not making this distinction leads to the preoccupation that I have observed in many project managers: relentlessly improving the content of the Gantt chart or endlessly tweaking the project plan with the naive expectation that these activities will improve the project's success in the mind of the customer. This is tantamount to upgrading the look of a travel brochure in the hopes of providing a better vacation experience. This fiction of project management has led to the formation of project offices and other project support organizations that have created monumental methodologies, tools, and practices that pump out bureaucracy and project documentation but have little to show for in the way of tangible results that customers see, feel, and put to use. There is lots of ceremony, but where's the cake?

The energy field definition means that project management is first and foremost an interpersonal, people-facing business. It's the creative and generative force behind valued outcomes. It includes, but is not primarily about, the flow of project documents and documentation and the application of project management tools and techniques. Project management is about management by eye contact and not by icon-tact.

Thoughts, emotions, and interactions are the wellspring of creativity. And the quality and flow of thoughts, emotions, and interactions determine the quality and value of the project deliverable.

The energy field definition says that project management is the life-giving force behind valued products, services, and the ultimate business outcome.

Projects are living, breathing things. They are people. They have moods. You can easily experience this for yourself. Think of several familiar projects and ask yourself, Which ones are in a good mood? Which ones are in a bad mood? When a project is in a bad mood, the flow of ideas is stifled, and the energy field becomes dense with a negative charge. Interactions among stakeholders turn to gossip, complaining, criticism, fault finding, whining, and sabotage.

When a project is in a bad mood,
the flow of ideas is stifled.

If project management—traditional or eXtreme, and anything in between—is really the facilitation and management of thoughts, feelings, and interactions that give birth to tangible products and services, then these are directly influenced by the emotional state of the project team and other stakeholders. If the team is soured, confused, conflict ridden, callous, and stressed out, these feelings and thoughts will taint and infect the quality of the project outputs. And a better-looking Gantt chart won't help matters. If the team is downbeat and the critical stakeholders perceive the project in a dim light, this attitude will reflect itself in the quality of the final product, just as the quality of sunlight affects the growth of a plant. How something is perceived changes that which is perceived. This is the primary significance of physicist Werner Heisenberg's uncertainty principle, which has been verified repeatedly by experiments with subatomic particles: we cannot observe something without changing it. The perception is the reality.

The new definition of a project and project management shifts the emphasis and focus of the project manager away from the management of the project artifacts to that of creating an environment that fosters good thinking, positive energy, fluid communication, and robust collaboration. This is the lifeblood of successful eXtreme projects. Detoxify the soil, create a greenhouse, and the flowers will flourish.

Creating an environment that fosters positive energy requires managing the flow of your own thoughts, emotions, and interactions under conditions of high stress. That's why self-mastery and leadership by commitment are crucial to your success.

What Is an eXtreme Project?

An eXtreme project is a special kind of localized energy field (comprising thoughts, emotions, and interactions expressing themselves in physical form). It is a complex, high-speed, self-correcting venture during which people interact in search of a desirable result under conditions of high uncertainty, high change, and high stress.

Self-correcting is a key phrase. It recognizes that there are many variables and unknowns both internal and external to the project and the sponsoring organization. No one can keep track of them all. No one knows enough to direct everyone else. This is not the command-and-control school of project management. An eXtreme project cannot be regulated from top down. It can only be guided from above and managed from below as individuals, pairs, and groups of stakeholders continually make self-correcting adjustments as the project goes along while keeping in mind the desired project outcome.

In search of a desirable result is another key concept. It means that an eXtreme project is a discovery process: both the content of the final deliverable and the path to get there will evolve throughout most of the project's life.

What Is eXtreme Project Management?

When faced with a demanding project, eXtreme project management loads the deck in your favor because it puts the emphasis on managing the project's energy field: the thoughts, emotions, and interactions that produce results. eXtreme project management *is the art and science of facilitating and managing the flow of thoughts, emotions, and interactions in a way that produces valued outcomes under turbulent and complex conditions: those that feature high speed, high change, high uncertainty, and high stress.*

In his book *Agile Software Development Ecosystems* (2002), Jim Highsmith uses the term *ecosystem* to describe a holistic environment that includes three interwoven components: a "chaordic perspective, collaborative values and barely sufficient methodology."

The term *chaordic* refers to an endeavor or organization that exhibits properties of both order and chaos in a way that defies management through linear cause-and-effect approaches.

eXtreme project management contributes to success in three ways. First, it recognizes that you don't manage the unknown and unpredictable in the same way you manage the known and predictable. It makes it possible for continuous self-correction to take place in real time. Second, it focuses on gaining and sustaining commitment to the project mission by instilling desire and confidence among key stakeholders. Third, it is much more than just a methodology or another set of software tools and templates: it takes an approach that is holistic, people centered, humanistic, business focused, and reality based.

- *eXtreme project management is holistic.* This is a holistic model that is built around an integrated set of principles, values, and practices that accelerate performance on all three levels: individual, team, and organization. It includes methods, tools, and techniques, but unless these are firmly rooted in the fertile soil of the quantum worldview, they are about as useful as tumbleweeds blowing across a barren prairie. Don't fall into the tool or methodology trap. This is not fill-in-the-blanks project management.
- *eXtreme project management is people centered.* It puts emphasis on managing project dynamics, which means the interactions and communications among the project stakeholders, as well as their changing expectations. Projects rarely fail due to the team's inability to produce a deliverable that is technically sound. Many elegant solutions, systems, and products sit there and rust because they did not meet the real needs of the intended customer. Nor do projects typically fail because the team didn't have the right project management software tool.

Projects rarely fail due to the team's inability to produce a deliverable that is technically sound.

- *eXtreme project management is humanistic.* It is based on the radical position that project success and quality of life are inseparable; that is, a satisfactory quality of life is planned into the project. If the team is demoralized, experience tells us that the project will suffer in terms of schedule, quality, or budget (or all of these).

From an organizational perspective, eXtreme project management should appeal to senior executives who recognize that if an organization runs its staff into the ground on project after project, they will eventually run out the door (even if customers are satisfied), and the business will be adversely affected in its ability to hold and attract good people. Eventually, there may even be a negative impact on the organization's competitive position.

eXtreme project management makes processes and tools the servants of people. It is ever mindful of the Sirens' call that lures people into becoming unwitting slaves to well-intended but cumbersome methodologies, templates, and software tools that stifle motivation, innovation, and high-quality work and otherwise contaminate the project's energy field, putting the endeavor in a bad mood.

- *eXtreme project management is business focused.* It recognizes that a project is first and foremost a business venture. The project team relentlessly focuses on delivering value early and often. And eXtreme project management incorporates the realization of business benefits after delivery of the project's output.

- *eXtreme project management is reality based.* It provides tools and methods that are practical and proven to work in project environments that feature constant change and high unpredictability. It recognizes that you are wasting your time trying to change reality to fit your project plan. Byron Katie, author of the book *Loving What Is* (2002), says in her workshops, "When you argue with reality you lose, but only 100% of the time." The motto for eXtreme project management is, "Reality rules."

How Is Success Measured on an eXtreme Project?

Since eXtreme project management is people- and customer-centric, it will come as no surprise that success is measured as follows:

- Customers are happy with progress and interim deliverables. There is a general feeling that the project is moving in the right direction despite the surrounding volatility. Tangible results are being produced—things that customers can see and feel.
- Customers are happy with the final deliverable. It meets the success criteria that have been agreed on throughout the project's life cycle.

- The downstream (postproject) benefits are realized. The intended business benefit for having undertaken the project in the first place is measurable and has materialized.
- Team members enjoy a satisfactory quality of life throughout the project. When asked if they would be willing to participate on a similar project, a majority of team members would answer yes.

A short way of saying this is that customers receive value throughout the whole life of the project and the project team feels good about the experience.

Who Holds a Stake in Success?

If projects are people—their thoughts, emotions, and interactions—then relationship management becomes the main focus of eXtreme project management. On eXtreme projects, the key to success is other people. It's stakeholder management, which means relationship management. It's politics.

On eXtreme projects, the key to success is other people.

Anyone who participates on a project or who is affected by the project (during or after completion) is a stakeholder. Stakeholders provide vital goods and services in many forms, including authority to do things, other projects you depend on, information, feedback, labor, cooperation, decisions, approvals, and advice. Other projects that depend on your project are also stakeholders. Stakeholders can also put up roadblocks and find subtle ways of sabotaging a project.

Because many eXtreme projects have high stakes and are organizationally complex, with impacts on multiple departments, systems, and processes, the size of the stakeholder community can be formidable. Managing their conflicting expectations is the biggest challenge facing eXtreme project managers. In Chapter Seven, I'll go into more detail on the major stakeholder groups. For now, I simply set out the magnitude of the challenge by showing this lineup of people who populate the project's energy field:

- You and your family
- The project sponsor
- Customers
    Business owner
    Functional ambassadors
    Delegate users
- Producers
    Project manager
    Core team
    Project contributors
- Suppliers
    Vendors and other outsourcers
    Consultants
    Contractors
    Resource managers
- Support staff
    Facilitator
    Project administrator
    Project office
- Dependent projects
    Projects you depend on
    Dependents on your project
- Influencers
    Upper management
    Review board
    Your boss
    Functional departments
    Unions
    Families
- External
    Competitors
    Government agencies and politics
    Special interest groups
    Media
    The public

In addition, there are organizational influences to contend with. These include the systems, policies, and procedures (no doubt all based on a Newtonian mind-set) that you have to live with unless you can find a guardian angel who can allow you to bypass those that get in the way.

An organization's culture—the way things are done in a particular organization—can also be a big influence. If you work in a command-and-control culture, you will likely encounter little tolerance for collaborative decision making, a key ingredient for success on eXtreme projects.

What Are the Elements of the eXtreme Model for Success?

To succeed on an eXtreme project requires gaining and sustaining commitment to the project mission through its life cycle. This is accomplished by applying the quantum mind-set: to facilitate, lead, and manage the project according to a set of principles, values, and practices that are compatible with change and uncertainty. These form the soft and the hard glue of eXtreme project management and are embodied in the form of these elements:

The 4 Accelerators—the principles for unleashing motivation and innovation

The 10 Shared Values—the components of the value system that establish the trust and confidence needed to succeed

The 4 Business Questions—the questions that when they are continually addressed ensure that the customer receives value each step of the way

The 5 Critical Success Factors—the essential skills and tools and the environment that make it possible to take action in a way that produces valued results for the project's customers

Orchestrated together, these elements make it possible to maintain control in the face of volatility and vastly improve the chances of delivering value early and often to customers.

The 4 Accelerators and 10 Shared Values are people oriented and form the bedrock of eXtreme project management. Unless this foundation is in place, the 4 Business Questions and 5 Critical Success Factors will stand on a bed of quicksand. All of these work together to keep the project's energy field vibrant and productive (Figure 2.2).

Figure 2.2. The Model for eXtreme Project Management

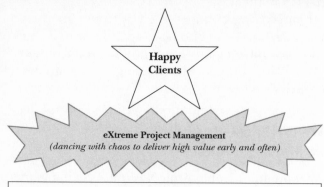

Happy Clients

eXtreme Project Management
(dancing with chaos to deliver high value early and often)

Quantum Mind-set
(choosing a worldview that is compatible with chaos and unpredictability)

The 4 Accelerators
(principles for unleashing motivation and innovation)
1. Make change your friend.
2. Build on people's desire to make a difference.
3. Create ownership for results.
4. Keep it simple.

The 10 Shared Values
(establishing the trust and confidence to succeed)
Client Collaboration . . . People First . . . Clarity of Purpose . . .
Results Orientation . . . Honest Communication . . . Fast Failures . . .
Early Value . . . Visibility . . . Quality of Life . . . Courage

---

Where The Rubber Meets The Road
• Continually address the 4 Business Questions
• Adapt the 5 Critical Success Factors

The 4 Business Questions
(ensuring the customer receives value each step of the way)
1. Who needs what and why?
2. What will it take to do it?
3. Can we get what it takes?
4. Is it worth it?

The 5 Critical Success Factors
(taking action: the tools, skills and environment to succeed)
1. Self-Mastery
2. Leadership by Commitment
3. Flexible Project Model
4. Real-Time Communication
5. Agile Organization

The 4 Accelerators and 10 Shared Values
are people oriented and form the bedrock
of eXtreme project management.

Unleashing Motivation and Innovation: The 4 Accelerators

The 4 Accelerators speed up the flow of positive energy through-out the project's energy field. They enable the stakeholders and the team in particular to be adaptive. Keeping these guiding principles in mind will go a long way in keeping a project moving and the team committed and creative. By *committed,* I mean a sense of ownership. Importantly, these accelerators also form the fertile soil that gives birth to innovative products and solutions. And they go a long way to establish the desire to succeed.

The 4 Accelerators, covered in full in Chapter Five, are summarized here:

1. Make change your friend. Change carries a negative connotation on projects. It disrupts things. It's not something that is typically welcomed, and that's why traditional project management makes a big deal out of change control.

eXtreme project management requires a different attitude about change—one that says change represents opportunity and that welcoming change improves the chances of delivering the desired result (which is likely to be vastly different from the originally planned result).

In practice, making change your friend means accepting what is and moving on from there.

2. Build on people's desire to make a difference. I don't think many people get up in the morning excited about getting back to their projects. In fact, the word *project* has a dispiriting sense associated with it. People are more likely to rise and shine if they know they are on a mission; that is, they see their project not so much as a project but as a cause. When put into practice, this second accelerator means showing people how their job contributes to the bigger picture by providing a sense of meaning and purpose.

3. Create ownership for results. People support what they create. I may feel good about being part of an important project, but if it is a risky venture, as are all eXtreme projects, I will want to have a voice in shaping the project. In practice, this principle means to trust in people's expertise and commitment and afford them the opportunity to influence how to succeed on the overall project, including how performance will be measured.

4. *Keep it simple.* The old KISS principle—Keep It Simple, Stupid—is much more than lip-service on an eXtreme project. It's taken seriously. In practice, it means less is more: less process, less project management overhead, fewer policies and standard operating procedures.

Establishing the Trust and Confidence Needed to Succeed: The 10 Shared Values

This is the value system that fosters a strongly held belief among project stakeholders that by working together they can succeed, even in the face of volatility and adversity. It comes down to what Henry Ford said: "If you think you can, you can. If you think you can't you can't. In either case you are right."

These 10 Shared Values relate to people, process, and business value (they are covered in full in Chapters Five through Seven):

People Values

1. People First—eliminating barriers so that people can do quality work
2. Honest Communication—acting with integrity and speaking the truth about the good, the bad, and the ugly without fear of reprisal
3. Quality of Life—ensuring that the project strikes a satisfying balance of work life and personal life
4. Courage—having the fear and doing it anyway; doing it scared because it's the right thing to do

Process Values

5. Client Collaboration—ongoing interaction and feedback with the customer throughout the venture as opposed to the customer's handing off the requirements and disengaging
6. Fast Failures—finding the quickest path to failure by tackling the most difficult, risky, or important work very early on

7. Visibility—keeping everything out in the open for all to see: plans, progress, work products, issues, who's accountable for what

Business Values

8. Clarity of Purpose—understanding not only the goals of the project but the bigger picture: why it's being undertaken in the first place
9. Results Orientation—focusing on the completion of deliverables rather than on tracking tasks
10. Early Value—giving customers something they can put to use as soon as possible

The 4 Business Questions

The 4 Business Questions serve as a constant reminder to all stakeholders that the project is first and foremost a business venture: the goal is to deliver value each step of the way, as well as during the benefits realization stage, which begins after the final project output has been produced.

These are the 4 Business Questions (they are covered in detail in Chapters Five and Eight):

1. Who needs what and why?
2. What will it take to do it?
3. Can we get what it takes?
4. Is it worth it?

In practice, applying the 4 Business Questions means continually updating the business case to reflect the latest expectations and projections.

Putting in Place the Skills, Tools, and Environment to Succeed: The 5 Critical Success Factors

The 5 Critical Success Factors (CSFs) are where the rubber meets the road. They employ the 4 Accelerators, the 10 Shared Values, and the 4 Business Questions by building them into the life of the project. They also speak to the skills, methods, and practices that are essential to lead, plan, manage, and track the project from start to finish and to assimilate change along the way.

CSF 1: Self-Mastery

CSF 1 recognizes that you cannot separate your project from yourself any more than you can separate the wet from the water. To stay sane over time means being able to keep a grip on yourself as well as on the project. An eXtreme project is stressful under any circumstances. It can follow you home at night and live rent-free in your head, depriving you of a personal and family life. Self-Mastery means the ongoing practice of leading oneself. In the absence of even a modicum of Self-Mastery, the eXtreme project manager will soon realize that he is out of control and no longer has a project; rather, the project has him. Unless you choose Self-Mastery, you are by default choosing self-misery. The goal is nothing less than inner peace. Self-Mastery is the subject of Chapter Three.

You cannot separate your project from yourself any more than you can separate the wet from the water.

CSF 2: Leadership by Commitment

The job of the eXtreme project manager is to gain and sustain the commitment of others. This person is able to unleash motivation and innovation, establish the trust and confidence to succeed, ensure the customer receives value each step of the way, and maintains control in the face of volatility. To do this requires that the project manager become the steward of the project's energy field and the process leader who manages and facilitates the flow of emotions, thoughts, and interactions in a way that produces valued outcomes. By effectively (or ineffectively) managing the project's energy field, the eXtreme project manager creates the circumstances for success (or failure). Because of the critical importance of leadership for eXtreme Projects, four chapters (Chapters Four through Seven) cover all aspects of leadership in detail.

CSF 3: Flexible Project Model

The Flexible Project Model is iterative and consists of four cycles plus one element called Disseminate. The model spans project start-up to project turnover. Its purpose is to provide just enough discipline to allow people the freedom to innovate and to get work done. Similar to the structure of a jazz composition, the flexible model provides the framework for people to improvise when needed but without losing control of the project. The four cycles are: Visionate, Speculate, Innovate, Reevaluate, plus the final element called Disseminate.

Part Three presents a complete guide to using the flexible project model. Here is a brief overview of each element.

CSF 3.1: Visionate: The What

A business problem or opportunity has been presented. Face-to-face sessions between the project sponsor and crucial stakeholders are held in which all come to a collective vision and clear understanding of the business opportunity to be pursued or the problem to be solved. During the initial scoping meeting, a prioritized set of requirements is agreed to, as well as how success will be measured. This is an initial definition and is expected to change as project work commences.

CSF 3.2: Speculate: The How

Some high-level planning is done very quickly to sequence the deliverables and identify milestones. This is documented and agreed to by all parties, along with the expectation that it will change as project work commences.

CSF 3.3: Innovate: The Doing

Innovate takes place within predefined time frames. The emphasis is on experimenting and rapid development, generating real-time feedback from the customer. At the end of the time frame, the results are prepared for review, which takes place during the Reevaluate cycle.

CSF 3.4: Reevaluate: The Reviewing

The customer and team review the results. Were the requirements met? Have they changed? The results are reviewed against the 4 Business Questions. And if there is still value in moving forward, the team cycles back to Speculate, to make the next time-framed plan in order to start the next round of innovating. The Speculate-Innovate-Reevaluate sequence is repeated until the time and cost budgets have been expended or the desired result has been achieved.

CSF 3.5: Disseminate: The Harvesting

When all the dust settles, eXtreme projects are about accomplishing something useful and turning that over to the project customer and beginning the benefits realization plan.

CSF 4: Real-Time Communication

Things happen fast on eXtreme projects. People need information about the good and bad so that they can self-organize into groups to make decisions. They need a forum for discussion and debate so that the best options are surfaced and addressed. They need to share documents and have ready access to project management tools. Stakeholders need to be kept up to date. Real-Time Communication means to put in place the project management infrastructure to ensure that information is available at any time to anyone who needs it in order to speed the flow of thoughts and ultimately decisions. Chapter Fifteen explains this CSF in practical detail.

CSF 5: Agile Organization

Projects are like flowers. If the soil is toxic, one or two flowers may survive, but sooner or later the crop will die. Agile Organization means putting in place a change-tolerant, project-friendly culture that recognizes and supports the special needs of different projects from traditional to eXtreme. The goal of a change-tolerant organization is not to ensure that projects are delivered on time, on scope, or on budget but rather to ensure that the project delivers the intended business outcome. This topic is covered in Chapter Sixteen.

Let's begin by examining the leadership skills needed for an eXtreme world, taking a look at the first Critical Success Factor: self-mastery.

Part Two

Leadership Skills for an eXtreme World

The primary role of the eXtreme project manager is to gain and sustain commitment to the project mission. Commitment occurs when stakeholders, including the core project team, have bought into the project. And buy-in occurs when there is a critical mass of desire to support the project, as well as confidence in its ability to succeed. You can tell that commitment is present when you have a stable and motivated core project team and the support of the stakeholder community at large.

When these two elements are present, the project gains forward momentum. It takes on a positive energy and stays in a good mood. And keeping the project in a good mood is the top priority for the extreme project manager.

When commitment falters or vanishes, the project's energy field turns sour, and the project drops into a blue mood. It then runs the risk of not meeting schedule, quality, or financial expectations, and total failure.

To gain and sustain commitment to the eXtreme project, and perhaps most projects these days, is no easy task. It requires strong, effective, consistent leadership.

Unlike in the Newtonian model, where power comes from position and hierarchy, project managers have little direct authority over people. Their power comes from the process they implement and the relationships they establish. In the quantum model, the eXtreme project manager is a process leader—someone who unleashes power rather than imposes power.

Good process facilitates the management and organization of ideas and translates them into concrete project deliverables. Good process transports people from chaos to clarity, from seeing themselves as irrelevant to experiencing that they are making a difference. Good process is able to turn conflict into cooperation. Good process connects the dots. Good process is not only the road map to success; it unleashes the energy to pull it off.

When you lead the process, you lead the people—all of them, regardless of rank or cultural background. Process and relationship management skills are the great equalizers in eXtreme project management. They enable you to:

- Unleash motivation and innovation.
- Establish the trust and confidence to succeed among key members of the stakeholder community at large.
- Ensure the customer receives value each step of the way.
- Maintain control in the face of volatility.

The next five chapters provide you with the perspective and tools you need to lead the eXtreme project process successfully.

Chapter Three explains why making a commitment to your own personal growth is the starting point for leadership. It details a three-step process for achieving self-mastery: (1) see yourself, (2) be yourself, and (3) assert yourself. This chapter also offers a variety of guidelines and tools to use on the path to self-mastery.

Chapter Four provides an overview of the organizational context of eXtreme projects and the project manager's role within that context in terms of leading the project team and managing relations with the project sponsor, key stakeholders, and other players.

Chapter Five explains why managing the project as an energy field is so important and offers guidelines for unleashing motivation and innovation and establishing the trust and confidence to succeed. I'll cover the foundational tools for putting the quantum mind-set to work: the 4 Project Accelerators, the 10 Shared Values, and the 4 Business Questions.

Chapter Six shifts the spotlight to the core project team and takes it from the point of assembling the team to moving it to the high-performing stage and keeping it there. The emphasis is

placed on what you can do to make it possible for the team to succeed, including getting the right sponsor, ensuring productive
working conditions, good meeting management, and effective
group decision making.

Chapter Seven explains why project stakeholders either make
or break the project—and details ways to identify and manage
stakeholders as well as how to build the stakeholder database.

Taken together, these chapters demonstrate conclusively that
eXtreme project management is a people business, not a template
or a canned methodology business.

eXtreme Project Management Model
Applying the Quantum Mind-Set

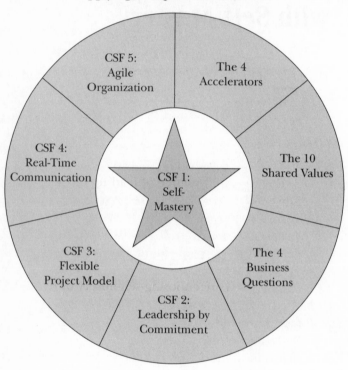

Chapter Three

Leadership Begins with Self-Mastery

Serenity is not freedom from the storm, but finding peace amidst the storm.
ANONYMOUS

Self-Mastery is Critical Success Factor 1 in eXtreme Project Management. It's the ongoing practice of leading oneself. It's the art of being self-directed. On an eXtreme project, this means being self-directed under adverse conditions. You can't stabilize the world, but you can stabilize yourself. It's your only hope. And when you stabilize yourself, the world around you, as if by magic, appears more stable. When working under adverse conditions, unless you choose Self-Mastery, you are choosing self-misery by default. Taken to its ultimate, the goal of Self-Mastery is nothing less than inner peace under any circumstances.

In the 1990s, according to the *New York Times* (Greenhouse, 2001), Americans increased their work year to an equivalent 49.5 weeks, surpassing the Japanese by 3.5 weeks, the British by 6.5 weeks, and the Germans by an astonishing 12.5 weeks. This is one reason that quality of life is one of the 10 Shared Values of eXtreme Project Management and why Self-Mastery is a Critical Success Factor on eXtreme projects. The demands can be so great that unless you get a grip on yourself—take charge of your psychoemotional state—your project will take hold of you.

As an eXtreme project manager, you can be only as good at managing and leading others as you are in managing and directing yourself. If you are constantly overstressed, anxious, lack self-discipline, have no life vision, and are fearful, you are out of control. You will have little credibility in front of others because you will have little credibility with yourself. By position, you may be able to get others to comply, but you will not motivate or inspire when the chips are down. So this journey starts at home. To be able to manage effectively and facilitate the flow of emotions and thoughts in a way that produces valued outcomes (the definition of what an eXtreme project manager does), you will better serve others when you have begun to master the ability to manage and facilitate your own emotions and thoughts.

In this chapter I'll cover:

- The project-crazy organization
- The formula of self-misery
- The formula for Self-Mastery, including how to see yourself, be yourself, and assert yourself
- What to do when all else fails

The Project-Crazy Organization

eXtreme projects are stressful under any circumstances. That may explain why eXtreme project managers tend to live lives that vacillate between frantic and quiet desperation. Yet the teachings of project management, at least until now, don't extend beyond the walls of our offices, although our jobs do.

In the absence of even a modicum of Self-Mastery, the eXtreme project manager will realize that he no longer has projects; rather, his projects have him. Why does this happen? Let's take a look at the project-crazy organization.

The loss of control, both real and imagined, can in part be attributed to what I call the project-crazy organization. The project-crazy organization makes it very difficult to succeed on projects. This happens because the pressure to compete causes management to launch too many projects given the people available. In the scramble to keep up and keep agile, a de facto set of worst practices comes into being. For many project managers and teams, the impact of these worst practices is high stress, anxiety, low morale, and burnout. These are the practices I've encountered all too often:

No priorities. "Project du jour" is practiced: projects are initiated and cancelled with no accepted criteria in place.

Communication avoidance. "Mushroom management" is practiced. Team members are kept in the dark on changes in strategy or project scope that send projects into unnecessary rework and put the team in a bad mood.

Disappearing teams. Now you see them; now you don't. In revolving-door fashion, team members are reassigned to other projects.

Murky roles. Decision-making authority is unclear. The project sponsor and functional managers simultaneously pull your project in different directions, leaving you stuck in the middle.

No project management process. There is no common approach across projects. As a result, management thinks nothing of adding more scope to the project, while at the same time cutting the deadline and reassigning team members to other projects.

No rewards. Somehow you perform a miracle and make it work. Your reward? You get to keep your job.

All of this project craziness not only lowers the success rate of all projects, it can have a negative impact on your quality of life on and off the job—if you allow it.

Nevertheless, I can tell you from having lived through this myself that in the project-crazy organization, there are no victims, just volunteers. A *victim* is someone who has no options left. There is always an option no matter how bad it gets. During his incarceration in a Nazi prison camp, Viktor Frankel (1984) discovered the ultimate human freedom: ". . . Everything can be taken from a man but one thing: the last of the human freedoms—to choose one's attitude in any given set of circumstances, to choose one's way" (p. 75). There are always options because if you can't change your circumstances, you can always change your mind about the circumstances.

The Formula for Self-Misery

If the scenario I've just painted rings true to you and you are feeling the brunt of all that project craziness, what can you do to improve your own sense of happiness and inner peace? A good starting place is to understand what *doesn't* work. I call this my formula for self-misery, and I know it well because I helped perfect it:

$$\text{SELF-MISERY} = CR + WH$$

where CR = change reality to fit your plan and WH = work hard to get better at something you don't like.

Trying to Change Reality to Fit Your Plan

I've come to the realization that for every plan I make, no matter how careful and detailed it is, reality seems to have a different plan in mind. That's why I make contingency plans: in order to adjust when reality's plan kicks in. Yet no one has ever been able to show me the contingency plan that reality has. What I've found is that reality doesn't have contingency plans at all. Reality *is* the plan. My own plan is just guesswork, with me trying to second-guess reality. In other words, reality rules, as I pointed out in Chapter One when I contrasted the quantum and Newtonian mind-sets.

In that chapter, you'll recall I mentioned two mental models for a project. The first is what I wish my project looked like:

Start ————————————————————————→ Finish

The second is what reality *says* my project looks like:

Reality: What my project really looks like.

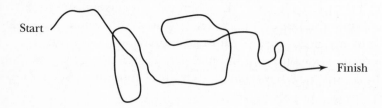

Start

Finish

In my speeches and workshops when I ask project managers to point to the mental model that best describes their projects, nearly 100 percent point to the squiggly line. (Those who point to the straight line can only be explained by having suffered a psychotic break with reality.)

Reality, like a child, is disobedient. Project managers who try to change reality to fit their plan end up spending most of their time committing project abuse: superimposing burdensome rules and policies, putting in place oppressive change control procedures, following people around to be sure they are on task, spending hours explaining discrepancies between the plan and the current situation, closing the door on new ideas.

These are some of the personal impacts of going up against reality (and I say this from my personal experience, as well as having worked with hundreds of project managers):

- Perpetual conflict with those doing the actual work and thus being the bad guy
- Constantly feeling stressed and under pressure, wondering if you are going to succeed
- Low energy
- Low morale
- Loss of health
- Loss of self-confidence
- Loss of self-esteem
- Guilt in not having time for family and personal life
- Anger
- Burnout

Add it up, and it spells suffering and misery.

I had to learn this the hard way. I got to a point where I recognized that when it came to going up against reality, I wasn't strong enough or smart enough to win. I had to learn to navigate reality, not try to change it. What I thought should be didn't matter.

I had to learn that I couldn't forcibly control my projects. I have to guide them, cooperate with reality, ride the horse in the direction it was going. And if I didn't like the direction it was going, I could jump off. Beating to death the horse I was riding was self-defeating. And ultimately I had to learn that plans don't cause reality to change. Just the opposite is the case: reality causes plans to change.

These principles are true for life in general, but they are exacerbated in the world of eXtreme projects. The eXtreme project manager is riding a horse in the middle of a stampede. The accomplished rider learns how to cooperate with the galloping animal and in the midst of his journey would never even think of trying to subdue its fury or turn against the stampede. Our plans and efforts are ineffective in getting reality to change its mind.

Working Hard to Get Better at Something You Don't Like

If trying to change reality were not enough of an exercise in futility, then try doing it in combination with a job you don't even like. Over time, the toll on your emotional and physical well-being—your quality of life—can be devastating.

At the time I didn't know it, but looking back I realize I was in the wrong job for twenty-three years. This was when I worked in the publishing industry. I kept advancing but never was happy. Deep inside I had a gnawing sensation that the fit wasn't right, but I didn't pay attention to that unease. Instead, I fell into the trap of thinking that when I knew more about publishing, gained more experience, and got more power, I'd feel better. The fact was that I was a fish trying to ride a bicycle. This means that becoming certified or getting an advanced degree in a profession that you don't really like only serves to lock in the misery. Doing more of what you don't like and thinking you'll eventually like it is perverted, if not insane.

Jean Davis, a psychologist I know of based in Evanston, Illinois, points out that if you're not living your own dream, you're living someone else's bad dream. She emphasizes that "our most productive work is an extension of our authentic self, but it has become laid over with someone else's nightmare." When the nightmare (the wrong job) becomes the norm, we sense that something isn't right.

Right livelihood means synchronizing what you do in life with who you are inside. It means being at ease (as opposed to diseased) with your work and life. It means not separating work from life, but in a positive sense; that is, our work becomes the natural expression of our innate talents and gifts both on and off the job. You know you are expressing your true self when you can say that being an eXtreme project manager is not something you do; it's who you are. Aristotle said, "You will find your vocation where your talents meet opportunity."

Right livelihood means synchronizing what you do in life with who you are inside.

The path to right livelihood starts by asking the right question. The *wrong* question to ask yourself is, "What kind of a job do I really want?" You're not out to get a job; you're out to get a life. A better question is, "What kind of a life do I want to live?"

When there is a good fit between who you are and what you do, the benefits are life changing. You will experience:

- Greater energy and enthusiasm
- Improved productivity
- High self-esteem
- Better family and interpersonal relationships
- Better emotional and physical health
- Inner peace

This is want happened to me when I left the magazine publishing business and got into the business of performance improvement. I was then able to leverage my natural talents for helping organizations achieve difficult business goals, teaching team leadership, and practicing Self-Mastery.

The Formula for Self-Mastery

Here's my three-step formula for Self-Mastery. Having perfected it, I know it well:

$$\text{SELF-MASTERY} = SY + BY + AY$$

where SY = see yourself, BY = be yourself, and AY = assert yourself. Each of the three elements in the formula deserves attention. And there are practical steps you can take to implement each.

Seeing Yourself

To see or to know yourself is to understand where your roots are.

Discovering Your True Strengths

Being well rooted in your strengths enables you to weather high change and high stress, two hallmarks of eXtreme projects. Without being well grounded, you will be blown around helplessly like a tumbleweed across the prairie. Seeing yourself involves understanding

your temperament, identifying your motivated abilities, and uncovering and eliminating self-defeating beliefs. Twenty minutes is
the time it takes to get the ball rolling by going to the Web and fill-
ing out the Keirsey temperament profile, an assessment tool that
identifies your dominant temperament, or predisposition to act in
certain ways. I'll cover this shortly.

A good first step, then, is to understand your temperament—
what makes you tick.

Understanding Your Temperament

Many of us have become strangers unto ourselves. We put more effort and anguish into figuring out others than we do in getting to
understand ourselves. And our greater fear is not that of meeting
others but of meeting ourselves. If we truly knew ourselves and
lived in a way that was congruent with our essential nature, our
lives would suddenly take on a new sense of meaning.

Many of us have become strangers unto ourselves.

Temperaments are preferences for behaving. They are not intelligences but are often related to intelligences. Understanding
your temperament style is a good starting point in making adjustments in your life's work.

The work of David Keirsey is particularly useful in helping people understand what makes them tick. Similar to the Myers-Briggs
Type Indicator, David Keirsey has identified four major temperament types and sixteen variations. It's easy and free to get started.
If you haven't done this, I strongly recommend it. Simply go to
www.Keirsey.com, and take the fifteen-minute temperament assessment. (An overview of Keirsey's temperaments is included in
the eXtreme Tools and Techniques section at the end of the book.)

My own temperament type came out to be Idealist. This means
that my interests lie in the areas of humanities, communicating
ideas using words, and making presentations. Moreover, the areas
I tend to focus on have to do with morale, self-esteem, self-respect,
and building confidence. As for my managerial intelligences, my
strong suits are diplomacy and strategy.

Knowing this helped explain why I was unhappy in my publishing career: a predominant part of the job required a Guardian

temperament. Guardians like rules, regulations, and details. They do best with budgets, deadlines, scheduling, record keeping, and keeping operations running smoothly. Their strongest managerial intelligences are logistics and tactics—just the opposite of diplomacy and strategy, which is what Idealists prefer and do best at. My recipe for self-misery was to be an Idealist in a Guardian job.

In my experience, a project manager cannot be all things and do them sufficiently well. It's important that your strongest suit be congruent with the dominant temperament required by the project, at least over time. That doesn't mean that if there is a mismatch you will not succeed. Many do. But if the mismatch continues project after project, a malaise will set in, and the formula for self-misery will take over. The project will be at risk.

Discovering Your Motivated Abilities

Many are chosen but few are called. The boss assigns Jessica to a project, and suddenly Jessica is a project manager. Most project managers wind up in their job by accident. It's rarely in response to a driving passion. We get there unintentionally, if not unconsciously. We might then become so invested in gaining the requisite skills to succeed that being a project manager now becomes our job identity. We might fool ourselves into believing that this is who we really are and what we want to do. Some would even seal their fate by becoming professionally certified. We now become so locked into this profession that we become hard-pressed to even imagine other viable options. This is a true identity crisis: somehow we've become distracted and disidentified from our real self. We've lost sight of our motivated strengths.

Everyone has his or her own unique natural abilities—things they do well and that they most enjoy doing. These are our motivated abilities; when we use them, we feel most involved and fulfilled. The key to personal growth is to build on your motivated strengths rather than compensate for weaknesses. Your motivated strengths or abilities are driven by your talents, "your naturally recurring patterns of thought, feeling or behavior" (Buckingham and Clifton, 2001). The key to personal success and job satisfaction is to use your motivated abilities, which are also referred to as success motivators. These motivators are enduring patterns that emerge early in life. They are constant and irresistible, meaning that we try to use them every chance we can.

Unfortunately, many people end up getting skilled at something for which they have no passion and then make it their livelihood. In the process, they lose sight of their natural talents. Unless you make the distinction between talent and skills, you can find yourself being like Tony, the Certified Public Accountant (CPA) who disliked numbers.

When he was in high school, Tony took a part-time job working in the local supermarket. He worked the register at one of the checkout counters. One day the head bookkeeper called in sick. The store manager asked Tony if he could help balance the register receipts with the cash. Tony was happy to pitch in and helped the manager. This went on for a couple of weeks until the bookkeeper returned. But Sally was only able to work part time until she got fully on her feet. Since Tony had done such a good job, the store manager asked that he fill in for Sally. Tony got a raise, and since he was a quick study, he soon learned the bookkeeping ropes. Tony's first love was working the cash register because he enjoyed talking to customers and bantering with the kids. The kids always wanted their moms to go to Tony's register.

Bookkeeping paid well, and the money went a long way to building his college fund. Sally's illness got to a point where she had to quit. Tony, the rising star, got the nod. Having just leased his first car and still needing money for college and dating, he gladly accepted twice his salary as head bookkeeper. He spent his hours in the back room crunching numbers. Every once in a while, he would go up front and try to spot the customers he used to make small talk with. At the end of his first two years in college, Tony had to declare a major. He thought about sociology and psychology. But he went with accounting because that was where the money was. And besides, he had the skills even though he didn't particularly like it. After all, he had to earn a living. (Are you getting the picture? Tony was perfecting his unmotivated strength.)

But that's not the end of the story. Tony got so involved in his accounting major that his love for human contact drowned in a sea of numbers. Upon graduation, Tony took a job at one of the Big 5 accounting firms. Despite his major in accounting, doing corporate audits for Fortune 100 companies was a real challenge and a far cry from keeping the books at the local supermarket. Tony felt pressed to gain more subject matter expertise. Plus, he had the added pressure of being engaged, and the wedding was only a year off. But getting up in the morning was tough. He could feel the knot in his stomach up to his throat. If he could only get his CPA and acquire more accounting skills, his struggle would be over. So he thought. And so he did. He got his CPA, and it was paid for by his employer. Newly credentialed, Tony was given even more challenging client assignments. He made a good living and sent his kids to college.

On his deathbed he hallucinated back to his supermarket days when he worked the register. He saw parents telling their kids, "No candy," at least until he could convince them with his special glance that just one piece wouldn't hurt. He still remembered the kids by name. He saw himself smiling shyly at Annette and the other young women who would flirt back with him. But those were the cash register days when Tony was a people person. Somewhere along the line, he became a numbers man.

Are you an accidental project manager? Do you love it? Do you want to make a living? Or do you want to have a life?

I know project managers who are in the same rut as Tony was, thinking that if they can just get that PMP® certification, things will be better. If you love project management, go for it. This book will take you to the next level. If you don't, then get a life. Reboot yourself. Using the tools in this chapter and the eXtreme Tools and Techniques section will show you how.

It's not hard to discover your success motivators. I recommend either the Jim Lewis method or, if you want a more formal approach, the SIMA method by People Management. Descriptions of both are included in the eXtreme Tools and Techniques section at the end of the book.

Eliminating Self-Defeating Beliefs

Writing in the early twentieth century, psychologist and philosopher William James wrote, "The greatest discovery of our times is that a man can change his life by changing his thoughts." Actually this was nothing new. Spiritual leaders have known this for thousands of years. James was just catching up with unconventional wisdom, but it was wisdom nonetheless. Remember Henry Ford's remark quoted in Chapter Two: "If you think you can you can. If you think you can't you can't. In either case you are right."

Your beliefs, conscious and unconscious, empowering and self-defeating, run your life. And unless you uncover and then investigate those self-defeating beliefs, you can remain stuck forever and never really know why. I had a self-defeating belief that helped turn me into a workaholic for twenty-three years. The belief was I needed to work sixty hours a week in order to succeed in publishing. Had I known how to investigate that belief, I might have had a better family life and saved myself from burnout.

I had another limiting belief, this one about management: management should provide me with sufficient resources to get my project done. That belief caused me to poor-mouth myself, which served to reinforce the basic belief. And since I didn't like to whine alone, I would lament to others, who were only too glad to echo that they were suffering the same management indignities. I now refer to this phenomenon of group whining as co-miserating—in other words, sharing the misery. I loved to find people to agree with me and help me prove that I was right.

Thanks to the work of Byron Katie, thousands of others and I have been able to transcend our self-defeating beliefs, which is the way out of self-pity and victimhood. It was the beginning of the end of suffering and self-misery. I'll show you how to do The Work, the term used to refer to Byron Katie's approach (2002) for ending suffering and creating inner peace.

To do The Work, do the following (more detail, including an example of a project manager using Katie's method to deal with self-defeating beliefs, can be found in the eXtreme Tools and Techniques section; also see www.TheWork.com):

- Describe and write down the situation: descriptions of people, circumstances, events, or behavior patterns that cause you stress or frustration.
- Identify underlying belief.
- Investigate each belief by asking Katie's four questions.
- Write turnaround sentences.

Uninvestigated beliefs are the primary cause of unhappiness. Investigating these beliefs frees you to come up with more options. And if there's anything an eXtreme project and project manger needs to succeed, it's alternatives.

Uninvestigated beliefs are the
primary cause of unhappiness.

Shattering and replacing self-defeating beliefs is fundamental for freeing yourself to be all you can be. It's the direct road to inner peace. It eliminates the middleman: having to rely on circumstances or others to change what is out of your control. You stay in control because you *can* control your beliefs. This is the ultimate freedom and empowerment: to rechoose what you want to believe. Change your mind; change your life.

Being Yourself

It's one thing to see and know yourself, including your underlying beliefs. It's another to actually *be* yourself. How can you bridge the gap between the knowing and the doing? This is an age-old question, and I don't pretend to have *the* answer. But I do have an approach that has worked for me and for countless others: putting your motivated abilities to work, which involves motivating yourself to change, discovering your life's purpose, creating an inspiring vision, and having an action plan.

Motivating Yourself to Change

Too many people wait for a crisis to hit before becoming serious about change. For example, you get laid off, rethink your life, and decide to pursue your dream of raising designer strawberries in North Carolina. As an Idealist by temperament, I tend to be introspective and motivated to self-search and reinvent myself. Most people, however, when laid off, go into high gear to find another job in their current profession even when they dislike their job. Given the need to meet their financial obligations, this is very understandable. Yet at some point, if they're lucky, they hit the breaking point. They get sick and tired of being sick and tired and make a change.

Waiting for a crisis to hit gives rise to what I now call the karaoke project manager (KPM). For the karaoke project manager, project management is not a true expression or extension of his or her authentic self. On the contrary, KPMs try to change their personality to match the requirements of project management. They do this by singing songs out of the PMBOK® (*The Guide to the Project Management Body of Knowledge*) instead of singing from their own hymnal. Rather than having their approach to project management become an expression of who they are, they become the unwitting parrot of someone else's material, not unlike the puppet speaking from the ventriloquist's lap. This is what happens when there is a gap between who you are and what you do. And when you're not authentic, you don't have the credibility to lead a team or lead a process. People will resist or just ignore you.

It's not necessary to wait for a crisis or become a KPM. You can be proactive regardless of your temperament. You can choose to make the time to discover your life's purpose and create an inspiring vision for yourself.

Discovering Your Purpose

Knowing your purpose and having a compelling vision to go with it can serve as the fuel to propel you to apply your motivated abilities.

Each of us has a heroic mission, a song that wants to be sung. When you are living on purpose, you go through the day feeling fulfilled and centered. Problems and setbacks still occur, but they seem to lose their punch because you have transcended them. In the absence of knowing your purpose, trivia prevails.

> *Each of us has a heroic mission,*
> *a song that wants to be sung.*

I discovered that my life's purpose is *to open myself and others to new possibilities.* How did I come to that conclusion? Someone recommended that I read Barbara Sher's book, *Wishcraft* (1979). I followed her techniques, and they enabled me to reinvent myself and, importantly, overcome my fears of the unknown. That was fifteen years ago, and I never looked back. And following her advice, I also made a mental movie of my ideal day and life, which helped reprogram my brain. Once I did that, I was able to pick a profession that made better use of my natural talents. Finally, my temperament and my job were congruent, and my internal struggle subsided.

To discover your purpose in life, take out the list of your motivated abilities that you developed from the eXtreme Tools and Techniques section. Find a quite place, and relax by taking a series of deep breaths. Then contemplate your list of motivated abilities and the patterns, and answer each of these questions by writing down the first thing that comes to mind (Sisgold, 1993):

- What is my purpose for being on the planet right now?
- What is uniquely valuable about me?
- What do I have to offer others?
- How can I express my purpose in my job right now?
- How can I express my purpose in my relationships?
- If I were starting from scratch and there were no limitations, how could I express my purpose in my career? That is, what professions—could I use to deliver my purpose?
- Where in my life am I already aligned with my purpose?
- Where am I not aligned?

Now create a concise purpose statement about who you really are. This is one that I did for myself: "I accept and express myself as a creative and dynamic person who is making a difference by helping people to open up to new possibilities in their work and personal lives. I do this through the vehicles of project management, team building, and Self-Mastery."

Creating a Compelling Vision for Yourself

Once you've written down your purpose statement (and you can do this on another day), find a quiet place and relax. Keeping your purpose statement in front of you, make a mental movie of your ideal: the perfect day from the time you get up until the time you go to bed. This is your compelling vision.

I define a vision as a set of thoughts, mental pictures, and feelings about an ideal situation. In this case, the situation is your life. By answering the following questions, you will begin to preexperience the life you want to have:

- Where are you living?
- What does the surrounding community look like?
- What's the weather like?
- Who's in the picture?

- What does your home look like, room by room? How is it decorated? What colors predominate?
- What do you see when you look out?
- How does your day unfold from the time you get up, hour by hour? Who are you interacting with during the course of the day? What are you doing together? How are others feeling having interacted with you? What are you feeling?
- What are some of the most rewarding things people would be saying about you?

The magic of visioning cannot be understated. Once you've saturated yourself with what your ideal day looks and feels like, an invisible hand will take over, and you will begin unconsciously to select those people and experiences that will lead you to your destination, even in the absence of a detailed plan. There's no need for self-misery. All you need is your imagination and a willingness to dream. Dare to dream.

Taking Action

It's not necessary to jump ship if you are unhappy. Once you have a sense of your life's purpose and a mental picture of your ideal life, you can incorporate some of your desired attributes into your everyday life.

Here's a minimalist action plan. Keep it simple. The idea is to get started doing just one thing that gets you more closely aligned with your purpose and vision:

1. Jot down three things you could do at work that would enable you to express your purpose and your vision more fully.
2. Do the same for your personal life.
3. Pick one or two things you can get started with in the next two days.

Expressing your unique purpose and motivated abilities though the vehicle of project management can be very satisfying and rewarding. I know from firsthand experience.

Asserting Yourself

The demanding nature of eXtreme projects can push you to your limits. To succeed, you need to draw the line when a peer or a superior wants to push you beyond what you are ready, willing, or able to do. It means knowing how to say no. I call this NoHow. You can't accommodate everything that everybody wants. Moreover, eXtreme project managers need to influence others without necessarily having sufficient organizational clout by virtue of job title or even by virtue of a strong enough project sponsor. Asserting yourself also means exercising your personal (intrinsic) powers, those that no one can ever take from you.

Exercising Your Personal Power

I never play into the victim mentality of those who bemoan their lack of authority to go with their responsibilities as project managers. The No Authority Syndrome is a trap. You have the power to get things done, even though you don't have authority, people, or money. In reality, you may have a lot more power than you realize.

You have the power to get things done, even though you don't have authority, people, or money.

Power refers to your clout. *Influence* refers to the skills and techniques you use to deploy your power and get what you want. Wielding your power and exercising your influencing skills go hand and hand. (I cover influencing skills in Chapter Five.)

Personal power comes from within. It's power that you have direct control over and is independent of external circumstances such as your position in the hierarchy or other people's opinion of you. Personal power is home grown. Since you are running an eXtreme project, you'll want to take advantage of every source of internal power you can.

Following are the different types of personal power that are important for those working on eXtreme projects.

Authentic Power. Authentic power is routed in a strong sense of personal values, principles, and practices. It is not a technique you use but a way of being. The hallmarks are self-esteem, self-confidence, and self-credibility. The test is your ability to direct yourself, whether it's about losing five pounds, or surviving seven years as a prisoner of war, or not compromising your values. It means being loyal to yourself rather than pleasing others at your own expense. It can mean walking away from an untenable situation.

People with authentic power participate in the fray, but they are much bigger than their jobs and Monday morning traffic jams. They are able to transcend the madness of everyday trials and tribulations, not getting crushed by the drama of it all. Their spirit is bigger than the drama around them. In terms of influencing others, there is no more potent source of power, because regardless of how bad things get, you are able to keep yourself intact and move forward. That alone will influence others. Churchill, Mother Teresa, and Gandhi exercised personal power. So can you.

I believe that authentic power is the most difficult source of power for people to tap into. That's because we've been conditioned to look to external sources—social norms, professional societies, even TV—to derive our personal values, if not our main identity. It's ironic: what we are looking for, our real, authentic self, is already inside us. We need to first reclaim ourselves. It's a question of tapping into the gold that's already there by putting into practice the first two elements of Self-Mastery: See yourself, Be yourself. These generate the self-knowledge and passion that unleash this, the third element: Assert yourself.

Self-Disclosure Power. This is where you open yourself up and reveal your vulnerability and your feelings. You ask for help. Here you might admit to your sponsor that you've tried everything and you are at your wit's end. Perhaps you made a mistake that set things back two weeks, and you need to extend the schedule. Or you have the courage to admit that you can't solve a particular problem and don't worry about saving face. Self-disclosure power is one of your most potent sources of power because it aims at the person's heart center and can enlist empathy, if not compassion. Self-disclosure power derives its effectiveness from the eXtreme project management Shared Value of honest communication and Accelerator 2: Build on people's desire to make a difference. That will help enlist them to help you.

Speak-Up Power. My personal opinion is that lack of assertiveness, which I call the good soldier syndrome, is a major cause of project failure. Project managers who willingly say yes to every new request and without examining its impact—put the project at risk. Worse yet, for fear of telling it like it is, some would even go along with a project that they know is doomed to fail before it gets off the ground. Niel

Whitten, a project management expert, is fond of saying that the number 1 problem of project managers is being too soft.

*The good soldier syndrome is a
major cause of project failure.*

Speak-up power means standing up for the truth and doing so in a constructive (as opposed to aggressive) way. Here are examples of assertive behavior and passive or aggressive behavior:

Passive behavior: Self-abuse (you win, I lose): "Yes, sir. Great idea. Wow. Let's go with it."

Aggressive behavior: Abuse of others (I win, you lose): "Shove it. We've been barraged constantly with your change requests throughout the entire project. Your committee continues to change direction and to be insensitive to the negative impacts these last-minute requests are creating."

Assertive behavior: Mutual respect for yourself and others: "Interesting idea. Right now, we're spread thin and other projects are at risk. Once I know the impact this will have on our schedule and budget, I'll get back to you with options and a recommendation for your final decision. I'll need forty-eight hours to do this."

Knowing how to say no with respect for yourself and others is what I call NoHow (see the eXtreme Tools and Techniques section for a step-by-step approach to NoHow). Speak-up power is one of your most important power sources. It is fueled by the shared value of courage, which means to have the fear and do it anyway.

Process Power. Here your power lies in your ability to establish and lead a project process that fits the project at hand. Process power connects the dots, making it possible for people to synchronize their work in pursuit of a common goal. To succeed at this, you need to be convinced that the process you will use has the best chance of getting the job done.

One of the biggest victim traps that project managers fall into is to believe that they need to get permission to practice good project management. Many people are given permission to practice project abuse or bad project management by virtue of official project management practices that are mandated but don't work and even make things worse.

So, who do you look to for permission to practice good project management? Look no further than the mirror. Nobody has to give you permission to practice good project management, to do the right thing. Again, the Shared Value of courage is the operative value here.

Take a look at the content in this book and you'll be hard-pressed to find an eXtreme project management tool, technique, shared value, project accelerator, business question, or skill for which you will need outside approval to put into practice. They can even be used in Newtonian cultures to accelerate projects and take the drudgery out of traditional and prescriptive practices. The test of a good practice is that it makes life easier and gets results. When you introduce a practice and it works, people will want more of what you got.

There will be times when you will run into a practice clash, meaning you would have to violate the prescribed internal practice because it is counterproductive to meeting the project's deliverables and business outcome. That's why you need guts power.

Guts Power. This power source is often invoked when all else fails. You simply refuse to do something or decide to break the rules. You step on toes, take the bull by the horns, annoy a few people, and get it done. You unilaterally defy the project management police and circumvent the 255-page imposed project management methodology. You don't ask for permission, just forgiveness. This takes guts.

Remember that personal power comes from within. It is independent of external circumstances such as your position on the organizational chart or other people's opinion of you. As an eXtreme project manager, you'll want to take advantage of every source of internal power you can.

Taking It to a Higher Court

There are three levels that we can work on to arrive at a place of inner peace, the goal of Self-Mastery. The levels parallel what are commonly referred to as body, mind, and spirit:

The physical: We seek peace by getting what we want by virtue of power and influence. Although we may reason and collaborate with others, when push comes to shove, we rely on our might, willpower, or prowess to win.

The mental: We strive to gain a sense of peace primarily by getting what we want through the use of our mind. We plan, set goals, outsmart the competition, figure things out, uncover and deploy our motivated abilities, and use many of the tools and techniques described in this book. We act smart.

The spiritual: We recognize that there is a higher order of things that ultimately we can't outsmart or power our way into getting our way. On the spiritual level, we surrender to and join forces with the unseen higher power, a force that we come to know as being greater than ourselves.

So far, I've been drawing mainly from the powers that come from the mental level. However, the volatile and unpredictable conditions characteristic of eXtreme projects can push us to a point of realizing that not even our most brilliant or collective mental efforts are enough to achieve our goal. We become blinded, seeing no way out. Under these circumstances, with no place left to turn, I find myself doing two things: asking for a miracle and repeating the serenity prayer. I can't explain how either of these works. To do so would be to attempt to explain the unexplainable. All I know is they work for me. Maybe they will for you.

Asking for a Miracle

When I ask for a miracle, I ask a higher power to show me how to perceive the current situation (or person) in a different way, a more peaceful way. A miracle doesn't mean asking for your desktop computer to be turned into gold bullion. A miracle is asking for shift in one's perception.

When I'm upset because someone was rude to me or even wronged me, I now turn to the something-that-is-more-than-what-I-am and ask, "How can I see this person (or situation) in a different way?" This doesn't mean that I walk away from the person or situation. It means that I deal with it from a place of peace rather than from a position of war, and do so even when I know I'm right.

In her book *A Return to Love* (1992), Marianne Williamson puts it this way, "Do you want to be right or do you want to be happy?"

When I ask for a miracle, I don't know why it works. It's way beyond me. I've gotten to a point where I no longer have to be able to explain the unexplainable or the invisible in order to enlist its powers. I've gotten to the point of realizing that faith is inescapable. If I don't have faith in something, I therefore have faith in nothing. It's still faith. So I've made a choice: I will have faith in the unexplainable, the invisible because it works for me.

Serenity Prayer

I find myself saying this prayer at least three times a day. I don't know why (and I no longer seek to know why) it works, it just puts me in a more peaceful state of mind. It bears repeating.

> Grant me the serenity to accept the things I cannot change,
> the courage to change the things I can
> And the wisdom to know difference.

◆ ◆ ◆

You can be successful using any one or more of the three levels of power. I use all three. I just want to hedge my bet. To discover how you can take it to a higher court, see "The Power of Meditation" in the eXtreme Tools and Techniques section.

The next four chapters take an in-depth look at Critical Success Factor 2: Leadership by Commitment. We begin with a description of the eXtreme project manager's leadership role.

eXtreme Project Management Model
Applying the Quantum Mind-Set

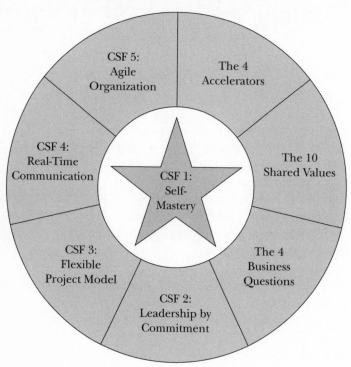

Chapter Four

The eXtreme Project Manager's Leadership Role

We can convert energy from one form to another.
THE LAW OF CONSERVATION OF ENERGY

The overarching role of the eXtreme project manager is to gain and sustain commitment to the project mission. Leadership by Commitment is Critical Success Factor 2 in the eXtreme project management model. Commitment is the energy that propels the project. Indifference and interpersonal conflict are energies that clog the project's energy field and stop it in its tracks.

eXtreme project managers gain and sustain commitment by being the project catalyst: the agent who takes action in a way that keeps the project's energy field fluid and productive. The project's energy field consists of the project's *content*—the thing or service that is being created—and the *context*—the internal and external environments that surround the content.

Although the eXtreme project manager oversees the project's entire energy field, her primary job is to manage the context, that is, facilitate and manage the flow of emotions, thoughts, and interactions in a way that produces valued outcomes. As an eXtreme project manager, you are the project's energy manager. The difference between the project's context and content is an all-important distinction. Not living up to this distinction is a major cause of failure for eXtreme project managers.

In this chapter, I'll explain the context for eXtreme projects in detail, exploring all the players and their roles and the eXtreme project manager's role and responsibilities regarding these players. I'll also take a closer look at what is meant by commitment and reinforce the need for process leadership, the major source of your power in your role as catalyst of the project's energy field. I'll describe the main sources of external power that you can unleash in order to help you get things done. Specifically, I'll answer these questions:

- Why is the context versus content distinction so critical?
- What does the successful eXtreme project manager know and do?
- Who are the key stakeholders in the eXtreme project manager's world?
- What is commitment?
- Who needs to be committed?
- Why does commitment falter or never happen in the first place?
- What is the difference between leading and managing?
- How do you keep the project in control?
- Why do eXtreme project managers fail?
- What are your sources of external power?
- What do you do when commitment is not obtainable?

The next three chapters then focus on the tools you need to be successful in your role as eXtreme project manager.

The eXtreme Project Manager's Role

In their book *Surfacing the Edge of Chaos,* Gioia, Milleman, and Pascale (2001) tell the story of a couple who inherited a cottage from their aunt. In redecorating one room in particular, they went through several iterations changing the upholstery and color scheme to get the room to their liking. But to no avail. Then one day the light bulb in the ceiling fixture burned out. When they went to change it, they noticed that the bulb's color was yellow. Then they understood: the yellow bulb was casting an unpleasant hue over the entire room and altering the color scheme and the effect they were trying to achieve. No matter what they did to manipulate the color scheme, it would always be influenced by the color of the light bulb.

In this story, the *context* (the yellow hue) had more to do with a satisfactory result than did the *content* (the fabric and wall coloring) of the room. In fact, manipulating the room's content wasted time and money and got the young couple nowhere.

In project management terms, success requires the integration of the business and political aspects with the technical aspects of the venture. The technical aspects deal with the project's content: the product or service to be produced. The business and political side has to do with the context (the surrounding environment) within which the product or service is being developed. Context management boils down to managing the expectations of stakeholders or, in other words, relationship management.

Success requires the integration of the business and political aspects with the technical aspects of the venture.

Think of Your Project as a Flower Garden

Another way of making this crucial distinction between context and content is to think of your project as a garden, an ecosystem made up of flowers, soil, and weather conditions (Table 4.1). In this metaphor the flower is the content; the soil and the surrounding weather conditions constitute the context. Both the soil and weather are critical for the survival, growth, and quality of the flowers. If the soil is toxic or the weather is inhospitable, the flowers won't live no matter how well they are tended. (This explains why palm trees won't grow on the streets of Alaska.)

A project's context is made up of the internal and external environments that surround the project. The external environment comprises the business conditions: the competition, government regulations, and third-party suppliers, for example. The internal environment consists of the thoughts, emotions, and interactions that surround and consequently shape the project content (the thing being developed). This takes the form of stakeholder expectations and opinions, including the politics of the project and the level of cooperation and support given to the project. The internal context also includes the organization's systems and policies.

All of the internal variables interact to form an overall attitude about the project. If the prevailing attitude (context) about the

Table 4.1. The Project as an Ecosystem

	Garden	Project Equivalent
Context: The conditions and volatility surrounding the content of the project	Weather: Sun, rain, sleet, temperature	External environment: Changes in competition, technology, government regulations, third-party suppliers, consumer tastes, economy, politics
	Soil: chemical makeup, fertility, depth, toxicity	Internal environment: Quality of thoughts, emotions, interactions surrounding the project; stakeholder expectations, systems, policies; the overall attitude about the project
Content	Flowers	The product or service being developed
Project role	The farmer: Detoxify the soil; build a greenhouse; manage the enterprise; work with a horticulturist to make adjustments (such as irrigation) due to weather	Project manager: Foster a positive attitude about the project; manage the energy by facilitating the flow of thoughts, emotions, and interactions; manage the project as a business
Tools	Tractor, fertilizer, watering system, shelter	Relationship management; facilitation, negotiation, interpersonal, political skills, technology infrastructure
Technical role	Horticulturist: Cultivate the flowers	Technical/development manager: Build the product or service

project becomes negative, any resultant flower will be perceived as a weed to be avoided or destroyed, with all the blame going to the farmer (also known as the project manager).

A major challenge to succeeding on eXtreme projects is that they live under turbulent conditions. Not only is the weather unpredictable and changeable, it's usually bad. Competition is disrupting plans, the political climate can shift, new government regulations have an impact on your project, technology can change midstream, outside vendors can leave you stranded. The role of the eXtreme project manager is to foster a positive attitude by creating a success-minded mentality (conducive internal context) and to enable the project to continually adapt to volatile external and as well as internal circumstances.

Job Description

The energy of a typical funeral is noticeably different from that of a bunch of people celebrating their team's Superbowl victory. The energy is palpable. So too a project's energy field is palpable. Commitment energy is palpable. Everyone feels something about the project. In case you didn't put it to the test before, try this now. Think of one or more current projects you are familiar with. Imagine the project is a person. How would you describe that person's energy field or mood? Upbeat, depressed? Positive, negative? Confident, fearful? Happy, doom and gloom? Vibrant, bogged down?

A positive energy field enables the project to move ahead with speed and confidence and creates a success-minded mentality. Perceived success begets success. Perceived failure begets failure. This is important because the perception of success or failure infuses the project's energy with that quality, just as the intake of nutrients and light determines the health of the plant.

Managing the project's energy field is accomplished by managing the project context. For the eXtreme project manager this is a fourfold role: navigating the political landscape, generating results, managing the mood, and ensuring business value (Exhibit 4.1).

By this time, the following definition should come as no surprise: the job of the project manager is to manage the project's energy field by facilitating and managing the flow of emotions, thoughts, and interactions in a way that produces valued outcomes.

Exhibit 4.1. The Role of the eXtreme Project Manager

Navigate the Political Landscape

- Get the sponsor you need to succeed.
- Establish good relationships and working agreements with key stakeholders.
- Ensure that the sponsor and critical stakeholders are continually aligned around the business case and the project's win conditions.
- Build win-win partnerships with suppliers and managers of interdependent projects.
- Influence and lead without authority.
- Negotiate *(for people, funds, capital equipment, time, and so on)*.

Generate Results

- Put the project management infrastructure in place *(eXtreme Project Management process, tools, templates, real-time communication capability)*.
- Facilitate decision making.
- Demonstrate early and ongoing results.
- Ensure customer acceptance of interim and final project deliverables.
- Track progress.

Manage the Mood

- Turn a disparate group into a functioning unit.
- Establish a working environment that empowers the team.
- Continually eliminate everyday barriers to doing good work.
- Find the WOW! factor.[a]
- Facilitate the resolution of interpersonal conflict.
- Recognize and reward individual and team behavior.
- Coach and encourage.

Ensure Business Value

- Maintain strategic (versus task) orientation.
- Focus on the business benefits.
- Continually address the 4 Business Questions.

---

[a]This is a term used by Tom Peters (1999). The WOW! factor is what will make the project exciting and memorable, with an important, even revolutionary impact. It unleashes the energy of people to want to participate.

A key word in my definition of project manager is *facilitate*, which means to make it easier to get things done. With respect to project stakeholders, the role of the project manager is to make it easier for them to resolve their own conflicts regarding scope, quality, and other business considerations. In this sense, the project manager is a catalyst in making things happen. The context of an eXtreme project has significantly more to do with project success than does the content, just like the soil and weather conditions have much more to do with the success of the plant than does the pruning. eXtreme projects rarely fail due to a lack of technical know-how. More often than not, we find a way to do it. Rather, eXtreme projects fail because the context defeats the ability to execute the technical know-how in a way that the deliverable solves the intended problem. And this is why eXtreme projects require a dedicated project manager and a separate manager responsible for product or technical development. As shown in Table 4.2, the development or technical manager is the subject matter expert.

The role of the eXtreme project manager is to till the soil; the role of the technical or development manager is to attend to the plant. This represents a major difference between the eXtreme project manager and the traditional project manager, whose emphasis is heavily oriented toward pruning plants rather than managing the farm to ensure good conditions for growth. Your job as eXtreme project manager is to detoxify the soil. Let the technical manager cultivate the plant.

A major reason eXtreme project managers fail is that they neglect to manage the project context by responding to the conditions surrounding the development effort: stakeholder emotions, thoughts, and interactions. In the energy field model, the role of the technical or development manager is akin to that of a horticulturist: to transform stakeholder thoughts (ideas, needs, objectives) into physical form.

A major reason eXtreme project managers fail is that they neglect to manage the project context.

Even if you are expert in the product or service being developed, you need to get off the case and ensure this function is placed

Table 4.2. The Domains of the
Project Manager and the Development Manager

Project Manager	Components Shared in Common[a]	Technical or Development Manager
Focus: Context— managing the flow of thoughts (decisions, facts, information, idea), emotions, and interactions	Shared: A common understanding of the collective vision for the project	Focus: Content— transforming stakeholder needs into a valued product or service
Project management	Objectives, deliverables, business outcome	Technical or product management (engineering, research, technical side)
Overall project leadership	Project mission statement	Technical team leadership
Relationship management		Requirements management
Emotional well-being of the project	Project boundaries	Design
Stakeholders and politics	Show stoppers	Specifications
Dependent projects	Requirements	Development, testing
Business value, benefits and costs	Win conditions	Prototypes, working models
Risks		Documents
Time line		
Documents		
Status reporting		

[a]These elements are covered in Part Three.

in the hands of another expert. Your job is to manage the energy called commitment and not meddle in the content. You need just enough knowledge to understand the technical issues and be conversant about the technology.

In practice, a project manager who also happens to be a subject matter expert for the product being developed may be called on for technical advice. That advice is best given as input for the technical team or subject matter experts to consider. When there is a change in scope and the business owner adds another requirement, the project manager's job is to look at the impact on cost and benefits, dependent projects, risks, and time line. The technical manager focuses on design, development, and other engineering and research implications. Both would work in concert, but each within his and her expertise.

Enlightened pharmaceutical companies, software development, and new product development organizations have made the context-content distinction and employ a separate project manager and development manager.

If you are in a position of having to be both context and content manager, the next best thing is to segment your time. Perhaps work mornings as technical manager and devote afternoons navigating the organization.

Stakeholders: The eXtreme Project Management Context

A stakeholder is anyone who can have an impact on the success or failure of your project either before or after the project has been completed. Stakeholders can be internal or external to the organization and can include those who will provide inputs to your project, such as needed products and services, funding, approvals, resources, and other projects that you will rely on for your own project.

Also important (and often forgotten until it's too late) are stakeholders who will be affected by your project once it is completed: the project's customers. The world is littered with well-intentioned projects that are ignored or circumvented once they are delivered to the customer, who says, "That's what I asked for, but not what I needed" or "I didn't ask for it and don't need it."

Stakeholders can also include individuals or groups who have information essential to the project, such as other project managers who have worked on similar projects and regulators who have information on impending legislation.

The people who populate the project's energy field wear many different labels and can have an impact on your project before or after completion:

You	Consumers
Your family	General public
Your project	Subject matter experts
The core project team	Project facilitator
Other project managers	Department managers
Project sponsor	Resource providers
Upper management	Outside suppliers
Steering committee	Government agencies
Business owner	Competitors
Internal customers	Project office
External customers	Your boss
Customer representatives	

The most important relationship you have is the one with yourself. Since eXtreme projects put extreme demands on your personal and professional life—demands to achieve, demands for time, demands to choose between work and family and between health and sanity—you need to take care of yourself. Unless you treat yourself as your most important stakeholder, you set yourself up for burnout. That's why Critical Success Factor 1, Self-Mastery, is an important part of this book. The project sponsor is your second most important stakeholder. Without strong sponsorship, your project is doomed to die.

The eXtreme Core Team and Subteams

Most eXtreme Projects involve multiple teams. Subteams are composed of technical and subject matter experts, including customer experts. A subteam has the following roles:

- Does the actual work of the project
- Is empowered to make technical decisions

- Is empowered to organize itself as it sees fit
- Coordinates its work with other subteams and resolves conflicts
- Ensures business value by continually addressing the 4 Business Questions
- Eliminates ongoing barriers that block progress
- Reports on subteam project status
- Adjusts and applies the eXtreme project process to its own work

In my client practice, the eXtreme core team is a team of teams, made up of the leaders or project managers of the various subteams, where each subteam representative speaks for one or more subteams. Core teams are typically cross-functional and cross-hierarchical. Not only is it rare that anyone on this team reports to you, often you will be outranked by functional managers who are on the team. Taken together, the different subject matter experts on the core team represent all the subteams comprising the entire project. You can think of the eXtreme core team, then, as a meta team. It has these roles:

- Oversees the entire project (or program)
- Ensures business value by continually addressing the 4 Business Questions for the overall project
- Serves as the interface with the project sponsor
- Reports on status for the project as a whole
- Synchronizes the work of subteams beyond what they themselves can do
- Resolves conflicting priorities among subteams
- Eliminates barriers that the subteams can't
- Makes business and technical decisions that have an impact on the project as a whole
- Champions the eXtreme project process
- Recommends that the project continue or not based on answers to the 4 Business Questions

As the core team's facilitator, your job is to lead the decision-making process, serving as catalyst to ensure buy-in among members on critical decisions. Critical decisions are those that will stop the project in its tracks or put it at risk unless there is sufficient support. Unless the eXtreme project manager takes on the role of core team facilitator and leader of the project process, she is abdicating her position to becoming the project number cruncher and scorekeeper, an administrative position that is important but insufficient for success. And in the absence of a process leader, the project will live its life in the storming stage: people working in an uncoordinated and uncooperative way. This is what happens when no one is leading the process. I'll return to the core project team in Chapter Six.

The eXtreme Project Sponsor

Your sponsor is the second most important stakeholder (you are the first). Without a strong sponsor, you and the project are doomed.

The effective eXtreme project sponsor has a vested interest in the project. This means that she has the organizational responsibility to ensure that the business benefits of the project are realized after the project deliverable is produced. The sponsor is also considered to be a part of the eXtreme project core team, and as is the case with other members, holds herself mutually accountable.

If you had to boil an eXtreme project down to the single point of failure or success, it would be the quality of the project sponsor. In theory, this means that the project manager is off the hook if the project goes down in smoke. But in reality, since project risk is typically assigned to the project manager, you are most often the scapegoat. You owe it to yourself and to the project to do everything in your power to ensure you have the right project sponsor.

If you had to boil an eXtreme project down
to the single point of failure or success, it would
be the quality of the project sponsor.

Job Description

As you examine the following project sponsor job description, you will see parallels with the eXtreme project manager's job description; in that sense, the project manager and sponsor work in concert at their respective organizational levels:

Ensure business value

- Ensure that postproject business benefits are realized.
- Throughout the project, continually address Business Question 4: Is it worth it?
- Have the final word when prioritizing the 7 Win Conditions (schedule, cost, scope, quality, return on investment, customer satisfaction, and team satisfaction, which are covered in Chapter Eight).
- Approve the scope of the project.

Navigate the political landscape

- Resolve conflicts among competing projects.
- Ensure crucial stakeholders are continually aligned around the business case.
- Defend the project.
- Serve on the steering committee.

Support the project

- Resource the project and fill gaps: people, funds, and capital.
- Review the project's vital signs.
- Empower a qualified project manager.
- Be accessible to the project manager at all times.
- Make unilateral decisions when required.
- Make timely decisions.

Here are a few notes about the sponsor's job description:

- The steering committee is composed of a cross-organizational mix of sponsors of interdependent projects. This topic is covered in Chapter Seven.
- In making timely decisions, we're talking minutes and hours, not days. A rule of thumb is that the sponsor needs to get back to you within two hours.
- Monitoring the vital signs includes changes in scope and business assumptions as well as gauging stakeholder satisfaction with results, ensuring risks are being managed, and reviewing status against budget and schedule.

• In addition to being accountable for the realization of business benefits, the other job responsibilities that distinguish the eXtreme sponsor from her counterpart on a traditional project are the constant availability, as well as making quick, and at times unilateral, decisions. In the ideal world, consensus might be the way to go. But under extreme conditions, the luxury of time is not available to round up crucial stakeholders and get to consensus or consult with the executive committee, which meets next week. Hence, the sponsor must have sufficient clout to be able to convince crucial stakeholders to support the decision after it's made.

• Another key point is the need for the sponsor to address conflicts among stakeholders, which typically revolve around adding or changing requirements. For example, the sales vice president wants to expand the project scope and make the entire product catalogue available on the company Web site. Marketing, however, wants to include only the auto parts and not the truck parts for now. You do a quick impact analysis to show how this would affect the schedule, cost, risk, and payback. Armed with that information, the sponsor's job is to make the call.

What You Should Expect from the Project Office

As manager and facilitator of the project's energy field (the project's flow of emotions, thoughts, and interactions), little is more important to success than focusing on relationship management. It takes desire, aptitude, and a willingness to deemphasize the traditional project manager's role of project administrator and scorekeeper in favor of ensuring that the conflicting needs of the project's crucial stakeholders are met or at least neutralized.

It is under these circumstances that the organization's project office (or whatever other name is used, such as project support group or project management organization) can be an invaluable aid to the eXtreme project manager. The support group can provide a project administrator who can handle the project bookkeeping tasks, freeing you to manage the project's mood and emotional well-being.

Making It Easier for Resource Providers

Develop your own personal working relationships with functional managers, and use your emotional intelligence to be sensitive to the demands being placed on them. When negotiating for people, it's generally best to give a description of the skills and level of experience you need rather than insist on a specific person by name. This gives the functional manager more options to meet your requirements. Importantly, whoever is granted to your team, you want to insist that he be the single point of accountability, avoiding a revolving door of loaned team members and complicating your job by having to work with two or more individuals.

Customers

Since eXtreme project management is people- and customer-centric, the eXtreme project manager ensures that the customer receives value each step of the way and is happy with the final deliverable. Indeed, these are critical measures of success.

Your Role as Process Leader

As process leader for the core project team, your primary role is to create an environment in which people become empowered to make decisions, solve problems, and do quality work. Fortunately, it's not about rah-rah speeches, which few people are good at anyway. And even if you were a motivational speaker, the engendered enthusiasm rarely lasts longer than the flavor of chewing gum. Your job is to make it possible for people to succeed by creating the circumstances for success.

In the Newtonian world, power comes from job title and position along the hierarchy. Because power and decision making are centralized, the Newtonian model saps the project of its vital creative energy by shifting control from the team and stakeholder community at large to the boss, who is considered to be the one in control. The centralization of power saps the project of the creative energy necessary for innovation and adaptability.

In this traditional model, the project manager sees her role as trying to get more out of people. In the quantum model, your role is to make it possible for people to do more. You do this through introducing appropriate processes and practices (such as good meeting management) and establishing a productive working environment, all of which facilitate the flow of emotions, thoughts, and feelings in a way that produces a valued outcome and speeds things up. On an eXtreme project properly run, no one is in control. Instead, everyone is in control. Leadership by commitment empowers. Leadership by control disempowers.

Fortunately, Newtonian-like control power is rarely available to the eXtreme project manager. You typically have little leverage by virtue of your organizational position or job title. So how do you lead a team of people who do not report to you in the organizational sense, have other allegiances, and don't even like the sound of the words *project management?*

In the quantum world, *your power resides in the process you use to empower people to get things done,* not in direct power over people. You are not leading people; you are leading the process. And by leading the process, you are leading the thinking. Your power also comes from the quality of relationships you establish with stakeholders. If blood is thicker than water, relationships are thicker than organizational charts.

This is a shift from the Newtonian to a quantum worldview. These two worldviews are similar to the reward/threat versus the organic model that Gerald Weinberg refers to in his book, *On Becoming a Technical Leader* (1986): "Instead of leading people as in the reward threat/model, organic leadership leads the process. Leading people requires that they relinquish control over their lives. Leading the process is responsible to people, giving them choices and leaving them in control" (p. 12).

This puts you face to face with the power paradox: you stay in control by distributing control. But watch out: the process you use needs to fit the problem. Newtonian project management is process heavy, whether you need it or not. It can put people in a straitjacket, sapping them of control and flexibility. Instead of the process working for them, they can end up working to feed the process. That's why you need to consider using a flexible project process. (See Part Two.)

You stay in control by distributing control.

In managing projects under extreme conditions, decision outcomes cannot be known with certainty. Outcomes are the result of multiple interactions. Even if you had all of the direct authority you wanted over people, this is potentially dangerous on eXtreme projects when it resorts to telling people what to do and how to do it or solving their problems for them or making decisions that others should own. No one is smart enough on an eXtreme project to have all the answers. By leading the process, you are making it possible for others to self-organize and self-correct, to discover and do right thing. You are the facilitator of disorder.

Tom DeMarco and Tim Lister (1999), summarize the essence of being a project manager:

- Get the right people.
- Make them happy so they don't want to leave.
- Turn them loose.

I've found that process power can be more powerful than even position power. You may know managers who have substantial position power but can't get people to work effectively toward a common goal. Process power saves the day every time. But all this does not mean that laissez-faire is *the* modus operandi when it comes to leading the core project team. There are times when consensus is best and times when a directive style is the way to go.

Process power is your way out of the storming and the chaos that goes with it. It makes senses out of nonsense, cuts a path out of chaos, and integrates the flow of thoughts and work toward achieving the intended outcome. It turns goals into reality. It unleashes motivation and innovation, produces tangible products, and fosters confidence and trust. It enables people to make a difference and ultimately to succeed.

Good process well applied makes heroes and heroines out of project managers. Seeing yourself as managing the process rather than leading people is a powerful new paradigm shift from the Newtonian to the quantum worldview. It makes you incredibly effective.

The sort of process that you should lead produces results under conditions of high change and high uncertainty. It builds commitment by fostering motivation, innovation, trust, and confidence and provides the customer with tangible value early and often. An effective process, like the one covered in Part Three of this book, makes it possible for people to make effective decisions and get work done. By leading the eXtreme project management process, you are expanding the capacity of the project energy field to get work done, and as a result, you are creating the circumstances for success.

But here's the rub: just because you know and love a particular process for managing projects, running effective meetings, and building teams doesn't mean that everybody will happily follow your lead. You have to know how to implement the process, to put it in play and prove that it works. In order for nonbelievers (and they are likely to be in the majority) to become believers, people need to *experience* short-term success with whatever process you use. Only then will you earn the right to be the process leader and gain the commitment of your team.

> *People need to* experience *short-term success with whatever process you use.*

Gaining Commitment

Commitment is a positive energy, an upbeat feeling that permeates and propels the project. Indifference or derision are negative energies that bog things down.

In my view, true commitment occurs when an individual or a group is emotionally compelled to move forward because he or she genuinely wants to achieve the intended goal or mission of the project. Typically, this means that combinations of two ingredients are present: desire and confidence. Desire is personal or internally directed. People desire to be a part of something when it meets their need for personal gain (for example, getting promoted, learning new skills, or being part of something important). Confidence is more externally directed. By confidence, I mean the belief that the circumstances surrounding the project are conducive to success, that the project is felt to be realistic for any number of reasons: realistic time frame, sufficient resources, solid sponsorship, the required tools, systems and processes available, strong stakeholder support, the right team, and so forth.

Commitment equals desire plus confidence. The more of each ingredient there is, the greater is the level of commitment. When team members are truly committed, they experience a sense of mutual accountability for their project and go the extra mile without being asked. They show up for team meetings. They get their work done on time. They do not have to be prodded and pushed each step of the way.

When commitment is not present, people act out of obligation or compliance, and may lack the extra drive to put the project over the top. As illustrated in Figure 4.1, the goal is to move your project into quadrant IV and keep it there. A quadrant IV project has both confidence and desire.

When the project lives in quadrant IV, it benefits from a good, healthy energy. And like attracts like. Successful project managers are able keep the project in quadrant IV. eXtreme project management boils down to the knowledge, skills, process, and tools for getting to and staying in quadrant IV. And that's what this book is about.

Gaining the commitment of team members and the project sponsor is only part of the equation. Without the commitment of customers, functional managers, and other stakeholders and influencers, success will be elusive: decisions will be delayed, team members will be reassigned to other projects, suppliers will miss deadlines, and politics will undermine the project in subtle ways.

Why does commitment falter or never happen? Here are some common reasons for low desire (lack of personal gain) and low

Figure 4.1. The Four Quadrants of Confidence and Desire

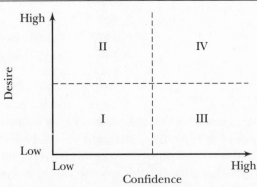

confidence (lack of trust in others and circumstances in general) among team members on a project (based on informal surveys taken during my workshops):

Reasons for low desire	*Reasons for low confidence*
• Been there; done that. Already working sixty-hour weeks.	• The team doesn't have the skills.
• Don't see the business value for the project.	• People spread too thin; competing priorities.
• My role is unclear.	• Project manager has dubious track record.
• Little or no say in how the project will be run.	• Unrealistic goals.
• High risk to my career.	• Project too complex.
• Don't like the people on the team.	• Project not politically favored.
• Too much project management bureaucracy.	• We have a high project failure rate [on this kind of project].
• They kill the messenger around here.	• Sponsor is not a champion; weak.
• I don't have the skills.	• Customer is not committed.
	• No faith in suppliers or other departments to deliver what we need.
	• Poorly run meetings.
	• Key issues and decisions go unresolved.
	• Insufficient support systems.
	• Physical environment not conducive.

Use this as a checklist, and ask yourself which of these demotivators are prevalent on your project. Do you even know for sure? Notice how many of these items you can have a direct impact on. Which can you influence? (Put down this book and start making some of these of demotivators go away.)

The Difference Between Leadership and Management

Warren Bennis, who has written much on the subject of leadership and management, is often quoted as saying, "Managers keep bad from happening. Leaders make good happen."

Another way of saying this is that managers are stabilizers and leaders are innovators. Managers want to do things the right way. Leaders want to do the right things. Managers tend to keep control close to the vest. Leaders distribute control. By now, you'll easily recognize these patterns as the difference between the Newtonian and quantum mind-set. Some things are to be managed, some to be led. You manage information and track progress. You lead processes, which in turn leads people.

Managers want to minimize change and tend to keep tight control over policies and procedures. They are taskmasters, a style that works better on stable projects. Leaders look for reasons to change and rely on guidelines and shared values and are relationship managers. To lead or to manage? It's not an A or B choice. All projects require a balance of both. For eXtreme projects, the balance tips heavily to the quantum side of the scale.

Since eXtreme project managers typically have little direct authority over people on the core team and zero authority over crucial stakeholders, the ability to influence is paramount. (Influencing skills will be covered in the next chapter.)

My definition of leadership as it applies to an eXtreme project is a composite definition. Leadership is the art of getting others to (1) want to do something you are convinced should be done and (2) make and implement decisions they are convinced should be made. (The first point is from Packard, 1962.) The key words are *want* and *convinced*. In other words, the goal of leadership is ownership. It results in commitment.

The second point recognizes that eXtreme projects are in flux, with new information coming in constantly, demanding that leadership be distributed. That is, team members and others need to have the latitude to adapt quickly by making intelligent, local decisions as situations arise without asking for permission each step of the way. This enables the eXtreme project to self-correct. In the heat of battle, you can't stop to check with headquarters all the time.

As we have seen, there are many variables and unknowns both internal and external to the eXtreme project and the sponsoring organization. No one can keep track of them all. No one knows enough to tell everyone else what to do. As such, eXtreme projects cannot be regulated from the top down. They can only be guided from above and managed from below as individuals, pairs, and groups of stakeholders continually make self-correcting adjustments as the project goes along, while keeping in mind the desired project outcome.

But you must use the right project process for the type of project at hand. On an eXtreme project, good process leadership will enable people to discover the best solution and to continually self-correct. Even if you had the direct power you might crave, it could be a grave disadvantage if it stifled the ability of those closest to the problem to solve the problem. A good motto is, "Disorder cannot be eliminated. It can only be navigated."

Keeping the Project in Control: The Law of Requisite Variety

I was doing project management consulting at the Portland, Oregon, Nabisco bakery, where a variety of cookies are made. During a tour of the facility, the plant manager told us that one of their goals was to improve throughput and reduce cookie breakage during the production and packaging processes. Despite extensive training and retraining of supervisors and their team members, they were getting nowhere slowly in achieving the hoped-for efficiencies. (My belief, by the way, is that if you are going to go nowhere, get there fast, and get it over with so you can try something else.) Although they were able to change the working habits and skills of production workers, it didn't seem to make a difference. Finally, they discovered there was still too much opportunity for variation.

One day management realized that the problem was not so much the variation in individual behavior; rather, it was due to an inefficient production process and the old equipment that people had to live with. The lack of a good process defeated the workers, even though they had the necessary expertise and skill set. The plant manager proudly summed up his Aha! moment when he said, "A lousy process makes a lousy cookie even when you have good people." It was not until they improved the process that they were able to improve performance.

Without realizing it, Nabisco had experienced the Law of Requisite Variety. Borrowed from systems theory, this law says that the element in the system with the greatest flexibility (or variability) will control the system. A system can be that of machines or people, or both. This helps explain why many project managers are not running their projects: their projects are running them. The challenge on an eXtreme project is that there are so many possible variables in behavior among the stakeholder community and external events that it is impossible to prevent all of the potential variation that will be encountered.

But you can increase the ability of the project to tolerate the volatility that presents itself. That's the beauty of process power. It's the great equalizer. It helps eliminate unnecessary variability by keeping the team out of the storming stage. It enables you to manage variability when it presents itself. In this way, process power increases your ability to roll with the punches.

In fact, that's what this book is intended to show you: how— through the application of the Accelerators, Shared Values, Business Questions, and the 5 Critical Success Factors—you can expand your bandwidth by having more tools at your disposal. By focusing on the process you use and the relationships you establish, the principles, values, and practices of eXtreme project management serve to harness the Law of Requisite Variety so that it works to your advantage and that of the project at large.

To summarize, in the quantum world of eXtreme projects, your power comes from the process you lead and the quality of the relationships you establish. Process and relationships are the two great equalizers. Your ability to lead the process and establish quality relationships is your unique effectiveness factor. Process power coupled with principles and values increase your bandwidth.

The Critical Success Factor of Self-Mastery goes a step further: it expands your personal power, which is the ability to psychologically and emotionally transcend the pressures of everyday events.

Nine Reasons That eXtreme Project Managers Fail

eXtreme project managers fail when they turn their sights inward and focus on technical and product development (content) issues and neglect the project's context: the general business environment, stakeholder expectations, and the project's emotional well-being.

The result is unresolved conflict, resulting in loss of commitment and ultimately failure to deliver an acceptable product or service.

The following project manager failure factors all relate to the project context. They are common to almost all projects but are intensified on eXtreme projects:

1. *No angel:* Not having the right project sponsor, one who is a champion and barrier buster.
2. *Poor soft skills* (communications, negotiation, conflict resolution, facilitation, and influencing skills).
3. *Hermit crab syndrome:* Sitting in front of a computer instead of in front of stakeholders.
4. *Good soldier syndrome:* Being too soft; not questioning authority or pushing back; simply following orders.
5. *Loss of business focus:* Not applying or misapplying the 4 Business Questions (which are covered in the next chapter):

   Poaching: Taking over the responsibility for answering Business Question 1 (Who needs what and why?). This question belongs to the project sponsor.

   Chickening out: Not taking ownership and full responsibility for answering Business Question 2 (What will it take to do it?); rather, letting the sponsor dictate the budget. This belongs to the project manager.

   Poor mouth: Unable to get what is needed to succeed (Business Question 3: Can we get what it takes?). This is a failure in negotiation.

   Malicious compliance: Moving ahead when the answer to Business Question 4 (Is it worth it?) is no. This means implementing a project or keeping it going knowing it doesn't have a chance of succeeding. Here the project manager gets blamed for the failure instead of a real reason: the business justification behind the project is not viable.

6. *Methodology mismatch:* Imposing a counterproductive methodology on the project.
7. *Totoolitarianism* (also known as management by template): Thinking that you can manage the dynamics of an extreme project by getting people to fill out forms, rather than putting the focus on unleashing motivation and innovation and estab-

lishing trust and confidence, all of which require a management style based on values and principles.

8. *Naive compliance:* Failing to detect that the project is not solving the real problem.
9. *Fish out of water:* Failing to recognize that eXtreme project management (and maybe any kind of project management) is not
   the job that best uses one's own natural talents and motivated
   strengths.

You Are More Powerful Than You May Realize

Despite having lots of responsibility without a lot of authority, you
nonetheless have more power at your disposal than you may realize. In contrast to personal power, project managers also have considerable external sources of power: sources outside your immediate
control. Sources of personal power (authentic power, self-disclosure
power, process power, guts power) are under your direct control;
they reside inside of you to use as you see fit. Draw on every one of
these external sources as you can.

> *Project managers also have considerable
> external sources of power.*

Position Power

When you have position power, you're the boss, and others know
it. This is the best-known source of power. It's nice if you can get
it; the chances are low for eXtreme project managers but nevertheless worth noting. A legacy of the Industrial Revolution, position power, is based on where you fall in the organization's pecking
order. It can be effective even when the subordinate is not your direct report. So if you're a director-level person, you are not likely
to disobey an executive vice president, even if she's not your boss
(unless you decide to use guts power). At its worse, position power
becomes coercive power, as in the reward-threat model. Sometimes
coercion is necessary; it gets things done, but can backfire if people do not buy in and instead practice malicious compliance (following instructions knowing the thing is going to backfire) or they

find ways to beat the system. The motto for those who abuse their position power might be, "Kiss up and kick down."

Referential Power

Referential power is clout by association. You ring up Jack, director of wireless technology: "Good afternoon, Jack. I'm the project manager for Joan, who is sponsoring the Headboomer project. [Joan is the senior vice president of engineering.] I need just five minutes of your time. Can we meet this afternoon? . . . Sure. I'm free at 3:30" You show up and after exchanging a few preliminary pleasantries, you pop the question: "We really need one of your audio gurus for a couple of months to help us on this mission critical initiative for Joan. Can you shake somebody loose?" "No, problem," says Jack.

Reputation Power

The word may be out that you really know what you are doing and have pulled off one or more miracles before. Here, your power is derived from your reputation. The idea is to name-drop an inarguably successful project you led or participated in. Because they believe history is likely to repeat itself, you find it easier than most others to get what you need. But reputation is not necessarily under your control. Some people will think highly of you, and others won't despite your past achievements.

Expert Power

With expert credentials, you are considered to be the subject matter expert in a technical or other discipline, including project management. In certain industries, among them pharmaceutical, information technology, and corporate and estate law, expert power is a major source for getting your way.

New Guy Power

You just joined the department or organization, or you've been brought in to save a project that's gone bad. People want to give you a chance to succeed and straighten out the mess. For the new kid on the chopping block, there is usually a window of opportunity where you can get more of what you want than after you've established roots. Carpe diem.

Precedent or Compliance Power

This approach (also known as conformity power) comes in handy when you want to influence someone above you who is new to the organization and doesn't know the ropes. It works well when there is an accepted third-party standard that must be adhered to—for example, "If we don't do this, the FDA will come after us," or, "We will be out of ISO compliance."

Payback Power

This is when you call in a favor or you tell the person you need something from them. "If you provide me with both Adam and Samantha for two full days this week, I'll get you some help when you're up the creek."

Insider Power

People like to be in the know, especially if it means getting privileged information ahead of others. Your argument might be, "By participating on this team, you will be getting and shaping inside information and making contacts that will give you a jump on others."

Per-Day Delay Power

What does it cost the company in lost revenues, profits, or recurring costs for every day the project slips? If you can come up with this number, you'll be surprised how much clout you will have to hire additional people or throw more technology at the problem to shorten the delivery date. Or if you want a good excuse to trim down the project of its nonessential features, you can frame your point in the context of how many weeks can be shaved off the schedule and the resultant revenues or costs savings per day that will be realized.

WOW! Power

WOW! power means to identify the overarching, common, compelling vision that makes the project a worthwhile venture. WOW! power energizes the venture because it elevates the endeavor from "just a project" to a cause. When people are on a heartfelt mission, they can become unstoppable. We only have to look at Martin Luther King Jr., Gandhi, and Mother Teresa, all vivid examples of people who will go to enormous lengths when they believe in a cause.

Scarcity Power

Some people are motivated by lack, fear, or missing out. You can influence them by saying, "We need to act by next Tuesday; otherwise we pay a penalty," or, "If we miss our window tomorrow with Jim, we won't be able to get approval until he gets back from Bali."

Reward Power

Money, other perks, and performance bonuses can get you what you want. This can be particularly effective when a vendor is given a bonus for early or on-time completion. It can also be used in conjunction with per-day delay power: once you know the dollar cost per day or week for a delay, you can reward accordingly. For instance, if the cost-per-day delay is $1,000 in lost profits, then giving the contractor a bonus of $500 per day ahead of schedule is a winner all around.

Begging Power

I don't recommend this power. It's bad for the self-esteem and ruins your kneecaps.

When Commitment Is Not Obtainable

Sometimes no matter what you do, you cannot gain and sustain sufficient organizational commitment, and the project is a risk. What do you do?

One afternoon I showed up at my regular time to coach Bruce, a project manager leading a massive project to reengineer the purchasing process for a public utility company. As part of the initial planning for the project, Bruce and the project sponsor-customer agreed that a critical success factor for the project was to assign two people from the purchasing department to work full time on the team during the engagement. About a third of the way through, the sponsor decided that other priorities prevailed and the two promised team members would have to be pulled from the project indefinitely.

When I walked into Bruce's office for our regular meeting, the first thing he did was announce that he had just stopped the project. "I lost two promised people for the project. At the outset, we agreed the project ran a very high risk of failure without them, so I brought it to a halt."

Bruce did the right thing. It's lunacy and irresponsible to the organization to continue a project that's doomed to fail.

◆ ◆ ◆

Now that you have a better understanding of your role as eXtreme project manager, you are ready to find out how to lead the process and focus on eXtreme principles, values, and interpersonal skills. Critical Success Factor 2, Leadership by Commitment, continues in the next chapter.

But first, consider this: After reading this chapter about the role of the eXtreme project manager, are you feeling like a fish out of water?

If you didn't do it earlier, this may be a good time for you to look at your motivated abilities. I covered how to go about this under Self-Mastery, Critical Success Factor 1, and provide some practical tools in the eXtreme Tools and Techniques section. If your first love is to work with technology and develop new products, then you may find yourself out of your element as a relationship manager, which is the primary job responsibility of the eXtreme project manager.

As a reminder, self-mastery means following your passion. Trying to get better at something you don't like is the path of self-misery.

eXtreme Project Management Model
Applying the Quantum Mind-Set

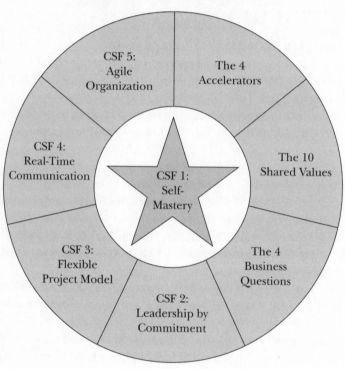

Chapter Five

Principles, Values, and Interpersonal Skills for Leading

The key very simply, is other people.
MARIANNE WILLIAMSON

The previous chapter focused on the role of the eXtreme project manager as energy manager: one who gains and sustains commitment to the project mission by managing the project's context. In this chapter and the two that follow, I continue my focus on Leadership by Commitment (Critical Success Factor 2), and put the spotlight on the principles, values, business focus, and skills you need to succeed.

If I had to summarize this and the next two chapters in a word, I'd say this is the touchy-feely stuff, the soft glue that holds the eXtreme project together. Critical Success Factors 3 and 4 (the Flexible Project Model and Real-Time Communication) put the emphasis on the hard glue practices of project management. Most of eXtreme project management is soft glue. As it turns out, the soft glue, which represents the project's dynamics, is really the hard stuff of eXtreme project management. And the hard glue (scheduling, analysis, technology and tools, and the like), which represents the mechanics, is really the easy stuff for most people. I'm hard-pressed to identify a project that failed because we didn't have the right scheduling tool or set of templates to fill in. Behind every failure lurks a people and communication problem.

As another reminder, if you don't like touchy-feelies, then eXtreme project management isn't your cup of tea. Instead, take a coffee break and ponder what you learned about your special motivated abilities and talents in Chapter Three.

This chapter covers the 4 Project Accelerators, the 10 Shared Values, the 4 Business Questions, and people skills (negotiating, resolving conflict, emotional intelligence, and getting your point across).

Taken together, the principles, values, and people skills that I cover here and in the ensuing chapters provide the foundation to create a change-tolerant environment. They enable you to manage the project's energy field by facilitating and managing the flow of emotions, thoughts, and interactions in a way that gains and sustains commitment throughout the venture. As a result, you will be better able to:

- Unleash motivation and innovation.
- Establish trust and confidence among the stakeholder community at large.
- Exercise power and influence others without authority.
- Ensure the customer receives value each step of the way.
- Keep the project under control in the face of volatility.

The 4 Accelerators and 10 Shared Values lie at the foundation of eXtreme project management. Together they serve to speed up the project by keeping the flow of thoughts, emotions, and interactions fluid. They are the bedrock of eXtreme project management. Constantly asking the 4 Business Questions will help remind you and all other stakeholders that the project is a business venture, keeping you oriented in a confusing environment.

The 4 Accelerators and 10 Shared Values lie at the foundation of eXtreme project management.

The 4 Accelerators: How to Unleash Motivation and Innovation

To unleash motivation and innovation is to make it possible for people to have an impact. Here are the principles that successful eXtreme project managers apply.

1. Make Change Your Friend

This principle refers to both responding to and creating change. Typically, change carries a negative energy on project because people have to switch gears. They want predictability, especially managers who are held to departmental budgets. The word *variance* is the first cousin of *change* and also carries a negative connotation. Although variance can be positive on a project that is (surprisingly) ahead of schedule or budget, most people think of it in the negative. Change, then, is not something that is typically welcomed, and that's why traditional project management makes a big deal out of change control. Note the word *control*. The message is that change is the enemy.

In highly competitive environments, change can be viewed as a weapon to cause chaos for the competition. For example, midway through a project, someone discovers a technical capability that will leapfrog the competition. In a typical project environment, one with a Newtonian mind-set that resists change, this discovery could be cause for alarm and generate resistance. In an environment that welcomes change, the discovery can be exploited without resistance to generate business value.

Many projects suffer from rigor mortis, which I define as death by rigor. Elaborate procedures are put into place to evaluate the impact of change requests to a point where the project becomes stalled due to drawn-out hierarchical approval processes. In fact, many traditional projects build in rigor mortis early in the project cycle with lengthy requirements-gathering processes, which can last six months to a year or more. The thinking behind this is that if we can find out what they *really* want, we can eliminate almost all change and take a straight path to the goal. This is a form of Newtonian neurosis—the attempt to bludgeon every project into a straight line. You can freeze requirements, but you can't freeze the customer's desire to change things. Persistent resistance places the project customer and project team in an adversarial relationship. It saps vital energy and puts the whole project in a bad mood.

eXtreme project management requires a different attitude about change, one that says change represents opportunity, and that by welcoming change you improve the chances of delivering the originally planned result. The desired result, which has to be discovered, is likely to be vastly different from the planned result.

An attitude that resists change also resists the processes that lead to discovery. Welcoming change keeps the project moving and makes discovery possible. And yes, eXtreme project management requires that you look at the impact of changing requirements so that the customer can make an informed decision about moving ahead. But it's done in a less bureaucratic way.

In practice, "make change your friend" means accepting what is and proactively moving on from there. In particular it means:

- Actively looking for opportunities to do things differently.
- Making it easy for new ideas to surface and be acted on.
- Performing a quick impact analysis when change occurs.
- Making continuous adjustments to the plan and the product along the way.
- Admitting that it's not working and taking corrective action.
- Being willing to junk the plan and start over at any time.

2. Build on People's Desire to Make a Difference

I was once doing a consulting assignment for a large U.S. government agency. As I walked through department after department, day after day, I noticed expressionless faces of bureaucrats pushing paper or waiting for paper to be pushed their way. Many would congregate to gossip and bemoan and share their misery—co-miserate if you will—with each other. They were demoralized, and their energy was low. Being demoralized may be a normal state, but it doesn't have to be an inevitable state. I believe these government employees had become disenfranchised from their jobs by the system they were faced with, which left little or no room for individual contribution. They could not see how their jobs made any difference to anybody. They just showed up and did the bare minimum, or nothing at all, by hiding behind bureaucratic procedures, resulting in a form of on-the-job retirement.

I also remember an engagement at a bakery for Nabisco. I was given a plant tour and had a chance to talk to Bill, who worked at the beginning of the Oreo cookie line, which extended about the length of a football field. Bill's job was to be sure the cookie dough was the right consistency before it was cut into wafers and baked. Bill had been working in the plant for thirty-two years. I asked him what his job involved, and he did not hesitate to reply: "My job is to make a quality cookie that families will enjoy." Notice he did not say that his job was to be sure the cookie dough was running at the correct consistency. That's because Bill had more than a job. He had a sense of purpose that continued to motivate him even after thirty-two years on the line. Bill was making a difference.

When put into practice, the second project accelerator, "Build on people's desire to make a difference," means:

- Showing people how their job contributes to a higher cause and providing a sense of meaning and purpose.
- Creating and recognizing small wins: seeing what's going right and recognizing successes no matter how seemingly small.
- Providing people with an opportunity to make things better, to leave their mark.
- Recognizing that people by nature want to be proud of their work.
- Removing barriers that prevent people from doing quality work.

3. Create Ownership for Results

Bill at Nabisco was quick to point out and brag about the new computer-based system he was using to monitor the Oreo cookie dough. He also had the power to affect the cookie baking process by speeding up or slowing things down or even stopping the entire line. I asked him who had designed the system. He told me and added proudly, "I worked with the design engineers to educate them on my job and the types of problems I run into." Bill was a fan of the computer-based system because he played a major part in creating it. Not only were his hands and heart engaged, so was his mind.

In practice, the principle of "create ownership for results" means to give people the freedom to determine how to do their job as well as the opportunity to influence how to succeed on the overall project. In particular, it means:

- Recognizing that people prefer to participate in change them-selves rather than to be changed.
- Giving people a voice so that they can be heard on the issues and topics that are near and dear to them, even if someone else will make the final decision. These issues and topics include

decisions regarding the content and quality of work products, the overall project goals to be achieved, the processes to achieve the goals, and how performance will be measured.

- Providing guidelines rather than strict rules so that people have the latitude to do what they believe is the right thing.
- Involving people in group brainstorming and decision making.
- Understanding who owns what decisions in the first place. Business folks make business decisions; implementers make technical decisions and operational decisions (estimating how long it will take and how much it will cost).

This accelerator is based on the principle that people support what they create. Here is an example from my own experience. In 1986, I was recruited by the ComputerWorld organization to start a high-tech newspaper known as *NetworkWorld*. I reported to Jim Povec, who was vice president of the publishing division I worked in. Jim was not one to tell me what to do or how to do it. He knew we had already agreed on a set of business goals and a plan to get there. He left the rest up to me and was always available for coaching when I needed it. Any time I went to Jim to get help with a decision, we'd discuss the options I brought to the table. After we batted things around, Jim would invariably say, "Doug, what do you want to do?" Whatever I decided is what Jim would go with. The ball was clearly in my hands, and Jim's style evoked a deep sense of responsibility and commitment on my part. Initially, I felt empowered. Then I would get a little scared when I realized I fully owned the decision, for better or worse, and I was on the line.

I later learned that people tend to live up to the expectations held for them. What I also learned from Jim is that a good leader is also a good follower. Jim would follow my lead and stand behind my decision. As result, I was a great follower of Jim, as were many others who worked with him. I concluded that two important hallmarks of a good leader are:

- A genuine willingness to follow the lead of those who work with or for them.
- To have willing followers—those who follow out of commitment rather than out of coercion or even compliance.

I also learned from Jim that leadership is a function (what you do) and not a position held by one person. In taking my lead from

Jim, I also led people who reported to me in the same way. I would follow their lead. As a function (and not a position), this meant that leadership could be practiced by many, not just the few anointed leaders. It also explains why holding the position of leader doesn't make one a leader.

4. Keep It Simple

The old KISS principle (Keep It Simple, Stupid) is not lip-service on an eXtreme project; it's taken seriously. In practice, this means less is more:

- Less project scope, less hierarchy, less process, less reporting, less rigor, fewer people, fewer forms to fill out, only the necessary documentation, and so on
- Doing the least amount of work to get the job done
- Meeting minimum requirements; building something more elaborate later

The Combined Effect of the 4 Accelerators

Taken together, the 4 Accelerators speed up the flow of positive energy among those involved on the project. They enable the stakeholders and the team in particular to be adaptive, committed, and creative, and they go a long way to establish the desire to succeed.

The 10 Shared Values: How to Establish the Trust and Confidence to Succeed

When you yourself live by the 10 Shared Values presented in Chapter Two, you foster trust and confidence. Trust, which is earned over time, is a mutual feeling that people can be depended on to keep their commitments and deliver the goods. When stakeholders experience trust, they gain confidence in the project's ability to succeed even in the face of great adversity. Trust transcends adversity. Confidence—and at best, conviction—is the strongly held belief among project stakeholders that working together will bring success, even in the face of volatility and adversity.

While all ten values apply all the time, in this chapter on leadership and interpersonal skills, People Values come to the forefront.

Here I present people values in more detail (process values and business values are examined in the next two chapters).

People First

In practice, *people first* means eliminating barriers so that people can do quality work:

- If methods, tools, and rules are not working, these are modified; energy is not wasted trying to modify the people affected.
- Relatedly, if methods, tools, and rules are getting in the way of progress, these are changed with input from the people who are affected, not unilaterally.
- Managing is by eye contact instead of by e-mail.
- A convenient working physical environment (the tools, lighting, space) is provided to get work done.
- Appropriate support is provided for team members who may be experiencing personal or family problems.

Honest Communication

In practice, *honest communication* means acting with integrity and speaking the truth about the good, the bad, and the ugly without fear of reprisal:

- Expressing facts as well as feelings about the project
- Being open to giving and getting feedback
- Telling the whole truth, not half truths
- Fully listening to others before judging what they have to say
- Not fooling yourself, that is, being in touch with what's true for you even if you don't like looking at it

Quality of Life

In practice, *quality of life* means ensuring that the project strikes a satisfying balance of work life and personal life:

- Recognizing that people have the right to do good work that they can be proud of

- Building in forty-hour weeks to the project plan and not assuming people have infinite time to spent at work
- Recognizing that out of every forty-hour week, ten to fifteen hours are likely to be spent on activities not involving direct work on the project (such as personal calls, administrative stuff, meetings related and unrelated to the project, bathroom breaks, coffee breaks, normal socializing) and staffing the project accordingly

Courage

In practice, *courage* means having the fear but moving ahead anyway—doing it scared because it's the right thing to do:

- Telling it like it is, including the bad news
- Being true to oneself and standing up for what's right even if you are the lone dissenter
- Being firm in asking management for what you need to succeed
- Being the lone promoter of an idea
- Being able to admit you were wrong
- Not waiting for permission before you do what you know needs to be done
- Disturbing the system by doing what's right versus what's established
- Pushing back, that is, a willingness to stand up for one's values versus being an accommodator and people pleaser
- Being willing to junk what you've done and start over with a better idea
- Being willing to change your mind; to do the right thing vs. having to be right
- Being outspoken about killing the project when no one else is willing to bring it up
- Being able to walk away from the project or even one's paycheck
- Having the strength to admit the truth about yourself to yourself (and not berate yourself for who you are or what you think)
- Acting with integrity

Using the Four People Values

These four values—people first, honest communication, quality of life, and courage—are important tools for combating fear, uncertainty, and doubt (FUD), which tends to accumulate in high-risk projects and gum up the works. FUD clogs the projects energy field, slows things down, and casts a negative spell over the endeavor. A project that has a high FUD factor stands little chance of success. This again is the self-fulfilling prophecy: if the project thinks it can't succeed, the odds are it won't.

---

*A project that has a high FUD factor
stands little chance of success.*

Getting the FUD out in the open makes the project manager the project exorcist. Although all four people values help combat FUD, my favorite way of exorcising the FUD is to use honest communication and courage and make it an everyday practice to ask three questions as part of routine discussions about the project:

1. What do you feel is going well on the project?
2. What are your worries at this point?
3. What do you think we can be doing differently?

Using courage and honest communication to exorcise the FUD brings the skeletons out of the closet in the form of risks that can be mitigated and issues that can be addressed. Their impact is that the project's energy field clears up, and the venture moves ahead with clarity and speed. As the saying goes, "What we don't face, we fear. And what we fear controls us."

How do you get your team and others to live by the 10 Shared Values and 4 Accelerators? You can't unless they see value in them. My recommendation is that when you kick off the project scoping meeting, you discuss these and ask which ones people in the room (the crucial stakeholders and core team members, including the project sponsor) are willing to live by. So expose them to the values and accelerators. But above all, *become the living* example, the role model. As Gandhi said, be the change you want to see.

The 4 Business Questions: How to Ensure the Customer Receives Value Each Step of the Way

eXtreme project management recognizes that every project is first and foremost a business venture and must demonstrate an acceptable return on investment. The goal is to deliver value each step of the way, as well as during the benefits realization stage, which begins right after the project deliverable has been accepted by the customer and the product or system has stabilized.

The successful eXtreme project manager will manage the project around the 4 Business Questions and relentlessly update the answers to the questions throughout the life of the project. The answers will continually change, sometimes weekly, sometimes even more often.

In practice, applying the 4 Business Questions means (1) ensuring that the appropriate party is held responsible for answering his or her own question; (2) continually updating the business case to reflect the latest answers and expectations; and (3) lobbying to kill the project when the answer to question 4 is no. Ownership responsibility for each business question is assigned as follows:

Question 1: "Who needs what and why?" is the responsibility of the project sponsor.

Question 2: "What will it take to do it?" is the responsibility of the project manager.

Question 3: "Can we get what it takes?" is a negotiation between the project manager and the sponsor.

Question 4: "Is it worth it?" is the responsibility of the sponsor.

Big problems result when the wrong people take ownership of each other's business question. This can happen when the project manager and team, consciously or unconsciously, make scope, quality, and financial decisions that should really be made by the customer organization, or when the project sponsor makes budget decisions and schedule decisions that should be made by the project manager and team.

Here's an example of how not to apply questions 1 and 2 (respectively, "Who needs what and why?" and "What will it take to do it?").

Mary Business Owner, and *not* Joe Project Manager, is supposed to own the answer to Business Question 1. However, when pinned down, Mary's requirements for the project deliverable and desired business outcome are too vague to work with. Joe lets Mary off the hook and decides that he and the development team will figure out (read, "second-guess") what's really needed. In other words, Joe caves in and takes over Mary's responsibility for answering question 1.

In the meantime, Mary has a business to run. Although she has little idea of what she really wants out of the project, this does not deter her from giving Joe a firm deadline and strict budget. Interpretation: Mary has just picked Joe's pocket by steeling ownership of Business Question 2: "What will it take to do it?" The bottom line is that insanity reigns: the most disadvantaged person is now running the other person's show. Worse, neither of them realizes what has happened.

If this is happening to you, here's what to do:

- Make a list of all the unknowns that will likely have an impact on the schedule and budget. Use this to educate the project sponsor. You are doing her a favor.
- Clarify that you own question 2.
- Insist on having representatives of the customer organization available throughout the project in order to uncover the true requirements. Point out that this will yield the answer to question 1, and it will also provide the basis for estimating question 2.
- Indicate to the project sponsor that go/no-go points will be set up so that she can make ongoing decisions in answer to question 4 ("Is it worth it?") and as a result keep the project in financial control.

Post the 4 Business Questions on your office wall—and while you're at it, the 4 Accelerators for unleashing motivation and innovation and all of the 10 Shared Values for building trust and confidence. Glance at them at the beginning of the day. At the end of the day, ask yourself how you did in putting the accelerators, shared values, and business questions into practice. This takes a total of five minutes.

At the end of the day, ask yourself how you
did in putting the accelerators, shared values,
and business questions into practice.

Developing Interpersonal Skills for an eXtreme World

Since eXtreme projects are always about people, interpersonal skills are critical. To exercise interpersonal skills, the eXtreme project manager needs emotional intelligence, respect for people, and acceptance of different personality types and thinking styles. The cornerstone of interpersonal competence is strong communication, including listening, influencing, negotiating, and conflict resolution skills.

Emotional Intelligence

As a project manager, the ability to apply emotional intelligence is one of your most powerful practices. One way to fully understand the importance of emotional intelligence is to look at emotional ignorance. Emotional intelligence is the ability to be sensitive to, and respond appropriately to, a person's feelings in a given situation.

I used to be a master at emotional ignorance. That was in the days when I was a workaholic, which played a big role in wrecking my marriage. One evening, or I should say, night, I walked in the door around 11:00 P.M. Waiting for me was my wife, Lucrecia. She was livid and lit into me full throttle. "Where have you been? You missed your son's Little League game today for the third time this year. Even when you're home and not on a plane, you still don't take the time to be a real father. Every other father was there rooting for his son. But not you. No, not you. You and your damned job are turning your son into an orphan!"

At the time, John Grey's book, *Men Are from Mars, Women Are from Venus* (1997), had not been published. But even if it had been, I would have been too busy to read it. So as the man from Mars, I calmly proceeded to reach into my suit jacket pocket and pull out the time line for my latest project, which was to launch a market intelligence service to be sold to computer equipment manufacturers. I then proceeded to explain the facts of the matter and told Lucrecia that if she looked carefully, she could see that I was on the critical path for this project and I had to finalize the direct mail package to meet the printer's deadline.

The words *critical path* were all she had to hear. "Critical path!" Incensed, she said. "I'm going to put you on the critical list!" She was about to haul off.

It took me years to realize what a jerk I had been in attempting to explain my position by giving her a minilecture on the facts of my job and my deadline. The lesson here is that when someone is in the feeling state and upset, throwing facts at the person only enflames the situation, just like throwing gasoline on a bonfire. It will invariably make matters worse. This is the height of emotional ignorance.

So how could I have responded to Lucrecia? Had I known better, I would have acknowledged her feelings: "I see my coming in late is really upsetting to you." And I would have postponed any discussion of (my) facts until the emotions had calmed down. Only at that point would I even be in a position to really hear her concerns and her mine. Until that happens, no solution is possible.

The process of emotional intelligence I am referring to can be summed up by this sequence: Feelings ➤ Facts ➤ Solutions. You can refer to it as the Feelings First Model. (I had it backward in my example with Lucrecia: I put the facts in front of her feelings.)

Like people, projects can be in a good mood or a bad mood. Unless the feelings running through a situation are addressed and relieved, people and projects will stay stuck. After all, projects *are* people. It's the touchy *feeling* stuff.

This means that if project stakeholders are upset and differences not aired, those suppressed feelings will block progress. The project's energy will be misdirected into underground activities that undermine the project. These include bad-mouthing, pulling people from the project team, delayed approval cycles, no-shows at team meetings, negative body language, and much more, all of which keep the project in a bad mood because the context has gone sour.

The typical response to these antiproject activities is to put in place rules and policies to get people to change their behavior.

These mandates can then be used as clubs for purposes of compliance and even coercion. But it's difficult to squelch the human spirit. People are creative and like to find workarounds, just like water will make its own way around obstacles in its path.

The moral is, "Feelings first." And this applies not only to your dealings with the people around you; it applies equally to how you deal with yourself. Unless you can first deal effectively with your own emotions about a situation, you are playing with a partial deck in making decisions and in managing, communicating, and leading others.

The importance of processing one's own feelings first was brought home vividly to me when I was the publishing director of *MIS Week*, a newspaper written for information processing professionals. My team and I had spent eighteen months of blood, sweat, and tears reinventing the failing newsweekly. We had turned the corner and were even ahead of plan. Then one day, out of the blue, my boss told me that management had decided to cease publication. He gave me two hours to "round up the troops" in order to give them the news of our demise, which he would deliver. Once the news was delivered, my job was to plan and manage the project to shut down the business. As chief undertaker, I was confronted with legal decisions, financial decisions, personnel decisions, public relations decisions, and a mountain of administrative details to be handled. For nearly two weeks, the emotional pain blocked my ability to think clearly and handle the hard, cold business aspects of the shutdown. I went from being an effective manager to one who was emotionally crippled. It was not until I had spent a good amount of time experiencing my personal feelings about our plight instead of avoiding those feelings that I was able to act in the best interests of all concerned.

The same principle works in less somber situations. I remember stopping at a discount consumer electronics store and seeing a demonstration for a camcorder. I got excited at the prospect and made an impulse buy for a cool $950 so I could record my speeches. I've had the camcorder for six years and have used it exactly three times. Had I let my initial excitement calm down until I was more rational, I doubt I would have made the purchase.

eXtreme project managers live in a world that is emotionally charged. To be effective, you have to deal with feelings before facts, and the first feelings to be dealt with are your own. If dealing with your own and others' feelings is not your strong suit, find other opportunities that suit you.

Become a Theory Y Manager

Are you a theory X or Y person when it comes to the supervision of people? The two contrasting approaches were first spelled out by Douglas McGregor in *The Human Side of Enterprise* (1985). A theory X manager has a fundamental belief that people don't like to work, can't be trusted, will try to get away with anything they can, and are out to get you politically. The theory Y manager has the opposite belief and holds that people are intrinsically motivated to do good work and will do so when they can satisfy their basic needs to make a difference and fulfill their aspirations. This manager also holds a belief that people are intelligent, have talents, and can be relied on to solve problems and take initiative and to do the right thing.

Theory X aligns with the Newtonian belief system that gave rise to the command-and-control management style and the reward-threat model. Theory Y aligns with the quantum mind-set, which is akin to the Weinberg's organic model (1986). A theory X manager is a taskmaster; a theory Y manager is a relationship manager.

There is a time and place for both styles, even on an eXtreme project, but the predominant management style needs to be theory Y. The need for speed, collaboration, creativity, and constant decision making and self-correction on eXtreme projects demands a quantum project manager.

If you are a theory X manager, that doesn't mean anything is wrong with you any more than it's wrong to be left-handed. It's not about guilt. Chances are you were brought up to be a theory Xer. Moreover, you may be a theory X manager due to your temperament. But you can adopt a quantum management style if you want to. Your ability to succeed on an eXtreme project that is organizationally complex requires it.

Learn to Be Accepting of Others

As manager and facilitator of the project's energy field, you will be dealing with a range of personality and thinking styles. Some will be draining, others energizing. You will likely have little to no control over who is on your team. Conflict is inevitable. Even if you could orchestrate the team to match your own management style (and reduce conflict), this would be a mistake. Extreme projects require diverse viewpoints and problem-solving styles in order to have a chance of being successful. You need to build an environment that fosters a conflict of ideas. You need to establish a free trait agreement (so to speak).

Yet many project managers become frustrated when people they interact with do not match their own personality or thinking style. Since you (or anybody else, for that matter) have limited ability to change a person's personality or thinking style, your options are to replace the person (which you might have to do when there is a major performance deficiency) or change your perception of the person.

One of the most important and humbling discoveries you can make is to come to the realization that your perspective and modus operandi are not the only viable way and that, in fact, this is a good thing. At the very least, you need to develop tolerance for people you have to work with. Compassion may be too much of a stretch, even for the most evolved among us. If compassion would be pushing the envelope, then strive for appreciation or even acceptance.

A good way to practice acceptance is to understand the underlying need the individual is trying to satisfy. All behavior is a desire to satisfy a need. And most of those needs boil down to a call for recognition and acceptance, which can be expressed in a variety of endearing or offensive ways (such as dress, voice tone, body language, or use of language).

If you have trouble accepting a particular person, at least try to make the distinction between the idea being presented and the personality of the individual who is delivering the idea. On an eXtreme project, you cannot afford to shut out ideas. Using this critical distinction, you can increase the flow of ideas and not have to change the fact that you still believe Joe is a first-class jerk even on a good day. A key point here is that acceptance doesn't mean you condone or like the person or behavior. Call it tolerance, which might be defined as begrudging acceptance.

The benefit of practicing acceptance or even appreciation is that it helps keep your own internal energy field clean. That is, if you take in toxic food, it does bad things to your physical system. And if you take in someone's toxic energy without practicing tolerance, it can do bad things to your own mood. It's important to control your intake of negativity. That's why I personally listen to the news in very small doses. A constant diet of negativity sours one's mood day in and day out.

The best shortcut I have found to develop tolerance and acceptance is to understand your own temperament style, which was covered under Critical Success Factor 1: Self-Mastery. Self-awareness and self-acceptance is the beginning of self-compassion. And as we are with ourselves, we are with others.

Principles of Effective Communication

How do you get what you want? Power (both personal and external) is the clout that you have. Communication skills turn power into action. The ability to communicate with others and to establish rapport with core team members and the stakeholder community at large are among the most important skills that the eXtreme project manager can acquire. Without rapport, there's conflict at worst and apathy at best. To succeed, you need 360-degree communication capability so you can communicate with those above you and below you, as well as those at your level.

I'd bet that most, if not all, of your communication is intended to influence behavior. Try this: pay attention to the messages you put out over the next several hours, both verbal and in writing. Ask yourself, What am I trying to influence with this message? Can you actually put out a neutral message, with no influence intended? And when you are not influencing others, take a moment to listen to your own self-talk: *Call so and so, finish budget forecast, lose weight, talk to Brian about his sagging performance.* How much of that internal communication is aimed at influencing yourself? . . .

When *don't* you need to exercise influence? You need to influence people to give you resources, show up at meetings, follow a sensible project management process, meet agreed-on deadlines, resolve conflicts over the project scope (its scope, budget, level of quality expected, schedule and business benefits), make timely approvals, make quick decisions to keep the project moving, and more.

We are always attempting to influence others and ourselves, whether we like it or not. But too often, we focus only on whether we are getting our message across. We forget that communication is most effective as a two-way process. If you want someone to listen to you, the best way to establish the proper environment for that is to demonstrate that you are willing to listen to them. And how do you do that? By actually listening to them.

The WIIFT (What's in It for Them?) Principle is one of the most effective communication tools you have: you get what you want by showing someone how what you want can get them what they want. It means you have to get out of your own way and see the situation from the perspective of the other person. And how do you do that? You talk to the other person and listen. For instance, many project managers I know get frustrated; a typical comment is, "My boss doesn't believe in project management, and I know we need it." I happen to agree with the boss. Why should she want project management? She's smart. What she really wants is what project management can do for her. So what's important to her? Getting her business objectives met faster? Reducing risk? Talk to her, and really listen to what she says. Don't just assume you know what it is.

Practice Reflective Listening

Reflective listening, also known as active listening, means to mirror back (rephrase) the other person's position and to do so with feeling rather than parroting. It doesn't mean you accept or agree with it. You are demonstrating that you understand.

When mirroring, care needs to be taken so that it comes across in an authentic and not a patronizing way. Good reflective phrases to use are, . . . "I hear you saying . . . ," "Let me be sure I understand . . . ," "In other words . . ."

Go to lengths to understand the other party before making yourself understood. Paraphrase back what the other person said until he or she is satisfied that you understand his or her thoughts and feelings. Stephen Covey (1989), put it this way: "Seek to understand before being understood."

> *Go to lengths to understand the other party*
> *before making yourself understood.*

Reflective listening, like other communication techniques, helps to establish rapport, and rapport opens the door to getting what you want. Practice your listening skills. (A guide to effective listening practices is included in the eXtreme Tools and Techniques section at the end of this book.)

Here are some overarching communication principles that apply in most all settings and go hand and hand with the specific practices that comprise the rest of this chapter:

- *The Relationship Consistency Principle:* You cannot effectively influence someone if your communication is out of sync with your relationship to the person you are communicating with.

Every communication has two components: the content (the message being delivered) and the implied relationship of the communicator to the other person. For instance, it's one thing to say to my seventeen-year-old son, "Get the car washed today." It's quite another to say to my significant other, "Get the car washed today." She would likely be incensed because our implied relationship is one of equals (called a symmetrical relationship). In contrast, my relationship with my son is by and large complementary. And as the parent, I also have an implied power advantage over him as well.

Or it may be appropriate to tell one of your peers about the wild weekend you just enjoyed, who you were with, and what you did. The same story told to your project sponsor could make him feel very awkward. It violates an implied relationship boundary.

In navigating the stakeholder community, it's important that you know the level of the person you are dealing with so that you communicate in a responsible way. Keep your communication consistent with your relationship.

- *The Message Wrapper Principle:* How you say it can have more of an impact than what you say.

From time to time I receive an e-mail that is written in blue. That tends to get my immediate attention. Since blue is now being abused as the attention-getting color, some people I correspond with have upgraded to red. That really grabs me. I'm just waiting for someone to escalate to red UPPER CASE letters. I guess that would be a cause to panic. Or it may also imply that they are shouting at me and turn me away.

Similarly, how we use our voice materially influences the result: pace, volume, emphasis, and the confidence with which we say it— "GET THE CAR WASHED, SON" versus, more politely, "*Get the car washed, son.*"

To influence people, be aware not only of what you say but how you say it.

• *The I Am Responsible Principle:* The communicator has full responsibility to ensure the communication gets through to the receiver.

We've all suffered through lectures where the speaker appears to be speaking a foreign language, showing no sensitivity to the audience. And the audience doesn't get it. The onus is always on the communicator to get the message across and to validate that the message hit or missed the mark. As a professional speaker, my most important step in preparing for a speaking engagement is to fully understand my audience: their working environment, their challenges, issues, frustrations, level of expertise in my subject matter, their hopes and what they want from me. When I do this well, I have an impact. It can be a disaster to talk down to an audience or to talk above their heads.

• *The No Technobabble Principle:* When speaking to a Roman, speak like a Roman.

This principle is related to the responsibility principle. You wouldn't get up in front of a first-grade class and proceed to quote from Henry Stapp's paper, "S-Matrix Interpretation of Quantum Theory." Yet I have witnessed presentations by experienced project managers in which they drag out twenty-seven overhead slides and proceed to quote from the PMBOK® (Guide to the Project Management Body of Knowledge) to explain the intricacies of earned value computations for the benefit of the project's sponsor and business team. As Wayne Dix who headed the PMO for AXA Financial, has said, "The project sponsor doesn't care about the PMBOK®."

Good communication joins; poor communication separates. The job of the eXtreme project manager is to unify crucial stakeholders in pursuit of a common mission that will produce a business benefit. The project is first and foremost a business venture that just happens to be undertaken using project management principles and tools. It's not a project management venture. You want to speak in the customer's business terms. Speaking project management technobabble separates the project (and the profession) from its customers, the ones paying the bills. It creates an us-versus-them split. If you want managers, sponsors, team members, and other stakeholders to be more inclined to embrace project management, find ways of talking the talk in everyday language. For starters, position project management as a "goal achievement process."

Speaking project management technobabble separates the project (and the profession) from its customers.

My friend Ravi tells the story of the first time he went into Starbucks for a cup of coffee. While he waited in line, the Starbucks sophisticates in front of him were confidently announcing their choices: "Venti skim late." "Café Macchiado, Tall." "Venti Americano with room at the top." (By the way, try leaving room at the bottom of the cup.) Intimidated by the jargon of the elite coffee clique, Ravi calmly walked out the door without his fix.

Rapport Is the Key to Communication

Almost everything in this chapter is related to establishing rapport, which is a prerequisite to effective communication. Rapport grows out of a mutual feeling that we are similar. Perceived differences inhibit rapport. (People like others who are like themselves.)

If establishing rapport is important to your success, remember to take a look at your personal appearance. What messages are being sent out by your dress? Hair style? At one financial institution I know, the project managers who staff the project support group all wear suits. They don't have to, but they need to relate to buttoned-down business executives and reinforce the point symbolically that the project is a business venture. The project manager's dress code also gives them greater credibility and readier access to managers who work in mahogany and brass settings. Showing up wearing a well-groomed ponytail or green hair (as might be appropriate at MTV) would be self-defeating.

Here is a list for getting your point across in one-on-one communications and small groups. It also summarizes key points made throughout this chapter:

- Know the outcome you want.
- Defuse yourself first if the subject is emotionally charged.
- Be authentic: speak from your heart as well as your mind.
- Speak with conviction in your voice; make statements rather than ask questions.
- Be congruent. Check to see that your verbal and nonverbals are in sync.
- Be concrete as opposed to ambiguous and hedgy. Avoid sugarcoating or disguising your message. Say what you mean.
- Be clear. Speak the language of your audience.
- Use a mix of visual and audio cues: words, numbers, graphics.
- Check to see that your intended message got across.
- If you are not getting across, try a different approach rather than merely repeating the original message in the same way.

How to Negotiate

Just about every influencing skill and power source I just covered will come home to roost in negotiation. And you'll need every edge you can get.

You can't be a project manager, eXtreme or any other, and not be a decent negotiator. Negotiation is a way of project life. It comes with the territory and is a critical skill. Yet few people are good at it. Negotiation is one of those in-your-face opportunities typical of eXtreme projects. It's yet another chance for you to facilitate and manage the flow of emotions, thoughts, and interactions, including your own, in a way that produces a valued result.

> *You can't be a project manager, eXtreme or any other, and not be a decent negotiator.*

In terms of the eXtreme project management model espoused in this book, negotiation is the guts of Business Question 3: Can we get what it takes?

The Four Types of Negotiation

If there is a bible for effective negotiation, it's the book *Getting to Yes* (Fisher, Ury, and Patton, 1989). The authors provide a practical method for negotiating anything. Importantly, they make the distinction between three types of negotiation: hard negotiation, soft negotiation, and principled negotiation. I've added a fourth because it's all too common: no negotiation.

Hard Negotiation

In hard negotiation, the participants are adversaries. The goal is victory, and the process is characterized by demanding concessions, distrusting others, digging in to one's position, intimidating, making overt threats, insisting on one-sided gains, and applying willpower and pressure. It is often long and drawn out and characterized by bad feelings, no solution, and a winner and loser or both losers.

At least in my experience, most of the negotiation situations that project managers on eXtreme projects face fall into the hard-ball style. It comes down to "them who's got the gold makes the rules," and the *them* isn't you. The deck is stacked in their favor:

- Those you are likely to have to negotiate with (department managers, suppliers, and other stakeholders) will have little allegiance to your project.
- Members of your project team, even those whom you outrank, don't report to you; you don't hold their paycheck.
- The project sponsor outranks you and will ultimately call the shots.

Later in this chapter, I'll give you some strategies for when you find yourself facing hard-core negotiation.

Soft Negotiation

This is the mirror opposite of hard negotiation. Here the participants are friends. The goal is agreement, and the process is characterized by making concessions. This takes the form of easily changing one's position, full disclosure, focusing on what the other party will accept, avoiding a contest of wills, yielding to pressure.

It yields faster agreement but usually a fuzzy or sloppy agreement and even a one-sided agreement where one party was needlessly overgenerous.

Both soft and hard negotiation styles are based on *positional* bargaining. I run into this situation a lot when I do workshops. It's hard to find a room temperature that's comfortable for everybody. For some, the room is too warm. For others, it's too cold. Frequently one of the participants will adjust the temperature during the break period. Then someone else will readjust it during the next break, causing a subtle power struggle. Solving the problem based on one's position might yield a one-sided solution: turn the temperature up in the morning to satisfy the people whose position is "too cold." Drop the temperature in the afternoon to satisfy the "too warm" people. The impact is an unsatisfactory situation for all.

Principled Negotiation

This form of negotiation shifts the focus from my position versus your position to one that's based on satisfying the *interests* of both parties, that is, each party's underlying concerns, needs, or desires. Principled negotiation shifts the game from me versus you to one of problem solving. It puts the emphasis on being hard on the problem and soft on the people.

Using the example of the workshop room temperature, the solution lies in getting people to recognize that the interest of each group is to be comfortable. Sometimes this can mean that certain people move to a warmer part of the room. But most often, it means that we will adjust the temperature to about 68 degrees and those who are too cold will keep their sweater or jacket on. The point is that focusing on interests and not positions offers more options.

No Negotiation

Here, the project manager simply accepts the project parameters as given and doesn't raise questions. This can happen if the project manager by temperament is too timid to speak up or is simply naive. Another excuse is, "It's not part of our culture to question management." Or it can be that a contract has already been signed and the project parameters are locked in, so the project manager feels she's stuck with the project as spelled out. Another possibility is that the project sponsor states he will not negotiate or simply won't make himself available.

It's at this point that the project joins the ranks of the walking dead. That's what happens when certain accelerators and shared values are violated, namely Accelerators 2 (build on people's desire to make a difference) and 3 (create ownership for results), as well as the Shared Values of client collaboration, honest communication, people first, and results orientation.

In a cynical sense, the no-negotiation situation arguably supports the Shared Value of fast failures in that for all intents and purposes, the project is dead from the start. The rest of the undertaking, so to speak, is merely the funeral procession disguised as a parade being led by a project management puppet.

No matter what the excuse, there is no excuse for not insisting on negotiating, even when a signed contract exists. If the party will not come to the table and you have exhausted all avenues of escalation, then you have a tough call to make. (See "When All Else Fails" at the end of the chapter.)

Principled Negotiation in Action

You're the eXtreme project manager for Project Headsup, a new liquid formulation for curing head lice. To round out the development team, you need to fill the key position of stability tester, the person who will measure the ability of the formulation to stay intact over a prolonged period before it goes out of date. It has been determined that stability testing will be particularly challenging due to the number and nature of the formulation's ingredients and packaging material options. The best person for the job by far is Kathy. You decide you want to get her on the team and need to negotiate her availability with Lorenzo, her boss. You know that Lorenzo is short-staffed and short-tempered and under pressure to meet the demands of multiple projects. The last time you needed someone, he provided you with Max, an inexperienced stability expert who did a poor job that resulted in costly problems with the Food and Drug Administration. You are understandably annoyed.

What you need to do is to separate the people from the problem and establish rapport with Lorenzo. This means to stick with attacking the problem, not the individual. It takes the form of seeing the world from Lorenzo's perspective, not assuming he is out to get you and not putting him under attack because of a past experience.

The problem you want to solve is how to get Kathy. But before you can tackle that, you have to deal with Lorenzo as a person who may have strong feelings, perceptions, and opinions about you, your department or organization, and what you are asking for. If you neglect dealing with these, they may block your ability to solve the problem. They can also stymie a solution if the discussion gets stuck at the personality level of exchanging wrongs with each other.

Lorenzo may unload his issues on you before you know it. Or you may anticipate them and acknowledge that you know he is short on staff and that you want to work toward a satisfying solution.

You can point out what's at stake on your project and explain why someone more experienced than Max is required (and not condemn Lorenzo for sending you a "loser" the last time). And that's why you want Kathy this time. Even so, that may not stop Lorenzo from going into a mini-tirade: "You guys always wait until the last minute to ask for help. And when you tell me you'll need them for three weeks, it turns out to be two months, and that puts me in a bind." At least now you know what his interests are: more lead time and a more accurate assessment of how long you'll need his staff member.

It's at this point that you want to remember to practice emotional intelligence as well as the applicable communication judo skills I covered earlier. In this situation, the Feelings → Facts → Solutions model is your friend. First, acknowledge your own feelings (anger, fear) to yourself and then deal with Lorenzo's through reflective listening. Be sure to focus on *interests* and not on positions.

Your position is that you want Kathy. Let's say Lorenzo's position is, "No way! She's already overbooked and can't be reassigned without causing major problems." If the negotiation were to be "I want her" versus "You can't have her," you would find yourselves playing the game of hard (power struggle) negotiation instead of principled negotiation. A more productive approach would be to leave your position out of the picture and examine your interests. For instance, do you want Kathy, or do you really want what Kathy brings to the table: her skills and expertise? The answer is the latter. What you want from a stability expert is experience with complex formulations, proven experience in meeting FDA requirements, reputation for meeting tight deadlines, and the ability to work well in a team setting. This allows you to reframe the game and provide more latitude for you and Lorenzo to get to a mutually satisfactory solution. It moves the negotiation from a battle to be won (a contest of wills) to a problem to be solved.

Now that you've reframed the game, you can move on to inventing options for mutual gain—for example:

- Lorenzo might have other people with the qualifications you want.
- Bring in a freelance expert. Lorenzo could screen the individual.
- Outsource stability testing to a qualified lab.

At this point, you need to insist on using objective criteria. You need to define what you mean by "experience with complex formulations and in meeting FDA requirements." How many years? On what types of stability projects and under what time constraints? Granted, you may have to negotiate these with Lorenzo, but with an open mind, he may convince you that someone with two years of successful experience, not five, will fill the bill. In this way, you both get what you need: Lorenzo gets to keep Kathy, and your relationship with Lorenzo is preserved.

Learning how to create winning value propositions can help boost your success in tough negotiations. (For a practical, step-by-step approach to crafting value propositions that will appeal to the person across the table, see the eXtreme Tools and Techniques section at the end of the book.)

Devious Negotiation Games

In hard-core negotiation, the deck is stacked against you by virtue of your position as project manager. And the participants are advisories or will soon be when pressed. There are no happy solutions for this situation. There are some strategies that you can use to try to mitigate the situation. You will still likely lose, but now it's a case of by how much.

This is especially true when you've been given a "death march project," a term that forms the title of Edward Yourdon's outstanding book, *Death March* (1997). Although it was written for software developers, the book has applicability to any project that qualifies as a death march. Not all eXtreme projects are death march projects, but some are. A death march project is one whose project parameters exceed the norm by at least 50 percent. The schedule, the budget, or staff is less than half of what would objectively be considered normal; the functionality, features, and performance requirements are twice what would be considered normal.

What can you do to maximize your minimized position? A starting point is to recognize the possible kinds of negotiating games that you are likely to encounter (Yourdon, 1997). These have been beautifully articulated by Rob Thomsett and summarized in Yourdon's book. Here I further summarize the more popular games that we have all encountered:

- *Reverse doubling.* Management recognizes that you will likely double your estimates. After all, they did the same thing in their day. Therefore, no matter what number you give them, they cut it in half. Imagine the plight of the novice project manager who presents an honest, undoubled estimate.
- *Guess my number.* Although the boss has an acceptable number, she doesn't disclose it, insisting you go first. Each time you overshoot the secret number, you're sent back to sharpen your pencil. When you eventually get the magic number, it's become *your* number and with that much more passion, she holds you accountable.
- *Double dummy spit.* This is hard-core intimidation at its best. *Dummy* is an Australian term for a baby's pacifier. You present your first estimate, and the boss turns red in the face, chokes, and then expels her dummy. Mortified, if not chastened, you cower off to revise your estimate, only to experience yet another tantrum. (Advice: when the dummy lands on the floor, don't pick it up and give it back. But if you must, then don't wipe it off.)
- *Spanish Inquisition.* I can remember being grilled at 1:00 A.M. as other business managers and I would line up one by one to

present our quarterly forecasts to the top brass of IDG Corporation. If they didn't like the forecast, they'd grill us relentlessly on our assumptions and expect a revised number on the spot. Asking for twenty-four hours to reforecast and come up with a realistic estimate only underlined our incompetence.

• *Low bidder.* The pressure's on: a competitor's bid to win the contract is more favorable than yours. Desperate to get the business, you become a writer of project planning and estimating fiction.

• *Cat and mouse.* A third party has been brought in to audit the project and check estimates based on their proprietary model. You don't have a clue and a chance, especially if the reason behind bringing in the cat is politically motivated.

With all of these games, you lose every time.

Project sponsors aren't the only ones who play devious games. Here are some that project managers play:

• *Doubling and then some.* This is the most common tactic for scheduling. After you use your own estimating technique, you at least double it. Many eXtreme projects and most death march versions are deadline constrained (not negotiable) in the first place, so doubling a drop-dead deadline is to no avail.

• *Gotcha.* You know it can't be done and also recognize you can't beat the system, so you don't even waste your energy. Instead, you realize that by the time they learn that the project can't be done within the mandated time frame or budget, it will be beyond the point of no return. Remember the new Denver airport? It was billions over budget and months behind schedule, but who was going to pull the plug? Government contract projects also fall into this strategy. Other examples are projects that must meet federal compliance requirements: if you don't comply, you are out of business. The upshot of the gotcha strategy is that the project manager becomes the sacrificial lamb. Somebody has to go.

• *Chinese water torture.* This is a popular ploy on short-duration projects (three to six months), but I've seen it used on longer projects. The idea is to dispense bad news in small doses. You do this by chopping the project into a series of small deliverables spaced a week or so apart (the requirements document, the design document, the first prototype). Then when these deadlines are missed, you ask for an extension. If you get it, great, but chances are that management won't allow the slippage. At any one time, a day or two slippage appears to be no big deal, until the cumulative impact takes its toll at the end and the deliverable is nowhere in sight. (The Chinese water torture and gotcha strategies are good examples of malicious compliance.)

• *Covert trade-offs.* Another form of malicious compliance, the covert trade-off is, in my experience, the most widely used strategy, sometimes by design and sometimes by default. You go ahead with the project knowing that it can't be done. The team also knows it's insurmountable, so they are forced by the system to cut corners behind the scenes. They do anything to get *something* out there as long as they won't go to jail for it. The rationale is, "We'll fix it later." I call this the kiss-and-make-up strategy. This can be expensive because the longer one postpones correcting errors, the more costly it is. Think of the cost to recall 1.2 million cars to fix a malfunctioning brake master cylinder. A very old saying is still true: A stitch in time saves nine.

That being said, those saddled with the inevitable postpartum headaches are typically not the ones who created the problem in the first place. So the project manager and team are off the hook because accountability for poor performance is handed off to the next in line. Moreover, organizational practices go a long way to perpetuate the kiss-and-make-up strategy: business owners are rarely held accountable for the realization of the project's business benefits after delivery. The buck stops nowhere except, that is, at the shareholders' wallet.

Above-Board Negotiation Strategies

Hope springs eternal, if not futile. Keep in mind that hard-core negotiation really means that you lose; nonetheless, your sense of integrity might compel you to negotiate in good faith. At best, you will be less worse off. You also honor the Shared Values of client collaboration, honest communication, and people first (you don't want to send your team on a suicide mission). And you take responsibility for Business Question 3 (Can we get what it takes?).

And even if you lose big time, at least you can say you tried. If this were baseball, would you rather be batting 0 for 3 or 0 for 0? By being proactive, you can at least light the candle and avoid cursing the darkness. After all, you have to live with yourself. Here are some strategies. They all involve making trade-offs. Recognize that these are all *rational* approaches but the people you will be facing are not likely to be rational at all, especially if this is a true death march project to meet a do-or-die business objective or is politically motivated:

- *Exposing the folly.* This involves letting them see just how ridiculous their demands are. It can be as simple as referring to the old project management saw by saying to your sponsor, "Everybody knows that you can have it better, faster, or cheaper, but not all three. Pick two. And if we find we can't make all two, which one is the top priority?" A tool that I provide eXtreme project managers for the purpose of exposing the folly is called the project uncertainty profile. It enables the manager to quickly assess the level of uncertainty associated with the project and demonstrate the impossibility of predicting the amount of scope that can be delivered and at what cost given the deadline. The project uncertainty profile is covered in Part Three.
- *Questioning the end date.* This is one strategy that I've seen work. You ask, "What is it about the date of May 1 that is key? What would be the consequences of delivering the goods a week later? Two weeks later? What opportunities would be missed? What costs would be incurred?" Often you'll find that there *is* flexibility. This strategy is useless for true drop-dead dates like Y2K, submitting a government bid, or if the deliverable is needed for demo purposes at the consumer electronics show.
- *Scope bleep.* In this classic approach, you press hard to uncover the absolute minimum acceptable product that you can deliver—in other words, finding Pareto's 20 percent that will give 80 percent of the bang. "If we did nothing else, what must we absolutely deliver?" This is another example of pressing for the worst-case scenario.
- *Buying time.* The guiding principle is never to give an estimate on the spot. Ask for time, even if it's for one hour. Your rationale, you proclaim, is, "If I gave you an estimate out of the blue, it might turn out to be too high and you'd decide not to go forward and possibly miss an opportunity. Or if I am too low due to all the unknowns, you'll have an unpleasant surprise at the end." Be prepared to rattle off a list of unknowns. Memorize a few standard ones so that you always have them ready. You could also exercise self-disclosure power and say something like, "To be honest

with you, I have no idea. I've never seen one like this before. Give me twenty-four hours."

Try it, but don't count on them buying it. Being rational may have nothing to do with it. Moreover, your situation might be so pressure packed that you have to come up with a number on the spot to support the big decision being made at that meeting.

- *Making time.* You may be able to get people to work overtime and get out of the jam that way. Chances are, though, that people are already working ungodly hours and have no slack. And if you are on death march project by Yourdon's definition, it's already assumed that people will be putting in eighteen-hour days and working around the clock. Effectively, you don't have overtime as an option.

- *Hedging your bet.* Here, the principle is to never give a point estimate. Use a plus-or-minus range: "Based on what we know now, I'd say twelve weeks plus or minus four." Always include the range in all forms of communication. The reality is that they will likely take the midpoint or earlier date and hold you to it.

- *I'm the expert.* This is an application of expert power. You're the project manager. You own Business Question 2: What will it take to get it? So you are given a dictated budget, a time line, and three people to get the job done. You tell them point-blank, "I'm the project manager. That's what you hired me for. I'll come up with the estimate and rationale."

This is where bedfellows of guts power and the Shared Value of courage come together. You demand respect. But this is hard to do if you don't respect yourself as the expert, or at least believe that you are smarter than they are when it comes to project management.

- *More people.* You can ask for more people, but recognize that it's one thing to cut in half the time it takes to build a wall by adding twice as many bricklayers to the project. For projects involving complex systems, the linear approach can be fallacious. Frederick Brooks, in his famous book *The Mythical Man Month* (1995), demonstrated that adding more people to an already late software project can make it later. More people means more variables, which means more interactions, greater complexity, more control policies, and this means greater overhead and more people. And this is compounded by the nature of the beast itself. In software development, R&D projects, and others that involve high levels of intellectual capital and many unknowns, we are dealing with a lot of complexity to begin with. More people compounds complexity with more complexity. The solution is to take the additional people and partition the project. This involves lopping off a discrete chunk of work and assigning it to a dedicated subteam. This minimizes or eliminates the number of cross-project interactions and can avoid escalating communications complexity.

• *Break the rules.* This has to do with policies, approval processes, and proscribed methodologies you are saddled with. Here, you ask your sponsor to give you permission to circumvent the bureaucracy. If you can't get relief, you simply bypass the system. The nice thing about some bureaucracies is that they trip over themselves, to your advantage. By the time they find out what you've been up to and then get you to mend your ways, you are way ahead of the game.

I remember working with one team that was saddled with a cumbersome project management scheduling and communication system mandated by the project office. The team decided to go to a third-party vendor of collaboration software services. For a few thousand bucks in subscription fees, they were up and running and collaborating. The money was a drop in the bucket and easily hidden in the project budget. The project office never found out.

Recognize that all of these strategies have consequences. You might make a few enemies along the way, maybe even get fired. But this is eXtreme project management, and you're in the game.

How to Resolve Conflict

Conflict of ideas is to be encouraged if we want the best thinking to come forward. Conflict is the womb of innovation, giving birth to a solution or concept that no one individual alone might have contemplated. Conflict can be the lifeblood of a team when the conflict revolves around differing viewpoints on how to solve a problem or how to proceed on the project. But as James Lewis points out his book *Team-Based Project Management* (1997), "Conflict of ideas may lead to interpersonal conflict, and when this happens, it must be resolved, or damage to the effective functioning of the organization [or team] will result" (p. 193).

When conflicts go unresolved, people hold on to bad feelings, which contaminate the project's energy field casting a negative spell over the endeavor and resulting in low morale, low productivity, and high stress.

An assertive approach to conflict resolution that I use with good results is the DDEENT model. Before using the model, you should establish the appropriate context. First, choose a neutral setting in which to discuss the problem. Going into the meeting, do not assume you know the other persons intentions, thoughts, or feelings.

These are the six steps of the DDEENT model (the first letter of each step forms the acronym):

1. *Diffuse yourself first.* This is the Feelings → Facts → Solutions sequence applied to you. Unless you calm yourself down before engaging the other person, you're likely to go into the meeting hot under the collar and enflame the situation.

When you find yourself in the midst of an interpersonal conflict, say to yourself, "I can picture myself doing [or saying] the same thing that he/she just did [said]." This will help you get to a position of tolerance for, if not acceptance of, the individual. If that doesn't work, I highly recommend you apply Byron Katie's four questions and the turnaround that are covered in the eXtreme Tools and Techniques section at the back of this book.

2. *Describe the conflict.* Be clear why you called this meeting, and state the problem as you see it. Deal with the issues, not the character of the other person. State your sincere desire to resolve the conflict to the satisfaction of both parties. Where value differences have caused the conflict, deal with the tangible effects of the difference, not the values themselves.

3. *Explore causes.* Build rapport and trust by applying active listening. Keep in mind that the other person is not bad, mad, or crazy just because you have differences. Try to work on one issue at a time when several exist. As part of this exploratory component, briefly state your needs, views, and feelings. A good way to do this is to say, "When this happens, I feel . . ." Always give the other person a chance to save face. And don't rush the process.

4. *Elevate the energy.* Refer to the higher good being served and the importance of the individual. You might say, "Building this ark is crucial for all mankind. And your role, Samantha, as the architect is fundamental to our success. That's why we need a faster

turnaround on the blueprints." In other words, appeal to your project's ultimate business purpose or some other redeeming value. By doing this, you are also helping to unleash motivation by invoking Accelerator 2: Build on people's desire to make a difference.

5. *Negotiate a solution.* The guidelines and strategies on how to negotiate discussed earlier in this chapter come into play here. State what you want as a request, not as a demand. Brainstorm ways in which the problem can be solved to free up Samantha from other priorities. What's important here is that Samantha picks the solution that works for her. You'll recognize this as Accelerator 3: create ownership for results. Once an agreement is reached, ask the other party if there is anything that might prevent his or her complying with the agreement.

6. *Take action.* "I'll talk to your boss right away and see if I can work something out to get you more time on my project." Don't make promises you can't keep. Samantha is asked to state her action item: "I will get you the first draft blueprint by Wednesday noon at the latest."

Being able to resolve conflict effectively is a prime example of the role of the eXtreme project manager as one who facilitates and manages the flow of emotions, thoughts, and interactions in a way that produces a valued outcome. The overarching principle to keep in mind is that effective conflict resolution means that one must first deal with the feeling, starting with your own, before dealing with the facts and heading for a solution. Again, Feelings → Facts → Solutions.

When All Else Fails

What do you do when negotiation is impossible or fails and conflict is intractable? The short answer is: Go home. It's also the long answer because it requires painful soul searching. You can't avoid it. You can only postpone it.

You can't avoid it because, whether invoked consciously or unconsciously, Business Question 4 will rise to surface and whisper in your ear day after day: Is it worth it (for me to stick with this project)? This puts you face to face with the shared values of courage and quality of life, along with your own personal values and principles. What is the impact of this insanity on your health, your family? Is it worth it? What's at stake? This is why a solid foundation in Self-Mastery (Critical Success Factor 1), including the use of personal power, is fundamental for quality of life.

When all else fails, the choices that are staring at you are the following: tough it out, quit the project, or quit your job. It's a personal decision. What is important is that you make it with your eyes wide open, understanding the implications of each option.

If you quit the project, you run the risk of getting fired anyway or maybe compromising your future in the organization. But, then again, it doesn't sound like a place you'd want to work. Yet I know people who have become so attached to misery that it has become their identity. They wouldn't know who they were without it. They've become so locked into themselves that short of a crisis, they are not likely to move. Some would rather do almost anything than give up the investment in their identity.

One sad example of this had to do with a young woman I was coaching who was a wreck about her job. When I prompted her to think about finding a new employer, she said. "There is only one thing worse than working in this organization." When I asked what she meant, she said, "Looking for a job." It gave new meaning to the saying, "The devil you know is better than the devil you don't."

If you are dealing with corporate lunacy, the experts will tell you that your best bargaining chip when negotiating is your sincere willingness to walk away. But you have to mean it. To give you the courage to walk, remember to keep your resumé up to date, build your network, and stash away three to six months of money to live on while you reboot yourself. If you have a family, it also helps to keep their pictures visible to remind you that they need you, all of you. Many of us, me included, have made orphans of our children and widows and widowers of our spouses while we were all still alive: we show up physically at home, but we are not present. To go home means to come home to ourselves first so that we can truly be home for our loved ones.

eXtreme projects can bring us to extreme realizations about ourselves and what's important in life. They can take us home. That's why I bless these ventures.

In this chapter, I covered the essential principles, values, and interpersonal skills for the eXtreme project manager. In the next chapter, I continue Critical Success Factor 2, Leadership by Commitment, and place the focus on the requisite skills for leading the eXtreme team.

eXtreme Project Management Model
Applying the Quantum Mind-Set

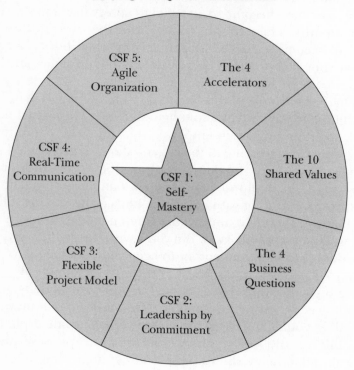

Chapter Six

Leading the eXtreme Team

Great people do not equal great teams.
TOM PETERS

If you don't have a viable team, you don't have a viable project. Period.

In the previous chapter, I focused on the principles, people values, and one-on-one skills that you need to succeed in leading in an eXtreme environment. This chapter looks at Critical Success Factor 2, Leadership by Commitment, by placing the spotlight on you and the team. This includes establishing the core team as well as putting in place an empowered environment that makes it possible for team members to succeed.

The very nature of eXtreme projects puts extraordinary demands on team members compared to the relatively more stable setting of the traditional project. Compounding the special challenges of high speed, high change, high complexity, and high stress associated with eXtreme projects, eXtreme project managers are typically faced with the following:

- An aggressive deadline imposed from above
- Skepticism among team members in the ability to succeed
- A dislike for project management and other processes
- Absentee project sponsor
- Unsatisfactory working conditions
- No direct authority over team members
- Part-time team members already overworked and stretched thin
- Turnover among team members through reassignments to other projects or leaving the company

- Multiple inputs from managers, sponsors, and customers who have vested and often conflicting interests in the project
- Lack of empowerment among team members to make decisions
- Significant personal stress due to working long hours and unexpected events

It's no wonder that being an eXtreme project manager is one of the most challenging jobs you can find.

I discussed the role of the core team in Chapter Four; here I show you how to put it together and get it running effectively. Specifically, I cover how to be the process leader of the eXtreme project team. It requires an understanding of these key characteristics:

- Characteristics of teams
- Creating the core team
- Getting the right sponsor and people on the team
- Becoming a high-performing project team
- Ensuring productive working conditions
- Managing meetings effectively
- Facilitating effective decision making and problem solving
- Earning the right to lead the process

By clearly focusing on your role as the process leader for your team, you will generate greater loyalty to the project, high morale, productive team meetings, effective and timely decision making and problem solving, and effective project sponsorship. Being the process leader also includes putting into practice the Flexible Project Model, Critical Success Factor 3.

Process Values

Remember the farming metaphor from Chapter Four: as the process leader, you are the tiller of the soil. Your job is to detoxify the soil so that those responsible for growing the plants (doing the work) can succeed. Process power along with your one-on-one interpersonal skills keep the soil fertile. Along with process power, you need to use process values. As I emphasized before, all ten Shared Values apply all the time. In using process power, however, process values come to the fore.

In addition to these values, the 4 Business Questions raise the critical issues you will need to address as you put together your team. As we will see, you will use them in many ways.

Client Collaboration

In practice, *client collaboration* means ongoing interaction and feedback with the customer throughout the venture as opposed to hand off and disengage:

- The customer has agreed to be available to make timely decisions and give approvals throughout the project as these relate to the business case, scope, budget, schedule, and desired quality.
- Listen closely to the voice of the client and not second-guess what the client wants.

Fast Failures

In practice, *fast failures* means finding the quickest path to failure by tackling the most difficult, risky, or important work very early on:

- Failing your way to success, which means knowing that every failure gets you that much closer to a better answer and believing that nothing succeeds like failure
- Enabling a continuous stream of adjustments by providing sample work products to the client (interactive models, vivid mockups, simulations) versus written descriptions or slide shows of what it will be like
- Gaining immediate feedback as to what works and doesn't
- Cultivating the practice that final specifications are a result of trial and error; the blind conformance to initial specifications can lead to dead-ends at a point too late to recover
- Knowing that getting it right the last time is more important than getting it right the first time

Visibility

In practice, *visibility* means keeping everything out in the open for all to see: plans, progress, work products, issues, who's accountable for what:

- Recognizing that people are visual
- Doing work on white boards and flip charts and using sticky notes
- Setting up a project war room if possible

In addition to these values, the 4 Business Questions raise the critical issues you will need to address as you put together your team. As we will see, you will use them in many ways.

Characteristics of Teams

There are many definitions of a team. The one I have found most useful over the years is that by John Katzenbach and Douglas Smith in *The Wisdom of Teams* (1993). I have modified it slightly so that it reflects the nature of eXtreme projects: "A team is a small number of people with complementary subject matter expertise who are committed to a common purpose, set of performance goals, and a common approach for which they hold themselves mutually accountable." As the process leader, your job, if not your mantra, is to enable your group to approach this standard and keep them there. Do this, and you will be successful.

This definition of a team has a number of important points:

- "Small number." Keep the number of members to a maximum of nine people. I prefer between four and seven. Once you get beyond nine, the communications and coordination processes become enormous and unwieldy.
- "Complementary subject matter expertise." Katzenbach and Smith used the term *complementary skills* in their original definition, which is usually interpreted as meaning just technical skills. In my use of the term, "subject matter expertise" includes both business and technical expertise.
- "Common purpose, performance goals, and approach." For a team to be committed, its members need to believe that the project is worthwhile. They also need to have a sense of joint ownership as to how they will be measured and how they will get to the goal (meaning the process and tools that will be used). Unless there is buy-in on all three elements (purpose, performance goals, and process), commitment will be elusive. When commitment fal-

ters, you may find yourself trying to manage by compliance and coercion instead. But since you are the project manager and have little to no position power, compliance and coercion are not options—unless you can get the sponsor to anoint you as Attila (or Sally) the Project Hun.

- "Hold themselves mutually accountable." In the mutual accountability model, team members do their job and support others in holding up their end of the project. The predominant attitude is that we either all succeed or we all fail.

A group is just the opposite of a team. There is no mutual accountability, just individual accountability for doing one's job but without feeling responsible for the whole project. In the group model, the group leader hands out assignments, rides herd, approves, and integrates the work. The group model, then, is highly directive and assumes the group leader has the authority, knowledge, and experience to get the job done. This model can be effective on projects that are stable and enjoy few unknowns: low complexity, familiar technology, set-in-stone requirements, and little change. Under these circumstances, the group model also works well when the team is inexperienced and can safely rely on the expertise of the group leader.

Unfortunately, many eXtreme project managers are process leaders for a group rather than a team. And because an eXtreme project features so many variables and unknowns, coupled with a lack of position power, the eXtreme group leader is in a low-win situation, putting the project at great risk: you can't possibly know the answers, and you have no power over those who do. That's why, as process leader, you have to win over the minds and hearts of others.

Establishing the Core Team

The sponsor is considered to be a part of the eXtreme project core team and the single most important factor in spelling success or failure on the project, which by definition are organizationally complex and politically sensitive. Given that the project manager has little direct power in the command-and-control sense, the real power to get things done needs to come from a project sponsor, who should be able to cut across organizational lines and influence people, including those not in the chain of command. (This does not absolve you from using your power sources and influencing skills covered in earlier chapters.) So the first and most important element in putting together your core team is the sponsor.

The eXtreme Project Sponsor

You know you have the right eXtreme project sponsor when:

- You are viewed as the project manager and not the content (development or technical) manager.
- You are able to get what you need to succeed on a consistent basis (including resources, timely decisions, and conflicts resolved with competing projects).
- You have the power to make your own decisions within predefined limits.
- You and the sponsor are both satisfied with the working relationship.

How do you get the sponsor you need and establish a strong working relationship with him or her? The 4 Business Questions are a handy, easy-to-use multipurpose thinking tool. I'll adapt them as framework to examine what is needed in the way of a sponsor for an eXtreme project.

What Does the Project Need and Why?

My favorite test of solid sponsorhood is the one Rob Thomsett came up with that appears in his book *Radical Project Management* (2002). It's called "the bag of money and baseball bat test." The project sponsor must have enough financial clout (bag of money) and organizational clout (baseball bat) to spend money and get things done quickly. A complication can be when the bag of money and baseball bat reside in the hands of two different people. This double-headed sponsor situation slows things and makes your job much more difficult when you need to get a quick decision or a conflict resolved.

If you are stuck with the dreaded double-headed sponsor, you should lobby hard that one of the heads be designated your single point of contact and whose job is to secure timely decisions from his or her counterpart. Otherwise you'll be playing monkey in the middle.

Another difficult situation occurs when you are given a sponsor that's at too high a level. It may sound great to have the CEO as your guardian angel, but unless you are heading up one of his top three priority projects, you may be hard-pressed to get timely decisions. Delays are killers on time-driven projects. Every day on an eXtreme project can be the equivalent of two weeks to a month on traditional project.

What Will It Take to Do It?

If your sponsor has the needed financial and political clout, you are fortunate, because without these qualifications, nothing else matters. The rest is relatively easy because you can always educate her on her sponsorly job duties and why they are crucial for the project's success.

If you assess your sponsor and she comes up short in having the necessary financial and political clout for the project to succeed, you are now in the unenviable position of having to do something about it.

Your strategy here is to make the case for why a certain level of financial and organizational clout and swift decision making are crucial for success, not only for the project but for the personal success of your sponsor as well. You are in the best position to do this once the details and politics of the project have come to the light during scoping and planning meetings that take place during the Visionate and Speculate cycles of the Flexible Project Model.

Your going-in attitude is that you have the interests of the business in mind and the substantial financial investment that is being made for this project. Your mind-set is also that you are doing your sponsor a favor, because you in fact are. If she doesn't have what it takes, she and the project are at risk.

In my practice, when this situation of insufficient organizational and financial clout comes up, the solution lies in having the existing sponsor find someone who can serve as an executive sponsor. I have never seen a case where the original sponsor bows out of the project. If your sponsor goes the route of an executive sponsor, then they need to work out their individual roles. The job sponsor description serves as the basis.

Some sponsors may dismiss this entire argument because they believe they can transfer their risk to you, or they simply reject the idea that they might not have the requisite clout. This is a case that if the project succeeds, you and they may get the credit, but if it fails, you get the blame. Watch out for being set up.

Also, remember the Shared Value of courage. So much of what it takes to move forward or stay stuck on eXtreme projects comes down to exercising courage. Courage can't wait for the fear to subside. That's why I say you have to "do it scared." The other Shared Value that is at a premium here is honest communication.

> *So much of what it takes to move forward or stay stuck*
> *on eXtreme projects comes down to exercising courage.*

In making your case to get the sponsor that's best for the project, it's important that you also take into consideration your sponsor's business and personal motivators, as well as her temperament style and managerial intelligences. (These are covered in earlier chapters and in the eXtreme Tools and Techniques section.)

Can I Get What It Takes?

Having made your case for what the project needs to succeed in the way of sponsorship, the answer will be either, "Yes, I can get it" or "No, I can't."

Is It Worth It?

If the answer is no, meaning you have made your best effort, then you are back to soul searching again because you are embarking on a no-win project. You need to take a serious look at your options and make an eyes-wide-open decision.

Negotiating Your Own Role

Assuming you have the right sponsor, your next biggest goal is to be positioned as the project manager as opposed to the technical or development manager. Most project sponsors do not make this distinction and simply appoint the technical manager to also be the project manager or vice versa. If this is the case, your job is to not let this happen and to make the case for a dedicated project manager.

By *dedicated,* I don't necessarily mean full time, although most eXtreme projects require it. It's quite possible that you will have another job to do or project to run. I mean dedicated in the sense that you are the project manager and not the technical manager for the eXtreme project. My experience is that if you cannot secure a position of dedicated project manager, then sooner or later, you will be "deadicated" instead: for all practical purposes, leading a dead-end project.

Timing is everything here. The best time to make the case for being the dedicated project manager is once the sponsor has a first-hand understanding of the project's context and requirements and risk profile, including its scope, time frame, cross-organizational dynamics, political sensitivity, technical complexity, degree of uncertainty and change, and critical success factors. This information will become quite evident as a result of the scoping and planning meetings that take place during the Visionate and Speculate cycles of the Flexible Project Model.

Although the project requirements and risk profile have become evident, the operational implications for the role of project manager are likely to come as a surprise to the sponsor. I have found that it is unlikely that the sponsor will have made the mental leap of translating project requirements and risks into what this implies for your role and even her role. Your job is to make the case. The eXtreme Tools and Techniques section contains a step-by-step process for creating a compelling value proposition to make the case for being a dedicated project manager.

Position Power

If you can get it, the ideal situation for the eXtreme project manager is to be granted position power by the sponsor, but run the project using process power wherever practical. In effect, this would make you the CEO of the project, with the clout to hold at least some team members accountable (peers and below) and to make certain decisions that don't require consensus or majority approval. Holding people accountable means that you have the power to influence their bonus or paycheck. Furthermore, to be credible in the role of project CEO, in some organizations you have to look and act the part: you need an office and salary on a par with the management level of those you will have to influence in order to get what you need. Few eXtreme project managers have the internal clout, preparation, and experience to pull this off.

A Partnering Agreement with Your Sponsor

When a consultant takes on an engagement, an important step is to agree on expectations, that is, what the client or sponsor can expect from the consultant, and what the consultant can expect from the sponsor. A project is an engagement. The same principle applies. The sponsor *is* your client, the one who must be satisfied with the end product.

Set the standard. Go over your job description as project manager as *you* see it and gain agreement as to what your job entails. Next, set expectations for communications. Find out what information your sponsor expects about project status, how often, and in what form. Then identify obstacles you anticipate where you will need your sponsor's support (for example, team members being pulled away, stakeholders likely to delay or undermine the project, delays in projects likely to have an impact on yours).

Recognize that one of your sponsor's most powerful motivators is likely to be that of keeping her boss happy. I remember Mike, a project sponsor I was consulting with. Mike had a penchant for adding more scope to the project, which was pushing out the schedule. Having sat through a review meeting with Mike and his boss, Charlie, the vice president of finance, I reminded Mike that Charlie said that being on time with the basics was more important than delivering all the bells and whistles. Mike quickly backed off from adding unnecessary scope. So find out what's important to your sponsor's boss. Use that as a legitimate lever to help you get what you want.

Recognize that one of your sponsor's most powerful motivators is likely to be that of keeping her boss happy.

Selecting Other Members of the eXtreme Core Team

As before, the 4 Business Questions provide a useful structure for determining your needs and those of your project.

What Will It Take to Do It?

Without the people power to get the job done, the project is doomed. Getting the right people and enough of their time is among your most important tasks.

Only when you have a handle on the job to be done are you even in a position to determine the critical subject matter expertise and technical skills that the project demands. Figuring out the job to be done is the primary purpose of project the Visionate and Speculate cycles of Flexible Project Model.

In the best case, you'll get to pick the people you need and get their bosses to shake them loose for as much time as the project requires, including full time if necessary. In the worse case, your project sponsor will tell you who has been assigned to the project even before the full scope of the project is determined. This shifts all the risk to you. On eXtreme projects, either by default or by intention, project risk is progressively passed down the chain until it lands in the project manager's lap. You have to be careful that you are not the last dummy.

At least you have the 4 Business Questions to serve as a reminder for you to press for what it will really take to succeed once you've completed the Visionate and Speculate cycles and have data to make your case. Data plus speak-up power fueled by the Shared Values of courage and honest communication are at a premium here.

In getting what it will take, your options are to press hard to reserve the right to pick the people you need (inside or outside the organization), and if you don't win on that, to reserve the right to veto anybody picked on your behalf.

If you have the opportunity to pick team members, it can be tempting to go to the star performers inside or outside the organization. That may sound good, but in reality, the stars are often spread too thin already. And, since they are really good, they are likely not to be inclined to want to be part of the stress and risk associated with your eXtreme project, even if you can get the resources to recruit them from the outside. You are unlikely to able to meet their conditions. You will be stuck with whomever you are handed unless you are very proactive. That's why you need veto power.

Another reality is that you are given nobody and are expected to scrounge up a team without any formal assignment to the team by the sponsor or even the functional managers. If that's the case, your job is to identify the people you need and then obtain a formal commitment from the sponsor that they will be officially assigned to the project.

Don't fool yourself. You may even succeed in getting volunteers to show up at the kick-off meeting because they think it's their job to be there, even though they have not been formally assigned to your project. This is slow death because you can succumb to the illusion that you have a real team to work with when you really have a phantom team on your hands. Months later, when you are hopelessly lost, you come to the realization. I prefer sudden death to slow death. At least it avoids the suffering.

Who *do* you want? You want competent people who have the necessary time. But *do* they have the needed time to spend? Don't take this for granted. Here are some probing questions to ask of would-be team members who have been formally assigned to the team:

- What are you working on that has greater priority than this project? Less priority?
- What do you foresee that could keep you from fulfilling your role on this project?
- How likely is this to happen?
- What personal commitments might take you away from the project? Family? Vacation?

I strongly recommend that you put together a short partnering agreement with the team member's boss so that there is no doubt. The partnering agreement is covered in Chapter Seven.

Can You Get What It Takes?

What if, after all is said and done, you still come up short and cannot field the right team to do the job at hand and you know you cannot meet your sponsor's goal? Assuming you are not allowed to extend the schedule, increase the budget, or cut the project's scope, you are embarking on a death march. You may temporarily fool yourself by thinking that once the project gets going, "I'll be able to get more of what I need once I prove myself." My experience shows that this is highly unlikely. If you don't get respect at the beginning, you won't get it later. Besides, if you prove that you can produce results through heroic efforts, you have proven your sponsor correct all along: you really didn't need more people.

It's not uncommon for a real team—one that has been formally assigned to the project—to mutate into a phantom team as time goes on and people get assigned to other work or leave the company. Are you able to compensate for team erosion? Has the eXtreme project turned from a good chance of success into a death march?

If you find yourself coming up with a "no" in answer to question 3, you are saying that you will fail. Proceed to Business Question 4.

Is it Worth It?

This is yet another opportunity to do some soul searching. eXtreme projects have a way of bringing you face-to-face with your personal set of values:

- Do I resign the project, or should I stick it out?
- What are the possible consequences of resigning? Of sticking with it? Look at the impact on personal health, family, and promotability.
- What other options do I have (for example, find another job)?

In addressing these questions, I have found it very useful to investigate my answers using the Byron Katie's "The Work," which is included in the eXtreme Tools and Techniques section.

Creating the Conditions for Successful Teamwork

Once you have the project sponsor and your entire core team in place, you need to establish the conditions that will enable the team to succeed.

Let's say that you're about to start your meeting. Look around the room as members of the core team assemble and take their seats. Glance at their faces, and look at the body language. What's the feeling in the air? What are you picking up in your own gut? What's the body language telling you? Now ask yourself, Is the project in a good mood or a sour mood? Is it energized? Do these people even want to be in the same room together? You want people to be saying to themselves, "I can win. We can win." To do this, you have to help the team move through the four stages of team development.

> *You want people to be saying to themselves,*
> *"I can win. We can win."*

It's well known that teams go through four stages of development: forming, norming, storming, performing (Figure 6.1). In the forming stage, when a team first gets together, individual team members have some pretty basic questions on their mind: What is the project all about? Why is it important? What's my role? Who are you, and what's your role? Since the team has just gotten together, no work is being done on the project. Once these basic questions are answered, the next logical stage is for the team to move into norming. This involves getting to know one another personally and setting up ground rules for communication and coordination of work. It also includes planning the project jointly.

What I find typically happens, especially on eXtreme projects with tight deadlines and short time frames, is that the team quickly gets eager to do work before the forming and norming infrastructure is in place. In other words, the team leapfrogs into the storming stage. They work hard but with little coordination and communication. This is the domain of the cross-dysfunctional team, where the team goes nowhere fast and keeps going and going, picking up pace and panic and tripping over themselves. Animosity and blame run rampant.

Figure 6.1. The Four Quadrants of Team Development

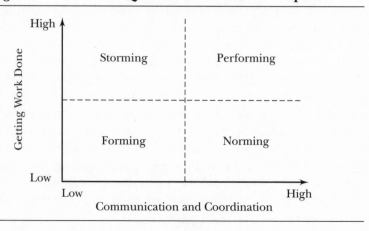

When a team is in the performing stage, it is not only getting work done, it is doing it in a coordinated way. When this happens, the project goes into a good mood and becomes energized. People know they are making progress, doing good work together, and having a few laughs along the way. The team feels and looks successful.

To be successful, a team does not have to be a love fest where everybody holds hands and walks into the sunset singing. They just need to work toward a commonly understood target in a coordinated way, even if several people can't stand each other. When I worked as a drummer in a jazz combo, I learned that what's important is that you all play the same tune and know your part. You don't have to like the trumpet player's style or personality.

Since we're dealing with people and not machines, there are no pat formulas and templates for moving a team from forming to high performing. Nonetheless, as the project manager, there is a lot you can do to vastly improve the odds of quickly moving the team to the high-performing stage and keeping them there. In fact, this *is* your job: to make it possible for people to succeed.

Finding the WOW! Factor

If the thought of "being on a project" lowers people's energy level, then "being on a mission" can get them excited. I'd rather sign up for a cause than a project any day. Causes give meaning. They energize and foster motivation and innovation because they unleash Accelerator 2: build on people's desire to make a difference.

One of the biggest motivators for being on a team is the desire for joint ownership: to do great work together, to be remembered as having made a difference, to have a great story to tell. When Steve Jobs was getting Apple Computer started, he unleashed enormous energy by giving people an opportunity to "put a dent in the universe." When I used to visit Apple, I could feel the energy and excitement in the air.

This is what Tom Peters (1999) is referring to when he uses the term "WOW Project!" Peters goes so far as to say you can take any task and redefine it into something exciting, even revolutionary, culture changing, and job promoting:

- An assignment to clean up the compensation time policy turns into a project to revamp the entire compensation program and reward system.

- A task to organize the library leads to a new companywide knowledge management system.
- Annoyance with scraps of paper used as bookmarks is the catalyst for the invention of sticky notes.
- Success in applying project management to several small projects escalates into a culture change as others contract project management envy.

Reframing a project can energize it. In 1985, I was hired by the IDG Group, an information technology industry publishing giant, to create and launch a new newspaper that became *NetworkWorld,* a weekly tabloid for buyers and advertisers of voice and data communications products and services. Giving birth to a new publication in half the usual time in a highly competitive publishing market can be overwhelming, even if you have a unique niche, as did our newspaper. In addition, the details and complexity of building a publication can be a nightmare. It's like trying to get five thousand moving parts to work together. The problem was that we initially saw our project as "starting a newspaper," an endeavor that at best had a flat energy wave associated with it. Getting up in the morning and thinking about the project was drudgery.

Then one day in a conversation I was having with Bruce Hoard, the editor, I realized that this was not about starting a newspaper. It was really about leading the world into the new age of information networking. WOW! I could get up for that. So could the rest of the staff. That simple reframing shifted the entire energy field of our venture. We were leading the world. How audacious. How exhilarating. How empowering. How unstoppable we were.

If your project is suffering from so-what syndrome, find the WOW! factor that is usually lurking under any project. Think of the impact that the project is intended to have: the outcome, the benefit, the change it will produce. What will be new and different? For example, ask yourself, your sponsor, and other advocates, "How will the project . . . shake up the competition? Redefine the game? Flatten the hierarchy? Keep us in business? Revolutionize our industry? Give people a better life? Make heroes out of us? Improve our standing on Wall Street? Save jobs? Dramatically improve the bottom line? Break into new markets? Deliver a blockbuster new technology? Set a new industry standard? Increase personal wealth? Take early retirement? Put a competitor out of business? Turn around a bad situation with an existing client? Liberate people from an age old, counterproductive business process?"

Push for Co-Location

A key component in the definition of an eXtreme project is that it is a self-correcting venture. And by now, it's obvious that a dominant theme of eXtreme project management is communications. To get the maximum benefit out of eXtreme project management, the core and subteams (those doing the actual work) do best when they are co-located. Even under the best circumstances, virtual teams that are spread across time zones are at a decided disadvantage over co-located teams. They are much more difficult to manage and generally take more time to get up and running and get things done. And when face-to-face communication is replaced by documentation and time lags, misunderstandings occur and delays arise. Co-location greatly speeds up the flow of communications so that problems can be resolved on the spot.

The most effective communication is face-to-face when people can read body language, grab a marker, and do a few squiggles on a flip chart. The greater the separation on a virtual team, the greater is the need for meeting preparation, coordination, documentation, and administration. Without the ability for instant feedback and correction, the greater the chances are of misinterpretation and going down dead-end streets.

Moreover, since product owners and product developers are separated by time and geography on virtual teams, several essential eXtreme project management shared values are compromised. The values of close client contact (client collaboration), the ability to discover real needs and quickly demonstrate potential solutions (early value), and the benefit of getting instant feedback on the spot (fast failures) are all sacrificed. Results orientation is another Shared Value that gets compromised since dispersed team members spend time generating documents instead of generating working models and prototypes. These distance practices also breed Newtonian-like fixed plans along with waterfall development approaches that lock out the ability to be nimble, resulting in greater risk of producing an obsolete or suboptimal end product.

Co-location also facilitates the ability to hold daily progress meetings that keep each subteam synchronized with itself as well as with other teams. Co-location supports the Shared Value of visibility and Project Accelerator 4, keep it simple, because it removes the administrative and other bureaucratic practices associated with separation.

If you are running a high-stakes eXtreme project, then you at least have a shot at convincing your project sponsor to pull strings and get the team co-located and dedicated at least for critical parts of the project (initiation, major reviews, and decision-reaching points) and house them in a physical environment conducive for collaboration.

If you have a deadline-driven, mission-critical project and a dispersed team, it will take all of your guts power to correct the problem, including breaking the rules. You will need to rely on your influencing skills. Your goal is a controlled environment for the eXtreme core team, one that the team can set up and call their own (Accelerator 3: create ownership for results).

Taking these steps takes courage, one of the most challenging Shared Values to live by. Even if you are not successful in sanitizing the working environment, you will earn the respect and loyalty of team members because you had the emotional intelligence to be sensitive to their needs and you had the guts to take a stand on their behalf. Actually, I think it takes courage not to stake a stand and not to assert yourself: by being passive, you are almost guaranteeing failure by tolerating intolerable working conditions.

If, despite your most strenuous efforts, virtual teams are a reality, then to succeed, team members and other stakeholders will require timely access to new and fast-changing information while keeping project management and communications overhead activities to a bare a minimum. This is the topic of Chapter Fifteen. You will also need guidance on the special challenges of leading a virtual team. See The Do's and Don'ts of Leading the Virtual Team in the eXtreme Tools and Techniques section.

Press for Conducive Working Conditions

An unfit working environment drains the project energy field, stifling productivity: it turns emotions sour, blocks the flow of ideas, and creates unproductive interactions, as when people continually barge in and interrupt your work or continually call impromptu meetings. I was sitting with a client one time, having an intense discussion, when one of her coworkers knocked and then walked right in without asking. No sooner had he interrupted our private meeting than someone else then butted in while he was interrupting!

In a study of six hundred programmers, DeMarco and Lister (1999) demonstrated that improving working conditions resulted in a 2.6-fold increase in productivity. Good working conditions translate into hard dollars.

It's your job to put in place a fertile work environment. Go to lengths to ensure the following conditions:

- Availability of refreshments
- Sufficient working and desk space
- Quiet
- Privacy
- Easy access to common supplies
- The ability for team members to choose their own work hours as much as possible
- Sufficient training
- Fully equipped meeting facilities
- The ability for team members to deviate from prescribed methods and policies if they can show they have a better way
- Reasonably up-to-date technology
- Clean air
- Concentrated time (rather than fractionated time, being pulled from one project to another)
- Policies that make it easy for people to take care of personal business

Set Team Operating Agreements

If working conditions deal with the basic infrastructure to get work done, operating agreements focus on how people will work together and behave in order to do quality work.

Team operating agreements or norms are created and agreed to by the team. Going back to Katzenbach and Smith's definition of a team, these ground rules enable the team to establish and live by "a common approach for which they hold themselves mutually accountable."

Specifically, team operating agreements cover how the team will administer its business and keep everyday communications complete and timely among themselves and with external stakeholders. The administrative component needs to reflect Project Accelerator 4: keep it simple. And the communication component puts into operation the Shared Value of honest communication. Team operating agreements can cover a number of areas—for example:

- Update the project milestone chart every Friday.
- Give advance warning if you will not meet your deadline.
- Welcome the messenger who brings bad news.
- Escalate to the project manager any issue you can't resolve in one hour.
- Minimize interruptions.

Make Small Wins a Way of Life

On pressure-packed, high-risk eXtreme projects, people need to experience success early and often. When working under eXtreme conditions, it's too easy to adopt a scarcity mentality and dwell on negativity and what's not working. The underlying principle here is that what you focus on will expand, be it positive or negative. Choose the positive. As the process leader, you have the choice at all times to focus on what's working and build a success mentality and momentum. This does not mean fooling yourself and others by neglecting problems; rather, it means making a big deal out of successes.

Small wins also mean fast failures. To fail early and learn what *doesn't* work is success indeed. Why wait until the end of the project and practice late failure when you discover that the system crashed on rollout or learn that a crucial experiment was postponed to do the easier stuff first, only to hold up the project indefinitely now that you are nine months into the game?

Any accomplishment can be considered a small win: getting the three new laptops that people have been crying for, running a productive meeting, successfully completing a crucial system test, winning over a project naysayer. Going after so-called low-hanging fruit—those things that require little effort but will have a big impact—is one way of building a momentum toward success. The question to ask is, "What can we do right away that will make a difference?"

Celebrate, Recognize, and Reward

The greatest reward for most people is doing quality work and being recognized for it. Even if you're working for a start-up company and have generous stock options and will be able to retire in seven years to southern France at the age of thirty-seven (if all goes well), you are not likely to feel enriched if your daily work life is miserable. Money is important, but rarely is it the number one reason people stay in their jobs.

Psychologists tell us that our top fear is rejection and that our top need is acceptance. On eXtreme projects, spare no opportunity to show appreciation for people who are below you, above you, and at your level. If your sponsor is doing a good job, create a plaque, get a special T-shirt made, give her a knapsack for carrying her weight on the project. Recognize people early and often. Contrive opportunities to do so.

Kathy, a project manager and participant in one of my eXtreme project management workshops, related how touched she was when she walked by the cubicle of a former project team member. Kathy had sent her a handwritten thank-you note recognizing her contribution to the project. That was two years ago, and the note was still being displayed. These seemingly little things count.

When I was launching *NetworkWorld,* the newspaper for computer network managers, I used to keep a case of champagne in my office. When the occasion presented itself, I would call a gathering, make a short congratulatory speech, and present the champagne.

At least half of the time when I work with a team to establish team meeting and operating agreements, someone adds to the list, "Have fun." The remaining half also want to have fun. It's just they forgot to mention it. So establish a morale budget. Microsoft believes in morale budgets. The team or group is given a budget that they can spend any way they want, from theater tickets to team outings to popcorn makers. When the stakes are high and failure is not an option, a thousand bucks for morale isn't even worth quibbling about.

The more demanding the eXtreme project is, the more reason to find opportunities for group celebration: beer parties after work or at conferences, team dinners, ski trips, bowling, and other social events that allow people to bond off the job. Such events generate stories that people tell the next day and keep retelling. They create folklore around the project, keeping it alive in the minds and hearts of people and making it special while extending the spirit to others. The main thing is to have the team pick the type of event that's most suited for its temperament.

The "mutual accountability" principle for teams means a balance between team and individual rewards and recognition. It might be a stretch to work out monetary rewards for your eXtreme project team unless there is a structure in place or you can influence your sponsor; nevertheless, it's worth a shot. But there is an abundance of nonfinancial team rewards that you can dream up: a long weekend after completing the first milestone, a field trip to a best practices organization, or a party. As the process leader, you don't even have to burden yourself with creative ideas. The team will support what they create.

Here are some tips for bestowing recognition and rewards:

- Have both team and individual rewards.
- Reward for appreciation, not as an incentive to do good work. (The latter is a demotivator and sends the message ahead of time that the person would not ordinarily do good work and needs to be manipulated or patronized.)
- Beware of creating a project culture that continually rewards heroic efforts. A culture of heroic efforts puts the project at risk and fosters internal team competition to outdo each other. The goal is to get people to outdo themselves, not one another.
- Let the team decide who should be recognized.
- Reinforce behavior, and reward results.
- Reward the right results. (Giving programmers twenty-five dollars for each bug they detect will likely end up rewarding the production of more bugs.)
- Recognize people in a way that creates a story to be told.
- Match rewards to individual preferences. What would be rewarding to a business manager may not be valued by a technical manager, for example.

- Make sure the reward is proportional to the level of achievement.
- Be timely and specific about what the reward or recognition is for.

Dealing with Overtime

Quality of life is one of the 10 Shared Values. Overtime is a case in point. The bottom line on working overtime, voluntary or mandated, is that eventually it will become counterproductive. For a short time, it may speed things up, but it won't over the longer haul. No one can work twelve- to eighteen-hour days week in and week out without adverse impacts: stress on personal life, decreased productivity, lower morale leading to increased mistakes, costly rework, resentment, and turnover. All put the project at increased risk.

Studies among both factory and office workers show that after working ten to fifteen hours of overtime for several weeks in a row, employee productivity drops to what would normally be accomplished in forty hours. That's the good news. The bad news is that error rates go up, leading to rework and costly mistakes, which pushes out the schedule.

Building overtime into a project plan also increases risk because no slack is available for the inevitable emergencies. On schedule-driven projects, excessive overtime is offset by reduced quality. On quality-driven projects, excessive overtime extends the schedule.

In the case of software developers (and undoubtedly other knowledge workers) who are pushed for more overtime than they are willing to work, when their motivation begins to drop, it affects not just the extra ten to twenty overtime hours, but their forty regular hours as well. Since motivation is the strongest influence on productivity, as motivation drops, so does total output (McConnell, 1996).

There are no easy answers to this one, especially in certain cultures that expect people to put in overtime as a badge of honor. Here are some things you can do:

- Negotiate for the resources you need.
- Build the project plan based on forty-hour weeks.
- Make it possible for people to do good work during regular hours by eliminating unpleasant working conditions.

The Keys to Running Productive Meetings

Now that you have your team up and running and have established the conditions conducive to success, you need to develop the skills for running team meetings and managing other work of the team. Beyond the basic interpersonal skills covered in the previous chapter, you need to become skilled at meeting planning, facilitation, and leading the team decision-making process. I think of a meeting as a mini project plan. It has all the components: overall purpose, specific set of deliverables, a flow of work, tasks, assignments, schedule, costs, and risks. It also has stakeholders: those who will be participating and may include friends as well as foes of the project. Moreover, the meeting environment—the context—has to be conducive. As the meeting facilitator, you're managing the context and leading the process, a perfect parallel to your overall role on the project.

Before the Meeting

There are some essential considerations for handling both the pre-meeting dynamics and mechanics. Exhibit 6.1 shows the list I use in preparing to facilitate a client meeting, that is, the mechanics. The items on the list may seem obvious, but common sense is not always common practice.

In planning your meetings, it is important to understand the risks of eXtreme projects. Not everybody affected by the project likes it. Some think it's a waste of money that saps them and their resources from their own pet project. Others will lose their jobs, especially if the project involves process reengineering. Before the meeting, ask yourself:

- What's the overall mood of the group likely to be?
- What's the chemistry between certain people?
- Who's likely to be enthusiastic?
- Who will be the naysayers? The disrupters? The dominators? The peacemakers?
- How will the mix of status or rank affect the flow of ideas?

If you see risks in any of these areas, your job is to diffuse these risks ahead of time as well as plan to address them in the meeting.

Exhibit 6.1. Meeting Planning Checklist

Agenda draft
- Meeting purpose summarized
- Meeting work products [or deliverables or outcomes] listed
- Meeting topics timed (start and end)
- How each topic will be facilitated (for example, small group presentations and recommendations followed by full group discussion and voting; full group brainstorming session on sticky notes, followed by categorization and prioritization within each category)

Participants identified and invited
- Team members
- Others who are needed to achieve the meeting's purpose and work products

Logistics
- Room, refreshments, equipment, enough flip charts, sticky notes, markers, masking tape
- Agenda distributed before the meeting, labeled "Proposed Agenda," sending the signal that I am open to suggested changes
- Participants advised of what to bring

During the Meeting

Here are some ways to create a conducive meeting environment from the beginning:

- Use a simple warm-up to get people focused. I like to use warm-ups that produce a tangible result that will further the goals of the meeting or detoxify the climate in the room if need be. Asking everyone what their favorite movie is may have its place as an icebreaker, but this type of warm-up is ineffective and annoying to some people.
- For meetings that are likely to be emotionally charged, I start with a warm-up that will acknowledge people's feelings, serving to unblock them so that the meeting can move forward in a positive vein. For example, if I'm working with an existing project, I go

around the room asking each person to write down on a sticky note one thing they feel is going well on the project. I then go around a second time asking them to jot down one thing they are concerned about. If by the end of the meeting, the issues haven't been addressed in the natural course of the agenda, then these issues and concerns are addressed and turned into action items if that is appropriate. If the group wants to modify the agenda to deal with significant challenges, then the agenda is modified on the spot (this is Accelerator 3: create ownership for results).

• Review the meeting purpose and proposed agenda. If you've prepared adequately, the meeting agenda will be accepted in substance by the assembled group. At times, people will want to add or modify topics, so I leave room on the agenda for other topics if time permits. On occasion, someone will bring up a meeting stopper topic, and if it is not addressed, the meeting will not be effective. In this case, the agenda will need to be modified on the spot.

• Establish meeting roles. Effective teams rotate these roles from meeting to meeting or within any one meeting: scribe (writes on the flip charts), recorder (transcribes and distributes the flip chart content, decisions, and action items), and timekeeper (keeps the group posted on time remaining for each meeting segment). At the end of the segment, the group decides if it wants to end the segment or continue.

• Establish a parking lot. Topics that are off the agenda will likely be sparked during the meeting. This is a good thing, but avoid taking the meeting off on tangents. Set up a flip chart labeled "parking lot." As topics come up, have participants name the topic, write it on a sticky note, and place it in the parking lot. At the end of the meeting, using the parking lot as input for determining action items.

• Agree on meeting agreements. Meeting agreements are intended to level the playing field by giving each participant an opportunity to influence the meetings outcomes and help to ensure that the meeting is productive. By creating the rules of acceptable behavior, participants take on ownership for the meeting's outcomes as well as for establishing and maintaining the climate in the room. Without meeting norms, you can easily lose control of the meeting.

An excellent icebreaker is to have each participant use a sticky note and marker to write down "one thing that would ensure a highly effective meeting." Typical items are one person talks at a time; cell phones on silent; if you disagree, give an alternative; leave rank at the door; no side conversations, make your point succinctly; start and end on time; no personal attacks.

Attach the sticky notes on a flip chart, and ask the group to reduce the suggestions to a set of themes. Then write these on a flip chart. Go around the room and ask each person if he or she can make a full effort to support the suggestions. Make modifications as needed, and finally post the final items for all to see.

Some agreements may not be possible for people to keep, such as "stay for the entire meeting," for example, because they have made prior plans. In that case, the norm is dropped since it can't be fully supported. If the same group will be meeting regularly, it may want to adopt this norm for future meetings where participants agree not to schedule themselves for other meetings.

By establishing agreements, you are transferring ownership of the meeting from just you to the entire team. It is therefore essential that you remind everyone that they are all co-facilitators and are expected to remind others if a member violates one of the agreements.

By establishing team meeting agreements and team operating agreements, you are enabling the group to create its own identity and project culture.

The Daily Huddle

Up until now, I have been referring to group settings where a formal and carefully orchestrated meeting or a problem-solving session is in order. Because eXtreme projects undergo so much variability, there is a need for daily formal meetings among subteams. These daily huddles are run by the subteam project managers. (The eXtreme core team, which is made up of members of the subteams, may not have to synchronize daily. Perhaps once or twice a week suffices.) The daily huddle strikes at the heart of the job for the subteam project manager: to make it possible for the team to do good work.

The huddle is based on an excellent practice that has come out of SCRUM, a form of agile project management used in software development. At the same time every day, the team conducts its huddle, a meeting of fifteen to twenty minutes in length that is led by the project manager. The purpose of this huddle is to focus on accomplishments and identify barriers to progress. Each team member answers four questions as they relate to the deliverable they are working on and the plan they have committed to:

1. What have you done since our last meeting?
2. What will you do between now and our next meeting?
3. What got in your way?
4. If we could wave a magic wand, what would make us more productive?

The project manager's job is to remove barriers. The huddle is a powerful project accelerator. It keeps the project energy field continuously clean by surfacing obstacles that dampen spirits and cause quality and schedule to suffer.

The elegance of the four questions emulates Accelerator 4: keep it simple. In fact, the huddle enables team members to live all 4 Accelerators and each of the 10 Shared Values.

Facilitation Skills

I once saw a cartoon that showed people sitting in a meeting with a banner hanging over the doorway that said, "You are here for no apparent reason." Most people hate meetings, and with good reason: they are often unnecessary, poorly planned, and inadequately run.

As the process leader, your job is to accelerate progress: to facilitate and manage the flow of thoughts, emotions, and interactions in a way that produces a valued outcome, and this applies to team meetings. Most meetings are either not needed or are so poorly run that plans are not formulated, decisions are not made, and problems remain unsolved. People leave the room even more frustrated than they were before the meeting began.

Facilitation brings into play Accelerators 1, 2, and 3: make change your friend, build on people's desire to make a difference, and create ownership for results. Good facilitation goes a long way in establishing trust and confidence (hence, commitment) in the team's ability to succeed because it puts into practice the Shared Values of clarity of purpose (we know why we are here), results orientation (we will produce specific meeting products), honest communication (it's safe for me to speak), and visibility (the group's accomplishments—are plastered all over the walls for people to see).

Good facilitation skills will earn you respect and even admiration. Meetings will be more productive because people will feel heard, and things won't get bogged down by going off on tangents.

For those situations when a formal meeting is essential, what follows is a crash course in managing the flow of emotions, thoughts, and interactions in a group setting. These techniques can be applied to a wide variety of meetings you will be called on to facilitate, especially, requirements-gathering, decision-making, problem-solving, and project coordination sessions.

The Facilitator's Role

If innovative ideas and speed are the lifeblood of eXtreme projects, then good facilitation makes them possible. The role of the facilitator is to create a collaborative setting in a way that unlocks and harnesses the group's collective wisdom. If the meeting environment is toxic, ideas and solutions won't flower. But there will be plenty of weeds in the form of bored looks, folded arms, potshots taken at ideas, side conversations, and no dialogue.

The goal of a collaborative environment is shared discovery and accomplishment leading to buy-in for a decision or for the solution to a problem or the resolution of an issue. A collaborative environment fosters open and honest communication of ideas and feelings, and it builds on a powerful human need: the desire to be heard, where each participant is given an equal opportunity to influence the outcome of a decision to be made or a problem to be shared.

As a facilitator, you are also a change agent, because you are creating ownership for change. It's not that people don't like change; rather, they don't want to be changed. As the neutral servant of the group, you are allowing participants to create and own the changes they want to see. There are a number of tools that help you move the team ahead while allowing participants to maintain ownership of the process, including the Six Essential Facilitation Techniques in the eXtreme Tools and Techniques section.

Here are some specific facilitator behaviors (adapted from Kayser, 1990):

Focus: Concentrate the group's energies on defining and accomplishing common, desired outcomes.

Appropriate approach: Use group decision making when buy-in is essential; allow unilateral or majority rule where this has been preagreed to by the group.

Open environment: Ensure everyone participates and feels safe in doing so.

Freedom from attack: Protect members and their ideas from attack so that all alternatives can be fairly discussed.

Although you are the process leader, everyone in the meeting is considered to be a secondary facilitator, another reason that it's important to establish meeting roles and meeting agreements. Besides, it's virtually impossible for a facilitator to be effective and not get diluted if she is attempting to facilitate discussion, write on flip charts, do the timekeeping, enforce meeting agreements, and manage the parking lot and action items at the same time.

Feelings ➤ Facts ➤ Solutions All Over Again

The key to running a successful group session is to put your main focus on managing the energy in the room and not on managing the time. "Let's put our feelings aside," said one project manager in a heated meeting. It was the wrong answer.

Having been a professional facilitator for thirteen years, I can tell you that the most important skill I have is to be able to deal openly with feelings in a group situation. The Feelings ➤ Facts ➤ Solutions model is important to keep in mind at all times during the meeting. If members of the group are upset, little progress will be made until the feelings can be addressed.

If members of the group are upset, little progress will be made until the feelings can be addressed.

I was once brought in to help a foundering team coalesce for their eXtreme project. The project mission was to introduce a new snack food and gain market share by beating the competitor. The team was expected to do the project in fifteen rather than the usual eighteen months. Compounding the challenge, they had lost the first three months in continuous storming, bickering, and blaming each other. In effect, they now had to do an eighteen-month project in just twelve months.

If this were thirteen years ago, when I was still practicing emotional ignorance, I would have walked in with my eXtreme project management process and gotten right down to business. Instead, we spent the first two hours getting their conflicts out in the open. After lunch together, we got down to business. The group's energy had shifted enough so we could move forward. Follow-on coaching was required, but the essential shift had taken place, and the environment was no longer toxic. We could turn to the project.

The Feelings ➤ Facts➤ Solutions model works every time. I'm vigilant about what the group might be feeling. When uneasy feelings prevail, it's fruitless, emotionally ignorant, and counterproductive to attempt to move forward and expect the group to bang out meeting work products in the interest of keeping to task and schedule. What's called for is relationship management, not task management. As a facilitator, I can manage the schedule and tasks only after I clear the feelings.

An approach I use in dealing with a group or several members who have moved into the feelings domain has proved effective in bringing feelings to the surface and clearing the air. I call it the 4 A model. A practical guide to using the 4 A Model is included in the eXtreme Tools and Techniques section.

The Power of Self-Disclosure

I've been in situations countless times when I'm completely lost in the conversation or the meeting dynamics are such that it is not possible to move the group forward. I feel helpless and incompetent.

When I get stuck, I call on my self-disclosure power. I open myself up, reveal my vulnerability, and ask for help. "Folks, I have to admit I am completely lost in these last conversations. I'm not sure what we are trying to do at this point and can't pick out the thread. Can someone help me?"

By admitting my vulnerability and my feelings of frustration and helpfulness (without blaming anyone), coupled with the Shared Values of honest communication and courage on my part, the group invariably bails me and themselves out of the situation. They support what they create. By giving group members the opportunity to self-correct, it also activates Accelerator 3: build on people's desire to make a difference.

Decision Making and Problem Solving

As the process leader, your value-added lies in making it possible for others to do good work, and this extends to making decisions and problem solving. This makes you indispensable because the only reason for establishing a team is to make decisions and solve problems.

---

*The only reason for establishing a team
is to make decisions and solve problems.*

On eXtreme projects where we are confronted with many unknowns, complexities, considerations, and options, no one individual can be smart enough to make all the decisions and solve all the problems. This can be tough to swallow among the scientific community. That's because scientists and other high-intellectual-capital and pedigreed professions are socialized to believe they are supposed to know the answers. They are esteemed for their intellectual prowess and expertise and may like to throw around their brain power rather than delegate technical or scientific decisions to subject matter experts on teams. This can result in bottlenecks where decisions are constantly bucked up the hierarchy, causing delays and often undermining the quality of the decision when the decision maker has not been privy to all the discussion, surrounding considerations, and potential impacts that the team has been immersed in. On eXtreme projects, the reality is that all of us together are smarter than any one of us. Good collaborative decision making and problem-solving processes are a must.

Are You Making a Decision or Solving a Problem?

To make a decision is to choose among a set of predetermined options. Problems are different. They involve figuring out how to achieve a goal where there are obstacles that need to be overcome and no predetermined set of solutions. Problem solving involves decision making at the end, but before decisions can be made, time is spent in identifying causes, postulating potential solutions and evaluating each one, and then deciding on the best choice.

A trap that teams fall into in the press for speed is to make decisions before the problem is understood. I worked with a client who was upgrading the company Web site because they had discovered that their sell-through rate had dropped from 11 to 7 percent. The team was in the process of evaluating different options for improving the site's graphics, response speed, capacity, and product search options. When they were asked how they knew that these were the reasons potential buyers were turning away, there was a stunned silence in the room. Then someone said, "That's what we were told to do." As facilitator, your job is to help ensure that the group is not making decisions without first understanding the problem. Understanding the problem means defining the problem, defining the goal, identifying causes, identifying likely solutions, and deciding on the best solutions.

Reaching an Effective Decision

A decision has two major variables: the quality of the thinking that goes into it and the level of acceptance for carrying it out. It's possible to have a very well-thought-out decision that nobody implements or to have a poorly thought-out decision that everybody implements. The facilitator's job is to ensure that there is a balance of quality thinking and level of acceptance. This idea can be summarized using a simple equation:

$$ED = QT \times BI,$$

where ED = effective decision, QT = quality of thinking, and BI = buy-in for implementing the decision.

The *Challenger* disaster in 1986 is a good example of not balancing the equation. Based on his analysis of the facts, one of the engineers objected to giving clearance for takeoff because he had reason to believe that one of the essential parts, the O-rings, might not be able withstand the amount of anticipated cold. Under the gun to execute the launch, management trivialized the engineer's concerns (poor QT on their part) and put considerable pressure on the engineer to give clearance. The engineer succumbed, being coerced into (forced to buy in to) agreeing (high *BI*), and the decision was made to launch. The engineer was correct in his assessment. The entire crew died as the *Challenger* decomposed shortly after blast-off.

In terms of the equation, the *Challenger* example works like this. Assume we rated each of the elements on a scale of 0 to 10, where 0 is a low score and 10 is a high score. We would score *QT* a 0 and *BI* a 10 because the decision was implemented. This would yield an *ED* of 0:

$$QT \times BI = ED$$
$$0 \times 10 = 0.$$

This is an example of everybody moving forward with a bad idea. It can also work the other way around, where nobody moves forward with a good idea.

As facilitator, your job is to ensure an effective decision with the appropriate level of quality thinking and buy-in. This does not mean all decisions are made by consensus. If the decision is trivial or in the case of an emergency, consensus is not appropriate.

Decision-Making Styles: Four Options

The goal is to maximize quality thinking and buy-in, but that doesn't mean consensus is always the way to go. Here are the major options and when to use each (Table 6.1):

One person: No others are involved.

Consultative: One person decides after actively listening to the opinions of others.

Majority rule: Fifty-one percent or more of the group is in favor.

Consensus: The group can support the decision, even though it's not the first choice of some.

Majority rule runs the risk of polarizing the group into winners and losers. Majority rule works best after everybody has voiced their opinion.

Table 6.1. Methods for Reaching a Decision

Level of Complexity Involved or Expertise Required	Level of Buy-In Required to Carry Out the Decision	Preferred Decision Method
High	High	Consensus with subject matter experts present
High	Low	Consultative
Low	High	Consensus
Low	Low	One person, majority rule

Consensus is often given a bum rap: "A camel is a horse designed by committee." Consensus does not mean compromise where you split things down the middle and wind up with a watered-down decision.

Consensus should not lead to groupthink. "I'll go along with it because I want to be a team player" can be dangerous words when they cause people to back down from arguing their point in the spirit of keeping things moving. This leads to false consensus. Under eXtreme conditions, you want to encourage a conflict of ideas so that the best solution might emerge, enabling the project team to self-correct. Groupthink also occurs when people decline to question authority. Groupthink was behind the Bay of Pigs fiasco. When President Kennedy told his assembled advisers that he wanted to invade Cuba, they all went along in a show of support. No serious questioning took place.

Under eXtreme conditions, you want to encourage a conflict of ideas.

A powerful way to help avoid groupthink is for the group leader to refrain from stating an opinion until after all others have come forward. Once there is a set of options to work with, the consensus process can be applied. Or the group leader may decide to take a consultative approach, reserving the final decision for herself after hearing all viewpoints.

Consensus involves robust debate. It doesn't mean that everybody has to be ecstatic with the final decision. It means that there are no serious objections and all are willing to implement the decision. Here are the steps for reaching consensus:

1. Post the question or topic.
2. Identify decision criteria.
3. Share background information.
4. Identify possible alternatives.
5. Discuss the pros and cons in the light of available information and the decision criteria.
6. Have each person or group advocate a preference.
7. Vote, discuss, and revote.

When the consensus decision is expected to have a major impact on the project, I recommend that the group be allowed to sleep on the decision and convene the next day to reconfirm their choice.

The 70 percent rule is a useful test for consensus and can save hours of endless discussion when one or more individuals are willing to move forward if they had only been asked. After robust debate and discussion, ask each of those who may not be in agreement the following question: "Even if this is not your first choice, would you say that you are at least 70 percent in agreement? And can you support it 100 percent?" If the answer is no, ask, "What would have to happen for you to reach the 70 percent agreement level?" Then put that up for group discussion. The goal is not to coerce the objectors.

When Consensus Isn't Obtainable

It's possible after sufficient debate and negotiation that consensus cannot be obtained. The issue becomes how important to carrying out the decision are those who, in good conscience, feel they cannot move forward, which means the decision will not be implemented and the project is at serious risk. If postmeeting negotiations still cannot reach consensus, then you need to take it to a higher authority, the project sponsor.

There are times when the call is up to you. You've done the analysis, and the choice is still not clear. My recommendation is to put the decision to the body test, to engage your gut and your heart in addition to your mind. Go to a quiet place, preferably outdoors in a natural setting, and take two to three deep cleansing breaths. Relax your body by letting it go limp, and put your attention on your heart. Make your choice.

Then tune into your body, noticing any sensation, however faint, of either comfort or discomfort. If you get an uncomfortable body sensation, that's not the right decision. In my own practice, I always make a decision twice. If it starts out in my mind, I subject it to the body test, and vice versa. I always go with the body.

Facilitation brings into play Accelerators 1, 2 and 3: make change your friend, build on people's desire to make a difference, and create ownership for results. Good facilitation goes a long way in establishing trust and confidence (and hence commitment to) in the team's ability to succeed because it puts into practice the Shared Values of clarity of purpose (we know why we are here), results orientation (we will produce specific meeting products), honest communication (it's safe for me to speak), and visibility (the group's accomplishments are posted all over the walls for people to see).

How to Earn the Right to Lead the Process

Just because you are the project manager doesn't mean that the project team and other stakeholders will want to go along with any process you'd like to introduce. To be successful, you need to build both your competence and self-confidence while earning the confidence of those who would follow your lead. Here is a three-step model that will earn you the right to lead the process and at the same time accelerate you to a point of Self-Mastery: the state of being unconsciously competent:

- Practice.
- Enlist their support.
- Go to bat for them.

These steps are not sequential as much as they are simultaneous.

Practice

You don't learn how to ski by reading a manual. It takes practice. In their book *Primal Leadership* (2002), Goleman, Boyatzis, and McKee cite a presentation made by Jim Loehr and Tony Schwartz in which they point out that athletes spend a lot of time practicing and a little time performing. But leaders spend a lot of time performing and a little time practicing. Learning good process leadership skills requires as much practice as learning athletic skills. Process leadership is not an adjunct to your job. It *is* your job.

Process leadership is not an adjunct to your job.
It is *your job.*

This is why classroom training in leadership has little impact. Classroom training can impart new knowledge, but leadership requires new behaviors and skills, and this takes practice and repetition. To get the point of Self-Mastery, you have to close the gap between the knowing and the doing. Make both happen simultaneously.

If you are new to facilitation, practice every chance you get. Take advantage of nonthreatening situations. Keep a flip chart in your office or get a white board. Put on your facilitator hat and use techniques I described for spontaneous brainstorming during impromptu meetings with colleagues.

Rehearsing in your mind can be as powerful as rehearsing in the flesh. Visualization is common practice among athletes. Mental movies can be made anytime, anywhere. They enable you not only to rehearse but also to preexperience success: to feel what it feels like beforehand. You literally preprogram yourself for success by programming both your thoughts and feelings.

Enlist Their Support

You don't have to pretend more than you know. That can really put you in a state of internal anxiety.

The best example of this I ever witnessed was by Kymm Bartlett, a product manager for General Mills. She had just taken the workshop in project management, saw the value, and wanted to use the process to relaunch a snack product the company had been trying to revive.

Until this point, her team was undisciplined in project management and tended to do projects in an ad hoc way. She wanted to improve performance but was sensitive to the freewheeling culture. Kymm's approach was along these lines: "I have a couple of new techniques that I've learned. I think they can help us improve the odds of our being successful on this project and save us time and maybe even some frustration. I'd like to try them out with you. If they work, great. If not, we'll go back to what we were doing."

Notice what Kymm did. She enlisted all 4 Project Accelerators. She introduced change in a nonthreatening way, recognized that people want to make a difference, gave people an opportunity to support the process, and kept it simple. Her straightforward approach emulated the Shared Value of honest communication, and her concern for people over the process activated the value of people first. She also used the Shared Value of results orientation ("save time and be more successful") to appeal to the team's desire to get things done. And if it didn't work (fast failures), she was willing to drop it. She also respected their concern for quality of life (eliminate "some frustration"). And above all, she had the courage to take a risk. The key to Kymm's success is that she made her project her laboratory and the team's as well.

Go to Bat for Them

One of the most powerful things you can do to earn your right to be the process leader is to make it possible for the team to do good work: to eliminate some of the everyday morale killers and poor working conditions. The principle is fundamental, but rarely is anything more than lip-service ever paid to it: stand behind them, and they will follow you.

The huddle provides ongoing opportunities to eliminate barriers. And what's amazing here is that even if you fail in getting all the barriers eliminated, you have the benefit of the Hawthorne effect working overtime for you. The Hawthorne effect came out of a study conducted by Elton Mayo and associates in 1927. They were studying the impact on productivity by changing the lighting at the Hawthorne plant of Western Electric. They discovered that when they turned the lights up, productivity went up (Huse, 1979). When they turned the lights down, productivity went up. How could this be explained? Mayo concluded that the simple act of conducting the experiments caused the increase in productivity. Why? Because workers became aware that people important in their work lives were taking care of them. This startling conclusion has three important implications:

- People are motivated by recognition.
- You are very likely to gain the respect of others if they see that you are actively trying to make their life better.
- Productivity will go up (at least for a while) even if you are not successful in making the desired improvements on their behalf.

Your sincere attempt to lobby and negotiate relentlessly on behalf of the team will carry you only so far. Unless you can win some concessions, the environmental factors will still hamper, if not defeat, the project.

In this chapter, I covered what it takes to lead the eXtreme team. In the next chapter, I'll extend Critical Success Factor 2, Leadership by Commitment, to include that of establishing and managing the stakeholder community.

eXtreme Project Management Model
Applying the Quantum Mind-Set

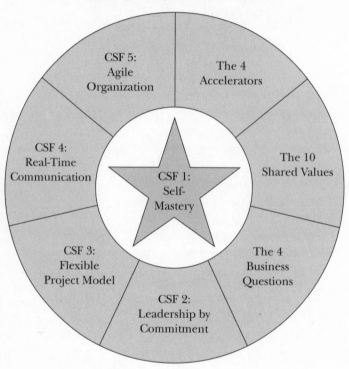

Chapter Seven

eXtreme Stakeholder Management

I keep my friends close, but I keep my enemies even closer.
ANONYMOUS

A stakeholder is anyone who can affect the success or failure of your project either before or after the project has been completed. Stakeholders can be internal or external to the organization and include those who will provide inputs to your project, such as needed products and services, funding, approvals, resources, and other projects that you will rely on for your project.

Stakeholder management is the soft glue that holds the eXtreme project together. Failure to manage the stakeholder community effectively is the primary reason that eXtreme projects come unglued and go out of control. Traditional project management focuses heavily on project mechanics: tools and templates and the design and creation of the product or service being delivered. eXtreme project management puts the emphasis on the human dynamics: managing relationships and facilitating interactions. Effective stakeholder management is at the heart of Leadership by Commitment, Critical Success Factor 2.

> *Failure to manage the stakeholder community effectively is the primary reason that eXtreme projects come unglued.*

This chapter covers the following topics:

- What makes stakeholder management so challenging
- Who your stakeholders are
- The benefits of good stakeholder management
- Who needs to be committed to what
- How to partition stakeholders
- How to build the stakeholder database
- How to establish stakeholder win conditions
- How to establish a partnering agreement
- Combating the phantom approval cycle
- Managing organizational change?
- Business Question 4: Is it worth it to you?

The Stakeholder Challenge

Not everybody will be enthusiastic about your project. In fact, my experience has shown that for every eXtreme project team, there is an equal and opposite project team hard at work, an antiproject team if you will, pulling the project in a counterdirection. The antiproject team is composed of individuals who feel that your project is affecting them, or will affect them, in some negative way.

eXtreme projects often cut across organizational lines and bring about change that disrupts entrenched systems, practices, and fiefdoms. Many of today's eXtreme projects are launched in order to give the organization a competitive advantage. Just like internal projects that cross organizational boundaries, eXtreme projects aimed at bringing innovative products to market strike at the organization's cash register and its relationship with customers and require the coordination of many functional departments. Change creates winners and losers. Some people may be out of a job when the project is over. Fear of job loss or job change is a major reason that the antiproject team is born. That's why, as the project manager, you are likely to be viewed as the enemy, even though it's not your project. (Remember that your project sponsor is the project owner. It's being undertaken to satisfy her objectives. You've been assigned to make it happen.) This is kill-the-messenger syndrome at its worst.

Not all members of the antiproject team are out to get you. Some are merely inconvenienced because your project will cause more work for them or their staff. Stakeholders who feel threatened by the project and cause problems drain the project of vital energy, just like weeds sap vitality from flowers in a garden. (Of course, there are fans of the project, although they are sometimes harder to find.)

Here's a partial list of what the saboteurs on the antiproject team can do:

- Not providing needed input and direction, leaving you to second-guess what is wanted
- Delaying approvals for needed decisions on policy and procedures, equipment, and people
- Continually finding flaws in work delivered
- Not providing needed feedback on interim project deliverables, causing delays
- Reassigning your team members to other projects
- Backroom politicking to kill the project
- Blatantly going on record and making a public case against your project
- Having team members they assign to your project act as unwitting spies, reporting back on project status and using or twisting that information against the project
- Starting a competing project to get it done their way

Beyond the stress and negative energy that high stakes and fear create, there are several other reasons that managing stakeholders is so challenging.

- *The sheer numbers.* If the primary role of the project manager is to manage the network of complex relationships among the stakeholder community, the sheer number of stakeholders can make this task overwhelming. Sara J. McKenzie, program manager for Sepracore, a pharmaceutical company, told me that relationship management can take up to 75 percent of her time. Her experience is typical. One project I worked on, installing a new clinical information system for a hospital, would have an impact on how two hundred stakeholders were going to have to do their jobs. Doctors, nurses, administrators, and technicians would have to learn new ways of working, often setting aside practices that they were brought up on ten and even twenty or more years ago.

As former president Richard Nixon once said, "The problem with politics is that it involves people." And when colleague Jim Lewis says, "Projects are people," I'm quick to add that the converse is also true: "People are projects."

- *Communication requirements.* Compounding the large number of potential stakeholders is all the interpersonal communication that that needs to take place: to resolve issues, get buy-in, get approvals, get feedback, report to management, and much more. Then there's the management and distribution of all the associated information about the project itself: the documents people are working on as well as information about the project itself: the time line, the stakeholder database, the risk profile, progress reports, team meeting notes and action items, templates, and more.
- *Matrix organizations.* Compounding stakeholder dynamics is that most, if not all, of the stakeholders will fall outside your boss's chain of command. This means you have no direct, and little, if any, indirect, authority over them.

In sum, on eXtreme Projects, you are dealing with a complex and confusing environment. It is easy to lose sight of where you are going. To maintain your focus, you need to rely on business values.

Business Values

Business values help you keep yourself oriented in a confusing environment and, just as important, help keep important stakeholders oriented as well. Here are the three business values, which are part of the 10 Shared Values of eXtreme project management.

Clarity of Purpose

In practice, *clarity of purpose* means understanding not only the goals of the project but the bigger picture too: why it's being done.

- Understanding throughout the project the intended outcome that lies on the horizon beyond the physical deliverable
- Remembering that there is always a higher order of things: a north star, or reference point, that will guide formal and informal decision making when you find yourselves mired in detail and muck

- Knowing that it is time to junk the requested deliverable when you realize that it will not achieve the ultimate outcome

Results Orientation

In practice, *results orientation* means focusing on the completion of deliverables rather than on tracking tasks:

- Distinguishing between activities and goals
- Recognizing that completing tasks may not be an indicator of progress
- Giving people the latitude to deviate from prescribed check-lists and strict procedures when these are not working

Early Value

In practice, *early value* means giving customers something they can put to use as early as possible:

- Providing incremental delivery in small packages early and often
- Meeting minimum requirements and avoiding goldplating

Managing Relationships

Paying careful attention to managing your relationship with your project's stakeholders will move the project along in several ways. Good stakeholder management:

- Fosters speed by keeping the project from being bogged down in politics
- Fosters innovation by ensuring that the project team stays intact long enough to collaborate and develop a sense of joint ownership
- Keeps resources (people, dollars, equipment) flowing to the project
- Keeps vital information and feedback flowing to the project as people cooperate to achieve the desired outcome
- Vastly increases the odds that the right thing is produced and that it will be embraced by the intended customers

The Stakeholder Universe

The stakeholder universe was presented and discussed in detail in Chapter Four. We looked at the role of the sponsor, the core team and subteams, the steering committee, and the myriad other people and units, such as the project office, resource providers, and customers. As a refresher, here is the stakeholder universe again:

You	Consumers
Your family	General public
Your project	Subject matter experts
The core project team	Project facilitator
Other project managers	Department managers
Project sponsor	Resource providers
Upper management	Outside suppliers
Steering committee	Government agencies
Business owner	Competitors
Internal customers	Project office
External customers	Your boss
Customer representatives	

One of the biggest mistakes in project management is to limit the identification of stakeholders to those who are affected by the project during the planning and execution stages. What about those who have to live with the project deliverable? These people are also part of the project context, and their opinions, needs, and reactions (in short, their thoughts and emotions) need to be taken into consideration.

I was once called in by the head of a company's project management organization (PMO) responsible for supporting software development projects that were undertaken for the firm's internal and external customers. The PMO had spent in excess of $1 million to bring in sophisticated project and portfolio management tools. After the tools had been in service for two years, they were being decommissioned. The software developers and their managers all but refused to use the project management system, and when they did use it, the data were unreliable for project tracking purposes.

Our research revealed that crucial stakeholders—key technology and software development managers—had not been part of the process to determine the requirements for the project management system and felt that the way they ran their operations was not reflected in the new tools. In fact, they were right. The motivation for bringing in the project management system was to satisfy the legitimate needs of senior management, who wanted to get a better grip on projects and how resources were being allocated. Management needed to plan and forecast. However, in focusing exclusively on what senior management wanted, the PMO neglected to consider the legitimate needs of technical managers and their staffs, who were already hard-pressed to keep up with their workloads. There was nothing in it for them except added work.

This project was unwittingly set up to create winners and losers. Gerald Weinberg sums it up wisely in his classic book, *The Secrets of Consulting* (1985): he calls it the Law of the Buffalo Bridle. "You can make buffalo go anywhere, just as long as they want to go." When it comes to project acceptance, people are like buffalo, not sheep.

Not bringing in postproject stakeholders early is an example of what happens when Accelerator 3 is forgotten: create ownership for results. And relatedly, it also represents a failure to live by the Shared Value of client collaboration.

The moral of the story is that those who have to live with the baby are just as important as those who give birth to the baby, and if you can't create a win-win situation for all crucial stakeholders, don't do the project. Without the commitment of customers, functional managers, and other stakeholders, decisions will be delayed, team members will be reassigned to other projects, suppliers will miss deadlines, and politics will undermine the project in subtle ways. Commitment doesn't mean just positive feelings for your project; it means that each stakeholder takes responsibility for the project in specific ways. Table 7.1 shows what each stakeholder group needs to commit to.

Although "Other Project Managers" come last on the table, don't underestimate their importance. Make them your friends. You will rely on deliverables from other projects to be used to complete your project. The quality, timing, and cost of those deliverables can have a significant impact on your project's well-being. And other project managers will likely depend on your project in order to get their project done.

Table 7.1. Key Stakeholder Groups and Their Commitments

Stakeholder Group	Commitment
eXtreme project manager	Apply the appropriate project management approach for the project at hand.
Steering committee	Fund the project based on its business value.
	Quickly resolve conflicts in project priorities where a change in one project's priority affects another's ability to succeed.
	Ensure realization of business benefits.
Sponsor	Ensure funding.
	Make timely decisions; make unilateral decisions when needed.
	Field the right team.
	Ensure realization of business benefits.
eXtreme core team	Agree to a common purpose, set of performance goals, and project management approach.
	Hold each other mutually accountable.
	Allow each team member an equal opportunity to influence team and project decisions.
Resource managers	Populate the core team and subteams throughout the project.
	Provide sufficient staff to produce required project deliverables.
Customers	Participate as a full-fledged team member as required.
	Provide timely feedback on work in progress and deliverables.
Other project managers (internal and external)	Meet agreed-on handoffs: timing, budgets, and quality expectations.

Do not assume that just because you have a partnering agreement with other project managers to deliver you the goods, this interface doesn't have to be managed. On the contrary, learn how to inspect tactfully what you expect.

Even a project with relatively few stakeholders is rife with conflicting objectives because people tend to act within their own self-interest. The following example illustrates the sorts of conflicts that naturally arise on eXtreme projects.

Babbot Labs has decided to enter the lucrative market for sleep-deprived adults who are looking to get twelve hours of uninterrupted sleep on weekends and holidays. To be sold in liquid form and over the counter, Zonk will be available in three sizes and three flavors. Industrial intelligence has revealed that a competitor, Wiser Unltd., has a six-month head start. In order to achieve the expected return on investment and market share, Zonk must beat Wiser to market and also unseat Blackout, the third-place brand, within twelve to eighteen months. Management has prioritized Zonk as a priority A project. To free up financial resources for project Zonk, it was decided to put project Nosey on hold. Nosey, a new, unique antihistamine with twenty-four-hour efficacy, was the pet project of senior vice prescient Adam Appleton, M.D., the head of Babbot's ear, nose, and throat product line. Appleton, a well-respected and powerful player, is not pleased to have his pet project bumped. Table 7.2 summarizes the conflicts among stakeholders.

Each group, looking out for its own interests and job responsibilities, can cause conflicts that need to be resolved within and across management groups. For instance, the senior management group wants to gain market share while improving profit margins, generally considered to be opposing objectives. Finance understandably wants predictable results, yet Zonk is in the early development stage and has many unknowns. The development team wants to work with stable product requirements, but marketing naturally wants to keep its options open as long as possible in order to keep ahead of the competition. The consumer wants low prices, which may be in conflict with the desire of some senior managers for higher profit margins. And as toxicology pushes for more time to test the drug, management is exerting schedule pressure.

Table 7.2. Project Zonk Stakeholder Conflicts

Senior Management	Financial Management	Development/ Project Team	Toxicology	Marketing	Manufacturing	Consumers
Reduce time to market	Efficient utilization of capital equipment	Work with stable product requirements	Sufficient lead time to test	Be low-price leader	Use existing equipment	No side effects
Gain market share	Predictable financial forecasts for Wall Street	Break new ground	Ensure safety, avoid lawsuits	Keep requirements fluid during development	Reliable volume estimates	Full twelve hours of sleep
No significant cost overruns		Time to test multiple options		Sufficient lead time to promote	Sufficient time to do test runs and scale up	Wake up refreshed
Improve profit margins		Minimal overtime				Low price, generics

Managing Your Stakeholders

We have looked at the challenges of dealing with stakeholders and the conflicts involved when different stakeholders bring different interests and agendas to the table. As an eXtreme project manager, how do you deal with all these people and their conflicting interests? The 10 Shared Values will help guide the way, especially the business value of clarity of purpose. Beyond these values, there are several key steps you can take here:

- Partition your stakeholders in terms of the size of their stake in your project and the amount of clout they can bring to bear.
- Work with the most critical stakeholders to reach agreement on the win conditions for your project.
- Set up explicit partnering agreements with everyone who is expected to provide resources, services, or other deliverables to your project.

Partitioning Stakeholders

With dozens and potentially hundreds of stakeholders, you will quickly find yourself up to your neck in stakeholders without a system to manage them. Some stakeholders are so crucial to the project's success that you need to drop everything whenever they have a question or a concern. Others will require attention but not so urgently. Many need just to be kept informed. You need to map out all the stakeholders on your project, partition them according to how much power and influence they can bring to bear on the project, and then manage them accordingly. Think of this as you would planning a marketing and public relations campaign, because it is. You need to know who your audience is so that you, the project team, and your sponsor can focus on those with the greatest influence on the project's success or failure. It's about influencing the influencers. Accelerator 3, create ownership for results, is at work here.

You will quickly find yourself up to your neck in stakeholders without a system to manage them.

The stakeholder database needs to be drafted just as soon as you know what the purpose of the project is and can begin to figure out who has the most to gain and lose and who will exert strong influence over the project. Since the eXtreme project manager's top priority is to manage the project's context, the stakeholder database needs to be updated continually. It's everybody's job to provide input. This includes the project sponsor.

There are three types of stakeholders who can be internal or external to the organization: crucial stakeholders, key players, and important stakeholders.

Crucial Stakeholders

These are individuals who can kill the project at any time. They have the power to pull the plug. As crucial stakeholders, they can do this by withdrawing funds or simply calling an abrupt halt to the venture. The project sponsor would typically have kill power at least or a very strong voice. Crucial stakeholders can also include other senior managers, all the way up to the CEO and board of directors. The overarching guideline here is that if they are not part of the solution, they are part of the problem.

It's very common to witness a project that no longer has any redeeming business value. Yet the project has taken on a life of its own and its proponents don't want to kill it for political reasons: it could raise embarrassing questions and cause heads to roll. So the project lingers on sucking up resources.

As a project manager, you may not want to be the nursemaid to a project that's in a coma. Assuming you have made the facts known to your sponsor and have still gotten nowhere, and wish to act in good conscience, you can use the killing power of those crucial stakeholders. This is a case where the antiproject team can be your ally.

You have two options. The first is to take your case to a higher court and see to it that these people get the facts. This is an opportunity to practice the Shared Values of honest communication and courage. The second option is to ask to be reassigned. As one Native American saying goes, "If you find yourself riding a dead horse, it's time to dismount."

Crucial stakeholders can also be active supporters of the venture. They can keep it going no matter what.

Key Players

These are individuals who can delay the project, sending it to a slow death. They can also ensure that the project is overlooked once it has been delivered. In the example I gave about the PMO and the new project management support tools, the software developers and techies were able to kill the project indirectly by neglect and by malicious compliance: providing inaccurate information. The functional managers who headed the software development and technology departments were accomplices by paying lip-service to the project management system and not pushing their people to use it. (They didn't want to upset their own stakeholders: their staff.) In contrast, the head of the PMO, along with his boss, were crucial stakeholders: they had the direct power to kill the project or keep it going.

Key players typically have intimate knowledge of the business domain that will be affected by the project, and they need to be given a voice throughout the project process. Their needs, issues, and expectations (in short, their win conditions) must be taken into consideration and reflected in the project deliverable or the project outcome. And when the crucial stakeholders approve a change to the project, the key players must buy in.

Important Stakeholders

These are people who need to be kept informed of what's coming and how it will affect their world. They want assurance that their needs are being represented by those who are planning the project. Keeping them informed can take the form of standup presentations, poster campaigns, e-mail, and other means of communication.

A Six-Step Process for Managing Stakeholders

In identifying the stakeholder community, the goal is to get to a point where they can be segmented into the three categories of crucial stakeholders, key players, and important people—and put into a database. There are six steps to this process. Like most of what we are talking about in this book, this is common sense, but it is uncommonly applied.

A good tool for building the stakeholder database is Microsoft Excel. On a project I worked on for a client, we ended up with a database of more than two hundred names. Table 7.3 provides an example of a filled-in database.

Table 7.3. Database of Crucial Stakeholders and Key Players

Job Title	Sponsor	Vice President of Finance	Vice President of Marketing	Head of Global Development	Director of Clinical Trials	Manager of Regulatory Affairs	Project Manager	Chief Scientist	Packaging Design	Head of PMO	Senior Vice President of Ears, Nose, and Throat
Name	M. Powers	J. Bucks	I. Spin	J. Travels	P. Oops	R. Tape	X. Treme	R. Beeker	C. Wrap	I. Gantt	Appleton
Stakeholder Type	CS	CS	KP	KP	KP	KP	KP	KP	KP	KP	KP
Role	Sponsor	Steering Committee	Core team	Department manager	Expert	Expert	Core team	Core team	Expert	Project office	Department head
Relationship manager	X. Treme	M. Powers	X. Treme	X. Treme	X. Treme	X. Treme	M. Powers	X. Treme	X. Treme	X. Treme	J. Travels
Project, decision responsibility											
Fund	F	F	F	F	F						
Project plan	A	C	C/E	C/E	C/E	C/E	P/E	P/E	C	—	—
Financial plan	P/A	P/A	C	C	C	C	C	I	C	I	—
Research	C	C	I	A	I	I	I	E	E	I	—
Development	C	C	I	A	C	I	I	E	E	—	—
Toxicology	I	I	I	C	I	I	I	E	C	—	—
Clinical trials	I	I	I	C	E	I	I	E	I	—	—
FDA approval	I	I	I	I	I	E	I	E	C	—	—
Staffing requirements	C/A	C	I	C/A	C	I	C/A	C/A	I	I	C/A
Manufacturing	A	I	I	C	I	I	I	C	C	—	—
Return on investment	E	E	E	I	—	—	—	—	—	I	—

Impact on job, career	Success would expand his domain	Possible negative impact if project overspends	Expands portfolio. Will have to increase staff, which will build department	Project can only help mobility	None. Business as usual. Greater job security	None. Business as usual. Greater job security	Promotion to program manager	Possible promotion. Peer recognition	None. Business as usual. Greater job security	None. Business as usual. Greater job security	Pet project bumped. Big cut in his product development budget.
Personal win conditions	Okay	Keep tight rein on financing	Okay	Okay	Okay	Okay	Okay	Okay	Okay	Okay	Allocate a small amount of money to do initial work on pet project
Major concerns about the project	Meet timeline, budget	Budget not predictable; short on staff to track costs	Product has clear competitive advantage	Can't be done in time frame; Insufficient time for exploration	Not enough lead time; insufficient staff	Lack of staff	Ability to resolve stakeholder conflicts; too many conflicts to resolve	Tight schedule, unstable specs; constant crunch	Lengthy approval process; time for securing approvals	Timely, accurate data; inaccurate reporting	Loan staff to project; already running short
Personal win conditions	No surprises	Frequent check points, fund in increments; Hire budget administrator	Keep specs flexible; agree with sponsor to review quota	Stable specs; agree on firm cut-off date for changes	Agree on firm cut-off date for changes, two more staff members	Three more staff	Get approval for administrative support person	Two more staff members in order to do parallel development	Permission to bypass standard approval process	Approve a project administrator	Free up staff but get management to put project earache on hold

Note: Influence level: **CS** = crucial stakeholder (has power to kill or continue the project); **KP** = key player (can seriously delay the project). Project/decision responsibility: **F** = fund the project (will come out of their budget); **A** = approve or veto major decisions; **C** = consult (must get their input); **E** = execute (responsible for doing the task or ensuring that it gets done); **P** = prepare (responsible for initiating the task); **I** = informed (no decision-making authority but must be kept informed); **$** = it's their money: they will pay for the project or the deliverable. **Impact on job/career:** How the project is expected, or perceived, to affect job mobility (a promotion, demotion, career enhancing, will be outplaced). Future prospects (move into a growth area, dead-end position). Power/span of control (will increase, decrease). Income potential (greater, lower)

The database in Table 7.3 is composed of crucial stakeholders and key players. To keep it focused and the size manageable, a separate database is typically set up for important stakeholders, who can run into the hundreds. Since important stakeholders need to be kept informed, this database should include how and when they will be kept up to date (for example, monthly e-mail, monthly briefing, reminders to check the project Web site for current status). This would be in addition to the information shown in Table 7.3 for crucial stakeholders and key players, although for important stakeholders, you will need to modify the left side of the table to fit your situation; it is still important to identify their major concerns and how they will be affected by the project.

In Table 7.3, the names and job titles of crucial stakeholders and key players run across the top. Specific stakeholder attributes comprise the left side. Importantly, each stakeholder is assigned a relationship manager—the individual whose primary responsibility is to ensure that the stakeholder's voice is heard and to either resolve issues that come up or find someone who can.

Although the attributes you use will differ according to the project at hand, the main point here is that they fall into several major categories: the stakeholders' planning and decision-making responsibility, their major concerns (that is, what they will tend to worry about), how the project will affect them during its life cycle and after completion (for better or for worse), and what their conditions of satisfaction are. (Conditions of satisfaction are discussed below. They answer the question, "What will make this project an acceptable experience for the stakeholder?")

At this point in the book, it should come as no surprise that much of the database is devoted to the emotional or feeling aspects of the project: these are represented by the bottom portion of the database starting with the "major concerns."

Start out the database by setting up columns and rows. Then follow these steps. If you want to change around the order, no problem. It's not dogma.

Step 1: Ferret Out the Stakeholders and Assess Their Clout

Ask, "Who will be affected either positively or negatively by the project?" Identify both organizations (business units, departments) and individuals. Stakeholders are *not* departments; they are *individual people*. Remember to include the less obvious stakeholders as well: your competitors, suppliers, and subcontractors; other projects that you will depend on; projects that will depend on your project. Also include key people in organizations who have information that can bear on your project, such as regulatory agencies and competitive intelligence services. Ask yourself, "Whose approvals will be required?" Initially the project manager and sponsor do this. It's vital to include the sponsor. Once the core team has been established, all members of the core team need to provide input.

Stakeholders are not *departments;*
they are individual people.

To assess their clout, ask how big their stake is. Size counts. Flag each stakeholder as to type: crucial stakeholder, key player, or important person. Do this by asking how much power and influence each has. Can they kill the project or keep it going outright? Kill it by slow death? I strongly recommend that you involve your sponsor in this assessment.

Step 2: Identify the Responsibilities of Each Stakeholder

This involves determining the project and decision responsibility of each stakeholder and is based on the work to be done, which will reveal itself during the Visionate and Speculate cycles of the Flexible Project Model. That's when the project scoping and planning meetings take place.

Step 3: Assess the Project's Potential Impact on the Stakeholder

The core question here is, "How will the stakeholder's world change as a result of this project?" Essentially, is this person likely to be better off? Worse off? More specifically, what will be the likely impact on his or her job or career? For instance, regarding power or span of control, will it increase, with greater responsibility or more people to supervise? Or will this person's world shrink because the reengineering project will reduce his or her staff? Will the result of the project be career enhancing (perhaps the stakeholder will be in charge of a new business in a hot market), or will he or she be outplaced? Will it result in a promotion or demotion? How will the project affect this person's future prospects: position him or her in a growth area or a dead-end street? What about income potential? Will the person be better or worse off in the long run?

Not all projects affect a person's job, at least directly. Some may have a bearing on quality of life or well-being in general. Public sector projects can have an impact on the community and can cause controversy (for example, running a new four-lane highway through a country town). The fundamental question to address is, "How will the stakeholder likely be better or worse off as a result of this project?"

The fundamental question to address is, "How will the stakeholder likely be better or worse off as a result of this project?"

At this stage, you are getting the lay of the land and making your own assessment, with the help of your sponsor, but in the absence of direct feedback from the stakeholders themselves.

Step 4: Assess Stakeholders' Likely Concerns and Personal Demands on Them

Given the nature of the project and the demands it will put on stakeholders or their staff, what are their major concerns? Will it drain scarce staff resources? Do they feel it's not possible to accomplish the project in the time required? Are they concerned about the small budget being allocated or the ability to meet quality requirements? Are they worried about the project's risk profile or even the overall viability? Where do they think they can get burned?

In Table 7.3, For example, the chief scientist for Project Zonk, who requires time to conduct a sufficient number of experiments, is likely to be concerned about the short schedule and unstable specs. The packaging design expert needs a long lead time to test different materials and is concerned about all the red tape that has held her up in the past, causing critical deadlines to be missed.

Step 5: Determine Personal Win Conditions

Here I use the term *personal win conditions* as distinct from the seven project-level win conditions discussed in detail later in the book. A project-level win condition determines how success will be measured on the overall project, as well as the relative importance of those success factors. These are schedule, budget, scope, quality, return on investment, stakeholder satisfaction, and team satisfaction. In contrast, *personal win conditions* refer to what can be done to mitigate the personal impact that the project is likely to have on the individual stakeholders. This includes its impact on job mobility, as well as their concerns about the project and any related fears. For key players, it calls for finding ways to meet at least a portion of their win conditions if possible. In other words, what can be done to keep them happy or at least keep them neutral so that they don't hold the project up? By definition, crucial stakeholders can kill the project outright. If you can't meet their win conditions, the project is dead.

In the Project Zonk example, J. Bucks, vice president of finance and a crucial stakeholder, is being held accountable for ensuring the project stays within budget. He was burned big time and embarrassed on the last big launch. He is concerned that the budget is not predictable and has no one available to track and audit expenses. His personal win condition is to have frequent check points, fund the project in increments, and hire a budget administrator. The win conditions for Appleton, who has had his product development budget cut in order to fund Project Zonk, is for management to allocate a small amount of seed money to his pet project. And to solve his staffing shortage, another of Appleton's win conditions is to convince management to put the earache project on hold.

Step 6: Assign Relationship Managers

Now that you know who's who, what do you do about these people? The database matters little until someone is assigned to keep on top of crucial stakeholders and key players. The burden falls mostly on the project manager and project sponsor. But other crucial stakeholders and key players will likely have a role as well. For example, in Project Zonk, Judy Travels, the head of global development, may be in a position to assuage the concerns of Dr. Appleton. Judy may agree to assign a researcher to at least begin work on Appleton's project. The role then of the relationship manager is to get resolution to concerns that can stop, delay, or kill the project. In addition to keeping bad things from happening, good relationship management can speed up a project that is already sailing along. I remember one project where the project manager was able to demonstrate that an additional expenditure of $100,000 for an expert in Java programming would likely shave four weeks off the schedule. And that translated into nearly $500,000 in additional revenues by being able to get to market one month early.

How to Set Up a Partnering Agreement

Can you get what it takes? This is Business Question 3, and answering it is the joint responsibility of the project manager and the sponsor. If the project manager is not able to secure the needed service provider, it then becomes the role of the sponsor, the project champion, to use his clout to obtain the service provider. It's easy for people to make well-intentioned promises, but they need to recognize just what they are committing to. This is a place where you do not want to take any chances and make naive assumptions about getting what you will need.

An important part of stakeholder management is to make explicit agreements with each stakeholder who will be expected to provide you with the resources, services, and other deliverables that your project depends on. These are mutual agreements (Exhibit 7.1).

On eXtreme projects, it's often not possible to predict with any accuracy the date by which you will need the service. It's not uncommon for Joanne to show up on March 15 ready to work, but the project is not ready to use her services. Rather than plan on a specific date, try working out an agreement based on lead time. For instance, the providing manager may say, "Give me ten working days lead time."

Organizational Interfaces

Besides people, there are other interfaces that will have an impact on your project. These include policies, procedures, systems, lengthy approval processes, and the prevailing culture. These can either defeat you or help you. And this is one reason that I have been stressing the key role of the project sponsor. On eXtreme projects that

Exhibit 7.1. A Partnering Agreement

Manager: Yolanda

Primary Service Provider	Service Customer	Type of Service to Be Provided	Expected Start Date	Expected Duration	Cost	Backup
Java Joe	Peter M.	Java programming	2/27	8 months	$55/hour	Andrea P.
Maria de la Joya	Matilda R.	Network design	3/1	6 months	$70/hour	Yusef M.

What is expected of us: _____

Manager: The person who will be loaning you the staff member

Service provider: This staff member who will be doing the work

Customer: The point person on your team who will be working with the service provider (and may even be approving the work performed)

Type of service: What work the provider will be doing

Backup: Someone who will replace the primary service provider if needed

What is expected of us: The agreement is two-way. Typical responses by managers are, "Give ample notice if your expected start or completion date changes."

are deadline driven, you will need special dispensation from standard organizational practices that will bog down your project—either that, or you decide to break the rules and take your chances. Hence, the Shared Value of courage, which is fueled by guts power, comes into play.

In certain organizational cultures, the words *project management* are akin to leprosy. You need to know this so you can frame what your job is in a positive way that will not cause people to remember suddenly that they are late for their root canal. Rather than calling it *project management,* refer to it as a *goal achievement process.* Then sanctify it with its own acronym and using your most solemn voice, say, "Yes, George, we'll be using Fast GAP on your project."

In certain organizational cultures, the words project management *are akin to leprosy.*

Another common cultural interface is that to get a decision made in hierarchical cultures, you may have to climb the ladder rung by rung. In collegial cultures, you can pop into the vice president's office and get a decision on the spot. The message here is to learn how to navigate the political waters.

The Role of the Steering Committee

eXtreme projects demand an agile organization. Beyond what your project sponsor must do for you, how does your project get the rest of the organizational support it will need to succeed when resources become scarce, when another project you depend on is reprioritized to a lower level and puts your project at risk, or when your project has a negative impact on another department?

The cross-functional nature of eXtreme projects spells conflict. It is not that departmental managers are malintentioned. Rather, they have limited people and time at their disposal and their own silo (departmental) projects, and other cross-functional project commitments can take priority over yours. These are legitimate needs.

Beyond these conflicts and in terms of the bigger picture, who will ensure that the benefits of your project are harvested now that your project sponsor has been sent to oversee operations in Bolivia in recognition of the fine job you did on her project? That is, another fundamental reason for having a steering committee is to ensure that responsibility is taken for benefits realization. In traditional project management circles, the project ends when the customer signs off on the deliverable. Rarely is anyone baked into the venture to ensure the organization sees a return on its investment.

The steering committee is the organizational construct that resolves these conflicts. It is made up of senior managers responsible for the organization's major stakeholder groups, among them, marketing, engineering, manufacturing, sales, product development, human resources, and information technology. Here is a sample steering committee charter:

- Resolve conflicts when reprioritized projects affect others.
- Reallocate resources to projects in need.
- Provide high-level business oversight by continually addressing the 4 Business Questions, especially number 4: Is it worth it?
- Ensure that the project's benefits are realized by the project sponsor and provide continuity if another sponsor needs to be appointed.
- Kill the project if it no longer makes business sense.

How to Combat the Phantom Approval Virus

You can probably think of a dozen reasons that a project gets delayed, but one of the greatest silent killers of projects is the phantom approval virus. This phantom takes the form of sign-offs and approvals that run rampant throughout the project and often go unanticipated. It can lurk undetected and eat away at your schedule, adding 50 percent or even more to the time line that was never planned. A six-month project can end up taking nine months, for example.

> *One of the greatest silent killers of projects*
> *is the phantom approval virus.*

Besides adding delay, approval steps can actually subtract rather than add value to the project by producing poor-quality decisions. This happens because the decision makers have not been party to all of the cross-functional discussion that the team had in considering the facts or preparing its recommendation. In addition, the team may spend hours generating documentation for the decision makers and even doing elaborate presentations. And if three functional managers are involved, the project can be pulled in that many different directions and become stalemated.

As part of the planning process, you have the responsibility to let the approvers (the project sponsor, customers, and anyone else) understand how their approval cycles will affect the project time line.

Here are some ways that you can protect your project from the phantom approval virus:

- The most important agreement is with your sponsor. As part of the sponsor agreement, the recommendation is that your sponsor agree to make decisions within a couple of hours, not days.
- Live the shared value of client collaboration. This helps ensure that those who count, the project's customers, are readily available to provide feedback and give approvals.
- Up front, reach agreement with the project sponsor, functional managers, and customers on those decisions for which the team has the authority to act. Examples are expenditure limits, recruiting additional team members, and selecting outside contractors.
- Explicitly define with your project sponsor those situations and limits over which the team has no authority for final approval
- Apply Critical Success Factor 3, the Flexible Project Model, which is built around short cycles with frequent review points.

Managing Change: You've Built It, But Will They Come?

eXtreme projects typically have an impact on the way the organization does business. These include projects that introduce new systems, technologies, and work flows. Often they are intended to make dramatic improvements in efficiencies and improve working relationships between the organization and its customers and suppliers. The most obvious example of this is the Internet and how it has changed the relationship between buyer and seller. In some cases, people have no choice about accepting the change. In other cases, they do have a choice and need to buy in. Consider these project failures:

- Why did a premier information services company have to decommission (throw away) a $1 million investment in project management software and tools?
- Why did a brand name in consumer goods fail after spending two years and several million dollars to centralize purchases of raw materials in order to create economies of scale?
- Why did a major utility spend close to $1 million in six months on leadership training and meeting management and not see any measurable change in behavior?
- Why do so many corporate empowerment programs intended to redistribute decision making down the organization fail to empower anyone?
- Why do upwards of 50 percent of process reengineering projects fail?

The common denominator is that people resist change, no matter how elegant and well planned the new idea is. Moreover, those of us who would initiate change often don't really understand how change works.

A key responsibility of the eXtreme project manager is to ensure customer acceptance of the final project deliverable. You yourself cannot convince people that they should love your sponsor's project, nor can your sponsor. But one thing you can do is to ensure that your sponsor and your crucial stakeholders know that acceptance of the project deliverable cannot be taken for granted and that the transition needs to be managed. Your role is to remind (and, if necessary, educate) your sponsor on both of these points.

The fact that you have developed your stakeholder database and thereby begun to identify pockets of resistance provides the initial evidence to get management's attention. In this sense, you are being the conscience of the project, acting as a catalyst in helping to galvanize those who are to orchestrate the change and realize the business benefits.

I will summarize five change models here, adapted from Weinberg (1997). Although Weinberg is referring to creating a culture change in how a software organization works, the models and principles apply to all projects that bear on the way people work.

Before you read about these change models, think of an example in your work experience where you were on the receiving end of a change that affected how you worked. As you read about these models, pick out the one that most closely resembles the model that your organization used, either intentionally or by default.

The Diffusion Model

In this model, change happens much like the way that dye dissolves into a liquid. Once released, the dye seeps through the solution on its own, perhaps penetrating some areas and not others. An example is a set of jokes that seem to crop up, like blonde jokes or certain ethnic jokes. They seem to take on a life of their own.

In the diffusion model, the underlying assumption is that change will happen, so no planning is necessary. The new system or policy is so obvious and needed (to those advocating it, that is) that people can simply not resist.

In practice, some people will take up the change faster than others. Other parts of the intended population may never get it. If there is any strength to the diffusion model, it is the recognition that change takes time to spread. The primary weakness is the belief that change will happen passively. This represents abdication by management to guide the process.

Hole in the Floor Model

This is also known as the engineering model. Those in the upstairs offices take control over the new idea by building well throughout and perhaps elaborate plans. The plans, which pinpoint the targets of change, are then dropped through a hole in the floor via a memo, slogan of the month, posters, or something else. The expectation is instant diffusion with little to no human contact and feedback perhaps with the exception of standup presentations here and there.

People who architect the hole in the floor model (usually left brain, logical engineering-type thinkers, perhaps "Rationals" in the Keirsey model) believe that all change programs are similar to the immediate and massive results you would expect, say, if you were to go to England and change the driving code from the left to right side of the road. This is not something you would do gradually.

Rationals believe that change will simply happen if there is structure behind it and people understand the rationale. In practice, the hole in the floor model usually boomerangs, or the desired change is simply ignored or gives rise to malicious compliance. The strength of this model is its emphasis on planning. The weakness is its sole emphasis on planning and ignoring the human factor.

In summary, this popular model is an example of emotional ignorance, having no regard for the feelings-facts-solutions model. Proponents believe that you just give them the facts, and change will happen.

The Carrot and Stick Model

This model begins to take into account the human factor and is based on the premise that you can push people in the direction you want them to go. The greater the desired change is, the harder you push. This is done through rewards and threats. This model can cause change to boomerang as people find unanticipated ways to push back. This, of course, is the modus operandi of project saboteurs. Rather than play your game, they will find other ways to outflank and attempt to defeat you.

The underlying belief is that people have a choice about change and can be motivated from the outside. If the carrot and stick model has strength, it recognizes that people are part of the equation. Built on the Newtonian view of the world, its weakness lies in its mechanistic and simplistic approach, treating people as if they were a variable in an equation.

The Learning Curve Model

A close cousin of the carrot and stick model is the learning curve model. Like its cousin, this model recognizes that people have a choice about change and can learn through large-scale training programs and by careful selection of personnel who are compatible with and embrace the new way.

This model has a good chance of working under circumstances where everybody will be affected the same way by the change. But this is rarely the case and explains why so many training programs are a dismal failure or take incredibly long for noticeable results. This is true for much of project management training. The organization decides that project management would be a good thing to do. Would-be project managers are sent off to training programs.

Upon returning from training, some (usually fewer than one in five) will attempt to apply some of what they learned. They quickly discover that they cannot make it work unless their boss and other departments play by the same rules. Yet these groups do not have the same incentive to learn and apply the skills as do those picked for the training. As a result, those trained get stymied, and the whole thing is labeled "program du jour." If the organization sticks with it, noticeable improvements can be seen in pockets over time. The weakness is that the learning curve model fails to manage change on a person-by-person basis, resulting in minimal impact on the organization's culture at large. Managing change, in addition to developing new behaviors and skills, works most effectively when each individual affected by the change is given a voice and can speak out about what's working and not working and how the change will be carried out.

The Satir Model

Named after the psychologist Virginia Satir, this model is based on a couple of key principles: human systems do not change unless individuals change one person at a time, and for change to take effect, the emotions must be understood and managed. Since you've read this far, this should not come as a surprise. I've been saying along that the role of the project manager is to manage and facilitate the flow of emotions, thoughts, and interactions. This idea applies to those who would orchestrate large-scale organizational change as well.

The Satir model consists of four stages:

1. Late status quo
2. Chaos
3. Integration
4. New status quo

In a way, this model changes how change is undertaken. It takes into consideration how people of different temperaments respond to change in each of the stages and how to manage this dynamic.

I was engaged in a project to turn around an ailing computer industry newspaper. When I was brought into the picture, *MIS Week* had been losing market share in advertising dollars, its only source of income, for three years. It had gone from fourth to sixth place and was in a death spiral. When I got there, I was amazed to find out that the staff had no appreciation for the severity of the problem. My project was to turn things around within twelve to eighteen months. Although I didn't know it at the time, this was a case that exemplified the Satir model.

Late Status Quo

Here, things appear to be in balance, but one part of the system is overcompensating for the other. In the case of *MIS Week*, the marketing and sales staffs were attempting to compensate for a newspaper whose publishing concept and content had been eclipsed by time and competition.

But everybody was in denial. To move out of late status quo requires the introduction of a foreign element. In this case, that was me. My job was to disturb the status quo. Rather than undertake a lengthy market study and waste time, I simply got everybody together and showed them the numbers and how much red ink we were running. I had to create a legitimate crisis. People initially dismissed the severity of the situation by suggesting what amounted to naive fixes, mainly centered around a new marketing program.

Less than two months later, when several advertisers pulled out (another "foreign element" and last straw), the situation could no longer be denied. The crisis that had been brewing all along had finally surfaced. This marked the end of late status quo.

Chaos

Our very foundation was shaken, but we had no place to go to, so panic set in and new ideas started to emerge. In our case, new advertising incentive programs, some of them ingenious, were proposed. But what you hope for is the transforming idea—the one that can change everything. We finally came up with one: to reposition the publication, defining it from scratch, and leapfrogging the competition by beating them into a new and burgeoning corner of the market.

Integration and Practice

Our transforming idea marked the end of chaos and the birth of a renewed computer industry newspaper. Rather than have a subteam go off and develop the new idea, I involved everyone who worked for the publication. All played a role in reinventing *MIS Week*. Everyone felt energized and creative. We were out of the woods. Integration and practice means putting the new idea to work. It wasn't easy. We hit roadblocks and had afterthoughts but persisted. What we had going for us was positive, creative, relentless energy, with everyone involved in shaping the end product as well as defining the process to get there.

The New Status Quo

Six months later (instead of the usual nine months), the new *MIS Week* was relaunched with a new look, information content, and circulation base. We got a lot of attention. People felt they were making a difference. Advertising volume improved.

The strength of the Satir model is that it brings together the strengths of the other models, while adding the personal dimension, giving individual stakeholders a voice, if not the ability to actively work on how the change will be implemented.

At the time, we didn't know that what we were doing approximated the Satir model. I had never heard of it. Here is what we learned from the *MIS Week* experience and from other projects I've worked with over the last fourteen years:

- Some people will resist change no matter how needed the new thing is.
- Even more, they resist being changed.
- Acknowledge the resistance rather than ignore or even resist their resistance.
- Set up forums so people can vent their feelings about the change, including their worst fears.
- Respond to their feelings with compassion.
- Show people what will still be the same and not focus exclusively on all that is new.
- Create small successes, and build on these.
- Eliminate the gap between training and practice by having people learn the new thing while doing real work in real time.
- Include a naysayer or two on the project team if you can.
- Recognize that some will never get on board not matter what you do. Move on without them.

The overarching principle for all these lessons comes from Project Accelerator 3: create ownership for results. People support what they create.

Business Question 4: Is It Worth It to You?

If you have read this far and have experienced a knot in your stomach or some other sinking or sickening sensation, you may be discovering that you are not cut out to be an eXtreme project manager.

Not everyone is overjoyed at the thought of succeeding or failing based on the politics of relationship management. Be thankful that you are getting a strong signal to find a livelihood that matches your natural talents and desires. Congratulations! What are you waiting for? If you want to end it here, Amazon.com remarkets slightly used books. But if you think you would relish the life of an eXtreme project manager, read on.

We're now ready to dig into Critical Success Factor 3, The Flexible Project Model.

| Part Three |

The Flexible Project Model

The Flexible Project Model is Critical Success Factor 3 of the eXtreme Project Management Model. People often have the mistaken notion that the difference between traditional and eXtreme project management is an argument about planning versus not planning. That's far from the truth. Both involve planning. And in both arenas, the goal is to keep the project under control.

The discussion really needs to center around which approach will give you the most control given the nature of the project. The Flexible Project Model is designed to enable you and the stakeholders to keep your project under control and deliver business value *in the face of volatility*. Under conditions of volatility, flexibility, not rigidity, is called for.

Another fundamental distinction between the traditional and eXtreme project management approach is that traditional project management looks at a project from design to delivery. In contrast, eXtreme project management and the Flexible Project Model look at a project more broadly: from concept to payoff.

The Parallel Universe Example

In presenting the Flexible Project Model in the chapters that follow, I combine a discussion of the steps and strategies of the process with an ongoing story about an eXtreme project from a parallel universe. The story, which continues across all five chapters in this part, is designed to serve several purposes:

- To show how the flexible model applies to eXtreme projects
- To convey the intertwined dynamics of a multiproject environment
- To bring in leadership lessons from Part Two by way of the story—and demonstrate that leadership is the glue that holds the model together
- To provide a variety of settings, such as information technology, pharmaceuticals, and construction, to which readers can relate
- To leaven the presentation of the process with some amusement and entertainment

The third point deserves emphasis. The Flexible Project Model is a tool box that consists of a bunch of templates and techniques. Together, these represent the implements and the mechanics of eXtreme project management. But a successful project is no more its implements than a piano constitutes a great concert. The Flexible Project Model will not play itself. Like any other method, it requires the discipline of Self-Mastery and the artful practice of Leadership by Commitment. These Critical Success Factors, along with those of Real-Time Communication and Agile Organization, plus living the 4 Accelerators and 10 Shared Values, are the fuel that powers the Flexible Project Model. The presentation of the parallel universe story highlights how all these soft topics are critically important and integrate in making the model work.

An Overview of the Flexible Project Model

Even the most creative endeavors have an underlying, if not invisible, flow to them; for example, emergency situations give birth to a process, often one that emerges spontaneously. The Flexible Project Model is intended to provide people with just enough structure to allow them to take advantage of unexpected events and changes without going off the deep end into project never never land, where the project spends the rest of its life hopelessly out of control. Another way of saying it is that the Flexible Project Model enables the project manager and stakeholders to take responsibility, that is, to respond with ability, allowing them to self-organize and self-correct, a necessity under conditions of high change and high speed.

The Flexible Project Model is a customer-focused, change-tolerant framework comprising four iterative cycles (Visionate, Speculate, Innovate, and Reevaluate) plus a final element called Disseminate. The term *cycles* is used to emphasize that the entire project, from Visionate through Reevaluate, is iterative, that is, one recycles through the process again and again. So too is the work that's accomplished inside any one cycle. The iterations continue until the desired result is achieved or a decision is made to kill the project or put it on hold.

The Flexible Project Model is a process: getting inputs from the right people, doing something with the inputs to produce outputs, and getting feedback that generates new inputs for the next cycle.

The following chapters delve into the essentials of each component. Until then, here's the big picture of the four cycles plus Disseminate.

Visionate: The What

This cycle puts the spotlight on Business Question 1: Who needs what and why? Visionate encompasses identifying and agreeing on the project objective: the problem to be solved or the opportunity to be seized. It includes the identification of business benefits and risks as well as identifying possible future scenarios that could affect the project for better or worse.

Chapter Eight explains the first part of the Visionate cycle, in which the project manager works with the project sponsor to capture and flesh out the sponsor's vision of the project.

The Visionate cycle also involves working with crucial stakeholders to produce a collective vision of the project and its deliverable, which is covered in Chapter Nine. A key outcome of the Visionate cycle is agreement among crucial stakeholders as to the Win Conditions for the project: how success will be measured.

Speculate: The How

The Speculate cycle addresses Business Question 2: What will it take to do it? *Speculate* means putting together a plan that includes interim deliverables and milestones, however tentative these may be. Chapter Ten covers this. Importantly, during the Speculate cycle, the work products that came out of the Visionate cycle are updated to reflect the latest information.

Before going on to the Innovate cycle, all 4 Business Questions are once again addressed in the light of the latest information, and if the project is still considered worthy (in answer to Business Question 4, Is it worth it?), resources are put in place to begin the cycle. This stage is covered in Chapter Eleven.

Innovate puts the emphasis on experimenting and rapid development and generating timely and real-time feedback with stakeholders, leading to their happy agreement: "Yes, that's what we really want!" or possibly, "We can't make it happen. Back to the drawing boards." Chapter Twelve describes the work during this cycle, which takes place within a series of predefined time boxes, usually one to six weeks. At the end of this period, the results are gathered and prepared for review, which takes place during Reevaluate, the next cycle.

Reevaluate: The Reviewing

The purpose of the Reevaluate cycle is to make a decision about the future course of the project. Chapter Thirteen focuses on answering a number of questions: Is it still the right project? Can we win? Should we keep going? The decision is based on the likelihood of realizing the project's postdelivery business benefits.

Throughout the entire process the quantum mind-set prevails. We've been looking to discover the desired result by doing a little aiming, firing the gun, and then redirecting the bullet based on the latest information. We are not wed to the Newtonian slogan that says, "Get it right the first time." The whole idea is to get it right the *last* time. We fail our way to success.

What you're seeing here is a continuous cycle of planning, deplanning, and replanning. The latest results drive planning. This is in contrast to the Newtonian approach, which holds the plan to be sacred and presses you to achieve the planned result. In eXtreme project management, the goal is not the planned result. It's to produce the desired result.

Disseminate: The Harvesting

Disseminate means releasing the project to the customer and kicking off the benefits realization process. Chapter Fourteen explains how to ensure that the deliverable does what it is supposed to as well as ensuring that the customer is ready, willing, and able to reap the business benefits.

How Much Process Is Enough?

I can't get give you a Newtonian, binary answer to this question. The short answer is, "Just enough." As a general guideline, when it comes to adding ceremony (more process, additional documentation), I recommend that you err on the side of Accelerator 4 and keep it simple.

Think of the components (templates and techniques) that make up the Flexible Project Model as a buffet. You take what you like and leave the rest. This will differ from project to project. Don't take this lightly. Unless it is so obvious that a component makes no sense for your project, my strong recommendation is that the team and crucial stakeholders spend some time trying each one. That's because they will not be in a position to appreciate the value until they actually sample it. If I had judged Indian food by the menu alone, I would never have eaten it. But now that I've tasted it, it has become one of my favorite cuisines.

If after applying the component, the team is adamant that certain formalities are adding too much overhead and their progress is being hampered, energy will start to drain from the project, a sign to scale down. When process becomes overbearing, people start working for the process instead of the other way around; the project goes into a funk, and the mood sours. Let the team decide how much process and tools are needed.

eXtreme Project Management Model
Applying the Quantum Mind-Set

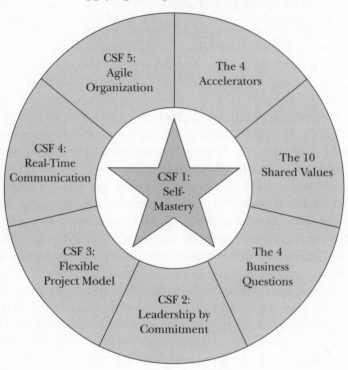

Chapter Eight

Visionate
Capturing the Sponsor's Vision

A small mistake in the beginning leads to a big mistake in the end.
—THOMAS AQUINAS

The Visionate cycle, the first component of Critical Success Factor 3, The Flexible Project Model, puts the spotlight on Business Question 1: Who needs what and why? The answer to this question drives the answers to the other three business questions: What will it take to do it? Can we get what it takes? Is it worth it?

The Visionate cycle consists of two interacting components: the sponsor's vision of the project and the collective vision. The sponsor's vision is captured initially by the project manager, before the project team is formed. The collective vision is a composite of the sponsor's vision as refined through discussion and collaboration with crucial stakeholders. This iterative process then is one of establishing a vision followed by a re-vision, which takes place at the scoping meeting where the collective vision is established.

This chapter focuses on capturing and clarifying the sponsor's vision of the project, the first part of the Visionate cycle. Chapter Nine covers how to translate the sponsor's vision into a collective vision of the crucial stakeholders and key players as well as the core project team.

In this chapter, I will cover:

- Getting in front of the sponsor, the first critical turning point
- How to uncover the true sponsor

- The Objectives-Deliverables-Benefit Model
- How to conduct the sponsor meeting
- How to draft the first iteration of the Project Prospectus, a summary of the major elements of the project, including the three-sentence project skinny, the project's ins and outs, project imperatives, the program breakdown structure, the product vision, and the 7 Win Conditions

Most organizations have an abundance of new ideas, problems to solve, and opportunities to pursue. As a result, projects often spring up like weeds and begin to take on a life of their own, draining nutrients from more worthy projects. Furthermore, without being officially sponsored, even the high-payoff projects will have a high risk of stalling or outright failure should they even manage to reach to the finish line.

Moreover, the project sponsor may have a very unclear idea as to what he or she truly wants and say something like, "Build us a Web site. Our competitors have one." Or he may have a very clear idea of what he *thinks* he wants, but this is likely to change frequently and abruptly throughout the course of the project as the competitive environment changes, input is gathered from crucial stakeholders, and the true requirements and underlying need are uncovered along the way.

> *The project sponsor may have a very unclear idea as to what he or she truly wants.*

Getting Answers to Business Question 1: Who Needs What and Why?

This chapter addresses the basic work products and other considerations that comprise the first part of the Visionate cycle. The work products of the whole cycle are summarized in Figure 8.1.

Business Question 1 provides the focal point for the initial discussion with the sponsor and is also the basis for the scoping meeting, which is discussed in the next chapter. Business Question 2 (What will it take to get it?) is the thrust of the Speculate cycle when it is addressed head on.

Figure 8.1. Critical Success Factor 3: The Flexible Project Model

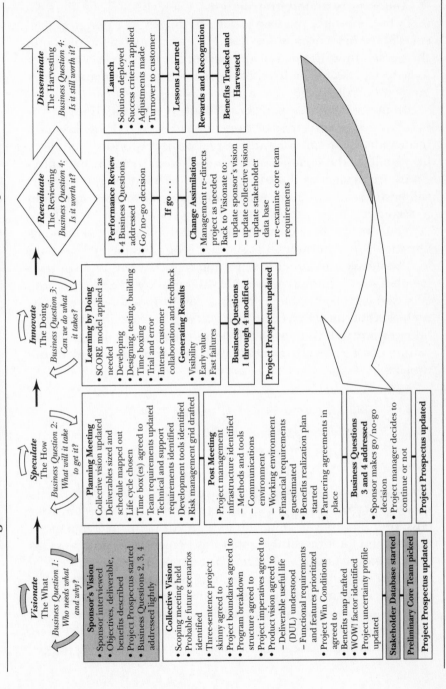

You want firsthand information. When you are recruited directly by the project sponsor, you are in the best position to get answers to the first business question. Here, you are looking right into the horse's mouth, which is the part of the horse you really want to be facing. Getting in front of the sponsor is the first crucial turning point on the project.

In many cases, the project will have been handed down (or over) to you by your boss or someone else who is acting as an intermediary between you and the real project sponsor. Neither is likely to have the same emotional attachment to and vested interest in the project as does the sponsor. Ultimately, the sponsor will have to live with the results long after you've gone to Hawaii to recoup.

You must get in front of the sponsor to get answers to Business Question 1. Furthermore, the sponsor is often in the best position to relax heavy bureaucratic reporting requirements and controls common to traditional projects but devastating to eXtreme projects. She is typically able to provide you with other concessions, such as a conducive working space as well as the equipment and other essential tools to get work done and foster rapid communication and fast feedback critical to performance on eXtreme projects.

You must get in front of the sponsor
to get answers to Business Question 1.

If you can't get an audience with the sponsor, the chances of being successful diminish dramatically. Getting in front of the sponsor can be tricky if you've been assigned to the project by your boss. Your boss may be reluctant to set up or participate in a meeting with the sponsor, thinking that this would reflect poorly on his understanding of the project and its business need.

There is a subtle bias in our culture that teaches us that asking questions of management is a sign of weakness or lack of business acumen. We think we're supposed to be psychic. Moreover, we might have the naive belief that if they are asking for it, they must actually know what they need. Or we may shy away, saying to ourselves, "They can't fault me for giving them what they asked for." But, yes, they can and they do. These beliefs can be fatal. To put it bluntly, if you don't get answers from the horse's mouth, you'll be the horse's ass.

To put it bluntly, if you don't get answers from the horse's mouth, you'll be the horse's ass.

At the start, it may not be clear who the true sponsor is, even to your boss. Let's say your boss assigned you to manage the project and you want to find out who the real sponsor is. Here are the key questions:

- Who decided we should be taking on this initiative?
- Whose department will be most affected by this?
- Who will be evaluating the results? And who must be made happy?
- Who will you need to go to for approvals?
- Whose budget will be funding the project?

You may have to persuade your boss that it is critical that you understand the project's objective, deliverable, and expected business benefits right from the sponsor. Your argument centers on your mutual desire to succeed. So if the sponsor will have to live in the house you are building, then it only makes sense to know what will make him happy before it's built and furnished. And this means getting a firsthand understanding of the objective, the deliverable, business benefits, how success will be measured, the constraints, what authority you will have, what the sponsor expects of you as project manager, and how she sees her role.

Ultimately, you may have to stand tall on the professional and ethical ground that you have a business and a moral obligation to understand the need and requirements as perceived by the sponsor before spending the organization's money. Courage. Without courage, nothing much else matters on eXtreme projects. Do it scared if you have to.

The First Sponsor Meeting

Assuming you have a commitment for a meeting with the sponsor, you'll need to prepare well for it.

Preparing for the First Meeting

You need to know what you want to come out with before you go in. In preparing, recognize that some sponsors will have a very concrete vision of the project and specify exactly what they want. These are potentially the most dangerous sponsors: they are so clear and emphatic that one may avoid questioning *why* the specified deliverable was even chosen in the first place to be the solution. It's quite common for a sponsor to say at the end of the project, "That's what we asked for but not what we need."

In other cases, depending on the sponsor's personality type and thinking style, her so-called vision may be very soft and difficult to get your arms around. This might be true if the sponsor is of the Idealist or Rational temperament whose dominant communication style is abstract. Such sponsors may have only a vague vision, one that's akin to a hallucination. Nonetheless, in deference to sponsors, we'll give them the benefit of the doubt and use the term *vision* to mean a picture, however clear or fuzzy, that includes the business objective, expected deliverable, and resultant business outcome.

Sponsors may have only a vague vision,
one that's akin to a hallucination.

The Objectives-Deliverables-Outcome Model

The Objectives-Deliverables-Outcome Model is an important mental model to keep in mind as you prepare for the meeting with the project sponsor. The questions you will be asking are designed to sort out answers to three critical pieces of information about the project (Figure 8.2):

The objective: The problem to be solved or opportunity to seize

The deliverable: The solution that is expected to solve the problem or exploit the opportunity

Figure 8.2. Objective-Deliverable-Outcome Model

Objective → *The What*	Deliverable → *The How*	Outcome *The Why*
What problem or opportunity does this project address?	*How will we solve the problem or seize the opportunity?*	*Why are we investing in this in the first place?*

The outcome: The expected business payoff (that is, benefit) in dollars and cents for having produced the deliverable

Here's an example of how a vice president of sales may frame a project to improve sales performance:

Objective	Free up salespeople to spend more time selling
Deliverable	A new streamlined order entry and call reporting system
Outcome	Two extra hours per day resulting in $300 per day on average in additional sales per salesperson × 500 salespeople = $150,000 per day additional sales

The distinction between project *objective* and *deliverable* is very important. It's possible to produce the agreed-on deliverable but fail to meet either the objective or outcome. For instance, the sales staff might use the extra time to take longer lunches, or the deliverable specified (a new order entry and call reporting system) may not be the only solution. What other options might be available to free up salespeople—for example, reallocating territories to save on travel time? Separating the objective from the solution (that is, the deliverable) opens the door for someone to come up with a brilliant solution at any time during the project. (Accelerator 1: Make change your friend). This is especially true for eXtreme projects when circumstances are fluid and complex, necessitating that one consider multiple options and even launch several projects knowing full well that one or more of them may have to be thrown away.

Conducting the Sponsor Meeting

A good way to start the meeting is to jump into the water and get the conversation moving. You can simply say, "Tell me about the project you have in mind."

The questions that follow are designed to create the clearest possible picture of the sponsor's vision of the project and your role in its success. The questions are organized around these topics:

- The business objective, project deliverable, and expected business benefit
- The project context, including political considerations
- Who the project is intended to affect
- Schedule and budget expectations
- Trade-offs that will have to be made

By addressing these issues, you are not only demonstrating your business savvy but also providing a valuable service to the sponsor and other stakeholders later on.

As part of the sponsor meeting, you will also want to gain an understanding of your working relationship and set expectations for next steps. Table 8.1 shows the questions to raise with your sponsor in your first meeting. You'll want to adapt these questions to your particular project.

You don't need to be Newtonian about this and ask all the questions or do so in the order given. The discussion is likely to jump back and forth. You can sort it out later. So let the discussion flow, but guide it so that you wind up with answers in each category. Asking these questions puts to work the Shared Values of client collaboration, clarity of purpose, and results orientation, as well as providing early value by helping the sponsor bring her vision closer to reality. The information you gather here literally means that the sponsor's vision is *in formation*: beginning to manifest in physical form.

Avoid Shooting Yourself in Both Feet Before the Project Starts

Act as if you were a journalist. In your first meeting with your sponsor, your role is that of an objective gatherer of information. Later, you will have an opportunity to negotiate gaps between

Table 8.1. Questions for the First Sponsor Meeting

Business Objective

- What opportunity are we going after?
- What's the business need that this project is intended to address?
- What is it that we are fixing, trying to improve, or solve?
- How will the project enable your organization to serve its customers better?

Project Deliverable Quality and Scope: These questions delve into the product or service that is to be produced: "If we had it in place right now [the process, the system, the product, the new service] . . .":

- What would you see as its main functions and features?
- Is this intended to be a stop-gap measure: We'll do it once, and if we replace it, will we start all over from scratch? Or are we trying to do something that we will attempt to fix and upgrade over time?
- What would be the absolute bare minimum functions?
- What would it physically look like to you?

Business Outcome: These questions are aimed at identifying the valued-added dollar-and-cents benefits that are being sought as a result of having produced the project deliverable. "Assuming we had completed the project and it was now up and running . . .":

- What is the most important payoff you are looking to achieve? Increased revenue? Better customer service? Greater market share? Decreased cost of doing business? Short-term profits?
- How would you quantify the dollar payoff you are targeting? ROI? Reduced cost? Over what period of time?
- What will you want to see to know that the business benefits have been achieved?
- Under what conditions would we shut down the project?

Context

These questions elicit information about the business climate surrounding the project:

- How does this project fit in with the organization's overall business strategy?
- Who's driving this project from above?
- Who will you be going to for approvals and funding?

Table 8.1. Questions for the First Sponsor Meeting, Cont'd

- What's driving us to do this now? What if we did nothing? Waited until next year?
- How does this fit into the overall priority of projects?
- If we have to let another project slip, what might that be?

Stakeholders: These questions relate to the politics of the project. Here you want to find out whom this project is intended to affect, for better or for worse. Those affected can be either internal or external to your organization:

- For whose benefit is the project being undertaken?
- What customer group or department is the project intended to affect?
- Who is likely to feel threatened by this project or have strong opinions?
- Who do we need to talk to that has to be happy with the results?
- Who are the strong supporters of this project?

Timing

- What's the time frame or deadline you have in mind?
- What's driving the deadline?
- What latitude is there?

Resources and Budget

- What would you expect to spend on this project?
- Whose budget is this coming out of?
- Who will I talk to when I need staff for the project?

Trade-Offs: When trade-offs have to be made, which one of the drivers for this project must be achieved (that is, it cannot be sacrificed)?

- ROI, time line, budget, functions and features, quality, customer/stakeholder satisfaction, team satisfaction?
- What is the second most important driver?

Working Relationship

- How do you see your role with respect to decision making? Funding? Staffing? Who else will you look to for this?
- How do you see my role on the project?
- What progress reporting information will be important to you?

what the sponsor wants and what you and the team think it will take to do it. In soliciting information from the sponsor, it is critical that you do not give the impression that the project being described is achievable (or not) in the time or budget she gives you. You will not know this until after the planning meeting (which takes place in the Speculate cycle), when you answer Business Question 2: What will it take to get it? Avoid giving off-the-cuff estimates.

Let the sponsor know that you will return with your notes consolidated in a summary of her vision of the project. The purpose of the second meeting is to make any adjustments. Once the vision is updated, that will form the basis for your third meeting before assembling the team and conducting the project kickoff, also known as the scoping meeting.

For the third meeting, you will return with ballpark data in answer to the question, "What will it take to get what you want?" namely, budget, resources, and risk profile. This will be very rough. And you will have better data after the scoping and planning meetings are held with the crucial stakeholders and the team who will be doing the work.

Between now and the second meeting, you may be back with a few other questions.

Once you've conducted the scoping and planning meetings, you will be in a better position to clarify your role and relationship in a way that will serve the best interests of the project. In the meantime, take good notes. For now, you are establishing a baseline. It's all going to change anyway.

How does this all play out in practice? Let's visit the parallel world of eXtreme project management to see.

The Project from Heaven Is Born

It was Monday in Mesopotamia, in a parallel universe. Noah arrived at Genetics Unlimited, where he managed research and development projects. He had spent the last two weeks wrapping up the project from hell and was ready for a little relief.

Out of habit, the first thing he did when he got to his desk was left-click on the MS Lookout icon. As he did, a new e-mail popped up:

Dated 2/1 Y2K BC

To: Noah

From: Gabriel

Subject: Confidential: Announcing the Project from Heaven

Good Morning Noah,

We will need your help on a new project. Meet me in my office at 3:00 P.M. today and I will fill you in.

Extremely yours,

G.

Noah turned away from his computer with a frown on his face. He had heard the buzz around halls about a top-secret, very big new project coming down the pike. And since Gabriel was close to the Sponsor of All Sponsors, no doubt this was considered a very big deal. Noah expected this to be an eXtreme project to end all eXtreme projects. But he was only mildly concerned, because he had read and used his eXtreme project management book, which had been published ten years before in the parallel universe, and it had helped guide him through some tough spots.

Well, he thought, at least he didn't have to fight to meet with the sponsor in person, which was always a big help. He rehearsed in his mind the questions he would need to ask Gabriel during the meeting so he could get the clearest possible picture of the sponsor's vision of the project and his role in its success. He listed the issues he would ask Gabriel about:

- The business objective, project deliverable, and expected business benefit
- The project context, including political considerations
- Who the project was intended to affect
- Schedule and budget expectations
- Trade-offs that would have to be made

In addition to getting his sponsor to answer these questions, he wanted to use the meeting to gain an understanding of his working relationship with the sponsor and set expectations for next steps. As Noah mentally prepared for his first meeting, he reviewed the questions in Table 8.1.

The meeting began promptly at 3:00 P.M. signaled by a lightning bolt and a loud clap of thunder. After exchanging a few pleasantries, Gabriel filled Noah in on his new project.

"We have been observing the people on the Planet Earth and are not pleased with how they have been treating each other. As a result, we wish to right-size the planet and start all over with a new crew. This has been personally approved by the Sponsor of All Sponsors.

On 11/9, nine months from now, the X-Virus will be released. This new and rare virus will afflict all living creatures. It attacks the central nervous system of both human and animal populations and causes a peaceful but permanent slumber. The virus spreads fast and is known to be fatal, causing death within forty-eight hours of exposure. All members of the human and animal populations are at risk."

Another downsizing project, thought Noah to himself.

The sponsor continued, "Preliminary research among members of VIA [Virus Information Association] indicates that it is possible to develop and deliver an effective anti–X Virus preventative vaccine. However, given the time available and the anticipated complexities of the research and development process, it is believed that the vaccine can be produced in only limited quantities. To ensure the preservation of species on earth, both animal and human, at least two qualified members of every ethnic and animal group must survive. A nominal fee for the vaccine will be charged to each selected human.

"Your job, should you decide to accept it, is to manage the X-Virus Vaccine Project. This project is part of the SOS [Save Our Species] program to be run by Donald Dirk, head of the Department of Earthland Security, and under the overall direction of F. Throckmorton, Jr., Earthland's chairman.

Noah swallowed hard.

Gabriel continued, "The minimum acceptable survival rate is 95 percent of the Selected Ones. Not achieving this minimal rate of survival will cause a serious imbalance in the sociogenetic, political, and economic makeup of future human and animal populations within four generations and return the planet to its present unsatisfactory state of affairs.

"We've budgeted $1.4 million drachmas for this project. A lot is riding on this. You've demonstrated strong leadership skills on your last three projects. I have every confidence that you will do another bang-up job on this one."

Noah then referred to notes he had brought with him, which consisted mostly of the questions he needed to ask the sponsor to clarify the business objective, the project deliverable, the business outcome, and all the other critical details about the project. He took copious notes on all of the sponsor's answers and later summarized the key points, which are shown in Exhibit 8.1.

Exhibit 8.1. Noah's Meeting Notes

Business Objective
- Save Selected Ones from dying.

Project Deliverable
- A vaccine for the X-Virus
- Being undertaken for the Selected Ones: two of every animal and human ethnic group
- Quality: 95 percent of Selected Ones must survive

Business Outcome
- To establish a 100 percent increase in peace on earth within four generations
- To increase per capita revenues from earth's inhabitants from 18,000 to 24,000 drachmas in four generations
- To decrease overhead costs to maintain planet earth from 18,000 to 16,000 drachmas per capita in four generations

Context
- Downsizing project. Very sensitive. Top secret.
- Part of larger program called SOS
- Takes priority over all my other projects

Stakeholders
- Highly political. Many will not get the vaccine

Time Frame
- Vaccine to be administered no later than 11/9 Y2K = drop-dead date

Resources and Budget
- $1.400 million drachmas

Trade-Offs
- Above all, must meet schedule, no matter what.
- Quality (efficacy) of vaccine must be optimized at all costs
- Budget, ROI, team satisfaction, happiness of non-Selected Ones and product scope (packaging and dosage sizes, for example) take back seat

Working Relationship
- I report directly to Sponsor
- Weekly progress reports
- Sponsor agrees to return decisions within two hours

Exhibit 8.1. Noah's Meeting Notes, Cont'd

Other Stuff

- No one has ever been able to develop on this time line before
- Untested technology
- A highly charged political environment—the Selected versus Nonselected Ones—means a turbulent, if not hostile, external environment resulting in more change and uncertainty
- High speed *plus* fixed deadline
- High change: many unknowns about the X-Virus. Impact: evolving requirements; new information will continue to make any plans quickly obsolete
- Quality can't be sacrificed

This looks like an eXtreme project.

Prior to leaving the meeting, Noah said to the Gabriel, "My next step is to develop a profile of the project and the project deliverable, the X-Virus Vaccine, and summarize it in the form of a Project Prospectus. I'll need to meet with you again to run this by you to be sure we have the same picture in mind. I will then return for a third meeting with a very rough ballpark estimate of what it will take to accomplish the project. At that point, I'll ask for your approval to move ahead with the scoping meeting during which your vision of the project will be extended to the crucial project stakeholders."

"Fair enough," Gabriel replied.

Now let's return to our own Planet Earth to see what the next steps should be.

Beginning Work on the Project Prospectus

Once you've had your initial meeting with the sponsor, you will want to consolidate your notes in the form of a Project Prospectus. Sometimes referred to as a project charter or the business case, it's a document that contains the essential information about the project.

The Prospectus contains the bare essentials of the project. It gets started right after you've had your first meeting with the sponsor and is updated throughout the venture. It's not official until it reflects the collective vision of the sponsor, crucial stakeholders, and the core team. That will happen during the scoping and planning meetings.

The Prospectus is always available in hard copy but is also made available through the project's Web site or stored in a virtual workspace shared by the eXtreme core team and other stakeholders.

The Three-Sentence Project Skinny

Once the project gets moving, things are going to get chaotic. A short, pithy description of the project goes a long way to keep people focused when all else seems to be out of control. The three-sentence project skinny is the lighthouse in the storm and the first step in sizing up the project.

The reason to avoid long-winded descriptions is that nobody remembers them, if they bother to read them in the first place. And besides, all those words create too much room for interpretation and confusion. They'll be plenty of time later for confusion.

At work here is Accelerator 4, keep it simple, as well as the Shared Values of clarity of purpose and results orientation. The three-sentence skinny achieves both. Exhibit 8.2 explains how to put together the project skinny—for example:

1. The Zonk team will develop a twelve-hour sleeping pill for sleep-deprived adults.
2. Our project will be considered completed when the formulation is turned over to manufacturing.
3. This project contributes to Babbot Labs' objective to increase share of market to 25 percent in the next three years among adults age twenty-four and older in the U.S. market.

The Ins and Outs: Delineating the Project Boundaries

The Ins and Outs establish the project's boundary. The Ins represent the major work to be done that is considered to be inside the scope of the project as defined by the first two statements of the project skinny. This in-scope work is what the eXtreme core team will be doing or ensuring it gets done by subteams and other partners (Table 8.2).

So that things don't fall through the cracks, it's a smart idea to identify the out-of-scope work: activities that are related to the project but are considered the work of other project teams. In practice, out-of-scope work represents related projects that, when

Exhibit 8.2. How to Write the Three-Sentence Project Skinny

First Sentence: Who's doing what for whom?

The Who: The name of the team or group undertaking the project. Later, during the scoping meeting, team members can pick their own team name. Something as basic as creating their own identity can give team members a special sense of importance. It also helps harness the energy of Accelerator 3: Create ownership for results.

The What: This is the project deliverable. On an eXtreme project, you never truly know what the sponsor wants or needs (at the outset); the sponsor rarely knows either, even if she hands you detailed specs. The real need—the desired result—will evolve during most of the project's lifetime. The proof will be in the pudding: the end customer has to have a direct experience with the project deliverable in order to know if it does what is expected. External factors, such as a competitor's move or new technology, will also shape the project deliverable.

Although the true deliverable will evolve, you need to understand what the sponsor is looking for. This means identifying the "what" that is needed. This can be:

- The thing to be produced
- The problem to be solved
- The opportunity to be seized
- The new capability to be put in place

For whom? The idea is to pinpoint the project's client and customer group—the set of stakeholders beyond the sponsor who need to be satisfied with the result. In some cases, the customer will be the end user (for example, the person who will be using the new computer printer you are building). The client can also be an interim user, such as the sales department that commissioned this project. It in turn may sell it to the final end user.

Second Sentence: What will constitute the completion of the project? That is, how will we know it is over?

Third Sentence: Why? The sentence answers the question "Why are we doing it?" It summarizes the underlying business case, the justification for undertaking the project (for example, market share, cost savings, profits, sales volume, improved service). As such, it provides the hook that links the project to a specific organizational strategy. Without the project, the organization would not achieve an important goal.

The content for this sentence comes from Business Question 4: Is it worth it? That's the question that specifically addresses the business value for the project and is the responsibility of the sponsor to answer.

Table 8.2. Project Boundaries

In-Scope Work	Out-of-Scope Work
X	Y
X	Y
X	Y
X	Y
X	Y

Note: X = agreed-on work of the eXtreme core team; Y = the work of the other teams.

taken together, form an entire constellation or family of projects (also know as the Program) of which your project is one of several. In the scoping meeting later on, the Ins and Outs, along with the project skinny and other items, will be modified by the stakeholders. The idea here is to give them a running start.

Project Imperatives

Project imperatives are the vital few make-or-break requirements that must be met for the overall project to succeed. Not meeting them will cause the project to fail or terminate. As such, they must be continually focused on by core team members, the sponsor, crucial stakeholders, and even third-party providers.

Project imperatives can relate to project schedule and the business case—for example, an end date that must be met or the project will fail, or a cost, risk, or payback threshold beyond which the project cannot be justified and will be cancelled. Most often, the project imperatives relate to the level of quality of the project deliverable—for instance, the new Web site must have an uptime rate of 99.5 percent, or the efficacy of the new cough syrup must provide twelve-hour relief.

In addition to being the essentials that must be continually focused on throughout the project by all team members, the project imperatives have these attributes:

- They provide the foundation for risk assessment.
- They empower team members with the basis to make crucial and timely decisions on the spot.

- They provide the basis for measuring success and provide inputs for the 7 Win Conditions of eXtreme project management.

Program Breakdown Structure

No project lives in isolation. There is always an entire constellation of projects that is required to achieve the overall objective. These related projects have to be commissioned by the project sponsor. Similar to an organization chart, the program breakdown structure (PBS) identifies the family of related projects that comprise the complete program. The PBS is usually a real eye-opener for the sponsor, who seldom realizes the extent to which other projects are needed for the entire program to succeed.

Product Vision

At this point, there is usually little to go on that would nail down the specifications of the ultimate deliverable. Nonetheless, in preparation for the second sponsor meeting, the project manager needs to get something started on paper no matter how tentative— the best description or profile of the final project deliverable possible at the moment as envisioned by the sponsor. It will, of course, change significantly during the scoping meeting. Ask yourself, "What is the project deliverable supposed to do? How well is it expected to perform? What else do I know about the deliverable?"

Pinpointing the Deliverable's Useful Life

The purpose of the deliverable's useful life (DUL) factor is to get an understanding as to the level of support for the product or system that will be required once it goes into service. There are three possible levels of commitment to the deliverable after it is produced. It's vital to know which level you are going after because that will drive the project's scope of work as well as the requirements for quality:

One-time fix: The project deliverable is a quick fix and is intended to solve an immediate problem. There is no intention of sticking with it. It will not be maintained or upgraded. Once the product or system serves its immediate purpose, we'll remove it and replace it with the real thing or it will not be replaced at all.

Deliver and fix: Deliver it now, improve it later. We know the project deliverable will fall short of what is needed, but we have to get something out there no matter what. Later, we'll reengineer it or rework the weak parts. I call this one "kiss and make up."

Long-term commitment: The deliverable must be perfect the first time out. We can't afford to ask for forgiveness. Once it's out there, it has to be solid. The new parachute has to work the first time. We'll be modifying or adding to it, but what we deliver out of the gate has to be done right. I call this, We're getting married."

If the strategy is a one-time fix, then you need to get a commitment from the sponsor to pull the plug. Otherwise, those who follow you will be saddled with time and money-draining efforts that can go on for years in a frustrating attempt to maintain a faulty product or system.

If the sponsor wants to play kiss and make up, then your job is to ensure that follow-on funding is available and that product support is in place. The DUL Factor contributes to the Shared Value of clarity of purpose.

The 7 Win Conditions

Win Conditions are a set of variables that define how success will be measured on an eXtreme project. They answer the question, "On what basis will we declare victory?" Following are the Win Conditions that apply to any project. Although the type of measure (money, time, or something else) is the same on all projects, each specific project will differ on how each condition is defined and how important the sponsor and crucial stakeholders consider each one to be for success. These are the 7 Win Conditions that are prioritized by those crucial stakeholders who are the project's customers or beneficiaries:

- Stakeholder (for example, customer) satisfaction
- Schedule (being on time)

- Budget (people, capital, other resources)
- Scope (the range of features or functions to be included in the project deliverable)
- Quality (how good the deliverable has to perform)
- Return on investment (the importance of meeting the targeted economic return)
- Team satisfaction (importance of team members having a fulfilling experience)

It's up to the sponsor and crucial stakeholders, not the project manager, to prioritize the 7 Win Conditions. The rule is that you can have only one must-meet and one optimize Win Condition at any one time. The other five are accomplished within acceptable parameters as defined by the sponsor and crucial stakeholders. Rob Thomsett (2002) uses a device called sliders to calibrate success. Each success slider can be set to on or off or graduated somewhere in between by stakeholders and the sponsor.

In practice, the Win Conditions also serve as a set of trade-offs. If the schedule is shortened, then more resources (budget) will likely need to be added. If the budget is cut, certain features or the level of quality will have to be cut to compensate. If more features are added or the level of quality required is increased, this will bear on customer and team satisfaction. Customers may be happier, but the team may not be if they are expected to work overtime to get it done, unless the schedule is increased or more resources are added. And if more resources are added, this may affect the project's return on investment. These decisions belong squarely in the sponsor's court.

eXtreme project management looks at all seven conditions, where traditional project management emphasizes the iron triangle ("bring it in on time, on scope, and on budget"). In eXtreme project management, we recognize the shortsightedness of this thinking. Even if you succeed in meeting the iron triangle criteria but fail to meet ROI expectations, the project has little redeeming value. This is equivalent to the operation being a success but the patient dies. That's why eXtreme project management extends from initial concept through the realization of business benefits. eXtreme project management, with its Shared Value of people first, also explicitly builds in team satisfaction as a measure of success.

In practice, the best time to have the Win Conditions discussion is after the skinny, project boundaries, project imperatives, program breakdown structure, and product vision have been agreed to. These elements, and especially the project imperatives, provide the context and input for a more focused discussion of Win Conditions.

As process leader, manager, and facilitator of the project's flow of emotions, thoughts, and interactions, you're off the hook here: you don't own the results of the Win Conditions discussion; your stakeholders do. And when they can't come to agreement, your sponsor makes the call. Identifying Win Conditions is among your most important project management tools and the process you lead for prioritizing the project's success factors, one of your greatest services to the project.

Identifying Win Conditions is among your most important project management tools.

Once the project is implemented, it's likely that the Win Condition priorities will change, as well as how each condition will be measured. For instance, the sponsor may determine that for business reasons, quality and not schedule is now the must-meet Win Condition. eXtreme project management continually calibrates project success against its expected ability to meet the intended business outcome. If the equation no longer works out, this is reason enough to kill the project.

The Second Sponsor Meeting

Once you have completed the first iteration of the Prospectus, you are ready to go back to your sponsor and review it with him or her, make adjustments based on the sponsor's feedback, and then get the sponsor to agree to the Prospectus as amended.

As you review each of the elements with the sponsor, you should not expect the sponsor to like or agree with everything. The sponsor may well want to change the Win Conditions. The program breakdown structure may be a real eye-opener. Your job is not to insist on your version of the Prospectus (remember that it is the sponsor's project, not yours), but to get these issues on the table and come up with a version of the Project Prospectus that the sponsor agrees to. Your job is to press the sponsor for decisions on each element of the Prospectus—decisions that you both realize may change as the project moves along.

Often a sponsor will refuse to be pinned down during the meeting and will say, "I'll get back to you." You cannot prevent this from happening, but you can insist that the sponsor really needs to get back to you. If your second meeting with the sponsor does not lead to the sponsor's agreeing to the Prospectus, you are headed straight for project hell. Moreover, if you can't even get the sponsor to sit still for the second meeting, you are already going down in flames.

Preparing for the Second Meeting

In order to begin to get his arms around the project and prepare for his second meeting with the sponsor, Noah drafted the Project Prospectus. He got out his copy of his favorite book, *eXtreme Project Management*, and refreshed himself on what elements of the Project Prospectus he would need to get started on right away. At this point, there was little to go on that would nail down the specifications or features of the vaccine. Nonetheless, in preparation for the second meeting, Noah wanted to get something started on paper, no matter how tentative. He expected it to change significantly during the second meeting with the sponsor, and change yet again when he brought in key players for the scoping meeting. With his notes from the first meeting and his copy of this book, he started to draft a preliminary version of these key items:

- The 3-sentence project skinny
- The in-scope and out-of-scope chart
- The project imperatives
- The program breakdown structure

- The product vision
- The 7 Win Conditions

Together, these formed the start of the Project Prospectus. Noah took his time with each item, and as he went along, it dawned on him that there was an entire constellation of projects that would be required to achieve the overall objective of saving the Selected Ones from the X-Virus. The PBS, in consequence, contained a great many things that the sponsor had never mentioned. The program included his vaccine project as well as all the related projects that were out of scope for the X-Virus Vaccine Project. These other related projects would have to be commissioned by the project sponsor. By following the guideline for questions to ask the sponsor, Noah was pleasantly surprised as to how much information he had already collected for the Project Prospectus.

Armed with the first draft of the Project Prospectus, he was ready for the second meeting with the sponsor. The purpose of the second meeting, in Noah's mind, was to clarify any ambiguities and to make modifications to the sponsor's vision for the project.

Conducting the Second Sponsor Meeting

As before, the second sponsor meeting began with a terrific volley of thunder and lightning. Noah and Gabriel enjoyed the show, but then got down to business. During the second meeting, Noah reviewed each of the elements he prepared with the sponsor. Gabriel did not like how Noah had worded the business outcome in the project skinny and made changes that helped clarify the project for Noah. The program breakdown structure was a real eye-opener for Gabriel, who had not realized the extent to which other projects would be needed for the entire program to succeed. He indicated to Noah that he would review the entire project structure after the meeting and either approve of each ancillary project or call Noah in to discuss it. After going through each aspect of the first iteration of the Prospectus and making numerous changes, they reached a common understanding on all items. Gabriel wanted to set them in stone, but Noah reminded him that on eXtreme Projects, it isn't wise ever to set anything in stone but rather consider it to be a baseline subject to change. Exhibit 8.3 is what Noah and his sponsor agreed to as a result of the second meeting.

Exhibit 8.3. First Version of the Project Prospectus for the X-Virus Vaccine Project as Approved by Sponsor

The Project Skinny

Objective (What?)	Save the Selected Ones from dying from the X-Virus
The Skinny	
Deliverable (How?)	*Who will do what for whom?*

1. The Anti-Virus Team will develop a vaccine and inoculate qualified humans and animals from contracting the X-Virus.

When will it be over?

2. This project will be considered complete when the Selected Ones have been inoculated.

What's the purpose?

Outcome (Why?)

3. To establish a 100 percent increase in peace and prosperity on earth within four generations

   • To increase per capita revenues from earth's inhabitants from 18,000 to 24,000 drachmas in four generations

   • To decrease overhead costs to maintain planet earth from 18,000 to 16,000 drachmas per capita in four generations

Project Boundaries Ins and Outs

In-Scope Work

• Profile the X–Virus based on the sample provided.

• Formulate the vaccine.

• Arrange for clinical trials in humans and animals.

• Test the packaging and stability of the vaccine.

• Circumvent FDA approval.

• Provide formulations, methods, and process requirements to manufacturing.

• Inoculate the Selected Ones.

Out-of-Scope Work

• Qualify and choose the animals and people to receive the vaccine.

• Produce vaccines for other (non-X) viruses.

• Research and develop preventions.

• Create antidotes or cures for those who contract the X-Virus.

• Develop preventions based on non-traditional medicine (Chinese medicine, new age healing and crystals, religion and prayer, metaphysics, psychology).

• Produce and distribute the vaccine.

• Repopulate the earth.

• Develop a public relations program.

Exhibit 8.3. First Version of the Project Prospectus for the X-Virus Vaccine Project as Approved by Sponsor, Cont'd

Project Imperatives

Sufficient time to test the vaccine's effectiveness

Side effects do not prevent the ability to reproduce

In time to inoculate Selected Ones

Program Breakdown Structure

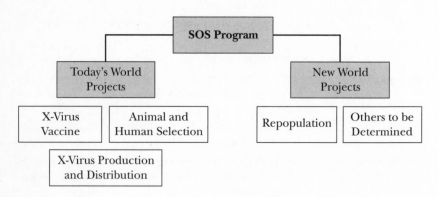

Product Vision

Capability   Arrests the virus in animals and humans

- Quality: takes effect in twenty-four hours maximum
- Side effects do not interfere with healthy reproduction
- Serum does not require refrigeration. Can withstand temperatures from $-60°$ to $+150°F$

Administration   By injection. What about other forms of intake? How about oral? Liquid? Pill?

Packaging   To be determined

DUL factor   Long-term commitment. Must be perfect the first time out. May need to inoculate again at some future date should the virus reappear once the new world has been established. May later be administered in other forms.

Exhibit 8.3. First Version of the Project Prospectus
for the X-Virus Vaccine Project as Approved by Sponsor, Cont'd

7 Win Conditions

		Metric
1. Schedule	Must meet	11/9: Selected Ones inoculated
2. Quality	Optimize	Vaccine to take effect within twenty-four hours. No adverse side effects regarding the ability to produce healthy offspring.
3. Scope (features: packaging, dosage size, and others)	Acceptable	To be determined
4. Resources	Acceptable	Not to exceed 1.4 million drachmas
5. Return on investment	Acceptable	To be determined
6. Stakeholder satisfaction (Selected Ones)	Acceptable	They don't have to like being vaccinated. It just has to work.
7. Team satisfaction	Acceptable	To be determined

In this chapter, we have described the first part of the Visionate cycle and, in the parallel universe, followed Noah through it, reaching agreement on the sponsor's Vision of the project. In the next chapter, we take The Flexible Project Model, Critical Success Factor 3, to the next step: translating the sponsor's vision into a collective vision shared among the project's crucial and other key stakeholders.

eXtreme Project Management Model
Applying the Quantum Mind-Set

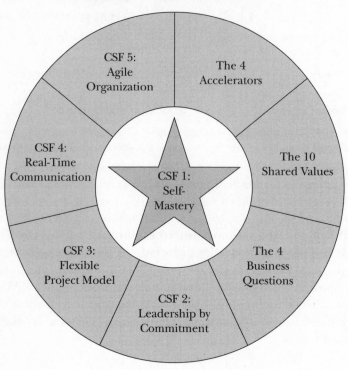

Chapter Nine

Visionate: Establishing the Collective Vision

Let your plan be for the best for all involved as well.
JAH

The Visionate cycle consists of two interacting components: (1) the sponsor's vision of the project and (2) the collective vision of the project. Once you have established a good understanding of the sponsor's vision, which should be the result of the second sponsor meeting, you need to begin laying the groundwork for translating it into a collective vision. The focus here is still on Business Question 1: Who needs what and why? Once the answer is expressed in the form of the collective vision, you can then move to the Speculate cycle where implementation planning takes place.

Creating the collective vision of the project is critical so that the venture can move forward with clarity, speed, and commitment. The collective vision is established in the scoping meeting, the landmark event that harnesses the collective intelligence of the group while extending ownership of the project vision from the sponsor to those whose support will be vital for the project's success. It's a major step in gaining and sustaining commitment to the project. Without it, an eXtreme project is doomed.

Sometimes (but not often enough) dead-end project ideas are killed or put on hold at the end of the Visionate cycle after the scoping meeting has taken place. A project is stopped when it becomes clear that it is unlikely to provide a satisfactory payoff in answer to Business Question 4: Is it worth it? or if the project is determined to be technically unfeasible.

This is a good outcome. When the Visionate cycle is done poorly or skipped and everyone rushes into planning, the result is usually that a half-baked idea gets planned and funded, wasting time and money and causing missed opportunities as more meritorious projects are abandoned or never see the light of day. If the answer to Business Question 4, Is it worth it? yields a favorable result, the project moves on to the Speculate cycle, where implementation planning takes place.

This chapter describes how the Visionate cycle, the first component of Critical Success Factor 3, the Flexible Project Model, moves from the sponsor's vision of the project to the collective vision. The results of the collective visioning process are highlighted in Figure 9.1.

- Preparing the Project Uncertainty Profile
- Estimating people and financial requirements
- Getting ready for the scoping meeting, including getting a go or no go from the sponsor, preparing the scoping meeting agenda, putting together the preliminary core team, identifying crucial stakeholders and key players, and preparing the sponsor for the scoping meeting
- Conducting the scoping meeting to create the collective vision: determining whether we are doing the right project, preparing the Benefits Map, and testing for answers to Business Questions 2 and 3
- Following up after the meeting

Preparing for the Third Sponsor Meeting

After the second meeting with the sponsor, you should have a fairly good idea of what the sponsor is asking for in terms of business objectives, deliverable, and business outcome. The next step is return to the sponsor with a good estimate of what it will take to deliver the project. The focus here is on Business Question 2: What will it take to get it? Start by making a general assessment of the risk associated with this project.

Figure 9.1. Critical Success Factor 3: The Flexible Project Model

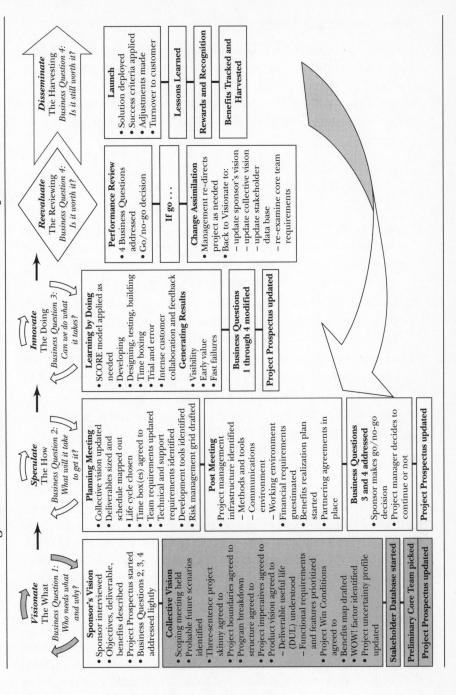

Project Uncertainty Profile

How risky is this venture? Sponsors and other key stakeholders rarely understand or want to face up to the extent of risk that surrounds their projects. Your job as eXtreme project manager is to expose the realities facing the project so that they can make informed decisions. There are four kinds of risk to address:

> *Your job as eXtreme project manager is*
> *to expose the realities facing the project.*

Business risk: What outside risks do we face? How strong is the competition? What could change that could have an impact on us, for better or worse? What about government regulations? How experienced are we in the target market?

Product risk: What risks do we face in being able to produce the project deliverable itself? Are we pushing the state of the art? Are we on the verge of a breakthrough?

Project risk: Do we have the ability to manage this project? The necessary resources? People? A qualified sponsor? How strong is the project sponsor? How great is our dependency on other projects?

Organizational risk: How politically sensitive or volatile is this project? How large is the stakeholder population? What priority is the project given?

Later, this quick assessment, called the Project Uncertainty Profile (PUP), will provide you and the team with the context within which you will plan and estimate the project in answer to Business Question 2: What will it take to get it? Exhibit 9.1 shows a sample PUP. Initiated by the project manager, the PUP eventually reflects input from the sponsor, crucial stakeholders and the core team.

Estimating Requirements

The estimates of the uncertainty associated with the project provide the background and context needed to begin thinking about what the project will require in terms of human and financial resources.

Exhibit 9.1. Project Uncertainty Profile

Low Risk				High Risk
0	1	2	3	4

Business Risk

	Factor		Rating
Clear and measurable	Ultimate business benefit	Unclear and not measurable	
Weak	Competition	Entrenched	
Local	Customer distribution	Global	
Established	Customer needs	Little known	
Veteran	Our market experience	Newcomer	
Stabilized	Government regulations	In flux	
Low	Financial exposure	High	
Flexible	Schedule	Fixed	
Stable	Market conditions	Volatile	
Total			
Mean			

Product (Deliverable) Risk

Clear	Functions and features	Unclear	
Clear	Quality and performance requirements	Unclear	
Stable	Core technology	Rapidly changing	
In place	Support systems and processes	Nonexistent	
Clear	Completion criteria	Unclear	
Attainable	Critical success factors	Unattainable	

Exhibit 9.1. Project Uncertainty Profile, Cont'd

	Factor		Rating
Low	Technical complexity	High	
Excellent	Track record with similar product	Poor	
Total			
Mean			

Project Risk

Reliable	Outside vendors	Unreliable	
Low	Complexity of the project	High	
Highly experienced	Team member expertise	Inexperienced	
Dedicated to this project	Team member availability	On multiple projects	
High	Project manager's control over resources	Low	
Expert	Project manager's experience	Novice	
Dedicated	Project manager availability	Multiple projects	
Light and flexible	Project management methodology	Bureaucratic and rigid	
In place	Project management infrastructure	Not established	
Satisfying	Likely quality of life on project	Dissatisfying	
Adequate	Incentives available	Not available	
Low	Dependency on other projects	High	

Exhibit 9.1. Project Uncertainty Profile, Cont'd

	Factor		Rating
Excellent	Track record with similar projects	Poor	
Clear	Who the sponsor is	Unclear	
Immediate	Sponsor availability	Delayed	
High	Sponsor's influence and reach	Low	
Total			
Mean			
	Organizational Risk		
Low	Political sensitivity	High	
Fast	Approval cycles	Slow	
Low	Number of stakeholder groups	High	
Low	Number of individual stakeholders	High	
Low	Crucial stakeholders' support	High	
Strong	Stakeholder participation	Weak	
Conducive	Team's working conditions	Distracting	
Co-located	Location of team	Dispersed	
Stable	Project portfolio priorities	Unstable	
Total			
Mean			

MEAN: ENTIRE PROJECT

No eXtreme project manager has all the answers to come up with a ballpark budget for the project. You will need to gather some colleagues in an informal meeting to get their input before returning for the third meeting with the sponsor.

People Requirements

The work to be done determines the people requirements. Having done your homework and drafted the project skinny, Ins and Outs, PUP, and other work products, you and your colleagues should be able to make a preliminary assessment of the critical skills needed on the project:

• The core project team. Not having the right skills and enough of them is a major reason for project failure. Now is the time to start thinking about putting together the core team. When you go to the next meeting with the sponsor, you want to be able to choose team members rather than being stuck with whomever you are handed or can round up. It's unlikely you will be able to assemble your ideal core team, but that should not stop you from identifying what the dream team would look like. If you fight for anything, it will be to have the right team in place.

• Other providers. Beyond the core team, project success will require the integration of many specialized suppliers (internal and external) in order to get the job done. Your project will also be dependent on the timely completion of related projects. You need to take inventory of these as well.

> *If you fight for anything, it will*
> *be to have the right team in place.*

Financial Requirements

Coming up with a budget is always tough at the early, vague stages of a project. Nonetheless, it is important to attempt to validate the sponsor's stated budget for the project. You will need to enlist help from others, especially those who know their way around budgets and have worked on similar projects.

When it comes to an eXtreme project, cost can never be predicted with much accuracy. That's why it can be essential to undertake the project in small chunks and establish a stream of short-term decision points (called time boxes) so that the sponsor can decide at multiple points along the way if it makes business sense to continue. (Time boxing is covered in the Speculate and Innovate cycles.) Here are some estimating tips that have proven useful on eXtreme projects:

- The term *exact estimate* is an oxymoron.
- An estimate is not a prediction.
- An estimate is not a commitment, a promise, or a guarantee (although it will most likely be taken as such). On eXtreme projects, there is no security. Your goal is to expose the folly of coming up with a secure estimate. Here, the PUP is your friend.
- The best estimates are those that are made by the people who will do the work *and* have a base of similar experience to draw on.
- Holding others accountable for your estimates goes a long way to demoralize the team; it practically guarantees failure.
- Avoid on-the-spot estimates. Ask the requester to elaborate on what is wanted. Indicate that there are a number of unknown factors that will go into the estimate and give a few examples. Point out that you don't want to give an off-the-cuff number that would discourage an otherwise good business decision or encourage a poor decision. Say you'll provide it tomorrow. This, of course, is the ideal. In the eXtreme world, you may not have this luxury and will be forced to come up with a number immediately.
- If you cannot buy time, provide an estimate range, for example: "We might be able to do it in eight weeks plus or minus three weeks. It will depend on our ability to shake loose a couple of people who are working on the Ramafranzit launch." *Never* give a single point estimate. Saying, "That will take us about eight weeks" is fiction given all the unknowns and puts you in the embarrassing position of holding yourself captive to a lie.
- When documenting your estimate in writing, always include the range. Say, "At this stage, until we know more, it could be from four to twelve weeks."

- No matter what you do or how you couch the estimate, the sponsor will take the most optimistic component of your estimate (or the midrange) and attempt to hold you to it. At the very least, knowing that you went on record with a range of numbers and did not capitulate to someone's fantasy number goes a long way in bolstering your self-esteem, if nothing else.
- Understand if you are being given a target or are being asked for an estimate. A target is when you are asked, "I want this by this date. What can you do for me by then?" An estimate is when you are asked, "Here's what I want. What can you give me by when and for how much?"

Go or No Go: The Third Meeting with the Sponsor

Once you have completed the PUP, decided on the skills that you will need on your core team, and put together at least a rough budget, you are ready for your third meeting with your sponsor. The purpose of this meeting is to:

- Review the level of risk associated with the project based on the PUP.
- Provide a very rough idea of the project's financial requirements, and discuss gaps compared with what the sponsor may have expected.
- Get approval to move forward and conduct a scoping meeting.

Many project managers make the mistake of starting out by focusing on budget issues. It is better to provide a context for the budget decision by starting out with a discussion of the risks associated with the project, using the PUP. Once the sponsor understands the risks, he will have a better understanding of, and appreciation for, the numbers in the budget.

Once the sponsor understands the risks,
he will have a better understanding of, and
appreciation for, the numbers in the budget.

When you do present the budget, emphasize that it is preliminary and based on the input of the several people you consulted. Remind the sponsor that you will have a better sense of the budget once the scoping and planning meetings are held.

At the conclusion of the third meeting, you need to press the sponsor for a go/no-go decision. In a very few cases, the evidence is simply overwhelming at this point that the project as framed makes no business sense, and the sponsor decides to end it right there or go back to the drawing board.

It is more likely that the sponsor will be suffering from sticker shock. In this state, she may simply declare a budget number and tell you to live with it (and not compensate by cutting back on the project requirements). If that's the case, your position is that you will have a better idea of what can be realistically done for the upper limit of her budget once the scoping and planning meetings are held. In other words, do not commit to the parameters, because neither you nor the sponsor knows the answer to Business Question 2: What it will take to do it?

It is also possible that you might suddenly find yourself in the middle of a negotiation. Nevertheless, there is no basis to negotiate because of all the uncertainty surrounding the project. Instead, refer to the PUP and say the numbers will be driven by the ability to mitigate some of the uncertainty as well as the information that comes up in the scoping and planning meetings about the work to be done and what it will take. In other words, your strategy is to postpone the negotiation.

All you are after is to ascertain if the sponsor wants to go to the next step: the scoping meeting: "Given what we know about the project right now and its uncertainty profile, is there enough business justification to continue or should we stop right here?" A go decision means that you will proceed to assemble your core team and move on to the scoping meeting. A no-go decision kills the project or sends you back to the drawing board to start over. Failure to get either decision leaves you floating in limbo.

Notice the Shared Values at play in this discussion with your sponsor: client collaboration, honest communication, results orientation, fast failures, and the one that drives the others: your courage.

Noah Gets Ready for the Third Sponsor Meeting, 2/8 Y2K BC

Having completed his second meeting with the sponsor and getting the sponsor to sign off on the Project Prospectus, Noah had a pretty good idea of what the sponsor was asking for. His next step was to return to the sponsor with a ballpark estimate of what it would take to deliver the project. He started out by making a general assessment of the risk associated with this project, using the guidelines set forth in his favorite book, *eXtreme Project Management*. Being a realist, Noah wanted to be sure that the sponsor and crucial stakeholders knew what they were in for regarding the riskiness of the X-Virus Vaccine Project. So he looked at all the key factors needed to complete the PUP: business risk, product risk, project risk, and organizational risk. He would use this quick assessment to provide his team with the context within which they would plan and estimate the project in answer to Business Question 2: What will it take to get it? Exhibit 9.2 shows how he assessed the uncertainty based on what he knew at this stage of the project. This was yet another eye-opener for his sponsor, who was not thinking at this level of detail.

Noah Asks for Help

After Noah completed the PUP, he soon realized that he did not have all the answers to come up with a ballpark budget for the project. There were too many variables, and too much specialized knowledge was required. He decided he needed expert advice, so he assembled some of his colleagues in an informal meeting to get their input before he returned for his third meeting with the sponsor. He knew he would soon have to put together the core team, and this would also be a good opportunity to sound people out about the project in terms of their interests and areas of expertise and to get ideas about other people to recruit. In thinking about Business Question 2, What will it take to get it? Noah considered what it would take in terms of people, including his core team and other providers, such as those on related teams and vendors, as well as financial requirements.

Having done his homework and drafted the project skinny, Ins and Outs, PUP, and other work products, Noah and his colleagues were able to make a preliminary assessment of the critical skills that would be needed

Exhibit 9.2. X-Virus Vaccine Project: Project Uncertainty Profile

Low Risk				High Risk
0	1	2	3	4

Business Risk

	Factor		Rating
Clear and measurable	Ultimate business benefit	Unclear and not measurable	1
Local	Recipient distribution	Global	4
Veteran	Global experience	Newcomer	4
Streamlined	FDA regulations	Lengthy	3
Low	Financial exposure	High	4
Flexible	Schedule	Fixed	4
Stable	Political conditions	Volatile	4
Total			24
Mean			3.4

Product (Deliverable) Risk

Clear	Vaccine profile	Unclear	3
Clear	Quality and performance requirements	Unclear	2
Stable	Core technology	Rapidly changing	1
In place	Support systems and processes	Nonexistent	3
Clear	Completion criteria	Unclear	0
Attainable	Profile attainable	Unattainable	4
Low	Technical complexity	High	4
Excellent	Track record with similar product	Poor	4
Total			21
Mean			3.0

Exhibit 9.2. X-Virus Vaccine Project: Project Uncertainty Profile, Cont'd

Project Risk

	Factor		Rating
Reliable	Outside vendors	Unreliable	3
Low	Complexity of the project	High	4
Highly experienced	Team member expertise	Inexperienced	3
Dedicated to this project	Team member availability	On multiple projects	4
High	Project manager's control over resources	Low	3
Expert	Project manager's experience	Novice	2
Dedicated	Project manager availability	Multiple projects	4
Light and flexible	Existing project management methodology	Bureaucratic and rigid	4
In place	Project management infrastructure	Not established	3
Satisfying	Likely quality of life on project	Dissatisfying	3
Adequate	Incentives available	Not available	2
Low	Dependency on other projects	High	3
Excellent	Track record with similar projects	Poor	4
Clear	Who the sponsor is	Unclear	0
Immediate	Sponsor availability	Delayed	1
High	Sponsor's influence and reach	Low	0
Total			42
Mean			2.6

Exhibit 9.2. X-Virus Vaccine Project: Project Uncertainty Profile, Cont'd

Organizational Risk

	Factor		Rating
Low	Political sensitivity	High	4
Fast	Approval cycles	Slow	3
Low	Number of stakeholder groups	High	4
Low	Number of individual stakeholders	High	4
Low	Crucial stakeholders' support	High	To be determined
Strong	Stakeholder participation	Weak	To be determined
Conducive	Team's working conditions	Distracting	3
Co-located	Location of team	Dispersed	3
Stable	Project portfolio priorities	Unstable	4
Total			25
Mean			3.6
MEAN TOTAL PROJECT			3.0

on the X-Virus Vaccine Project and help Noah to build a fact-based case for his next meeting with the sponsor.

From past projects, Noah realized that not having the right skills and enough of them was a major reason for project failure. He began putting together a list of people he wanted on his core team. Later, his position with the sponsor would be to choose his team members rather than being stuck with whomever he was handed or could round up. "If I fight for anything," he thought, "it will be to have the right team in place."

Estimating the financial requirements was a tough job given just how vague the project was at this point. Nonetheless, Noah felt it was important to attempt to validate the sponsor's stated budget for the project. He enlisted the help of Feldon from finance.

From experience, Noah knew that sponsors always have a maximum dollar figure in mind for their project, even though they might not come right out and say so. And if they didn't mention it, it was his job to pry it out. Noah would do this by asking, "What if this project cost 250,000 drachmas?" "What if it cost 500,000 drachmas? What if . . . ?" When the sponsor started to twitch and stutter or get red in the face, he would know that he had discovered the sponsor's threshold of perceived business value for commissioning the project.

Noah had wondered how sponsors came up with their budget numbers. Sometimes they were based on hard data or a vague recollection of a similar project. But most of the time, he found that they had pulled it out of their left ear. And that was okay with Noah at this point. His goal was to identify the gap between what he thought and what the sponsor had in mind. Establishing that there was a gap was his way of interjecting reality into the situation from the beginning.

Once before, Noah had been burned badly by not questioning the schedule or the budget. On one project when he didn't question the budget or the completion date, both had turned out to be wildly unrealistic. In effect, he had committed to a pipe-dream and was doomed from the outset. And at the end, *he* was held accountable for someone else's fiction.

Estimating was one of the more slippery slopes Noah had encountered. His saying was, "You're damned if you do and more damned if you don't." And when it came to an eXtreme project, he found that the cost could never be predicted. His philosophy was not to give unpleasant surprises a chance to take root. This practice also helped him sleep better at night. The Shared Value of quality of life was practically tattooed on his forehead.

Over time, Noah had come to rely on the list of estimating tips found in favorite project management book.

Noah's Third Meeting: Business Questions 3 and 4

Having done his homework, Noah was ready for his third meeting with the sponsor. Its purpose was to review the level of uncertainty associated with the project, acquaint the sponsor with the rough budget outline, and get the sponsor's decision on whether to move forward.

Noah felt a normal amount of stress as he approached the sponsor's office. He reminded himself of the Shared Value of courage, which means to have the fear and do it anyway—"Do it scared," for short. The customary clap of thunder and bolt of lightning signaled that he was to enter Gabriel's chamber.

Noah made the classic mistake of starting out by showing the sponsor the numbers instead of first reviewing the PUP that he had drafted (and would later be updated during the scoping meeting):

Noah's range:	2.4 to 4.4 million drachmas
Sponsor's budget number:	1.4 million drachmas

Gabriel had an adverse reaction and was quick to respond? "What! Where in creation did you get those numbers?"

Remembering the Feelings → Facts → Solutions model and the importance of practicing emotional intelligence, Noah agreed with Gabriel that there was a significant gap: "Yes, I can see why you'd be taken back. My numbers are quite different." And practicing a little self-disclosure power plus honest communication, Noah said, "I felt the same way when I saw my numbers. The gap was so large that I had quite a bit of trepidation about showing you these figures."

Gabriel seemed to calm down. Having dealt with the feelings surrounding the numbers, Noah then proceeded to go over his rationale for his budget estimate and started out by going over the PUP. Once Gabriel saw the connection between Noah's numbers and the PUP, which Gabriel agreed was fundamentally on target, he calmed down. It also didn't hurt that Noah mentioned that he did not come up with his estimate alone. He went on to say, "We will have a better set of numbers once the scoping and planning meetings are held. At that point, they will be based on the experience of those who will be doing the actual work."

After the stardust settled, Noah asked Gabriel if he should proceed to schedule a scoping meeting. He got the white light to go ahead.

Getting Ready for the Scoping Meeting

If you receive a go from the sponsor, you need to move ahead to the scoping meeting, a good example of where the 4 Accelerators are really needed. The accelerators, as you will remember, serve to unleash motivation and innovation, essential for projects that are high stress and demand creative approaches:

1. Make change your friend.
2. Build on people's desire to make a difference.
3. Create ownership for results.
4. Keep it simple.

In preparing for this meeting, I suggest looking back at Chapter Six to refresh your memory of how to get ready for and conduct a good meeting. Also, review the facilitation tips found in that chapter and in the eXtreme Tools and Techniques section at the end of the book.

Preparing the Scoping Meeting Agenda

You'll recognize that you already have done a lot of preparation for the scoping meeting: all of the work you've put into the Project Prospectus forms the basis for the scoping meeting agenda. Your agenda, then, will list a set of tangible work products that will be subjected to discussion, clarification, and modification by the meeting participants. In keeping with the Shared Value of results orientation, I recommend you express work products in the past tense, which makes them more tangible and gives people in the room a feeling of closure:

- Three-sentence project skinny, Ins and Outs, and Project Imperatives revised
- Product vision agreed to
- PUP updated
- Win Conditions agreed to
- Benefits map understood
- Probable future scenarios identified
- Action items agreed to

Among the other topics to include on the agenda are these:

- An assessment of Business Questions 2 and 3: What will it take to get it? Can we get what it takes? Given the budget estimating work you did in preparation for this meeting with the sponsor, you again have a head start here.
- A rough assessment of Business Question 4: Is it worth it?

You may have noticed that the scoping meeting has been roughly organized around the 4 Business Questions, where the work products focus primarily on Business Question 1: Who needs what and why?

All told, a scoping meeting can last anywhere from four hours to up to two days, depending on the project. In addition to the work products, allow thirty minutes at the start for the sponsor to express his vision of the project and answer questions. Also, slot a time at the end of the meeting (usually sixty minutes) for the sponsor to return and review the latest version of the work products.

To get ready for the scoping meeting, you need to pull together your preliminary core team, identify crucial stakeholders and key players, and put together the scoping meeting agenda. You should then review all of these items with the sponsor and enlist her help in recruiting people to come to the scoping meeting.

Putting Together the Preliminary Core Team

Most eXtreme Projects involve multiple teams. Subteams do the actual work of the project and are composed of technical and subject matter experts, including customer experts. In my client practice, the eXtreme core team is a team of teams, that is, the leaders or project managers of the various subteams. Core teams are typically cross-functional and cross-hierarchical. The subteams are typically chosen after the scoping meeting. But the core team, although tentative, is chosen to participate in the scoping meeting.

In putting together your core team (see Chapter Six), your options are to press hard to reserve the right to pick the people you need (inside or outside the organization) or, if you don't win on that, to reserve the right to veto anybody who has been picked on your behalf. You want competent people who have the necessary time to spend on the project, and you need to verify that they have the time.

Identifying Crucial Stakeholders and Key Players

A stakeholder is someone who can affect the success or failure of the project either before or after the project has been completed. They can be internal or external to the organization and include those who will provide inputs to the project, such as needed products and services, funding, approvals, resources, and other projects that you will rely on for your project. Stakeholder management is the soft glue that holds the eXtreme project together. (Chapter Seven addressed how to identify and manage relations with stakeholders.)

Reviewing the Agenda and Preparing the Sponsor

The draft agenda of tangible meeting work products is another opportunity to demonstrate the value added of project management, as well as to reinforce your role as manager and facilitator of the thoughts and interactions that keep the project moving toward its business goal. By gaining the sponsor's input, you are creating ownership for the meeting results. Again, it's her project and her meeting. You are the catalyst.

Impress on the sponsor the need to show up at the meeting for at least thirty minutes to introduce the project and to come back later at the end to spend sixty minutes to review and approve the work products generated by the participants. An absent sponsor demonstrates a lack of commitment to the project and will quickly undermine the commitment of crucial stakeholders and the core team. If the sponsor is unavailable, it is better to postpone the meeting until the sponsor can participate. Avoid the trap of being the spokesperson for the sponsor. It's her project. If the sponsor can't make it and you can't postpone the event, then insist that she send a stand-in with sufficient organizational clout.

More often than not, project sponsors don't have a good understanding of their role in general; in particular, they can use help in being prepared for the scoping meeting. In this sense, you can see yourself as an unofficial, undesignated coach. Provide the sponsor with a brief outline to summarize her vision for the project (notice how the outline follows the objective, deliverable outcome model discussed earlier):

- The problem to be solved or the opportunity to be seized
- The deliverable that is expected to solve the problem or seize the opportunity
- The intended business outcome (added value to the business; financial benefit)

The intended outcome is where the WOW! factor fits in: that which makes the project exciting or compelling, serving to energize the stakeholders. If the WOW! factor is not already evident, you might be able to coax it out of the sponsor. (Chapter Six has a list of joggers that can help you help your sponsor uncover the project energizer.)

Recognize that one of the last things that crucial stakeholders and core team members want is another project to work on, so have the invitation to the scoping meeting go out under the sponsor's signature. You can include an advance copy of the Project Prospectus, although most will not read it, or at least state the three-sentence project skinny. Remember to schedule the sponsor to return at the end of the meeting to review the scoping work products.

Conducting the Scoping Meeting

Armed with an agenda, flip charts, markers, large sticky notes, snacks, and drinks, you work your way through the agenda in order to reach consensus on the meeting work products.

At the beginning of the meeting, it is very important to exercise Accelerator 3: Create ownership for results. Do this by letting all know that although preliminary work has been done to define the project, all items on the agenda are open for discussion and modification and that the prework was undertaken in order to give the project a head start by providing clarity and focus for the scooping meeting.

Getting agreement on the 7 Win Conditions usually causes the most discussion, and that is the very purpose. Unless conflicting expectations and opinions are reconciled, the project will be fraught with insidious conflict that strikes at the heart of the project: agreement on what constitutes success. The impact: the holy grail of commitment to the project will be illusive.

If the project cannot meet the Win Conditions of crucial stakeholders, then by definition it is dead. (You may recall from Chapter Seven the different ways that stakeholders can sabotage your project.) Your job as project manager and process leader is to expose the conflicting Win Conditions among the crucial stakeholders from the start, during the project scoping meeting, so that your sponsor can resolve them if others cannot reach agreement. The goal here is to foster a healthy discussion of differences, resulting in a set of critical priorities and basis for making trade-offs. Here are some tips to facilitate the process:

If the project cannot meet the Win Conditions of crucial stakeholders, then by definition it is dead.

- Display the project imperatives that have already been agreed on. These provide valuable input for the Win Conditions.
- Review the meaning of each of the Win Conditions as agreed to earlier with the sponsor.
- Have the stakeholders individually pick their top two. Tell them that their number one pick is their must-meet condition, and their number two pick is the optimize condition. All the rest will have to meet acceptable criteria to be defined later (during either this meeting or during the planning meeting).
- Open the discussion.

After the stakeholders have had a robust discussion of their initial rankings, a revote is taken. In the eXtreme scheme, you can have only one "must meet" priority and one "optimize" priority. Recall that the must-meet condition is defined as the overarching requirement: if it is not met, nothing else matters. "Optimize" is the next most important requirement. The other variables must stay within acceptable limits as agreed to by the sponsor. As the project progresses and the competitive climate and other factors change, it is not uncommon for Win Conditions to shift.

Are We Doing the Right Project?

One of the bigger traps in project management is to assume blindly that the project as initially defined is the right project to undertake. Although it's never too late to introduce this topic, the time to do so is early—either here in the Visionate cycle or later during the Speculate cycle.

*One of the bigger traps in project management
is to assume blindly that the project as initially
defined is the right project to undertake.*

For instance, if a project is a solution to a problem or opportunity, there are usually several possible options for achieving the desired result. Left unchecked, people will typically grab the first solution and run with it. I remember reviewing a project intended to reduce customer defections by upgrading the Web site, making it more user friendly. On closer examination, it turned out that the root causes of customer attrition had more to do with the shallowness of the product line and pricing structure, but no projects were planned to solve these problems.

As the conscience of the project, your role is to ask, "What other options are available to us to address the objective [the problem or opportunity] before us? What about outside forces?" eXtreme projects are subject to the volatility of external events, which can change the very nature of the project—render the project obsolete after a lot of work has been done or give it new life. What if a new competitor beats us to market? What if one drops out? What if the Federal Communications Commission decides to regulate cable TV? What if unsolicited telemarketing calls are banned? What if wireless Internet takes over?

At this meeting, your role and value is to ask the unasked questions and open eyes to possible future scenarios. Ask, "What if . . . ?" Or ask a more general question: "What events over the next few months to two years could change the direction we are going in with this project?"

The Benefits Map

The Benefits Map is the starting point for the benefits realization process. The purpose of the map is to ensure that there is a clear link between the project deliverable and the intended business outcome. Importantly, it shows how interim outcomes link to the end outcome. And finally, it flushes out major assumptions that must be validated.

The map also clarifies that it may take multiple projects to achieve the intended final outcome. That is, any one project alone may not result in delivering the business outcome or benefit to the organization. That's why eXtreme project management looks at the project from concept to the point of final outcome.

A Benefits Map uses different symbols with different meanings (Figure 9.2):

Boxes: Projects that contribute to one or more outcomes

Circles: Outcomes, that is, the results being sought, including interim outcomes that lead to the outcome or benefit

Arrows: Contributions, that is, the role played by elements of the chain in contributing to outcomes

Hexagons: Assumptions, that is, conditions necessary for the organization to realize the intended benefits (we may have little control over these)

The development of the Benefits Map is also an opportunity for the sponsor to begin to identify individual stakeholders who will be held responsible for realizing the intended benefits.

Figure 9.2. Sample Benefits Map

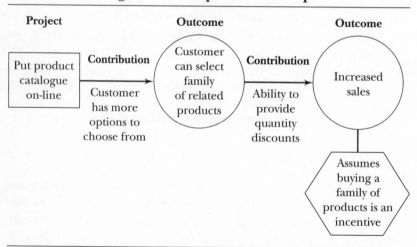

Source: Adapted from Thorp (1998). For another approach to benefits tracing, see Thomsett (2002).

Testing for Answers to Business Questions 2 and 3

Now that the project has been examined and modified, the timing is right to take an assessment of what crucial stakeholders and core team members think in answer to the business questions, "What will it take to do it? Can we get what it takes?" Although implementation planning will not be done until the Speculate cycle, people always seem to have an idea as to what a project will take in terms of time, money, and people. What's important here is not the numbers that people throw out, but their reasoning behind those numbers. Be sure to ask, "Tell us what your thinking is behind the number or range that you gave."

Also get an assessment to Business Question 4. Ask something like this: "Based on what we know now, does it appear that this project can achieve the desired business outcome? Why? Why not?

In asking Business Questions 2, 3, and 4, be prepared for emotionally based responses. This is your clue as to the real concerns, hopes, and aspirations of crucial stakeholders; they provide you and the sponsor with big clues as to what motivates these key people.

X-Virus Vaccine Scoping Meeting, 2/11 Y2K BC

In preparing for this meeting, Noah quickly refreshed his memory by checking back to Chapter Six in this book. There he found material on how to get ready for and conduct a good meeting. He also reread the material on facilitation tips.

Noah realized that the scoping meeting would be critical in gaining and sustaining commitment to the project, without which an eXtreme project is doomed. But Noah almost cancelled the meeting because Gabriel had a last-minute scheduling conflict. Having personally experienced the debilitating impact of a no-show sponsor on a project's mood and emotional well-being, Noah did not want to be party to a zombie project, one that had joined the ranks of the living dead. No sponsor is no way to kick off a project. Besides, Noah realized that this was not his project anymore than the general contractor owns the house he builds for another. It's the sponsor's project. Mustering up his courage, Noah was able to impress on Gabriel the need to show up at the meeting for at least thirty minutes to introduce the project and return later at the end to spend sixty minutes reviewing and approving the work products generated by the participants.

Because everybody's time was valuable (most in the room were working on at least four other projects, plus having to do their regular job as well), Noah took seriously the Shared Value of results orientation. He put together an agenda listing tangible work products that were expected to come out of the meeting for the X-Virus Vaccine Project.

Noah also set time slots for each work product and topic to be discussed over the day and a half they would be together. Some people were not pleased about having to spend the time, even though the initial announcement went out under Gabriel's signature. That e-mail concluded with, "If we don't have the time to figure out what we are doing, then we won't find the time to succeed."

The crucial stakeholders and other key players, including several members of the eventual eXtreme core team, settled into their seats. The four flip charts Noah ordered were standing there erect, ready to be called into action. The flip charts put into practice the Shared Value of visibility. Noah made sure that all twelve people in the room were armed with large sticky notes and black markers and a copy of the Project Prospectus that Noah and the sponsor had agreed on.

Gabriel sat down. A thunderbolt signaled the start of the meeting. After participants introduced themselves, a set of meeting norms were agreed to, and a timekeeper, scribe, and recorder were selected. Attention was called to the parking lot, where participants were able to use their sticky notes to post any open issues that would be better addressed after the meeting.

Gabriel, as the project sponsor, took twenty minutes to present the project, explaining what was driving this project to right-size Planet Earth in the first place. Gabriel then outlined the deliverable, that is, the solution that the project team was to come up with, to develop a vaccine, as well as the expected business outcome. Being sensitive to the concerns of those in the room who might not be among the Selected Ones, Gabriel indicated that golden wings would be made available to make the transition to the other side easier. He also stressed the drop-dead schedule for the project as well as what it was expected to cost. After an uncomfortable silence, fifteen minutes of questions and answers followed. With that, Gabriel left.

After the morning break, the twelve participants returned to examine Noah's draft of the three-sentence project skinny, the Ins and Outs, and project imperatives and then updated the vaccine's profile.

Are We Doing the Right Project?

Trinity, the head of global development for Genetics Unlimited, had been quiet, if not troubled, all morning. Something didn't compute. She glanced at the PUP and realized how much risk was associated with the X-Virus Vaccine Project. Then, leafing back to the front page in her Project Prospectus, she took a closer look at the stated business objective, which the sponsor had reiterated just few minutes earlier: "Business Objective: Save the Selected Ones from the X-Virus."

Then she got what was troubling her. "Scuse me, scuse me," she piped up, just as Noah was trying to turn people's attention to the Benefits Map. "Something's bothering me." (Women seem to be more at ease with self-disclosure power than men.) "If the business objective is to save the Selected Ones from the X-Virus, why are we limiting the solution to producing a vaccine? According to the PUP here, look at all the unknowns! We don't have a chance in hell. How many other, more certain ways might there be to save the Selected Ones?"

People started buzzing. Then Ezekiel, head of toxicology and a Guardian by temperament, and not one to be friendly to change, stood up and reminded the group, "We just heard from the sponsor, Gabriel, who is right up there with the Sponsor of All Sponsors. The sponsor said 'vaccine.' Who are we to question the sponsor? We have our marching orders. Let's not go off on tangents. Time is short enough."

Noah realized that this is the kind of confrontation that can happen when a quantum thinker and personality style like Trinity meets up with a Newtonian like Ezekiel, who likes to have things nailed down. Noah also realized that this was a good thing, although the conflict may feel uncomfortable at the moment.

Joshua, director of clinical trials, said, "Who are we *not* to question Gabriel? There's nothing more dangerous than a problem with just one solution, especially under these eXtreme circumstances. Failure is not an option. We need to hedge our bet. We need to consider our options here and bring them to our sponsor."

With the power bestowed in him as facilitator, Noah departed from the agenda and said, "Okay. Let's take a twenty-minute break from the vaccine project and do a quick brainstorm of possible other options to save the Selected Ones from the X-Virus. We can run these by Gabriel along with our recommendation on how to proceed in further exploring any of the options."

When Ezekiel and a few others started to object, Noah reminded them of the definition of an eXtreme project: "a high-speed, high-change, self-correcting venture in search of a desirable result. It's a *discovery* process. You need options. Locking into a solution too early can literally be deadly for all of us."

Considering Options

A quick brainstorming session ensued. Each participant jotted down their alternative ideas on sticky notes. Ezekiel sat there with arms crossed and never lifted his marker. At the end of the session, the group had come up with a list of options that was later organized into categories during lunch. The resultant flip chart page looked like this:

Sponsor's Objective: Save the Selected Ones from the X-Virus

Possible solutions to the problem

1. Develop X-Virus vaccine.
2. Prevent the virus.
3. Quarantine Selected Ones.
4. Develop an antibiotic.

Judith, in charge of clinical trials, took the initiative to write on a sticky note, "Ask sponsor if we should pursue options 2 through 4," and stuck it on the parking lot.

Scenario Planning

After wolfing down a lunch of hummus, tabouleh, and assorted veggies, the team reassembled. The next item on the agenda was to identify possible future scenarios.

From past projects, Noah realized that eXtreme projects are subject to the volatility of external events, which can change the very nature of the project and even render the project obsolete after a lot of work has been done. He thought to himself, "Gabriel is pretty close to the Sponsor of All Sponsors, but it's always dangerous to assume you know what was really going on. What if the team had done its work well and three weeks before the X-Virus was to strike, the strain was caught ahead of time by the folks at McIffy, the antivirus police? And then, in place of the X-Virus, the Sponsor of All Sponsors decided that right-sizing of the earth would now take place by an earthquake instead? With three weeks to go, there's no chance to recover from the news. How can we improve our odds?"

And that's how he explained it to the group, which gave him a perfect lead to the next item on the agenda, a brainstorming session to identify possible future scenarios that need to be anticipated because they could change the fundamental shape of the project. Noah broke the group into three subgroups. Each one was to identify up to five possible scenarios: catastrophic events that could wipe out the earth's population of humans and animals. The consolidated list of all three groups came out like this:

Biological disasters

- X-Virus
- Bubonic plague
- AIDS
- West Nile disease
- Lyme disease
- Hepatitis
- Yellow fever
- Smallpox

Human disasters

- Global war
- Holocaust
- Terrorism

Physical disasters

- Meteorite attack
- Invasion by extraterrestrials
- Massive earthquake
- Flood

Everybody's head was spinning. The group was feeling overwhelmed at all the possibilities, and a heavy blanket of FUD (fear, uncertainty, and doubt) descended over the room and sombered the mood.

What Project *Are* We Doing?

Donald Dirk, head of Earthland Security, was feeling the brunt of it all: "This is getting out of control. We can't possibly protect against all these eventualities."

All heads nodded in agreement.

"But," Noah said, "we can do some research and pick the top three to five most likely and plan for those." Judith wrote up a second sticky note, "Identify the highest-probability catastrophic events," and stuck it on the parking lot flip chart.

The day was coming to a close. People were worn out and confused. The meeting had raised more questions than it had answered. What is our project? Do we develop a vaccine? Or do we quarantine the Selected Ones? What if another disaster replaces the X-Virus? Are we supposed to assume it will be a flood? A meteorite storm? What *do* we do?

Given all the discussion and heated arguments that took place, Noah recognized that it is easy to lose track of what was actually accomplished during the day. He saw the need to reinforce the Shared Values of results orientation, visibility, and early value. To do this he referred to everyone's agenda and did a quick meeting audit. As he went through each agenda item, he simply asked the group to point to physical proof in the room that the topic had been addressed. The evidence was all over the place. They had updated the project skinny, modified the Ins and Outs, clarified the project imperatives, and identified the Win Conditions for the X-Virus Vaccine Project.

Finally, it hit Noah that his job as project manager was to facilitate the flow of both thoughts and emotions. Given the emotional content of the meeting and the stress associated with this eXtreme project, Noah went around the room and asked each participant to say in one or two words how they were feeling in view of the day. He did not comment on what each said. He simply acknowledged with, "Thanks."

Finally, he reminded everyone that the first item on tomorrow's agenda was to prepare for the sponsor review session that would take place at 11:00 A.M. That would be their opportunity to get answers to what options they should consider besides the vaccine and what catastrophic events they should prepare for.

The Next Morning

Just before Dirk left his office to join the scoping meeting, he fired up his Lookout Express to check any last-minute e-mails. He had a message from his boss:

Re: Save Our Species Program: New threat likely

Hello Dirk,

A late-breaking intelligence report indicates that a massive flood is nearly certain to immerse the planet just about the time the X-Virus is expected to hit.

Advise you take all precautions and make plans to build a flotation device to save the Selected Ones.

Sincerely,

F. Throckmorton

Chairman, Earthland

Late getting back to the meeting, Dirk entered making a dramatic appearance. "I've got news. I've got news." And he read Throckmorton's e-mail to the group.

A loud hush fell over the room. Then everybody broke into conversation at once. Noah let people talk and vent to each other before attempting to call the meeting back to order. Knowing the importance of managing the feelings before getting down to business and using self-disclosure power, Noah first acknowledged his own feelings to the group: "At this point I'm confused and uncertain about what we should be doing next. It's one thing after another."

Making that statement was enough to free up his own mind to compose two general questions for the group. He went around the table one by one. He asked, "Given this latest news, how are you feeling about this? What should we be doing now?"

After the last person spoke, it became quite evident that the group wanted to wrap up the work it had done on the X-Virus Project and prepare for the sponsor feedback session at 11:00.

Judith then generated a third sticky note for the parking lot: "Validate with the sponsor that a massive flood is coming." At the same time, the scribe added "Massive Flood" to the potential physical disasters already listed on the flip chart.

The Sponsor's Review of the Scoping Work

In preparation for the review session, the group quickly organized the flip charts and determined who was going to present what. They decided to pay special attention to the presentation of Win Conditions because these would determine exactly where the team would focus its efforts to ensure that the project deliverable, the vaccine, was successfully achieved.

The usual clap of thunder and flash of lightning signaled Gabriel's arrival. The team was particularly concerned about balancing the two top-priority Win Conditions of the project: the schedule was "must-meet" and the vaccine quality was "optimize." They were hoping to reverse these so that the end date would be declared flexible, allowing them time to focus primarily on the vaccine's quality as the must-meet condition.

Gabriel would not budge: "The date cannot be postponed. It is synchronized with other projects and cannot be moved. The X-Virus will hit on that date. This is no different from the Y2K BC project you all worked on, the one that saved all the world's computers from crashing at the stroke of midnight. Either you are ready or you are not. The drop-dead date of 11/9 is your single point of failure."

So be it. The room didn't like the answer, but at least there was clarity of purpose.

Trinity then proceeded to address the first of three parking lot topics and summarized the team's case for wanting to hedge their bet given all the uncertainty and risk surrounding this project. She indicated that there were other possible means to achieve the objective of saving the Selected Ones from the X-Virus. On the surface, several seemed to have a better chance for success, for example, quarantining the Selected Ones and developing an antibiotic.

The list of potential options was a real eye-opener for Gabriel, who started to appreciate just how complex this project was. Gabriel then recognized that the decision to develop an X-Virus vaccine in the first place was more of a knee-jerk reaction to the problem than a thoughtful examination of the options.

Noah was pleased with himself. One of his goals was to help stakeholders, including the sponsor, to identify options and begin to realize just what they were getting into. Noah could see from Gabriel's body language that they were getting through.

Gabriel agreed with Trinity: "Get back to me by Wednesday with your prioritized list of options to save the Selected Ones from the X-Virus. I like the PUP that Noah showed me. Use it to examine each of your options. Show me a list that ranks the options from least to most risky."

The next topic for discussion seemed to be the scariest of all: Which catastrophic event should they prepare for? Again, Gabriel's eyes were opened. Although he was aware of the high probability of a massive flood, little attention had been given to the possibility of other disasters. Somewhat embarrassed, Dirk nervously jumped in and stated that Earthland Security was in the process of identifying likely adverse events besides the X-Virus.

"It's now or never," said Gabriel. "Given the evidence I've seen, I'd put the massive flood at the top of the list of possibilities in addition to the X-Virus. Oh, and Dirk, have your group assess the likelihood of the other disaster events on that list by Thursday. The Sponsor of All Sponsors needs to start allocating funds and setting priorities before the project portfolio gets out of hand."

Noah asked the scribe to review the action items and then did a quick meeting audit by checking accomplishments against the agenda and the parking lot. The essential items had been covered, except for the Benefits Map, which had basically been overtaken by events. With his quantum mind-set, Noah wasn't about to go through an exercise that wasn't needed simply because he had a template for it.

The group left with mixed emotions: they felt good about what was accomplished, but also were feeling a great deal of stress about the work and uncertainty that lay ahead. Were they still doing the vaccine project? And what catastrophic event should they plan for? eXtreme projects seem to have more unknowns than knowns.

Despite the ambiguity, Noah was feeling pretty good about the meeting results, and he had realized the power of Accelerator 1: Make change your friend. The questions that Trinity had raised opened up new options. He now realized the importance of process power. It was clear from the meeting and the results that were produced. Anybody can be appointed project manager, but Noah had *earned* the right to be the project manager and to lead the process. He had the confidence of the crucial stakeholders and the sponsor.

After the Meeting

You're now a lot smarter (and perhaps a lot more anxious) about the project. But by definition, eXtreme projects don't go according to plan, which is why a quantum mind-set is critical. Nor do they exist in a vacuum. They exist in a web. Your eXtreme project will be affected by other projects, and other projects will depend on yours. For an example of just how complicated life can become in eXtreme project land, let's return to Noah.

> *By definition, eXtreme projects don't go according to plan, which is why a quantum mind-set is critical.*

Fast-Forward: The Plot Thickens, 2/13 Y2K BC

Noah and the Vaccine Team met the next day to reexamine their options. Was the vaccine solution *the* viable one? Or were there other more feasible options? Applying the PUP to each of their options, they ranked their choices in terms of greatest likelihood of success in saving the Selected Ones given the strict deadline:

Preventatives

1. Quarantine
2. Vaccine

Cures

1. Antibiotic
2. Massive doses of sunlight

On the side of preventatives, developing a vaccine turned out to be a far second choice, a real long shot. They also decided that they had a better-than-average chance of coming up with an antibiotic. As a result, they discarded their original project skinny. Instead of developing a vaccine, they decided to self-organize into two smaller teams, each with its own three-sentence project skinny. When it came to planning, Noah gained renewed interest in the Shared Values of fast failures and results orientation (Exhibits 9.3 and 9.4).

Vaccine Project Cancelled

Before proceeding to scoping and planning, Noah ran the team's new strategy by Gabriel. Looking at the PUP, Gabriel agreed the quarantine and antibiotic projects were much more viable options and ordered that the X-Virus Vaccine Project be "null and void." He then gave Noah the white light to proceed to scoping and planning each project.

Exhibit 9.3. The Quarantine Project: Three-Sentence Project Skinny

1. The Q Team will develop and implement a plan to quarantine the Selected Ones from the X-Virus.

2. Our project will be considered complete when the Selected Ones are safely protected from the X-Virus.

3. This project contributes to the sponsor's objective:

   • To establish a 100 percent increase in peace and prosperity on Planet Earth within four generations

   • To increase per capita revenues from Planet Earth's inhabitants from 18,000 to 24,000 drachmas in four generations

   • To decrease overhead costs to maintain Planet Earth from 18,000 to 16,000 drachmas per capita in four generations

---

Exhibit 9.4. The Antibiotic Project: Three-Sentence Project Skinny

1. The Antivirus Team will develop an antibiotic to cure the Selected Ones of the X-Virus.

2. Our project will be considered complete when the antibiotic is turned over to those who will administer it.

3. This project contributes to the sponsor's objective:

   • To establish a 100 percent increase in peace and prosperity on Planet Earth within four generations

   • To increase per capita revenues from Planet Earth's inhabitants from 18,000 to 24,000 drachmas in four generations

   • To decrease overhead costs to maintain Planet Earth from 18,000 to 16,000 drachmas per capita in four generations

---

Trinity was beaming to herself. If she had not raised critical questions during the scoping meeting, the team and sponsor may still have been pursuing the vaccine project, literally, a dead-end venture.

Noah learned a big lesson. When working under eXtreme conditions when information and circumstances change rapidly, you have to have the courage to junk the plan and start over again. Doing a great job of the wrong project is irresponsible. Noah made a note to himself on the inside front cover of his Project Prospectus:

I have 2 jobs:
1. To be sure that we are doing the right project
2. To be sure that we are doing the project right

Thursday: Dirk Returns with Evidence

By Thursday, Dirk was ready to present his findings to the sponsor. He had enlisted the research powers of the Global Intelligence Agency (GIA) along with the SBI, unaffectionately known as the Secret Bunglers of Investigations. Although neither agency was talking to each other, Dirk was nonetheless able to put "1 plus 1" together, as he would say it. Which potential disasters should Earthland Security be preparing for? According to the research, there was an 80 percent certainty that both disasters would strike by 11/9: the massive flood and the X-Virus.

The other disasters were also possibilities, but they were seen as several hundred years off and likely to hit after the Selected Ones had substantially repopulated in the new world.

Dirk recommended that any action on these events be postponed and that the focus of the SOS program be on saving the Selected Ones from the flood and the X-Virus. Gabriel bought the recommendation: "Good work, Dirk."

Noah Gets Another Project

No sooner had Dirk left than Gabriel grabbed his cell phone and called Noah: "Noah, I'm particularly concerned about the threat of a massive flood. Given your family's history of making wine casks for the Mesopotamia Brewery, I think you would be ideal to head the project to build a submarine to protect the Selected Ones from the flood."

Having said that and having learned from Trinity and the X-Virus experience, Gabriel immediately recognized that it was wiser to pose a project in terms of a problem to be solved or an opportunity to be seized rather than providing a singular solution.

Gabriel quickly rephrased his marching orders. "Noah, on second thought, let me put it this way: I want you to head the project to save the Selected Ones from the massive flood. That's the objective."

Noah was really feeling the stress of having to manage a third project in addition to the quarantine and antibiotic projects. He was overwhelmed with anxiety and that sinking sensation. By this time, he had learned to acknowledge and accept these feelings even though he didn't like having them, and as a result, he was quickly able to respond assertively and with clarity: "The quarantine and antibiotic projects will take up all of my time and more, especially because of all the stakeholder groups that will be affected. There's a lot of relationship management that will have to be done on these projects."

"Any ideas?" Gabriel asked. "Well, Trinity has led several other successful drug development projects recently. Plus, she brings a strong business perspective and has always been good at getting people to collaborate."

"Okay. Sounds like a good idea. I'll tell Trinity to go ahead and start scoping and planning for the antibiotic and quarantine projects. Oh, one more thing: I like the way you ran the X-Virus Vaccine scoping meeting and used those Project Prospectus and templates to capture the work products. We got quick results. Early value. I'd like you to coach Trinity on the way you did it. That way we can develop our own home-grown project management practice by working on real-life projects rather than wasting time sending people off to training classes and never seeing any substantial change in behavior and project performance."

Noah felt a huge burden lift off his shoulders. "Coaching was one thing. That way I can at least make a difference. But having to run three eXtreme projects was a no-win for everyone."

Noah was quick to call a meeting in order to evaluate options for meeting the objective of saving the Selected Ones from the flood. The group brainstormed these options:

Save the Selected Ones from the flood options
- Submarine
- Hot air balloons
- Ark
- Go to the moon
- Cryogenics
- Cloning

After completing a PUP on each option, they decided their best shot was to recommend building an ark given the state of technology and the time available. By now, Noah had established credibility with Gabriel. He was given the white light to proceed to scope out the ark project.

Web Site Project Introduced

Up until now, all attention had been riveted on protecting against the catastrophic events expected to take place on 11/9. Trinity was heading the antibiotic and quarantine projects, and Noah was managing the ark project. In a routine Huddle of Huddles meeting chaired by Dirk to synchronize the various SOS projects, Trinity raised a new set of questions:

- How would the Selected Ones be contacted, qualified, and kept informed before the disaster struck?
- What about *after* the disaster? Where would they go for information to orient themselves to the new world, to make the transition? They would need information to set up commerce, and if the flood came, they would need to begin to farm again and rebuild the infrastructure. How was this transition being handled?

Dirk raised the issue to Gabriel at the SOS steering committee meeting.

The Sponsor of All Sponsors and the others were quick to jump on it, and as a result, yet another project was added to the portfolio: to establish a full-service Web site to serve the Selected Ones before and after the disaster. The service was to be a profit generator, with revenues coming from subscriptions and transaction fees. Transactions fees would be charged for handling all purchases made through the site, which was expected to turn a profit within five years.

"Dirk, we'd like you to sponsor the SOS Web site project. Find yourself a project manager and go with it."

Rananda Gets the Nod

Dirk knew just who to pick: Rananda, head of Information Systems for Earthland Security. Rananda had led the team to develop Earthland's first Web site after being recruited from Mamazon.com, an Internet seller of anything and everything to anybody, anytime, anywhere.

That afternoon, Dirk called Rananda, told her he had a new project for her, and asked her to meet him at 10:00 A.M. the next day in his office to get the details.

Over dinner with Trinity the night before, Rananda had learned about the three-sentence project skinny. Trinity also mentioned that Noah, her coach, had a useful set of questions he used when meeting with a project sponsor for the first time: "I'll e-mail them to you tonight."

Rananda was prepared for her first meeting with Dirk. The interview questions she got from Trinity helped to keep Dirk focused, which was especially important that day since he felt quite scattered. Rananda left with her sponsor's answers pretty well nailed down to Business Question 1: Who needs what and why? At the meeting's end, they set a time for her to return and review her preliminary findings to Business Question 2: What will it take to get it?

As soon as she got to her office, she wrote down a draft of the project skinny to get her arms around the SOS Web Project and have a reference point for future discussions.

1. The SOS Web Team will build and launch a Web site that delivers vital information and e-commerce capabilities for the Selected Ones before and after the catastrophic event.

2. Our project will be considered completed once the Web site has stabilized.

3. This project contributes to the objective of establishing a 100 percent increase in peace and prosperity on Planet Earth within four generations.

She also noted, "The Web site needs to be up and running by 5/15, 11 weeks from today!" That was the date that would be required to begin the process of selecting, qualifying, and registering the Selected Ones.

Two days later, Rananda returned with her preliminary answers to Business Question 2: What will it take to do it? Dirk nearly choked on Rananda's SWAG (statistical wild ass guess) for what it would cost to establish the Web site. Not only that, Rananda provided a wide cost range, which did not sit well with Dirk's Newtonian temperament: he could deal with only single point estimates.

Armed with her completed version of the PUP, she was able to defend her estimate. She got the green light to call a scoping meeting, which was held the following Monday.

The SOS Web Site Project Scoping Meeting

Working together, the team and crucial stakeholders established a good-enough collective vision of the Web site project: possible future scenarios were prioritized, the project skinny was modified, and project boundaries and project imperatives were agreed to. As is typical, the most heated discussions were around the 7 Win Conditions.

The 7 Win Conditions

Everybody seemed to want all seven conditions to be number 1 priority. What were to be the must-meet and optimize conditions? Dirk, as project sponsor, ended up making the final call (Exhibit 9.5).

Rananda thought to herself, "Dirk may be a pain in many ways, but at least he's a sponsor who makes quick decisions."

The Benefits Map

Of all the work products that came out of the scoping session, the Benefits Map really got Dirk's attention (see Figure 9.3). When Rananda introduced the concept, Dirk was dumbfounded. "What in Earthland's name is that?" he asked pointedly.

Although he had never heard of a Benefits Map before, the visual nature of it made a good first impression. Moreover, as a Guardian-type personality, his well-honed Newtonian management style really liked the idea of arrows connected to circles and hexagons. It appealed to his penchant for wanting to link cause and effect even when there was no sure link.

Rananda explained that the map helped to ensure that there was a link between the project deliverable and the intended business outcome. Responsibilities were assigned for realizing the benefits.

Peering over his bifocals, Dirk observed, "In the past we just assumed that there was a link between the objective, the project, and the outcome. How do you read the map?"

Exhibit 9.5. SOS Web Site Project: Win Conditions

1. Quality	Must meet
2. Schedule	Optimize
3. Scope: Functions and features	Acceptable
4. Resources	Acceptable
5. Return on investment	Acceptable
6. Customer satisfaction	Acceptable
7. Team satisfaction	Acceptable

Figure 9.3. SOS Web Site Project: Benefits Map

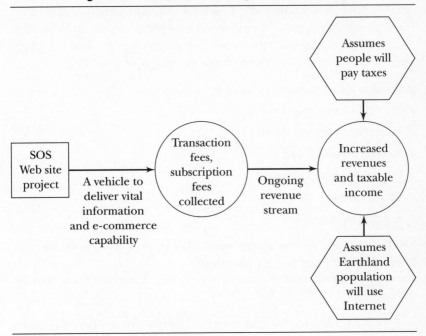

Everyone listened closely as Rananda explained. "The map reads as follows. The objective of the SOS Web Site Project is to be a vehicle for delivering vital information and e-commerce capabilities to the Selected Ones. This vehicle is expected to contribute by generating transaction fees and subscription revenues. These fees and revenues are intended to contribute ongoing revenue streams, which will contribute to the end benefit of increased revenues and taxable incomes from Earthlanders. The final benefit of increased revenues is predicated on the assumptions that Earthlanders will use the Internet and actually pay their taxes."

Feldon from finance interjected, "Can we really assume that people will pay their taxes? Do we need to put in place a collection mechanism?"

Dirk was quick to reply, "Chairman Throckmorton and his staff don't have enough bandwidth to focus on the postcatastrophic event projects. We'll cross that bridge when it collapses. Let's just worry about what we have in front of us now."

An uneasy silence blanketed the room. Something didn't sit right. What *do* we need to put in place *now* to bridge the gap between the catastrophic event and the new world? But before any one could raise a question, War-ren Windbreaker, Earthland's Chief Information Officer, jumped in: "Enough scoping already. I've got another meeting." So did everyone else.

Rananda proceeded to summarize the meeting. She and the group went down the list and checked off the meeting work products:

✓ Possible future scenarios prioritized

✓ Project Skinny agreed to

✓ Project boundaries agreed to

✓ Product vision agreed to

✓ Project imperatives agreed to

✓ Win Conditions decided

✓ Benefits Map updated

The last item on the agenda was to schedule the planning meeting. They agreed to meet the day after next.

We have seen in this and the preceding chapters how the spon-sor's vision is captured by the project manager, and then translated into a collective vision—a composite of the sponsor's vision as re-fined through an iterative process discussion and collaboration with crucial stakeholders.

Once the dust has settled on the Visionate cycle and you've up-dated the Project Prospectus, you have another opportunity to see if the sponsor wants you to take the project to the next step: the planning meeting. Here, you can test the sponsor's responses to Business Questions 3 and 4. This is also an opportunity to test your own answer to Business Question 4: Is it worth it to you?

I've seen many projects get to the point where it is clear that the project can't succeed in meeting the Win Conditions and the sponsor is not willing to make trade-offs that would give the project a fair shot. It's time for self-mastery and self-examination. Courage and quality of life will patiently await your call. You have the option and the consequences of staying on or asking to be reassigned. It is not an easy choice, but it is an inescapable one.

You're now ready to move to Speculate, the second cycle of the Flexible Project Model.

eXtreme Project Management Model
Applying the Quantum Mind-Set

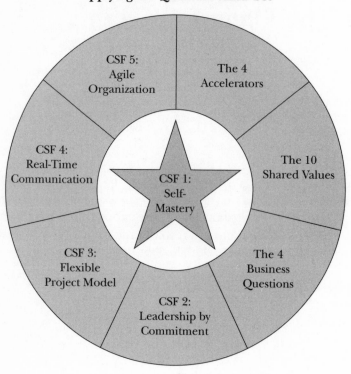

Chapter Ten

Speculate: The Planning Meeting

I know coaches who spend seventeen hours planning the perfect game only to lose because the shape of the football isn't round and they can't control the bounce.
BUD GRANT, COACH

The Speculate cycle addresses Business Question 2 head-on: What will it take to do it? The "it" refers to the collective vision of the project, the vision that started with the sponsor and was extended to the crucial stakeholders as a result of the scoping meeting. Speculate is the second cycle of the Flexible Project Model, Critical Success Factor 3, of the overall eXtreme project management model. If the Visionate cycle is the big picture stuff—where the rubber meets the sky—then the Speculate cycle is where the rubber meets the road.

eXtreme projects exacerbate conflicts in temperaments and thinking styles. Team members with a quantum mind-set are likely to say that eXtreme projects are so volatile that they can't be planned and scheduled; they say, "Just do it." The Newtonians in the group will shout, "Because eXtreme projects are subject to so much change, they need to be planned in detail in order to keep them under control."

Failure to plan and schedule the eXtreme project before rushing ahead and doing it will quickly send the venture into chaos. But overplanning the project will not only waste valuable time; the resultant detailed plan will be a group exercise in fiction writing.

Overplanning also has the effect of making everyone a prisoner to the plan. It puts the project in a straitjacket, disabling it from initiating or effectively responding to change. On an eXtreme project, we favor generating tangible results over generating Newtonian-like plans.

On an eXtreme project, we favor generating tangible results over generating Newtonian-like plans.

Moreover, because the sponsor and other senior management have a legitimate need for predictability, they will likely pressure the team for tight estimates of schedule, costs, and milestone dates. Although the team members understand this need of the sponsor, they will be reluctant to provide such predictability because of all the unknowns they anticipate and fear.

The role of the eXtreme project manager is to embrace this inevitable, necessary, and even beneficial conflict and do so by managing and facilitating the emotions and the thinking that needs to take place among three competing energy fields—the Newtonians, the quantonians, and reality—each of which has its opinions of how long it should take, how much it should cost, and how to go about it.

In addition to producing tangible planning work products, a critical psychoemotional goal of the Speculate cycle is to engender the trust and confidence among crucial stakeholders that they can succeed. Achieving the goal of trust and confidence is facilitated when the eXtreme project manager acts as a role model by living the 10 Shared Values and the 4 Accelerators. Although Project Accelerator 4, Keep it simple, is the cry of the Speculate cycle, the other three Accelerators also kick in.

This chapter covers the following topics:

- Getting ready for the planning meeting
- What goes on in the planning meeting
- Completing the Win Conditions metrics
- Breaking the project into deliverables
- Estimating the size of the project
- Applying the Project Uncertainty Profile

- Estimating the effort using the Delphi technique
- Selecting a life cycle for developing the project deliverable
- Engaging in the wall exercise for generating a first-cut schedule
- Developing the Risk Management Grid

The results of the Speculate Cycle are highlighted in Figure 10.1.

Preparing for the Planning Meeting

Before initiating the planning meeting, take stock of where you are after the scoping meeting by updating the Project Prospectus. On most projects, the scoping meeting will have identified aspects of the project that weren't considered previously and reveal critical skills that the core team will need. Reviewing the updated Prospectus will help you to identify these needs on the core team and recruit new people to meet them. When you have made the needed additions to the team, you are ready to send out the invitation to the planning meeting and prepare the meeting agenda.

The purpose of the planning meeting and that of the post-planning meeting work is to determine what it will take to bring the collective vision into reality: time, people, technology, methods, tools, and financial requirements. The planning meeting is attended by the core team (those who will be doing the work or overseeing the subteams doing the work) as well as others who may have information essential to the planning cycle. These can include certain crucial stakeholders and key players.

The Twelve-Step Planning Meeting Process

The following twelve-step process outlines the planning meeting and serves as the basis for the meeting agenda. Each step is summarized here and then treated in more detail:

1. Review and update the collective vision. The collective vision that was developed in the Visionate cycle serves as the foundation for planning.
2. Review the Project Uncertainty Profile (PUP). The level of uncertainty facing the project is a big driver for estimating the schedule. It also serves as an important input for completing the Risk Action Plan, step 12.

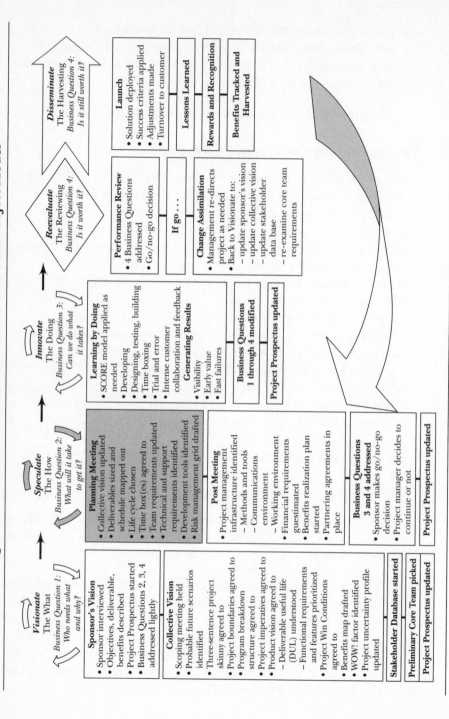

Figure 10.1. Critical Success Factor 3: The Flexible Project Model

3. Decompose the project into a set of deliverables. Every eXtreme project requires multiple streams of intermediate deliverables to come together in the right way at the right time to produce the ultimate project deliverable. Deliverables are actual achievements and should be expressed in the past tense, such as, "Wiring blueprint completed."

4. Estimate the size of each deliverable. Depending on the type of project, size will be measured in different ways. Lines of code or "function points" are useful measures in software projects; miles of highway and number of patients interviewed could be appropriate measures on other kinds of projects.

5. Estimate the effort to produce each deliverable in person-days. This requires technical experts in each area to make judgments based on their experience, as well as taking into consideration the level of quality required (based on the Win Conditions) and the amount of uncertainty (based on the PUP). The Delphi technique (described below) is then used to bring together the estimates.

6. Select a development life cycle. The development life cycle refers to the approach, that is, the method that will be used to build the final deliverable. Will we build it sequentially? Concurrently, doing different parts in parallel? Iteratively?

7. Schedule the deliverables. Scheduling the deliverables is a group exercise.

8. Agree on time boxes. The purpose of a time box is to force frequent decisions on the future course of the project and avoid endless experimentation. It answers the question, "How doable is this?"

9. Assess technical and support requirements. Beyond the deliverable itself, what infrastructure and follow-up support will be required to make it viable?

10. Assess team requirements. Knowing what you know now about the project and what it will take, this is the point to decide if the current team has all the requisite skills and time available to get the job done.

11. Identify development tools. Do you have access to the tools you will need?

12. Produce a Risk Management Grid. Risk management is the process of identifying, prioritizing, and actively managing the events that are likely to have a negative impact on the project.

Step 1: Review and Update the Collective Vision

Chances are that something has already changed, so you want the planning meeting to be based on the latest information available. The meeting is also an opportunity to ensure that newcomers are on common ground with the rest of the team. Cover the project skinny, project boundaries, project imperatives, Win Conditions, and especially the product vision.

Step 2: Review the Project Uncertainty Profile

Understanding the amount of uncertainty surrounding the project is achieved by having the planning group update the PUP. This provides new information about risks that did not come up before and greatly influences the precision of the team's estimate of effort.

Focusing on risks also acts as a catharsis, enabling team members to express their concerns and fears about the project, getting these out in the open so that they can be addressed directly. This step helps to reduce the FUD factor (fear, uncertainty, and doubt) on the project and put the project in a much more positive mood. In addition, not understanding the project risk profile is one of the biggest causes of poor estimates, which cause projects to fail, especially when projects are underestimated. Underestimated projects cause big problems, resulting in unpleasant surprises at a point where it can be too late to recover. This can be compounded when a team suffers from kill-the-messenger syndrome, forcing people not to provide bad news early enough when something can be done about it.

> *Not understanding the project risk profile*
> *is one of the biggest causes of poor estimates,*
> *which cause projects to fail.*

Step 3: Decompose the Project into a Set of Deliverables

A deliverable is a completed work product or result that is mutually agreed on by both the producer and the customer. Taken together, the deliverables add up to the entire project or final deliverable.

A critical requirement on any project is to decompose the product vision and the in-scope work by breaking it down into a manageable set of deliverables, with each deliverable having both a producer and a customer. The functions of the deliverable, along with the quality requirements and risks associated with the deliverable, are defined before any date is committed.

To come up with a set of project deliverables, the participants in the planning meeting break the project into several logical chunks. People are then assigned to a chunk based on their particular expertise and are charged with writing up a sticky note for each deliverable in their chunk. Reflecting the Shared Value of results orientation, the eXtreme project management practice is to express the deliverable as an accomplishment and to use the past tense such as "Home Page designed." Remember that a deliverable doesn't have to be a thing. It can also be the result of an action taken, such as budget approved or testing completed.

Each deliverable should be written on a large sticky note with a broad marker. The likely producer and customer of each deliverable should also be indicated, as shown in Figure 10.2.

Figure 10.2. SOS Web Site Project: Deliverable Sticky Note

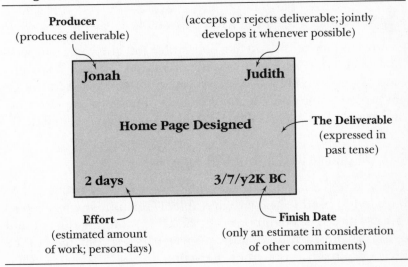

Identifying a producer and customer for each deliverable is extremely important to help keep the project under control. Any one deliverable can have myriad tasks associated with it. Unlike the Newtonian mentality of traditional project management, which is tempted to capture every task associated with every deliverable, eXtreme project managers are interested in tracking and managing the project plan at the deliverable level. It's up to the deliverable producers and customers to manage the detail of their own deliverables. If you try to micromanage each deliverable on an eXtreme project, you are guaranteed to fail. Even if you could find the time, you would become an unwitting bottleneck. eXtreme project management spares the project manager the unnecessary quagmire of endless detail.

In order to stay in control, you empower others to manage their own deliverables. The deliverable producers and customers need to constantly coordinate and manage their own work as things change without running to you as an intermediary. Producers and customers must own their own deliverables, which follows Accelerator 3: Create ownership for results.

---

*In order to stay in control, you empower
others to manage their own deliverables.*

Step 4: Estimate the Size of Each Deliverable

Getting an idea of the size of a deliverable will give you a clue as to how much effort and money will be required. The size or magnitude of a deliverable will be measured in different ways for different projects—for example, lines of code, number of experiments, number of clinical trials held, or number of systems installed.

Step 5: Estimate the Effort It Will Take

The next step is to estimate how much work in person-days will be required to produce each deliverable. Estimating the level of effort has three considerations. The first is considering the amount of uncertainty surrounding the project, which is contained in the PUP and already reviewed by the team.

The second is factoring in the level of quality required by the Win Conditions. Failing to take into consideration the cost of quality, in time and effort, can doom a project. Experience has shown that the level of quality required can double the amount of effort involved. Ask the team to consider the Win Conditions, and make sure that the quality metrics are spelled out, understood, and agreed to.

The third consideration is estimating the effort required for deliverables. The Delphi technique is a well-known estimating approach that capitalizes on the wisdom of those who have experience. It also works well in situations where there is very little experience because it fosters discussion and discovery. The prevailing principle is that all of us are smarter than any one of us. In this technique, each individual independently makes an estimate. Then all estimates are compared and reconciled. The key to success in using the Delphi process is to allow everyone an equal opportunity to explain the rationale behind the figures they came up with.

For each deliverable, estimate the best, worst, and likely case in six-hour person-days of effort. Realistically, at least two of every eight hours is spent in nontask work—answering e-mail, phone calls, breaks, administrative stuff, and so on:

1. Display all estimates by ranges: best, worst, and likely.
2. Reconcile differences by having each participant discuss his or her rationale. Then make adjustments based on the discussion.
3. Average each range, leaving out numbers on each extreme.
4. Record the range, for example, "Web page designed: 2–8 days."

On high-risk projects, it is often advisable to average toward the worst-case estimates. On low-risk projects, it is safe to average the likely estimates. It is never safe to just go with the best, most optimistic estimates all the way through.

Step 6: Select the Development Life Cycle

The life cycle answers the question, "How will we create the deliverable?" The choice of life cycle model depends on multiple factors, including how fast the product or service needs to be delivered and to whom, as well as the scope and quality of the deliverable and the budget. Other factors include how well defined and stable the requirements are, along with the complexity of the deliverable and the associated risks to schedule, budget, scope and quality. Figure 10.3 provides a graphic illustration of the most widely used life cycles. The life cycle has a direct impact on the Win Conditions and is a strategic decision that the sponsor makes once you explain the options.

The waterfall is the classic approach to development. It reflects the time-honored plan-and-control approach to getting results and works well under conditions of relatively low speed and low uncertainty, such as traditional construction and engineering projects. In the waterfall approach, nothing is delivered until everything is delivered. It is sometimes known as the big bang approach or Ta-dah! product development.

In the sequential model, the product or service is delivered in stages (sometimes called releases, versions, or models) rather than giving it to the customer all at once. Once the first version is out, the team begins work on the next one.

In the concurrent model, different teams work in parallel on components of the deliverable and closely coordinate their efforts so that the pieces integrate. This is the divide-and-conquer approach.

There are two variations of prototyping. Evolutionary development prototyping involves developing the primary features as defined by the project sponsor, demonstrating results, getting feedback, making modifications, and refining until the customer is satisfied. Evolutionary delivery prototyping is closely related to the evolutionary development approach. The difference is subtle and involves the amount of change that will be allowed before the deliverable is released. This model is more deadline driven than evolutionary development. Here, the philosophy is often to get something useful out then supplement or fix it later.

Finally, the fast-track model is the "pedal to the metal" approach. Isolate the team, minimize involvement with stakeholders, circumvent standard corporate practices and policies, and throw money at it. Although potentially attractive, this model eschews several important tenets of eXtreme project management: create ownership for results and client collaboration.

Of all these life cycles, the waterfall model is least appropriate for eXtreme projects. These projects are characterized by changing requirements, dead ends, unpredictability, messiness, speed, and innovation, which do not fit the waterfall model. Table 10.1 outlines the benefits and drawbacks of different life cycles. (For an

Figure 10.3. Development Life Cycles

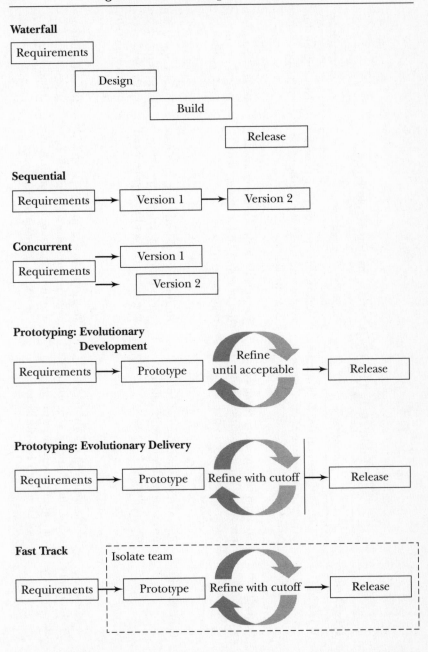

Table 10.1. Life Cycle Strengths and Weaknesses

Life Cycle	Strengths	Weaknesses	Comments
Waterfall	Reliable if used on the appropriate project and managed effectively; well known	Not good for poorly understood requirements; heavy overhead on large projects	Not suitable for eXtreme projects
Sequential	Focused on short-term results; provides customer with visibility, early value; easier to manage than waterfall	Requires careful coordination and documentation for subsequent teams and releases	Works best when requirements are fairly stable
Concurrent	Focused on short-term results; provides customer with visibility, early value	Requires experience in coordinating interdependencies, resulting in greater risk and more overhead	Works best when requirements are fairly stable; requires experienced team
Prototyping: Evolutionary development	Works well with poorly understood and changing requirements; customer experiences progress; quickly learn what works and doesn't	Tendency to overprototype and experiment; difficult to predict schedule and budget; performance less visible to management	Requires intense customer collaboration

Prototyping: Evolutionary delivery	Works well with poorly understood requirements; keeps focus on most important requirements; customer experiences progress; deadline orientation helps limit costs; schedule more predictable than evolutionary development	A limit to amount of change that will be accommodated; post-delivery maintenance can be high if quality is compromised during development	Requires intense customer collaboration
Fast track	Short time to delivery; emergency or catch-up situations	Low stakeholder involvement, with risk of not producing the desired result; possible postdelivery clean-up; requires experienced team, strong sponsor	Riskiest of all; often misapplied when more deliberate approaches would work

excellent description of various life cycle models used in software development, see McConnell, 1996.)

Step 7: Schedule the Deliverables

Once you have identified all the deliverables and have the estimated effort required for each, you can come up with a rough draft schedule. The wall exercise is a good way to do scheduling in a team setting and can be very useful in planning meetings.

In the wall exercise, the team collects each deliverable sticky note, including the estimated number of person-hours they had calculated for each deliverable, and organizes them. Divide a large wall in the meeting room into columns, each one representing one month. The team can then sequence the project deliverables over time by posting their sticky notes in the appropriate place. Again, you want to create ownership for results, so let the producers and customers of the deliverables figure out and negotiate the scheduling among themselves. Your job is to facilitate the process, not direct it.

Step 8: Agree on Time Boxes

A time box is a short, fixed period of time—anywhere from a week to six weeks—during which team members attempt to meet a set of agreed-on requirements that have been identified by the business customer. Once implemented (during the Innovate cycle), its purpose is to shed light on Business Question 3: Can we do (or get) what it takes? At the end of the time box, an assessment of results achieved is made by the sponsor and other crucial stakeholders. Because the time box involves real-life experience (rather than plans about life), the sponsor and team are better able to make fact-based decisions regarding implications for schedule, cost, and the level of quality that can be delivered.

Because time boxing forces frequent decision points, it is one of the most effective ways of keeping an eXtreme project under control. As such, it is a mechanism that puts into practice the Shared Values of fast failures and early value.

Because time boxing forces frequent decision
points, it is one of the most effective ways of
keeping an eXtreme project under control.

Here are guidelines for planning a time box:

- Have the sponsor or designated crucial stakeholders indicate their top-priority requirements for the time box.
- Have the team take its best shot at estimating how long it will take to meet the prioritized requirements.
- Plan the work using forty-hour weeks. The Shared Value of quality of life is operative here.
- As a rough guideline, assume that the first 20 percent of the time box is dedicated to the detailed planning of the work (which takes place during Innovate) and the last 10 percent for stepping back and preparing recommendations to move forward based on what was learned.

I look at a time box as a microproject within the larger project.

Step 9: Assess Technical and Support Requirements

It's one thing to write a symphony, but what good is it if the instruments you've scored haven't been invented or are not available? Assessing technical and support requirements involves looking at the feasibility of the available technology to deliver your deliverable. I once consulted on a project to implement a computer-aided design and engineering system. When the software went into live testing, it brought down the organization's entire network for four hours. Technical and support requirements differ widely by project. Introduce this topic into your planning meeting by asking, "What other systems and services will be needed to support our project deliverable?"

Step 10: Assess Team Requirements

At this point in the planning meeting, you know a great deal about the project. Have the group step back and make a list of the critical skill sets that will be needed on the project: those skills that if you didn't have them, the project would likely fail or be put at high risk. Then do a gap analysis by comparing the needed skills versus those already assigned to the project. Although this, like so much else in eXtreme project management, is common sense, this step is commonly overlooked.

Step 11: Identify Development Tools

This is another item that differs widely by project. Engineers, scientists, software developers, and others require special tools and systems to get their work done. Given what you now know about the schedule, PUP, and level of quality expected, what does the team need that it doesn't have (for example, computers, software, scientific apparatus, capital equipment)? People do know what's missing. Just ask, and go to bat for the team.

Step 12: Produce a Risk Management Grid

eXtreme projects inhabit a volatile and uncertain world full of risks. Moving ahead on a plan—without a consideration of the potential risks is to operate with blinders on. The last work product of the planning meeting is the Risk Management Plan. The purpose of the plan is to prevent or prepare for the high-probability, high-impact risks. Producing the risk grid has an important psychological effect. By externalizing the fears, uncertainty, and doubts of team members and then taking action to mitigate the associated risks, the resultant catharsis frees up energy and commitment to move ahead. As the saying goes, what we don't face, we fear, and what we fear controls us. Risk management is a perfect opportunity to facilitate the flow of thoughts and emotions.

Producing the risk grid has an
important psychological effect.

All of the discussion and work that has been done up to this point provides the fodder for identifying and evaluating the severity of likely risks. A simple and effective four-step risk planning technique is called, appropriately enough, RISK:

R—Research causes of risk.

I—Identify impacts.

S—Spell out solutions.

K—Keep on top of it.

To facilitate the RISK assessment, do the following:

1. Put two flip charts side by side (or tape blank flip chart pages to the wall), and set up a table that looks like Exhibit 10.1.

2. Using sticky notes, have the group brainstorm possible adverse events associated with the project, including both internal and external risks. They do this by writing one risk per sticky note. Ask, "Knowing what we know now, what could cause us to fail?"

3. Assign a handful of risk events to subgroups. Have each subgroup use sticky notes to indicate the impact the risk is expected to have on one or more Win Conditions.

Exhibit 10.1. SOS Web Site Project: Risk Management Plan

Score the probability and impact on a scale of 1 (very low) to 10 (very high).

Risk Event	Impact of Event on Win Conditions[a]	Probability (P) of Event	Impact (I) of Event	Factor (P × I)	Solution: Accept It? Prevent It? (How?) Mitigate It? (How?)
The network vendor cannot meet our spec in time.	Will delay launch of Web site; estimated loss of revenues per week delay is 75,000 drachmas	8	10	80	Requalify Kato, Inc. for this project; qualify at least two other backup vendors

[a]As applicable to schedule, quality, stakeholder satisfaction, requirements and features, resources, return on investment, and team satisfaction.

4. Have each subgroup score the risk as to its likely probability and impact (1 = very low probability or impact, 10 = very high). Multiply the two numbers to get the overall risk factor.

5. Each subgroup indicates the action to be taken to manage the risk: prevent it, mitigate it or accept it.

Pay closest attention to the highest scoring risks in the Factor column. Any risk that could impact one of your must-meet or optimize Win Conditions should be given special consideration. At the conclusion of this process, assemble the work products of all the subgroups together and transfer the key information required by the Risk Management Grid shown in Exhibit 10.1.

With this much of the planning meeting process outlined, let's go back to the parallel universe and see how they are getting along with their eXtreme projects.

Back in the Parallel Universe, 2/28 Y2K BC

Noah and his team have finished scoping the ark project. Trinity and her two teams have just wrapped up their planning meetings for the quarantine and antibiotic projects. Rananda and the Web site project are just about to start planning in earnest.

Rananda Prepares for the Planning Meeting

The Global Express driver handed Rananda a parcel from Mamazon.com. The book, *eXtreme Project Management*, was a gift from her friend Trinity. It seems that when you truly need information, it turns up just in time. The book broke open to the chapter that covered how to plan and facilitate meetings. Not having done much facilitation in the past, this would be Rananda's guide.

Rananda gave the upcoming planning meeting a theme, which was nothing more than an adaptation of Business Question 2: What will it take to do it?

Rananda updated the latest Project Prospectus based on last week's scoping meeting. The Prospectus also came in handy as a basis to identify who should be included in the planning meeting. With invitations to the planning meeting, she included her agenda using the twelve-step process.

She also e-mailed the Prospectus to all participants, fully recognizing that not all would read it ahead of time. Nonetheless, this sent a strong signal that she was thoroughly prepared, an important confidence builder among crucial stakeholders. She was starting to get the picture: an eXtreme project manager needs to earn the right to lead the project process. Every day.

> *An eXtreme project manager needs to earn*
> *the right to lead the project process. Every day.*

The Planning Meeting Begins

Since this was Rananda's first planning meeting as facilitator, she was understandably nervous. "What if I lose control of the meeting? What if it's a bomb?" Rather than go down that dead-end path and try to talk herself out of any of her feelings, she spent a few quiet moments alone. She went into her alpha state, a meditative frame of mind. She then acknowledged her fears by simply letting them run their course and having their way with her. She found that whenever she did this, she was never worse off, and most of the time she was better off.

There was quite a bit of tension in the meeting room. After all, the world was expected to come to an end.

She was gratified to see new faces in the room: people she had asked to join the core team and new stakeholders. A brief warm-up exercise gave everyone a chance to introduce themselves and provide a one-sentence description of their job. Each person was also asked to write and then read a sticky note on which they had written the one thing they wanted to get out of the meeting. The sticky notes were stuck on a flip chart for all to see, with the caveat from Rananda that "if the meeting is not meeting your expectations, you have the responsibility to speak up."

The Warm-Up

The warm-up exercise and sticky notes broke the ice and relieved some of the tension so people could begin to open up and focus on getting real work done. It also gave them a sense of control over the meeting: they were assured it was important for them to leave with their expectations being met and that they had a role in shaping the meeting. As Accelerator 3 extols, Create ownership for results.

The meeting agenda contained a list of work products that Rananda carefully phrased in the past tense, such as "Updated the Ins and Outs," rather than in open-ended form. By expressing them in the past tense, she was picking up on results orientation, the Shared Value that reminds people to keep the end point in mind at all times.

The meeting would last a day and a half, the time needed to bang out all the work products and get everyone on the same page in the process. By not getting everyone in the same room for a concentrated period of time, the project would waste months due to misunderstandings as to who would do what by when. And importantly, there would be little sense of shared ownership for the venture. The project would become unglued from the start and spend its life in the storming stage and doing unnecessary rework.

The Meeting Begins

After getting volunteers for timekeeper, scribe on flip charts, and recorder, Rananda posted the meeting norms from the scoping meeting and asked the group if they could live with these. The group added one norm: "Cell phones on silent ring."

After going over the agenda and reviewing the Web site project skinny and project imperatives, Rananda introduced Dirk, who would give "a word from our sponsor."

To orient the team and the newcomers, the first big item on the agenda was to review the collective vision. Remembering the Shared Value of visibility, Rananda had already posted the SOS Web site three-sentence project skinny (Exhibit 10.2), the project boundaries, and project imperatives on flip charts. These anchors would be a constant reminder throughout the meeting, helping to ensure that the Shared Values of clarity of purpose and results orientation were constantly kept in mind.

The next step was to gain a common understanding of the work to be done. Rananda accomplished this by having the team discuss the project boundaries and product vision and then update the project Ins and Outs. This was greatly facilitated by her insistence that representatives from Earthland Security's public marketing and relations team be in the room for the planning meeting. This team was the internal customer for the SOS Web site. It would be responsible for determining and prioritizing the functions and features of the Web site for the eventual users: the Selected Ones and their representatives. By exercising the Shared Value of client collab-

Exhibit 10.2. SOS Web Site Project: Three-Sentence Project Skinny

1. The SOS Web team will build and launch a full-service Web site to serve the Selected Ones before and after the catastrophic event.

2. Our project will be considered completed once the Web site has stabilized.

3. This project contributes to the sponsor's objective:

   - To establish a 100 percent increase in peace and prosperity on Planet Earth within four generations

   - To increase per capita revenues from Planet Earth's inhabitants from 18,000 to $24,000 drachmas in four generations

   - To decrease overhead costs to maintain Planet Earth from 18,000 to 16,000 drachmas per capita in four generations

---

oration, the SOS Web site team saved days, if not weeks, by getting on-the-spot answers to critical questions and avoiding second-guessing and unnecessary rework and false starts.

Rananda took great care to ensure proper ownership of Business Questions 1 and 2. The Marketing department owned the requirements that are the answers to Business Question 1: Who needs what and why? As project manager, she owned the answer to Business Question 2: What will it take to get it:

After discussion, the working draft of the product vision was updated (Exhibit 10.3). And based on the updated product vision, the group updated the Ins and Outs (Exhibit 10.4).

The Sponsor Kicks It Off

Dirk made time to come to the planning meeting and spend twenty minutes to introduce the project to the newcomers. He did a good job of reviewing the purpose of the project as well as the product vision, which was included in everyone's Prospectus.

But then Dirk's Newtonian nature came gushing out. "I'd like to introduce Ezekiel, who has been promoted to head our new SOS Program Office. Ez's job is to be sure that all SOS projects follow the prescribed M4 model. M4 stands for the Mother of all Monumental Maturity Models. It's the model promulgated by the Earthland Engineering Institute. We want to be M4 level 3 certified by the end of this project."

The group was incredulous. Who cared about M4 certification? They had other stuff to worry about.

Exhibit 10.3. SOS Web Site Product Vision: Functional Requirements

Before the Disaster	After the Disaster
Qualification	**Facilitate survival**
Qualify who gets chosen.	**How to live in peace**
Issue name tags.	**Food, shelter, clothing**
Travel	Where to eat.
Provide weather reports.	Real estate guide.
Provide information on where to assemble.	What to wear where.
Provide information on what to bring.	**Medical help**
Issue travel tickets to the ark and the quarantine facility.	Pharmacies.
	Hospitals.
Life on the ark	**Employment opportunities**
Post the floor plan.	**Government and elections**
Post activities.	**World religious services**
Post the meal plan.	**Facilitate commerce**
Life under quarantine	Enable shopping on the Web.
Do's and don'ts.	Dispense credit to qualified Selected Ones.
Animal husbandry	**Facilitate repopulation**
Maintain veterinarian files.	Provide Web-based dating services.
Post the diets.	
X-Virus antibiotic	
Be able to process orders.	
Maintain inventory statistics.	
Provide information on dosage and side effects.	
Subscriptions and fees	
Accept all major credit cards.	
Set up electronic funds transfer capability.	

General Capabilities to Be Included

Secure/Interactive/Seamless integration with subcontractors (travel agents, clothing providers, others)

DUL factor (the intended useful life of the deliverable):

[　] One-time fix; a patch: will junk this or replace the entire system

[X] Deliver and fix: Deliver now, fix flaws later; upgrade

[　] Long-term commitment: Must be perfect first time out

Exhibit 10.4. SOS Web Site Project: Ins and Outs

In-Scope Work	Out-of-Scope Work
• Determine technical requirements	• Maintain and upgrade the site after it's stabilized
• Keep product vision up to date	• Determine qualification criteria for Selected Ones
• Design user interface and Web pages	
• Outsource software development	• Administer antibiotics
• Test software	• Provide documentation
• Launch software	• Host it ourselves
• Provide e-commerce capability	• Do programming
• Put in place IT infrastructure	• Provide the information to populate the Web pages
• Arrange for hosting	
• Ensure integration with other systems and databases	
• Contract with third-party suppliers as needed	
• Plan and manage the project	

Track hits and transactions: Not sure if in or out. Get clarification from the sponsor.

"Ez will now run you through the M4 project management maturity model," Dirk added. "Next week you'll all attend the two-day M4 workshop for an in-depth understanding."

Neither M4 nor Ezekiel was on the agenda, and Rananda was caught by surprise. This would be her first big test as project manager. She said, "I wasn't aware we were to follow the M4 maturity model. Learn something new all the time. I will find out more about it after the meeting. In the meantime, let's give Ez his fifteen minutes to give us the big picture."

EZ enthusiastically flashed his three-inch M4 binder for all to see. He pointed to the templates, the procedures, and the documentation that were required to help the team define the project and keep it on track. Ez, an oxymoron in the flesh, made things look difficult. Everyone in the room got that sinking feeling. Jessup whispered to Beth, "Are we suppose to be building a Web site or building documentation?"

When he finished, Rananda was ready to exercise both her assertive and expert powers. She drew a line. This took courage. Her palms sweating mildly, she simply said it scared. "Thank you, Ezekiel. I want to find out more about M4 after the meeting. As project manager, my job is to ensure that the methodology we use for this project is the one most likely to help us succeed. So we need to talk about it. In the meantime, let's move on with the agenda."

She realized that had she not taken a stand here, her job as project manager would have been over for all practical purposes. She would have had no credibility. Moreover, she would find herself leading an uphill battle to get people to adhere to a methodology that they would resist and defeat in subtle ways each step of the way. Attention and energy would be diverted.

Ez left the meeting to terrorize one of the other projects. Rananda picked up where she left off and reviewed the remaining work products from the collective vision.

Before breaking down the project into a set of deliverables, Rananda had the group update the project imperatives, Win Conditions, and PUP. Along with the project skinny, boundaries, and product vision, these would serve as key inputs for the rest of the meeting.

Updating the Project and the 7 Win Conditions

The previous night after dinner at Wok and Roll, Rananda had had an insight. At first she didn't understand her fortune cookie: "Begin at the end, and end at the beginning." It sounded like a Zen koan. Being in a hurry, she crumpled it up and ran off. But the saying wouldn't let go of her. "Begin at the end . . . Begin at the end . . ." Then she got it: the time to define success on any project is at the beginning of the project, not at the end. The team needed to begin with the end in mind. Waiting for the end to define success could be fatal.

Rananda put it simply to the group. "We all want to be sure we are measuring success the same way." The team then went on to put metrics against each of the Win Conditions (Exhibit 10.5). They didn't have enough information for the ROI metric, but this wouldn't hold them back.

There was quite a bit of discussion as to why quality, and not the 5/15 target date, was the must-meet condition. Rananda pointed out that if the target date were hit but the imperative quality requirements were not met, the system would not be useable for the intended purpose. She added, "At some point, any date will eventually become a project imperative [Exhibit 10.6], but for now quality is at the top of the list. We'll do everything we can to optimize the schedule."

Exhibit 10.5. SOS Web Site Project: The 7 Win Conditions

Win Condition	Metric	Priority
1. Quality	See project imperatives	**Must meet**
2. Schedule	5/15 (target)	**Optimize**
3. Scope (functions and features)	See project imperatives: Sufficient functionality	Acceptable
4. Budget	Outside limit: 200,000 drachmas	Acceptable
5. ROI (for this project)	ROI; to be determined	Acceptable
6. Customer satisfaction	No less than 4 on scale of 1–10	Acceptable
7. Team satisfaction	Rated no less than 6 on scale of 1–10	Acceptable

Exhibit 10.6. SOS Web Site Project: Project Imperatives

	Metric
Sufficient functionality	Predisaster: Be able to qualify Selected Ones; order processing for antibiotic
	Postdisaster: Information about food, shelter, medical help; e-commerce capability
Multiuser friendly	Intuitive. All languages worldwide
Information integrity	98 percent accurate on sex, ethnicity, species, and health information
Secure	Impervious to viruses and hackers
Sufficient capacity	Able to withstand 10 million hits per minute
Reliable	98 percent uptime

And finally, the PUP was reviewed as another important piece of information that would influence the schedule, the work effort, team requirements, and risk management plan (Exhibit 10.7).

Defining the Deliverables

Rananda quickly explained how to use sticky notes to break the project down into manageable deliverables, stressing the importance of using results-oriented thinking and expressing each one in the past tense. In the past, Radavie spent hours and weekends breaking the project into deliverables and

Exhibit 10.7. SOS Web Site Project: Project Uncertainty Profile Summary

Risk	Risk Level (0 = low, 4 = high)
Business risk (for example, financial exposure, market, schedule)	3.5
Product risk (requirements, technology, support systems)	3.4
Project risk (for example, vendors, methodology, sponsorship, team stability, dependence on other projects)	3.2
Environmental risk (for example, stakeholders, working conditions, project portfolio stability)	3.8
Mean	3.5

tasks and then attempting to dole them out. But her days of traditional project management were over.

As the team went through the sticky note exercise, discussing deliverables and determining the producers and their customers, a loud buzz filled the room. Rananda was amazed to see all the discussion going on. Then it clicked in for her, "Aha! An eXtreme project is a self-correcting venture. The deliverable producers and customers need to constantly coordinate and manage their own work as things change. What a relief from the traditional project management approach I have been following. I don't have to be the hub for everything that goes on." Then she had a second Aha! "Now I see the beauty of Project Accelerators 2 and 3: Build on people's desire to make a difference and create ownership for results. All I have to do is to get out of the way." She had stumbled on the power paradox: "You gain power by giving power to others."

Sizing Up the Work to Be Done

Now that the team had a set of tangible deliverables to work with, they were in a good position to estimate how big the software component of the SOS Web Site Project would be. This was typically done by estimating the number of so-called function points, a specialized way of sizing up software projects. To aid the group, Rananda handed out some standard function point tables that she got from IFPUG, the International Function Point Users Group. This was an approximate measure but a lot better than sticking one's finger in the air.

Estimating the Effort It Would Take

Before the project could be rough-scheduled, Rananda would have the team generate an estimate of how much work in person-days would be required to produce each deliverable. Following her copy of her new eXtreme project management book, she asked the group to update the PUP, review the Win Conditions and quality metrics, and use the Delphi technique to estimate the time needed for each deliverable.

Scheduling the Deliverables: Going to the Wall

Rananda pointed out that this was a project to schedule from right to left since the end date is a big driver. But she also pointed out that rather than go down the path of doing a phony exercise of trying to force-fit all the work to meet the 5/15 deadline, it would be better to begin with a realistic assessment of how much work there really was in order to execute the product vision and see how long it would take without the constraint of the 5/15 target date. If they found that the work to be done could not be compressed to fit within the time available, they would have to make trade-offs to meet the 5/15 date: leave out noncritical Web site functions and features, add more resources, or come up with some other solution.

Rananda had participated in the wall exercise on a previous project. The exercise began with what seemed to be a mass of confusion as people put up the sticky notes, discussed them, moved them, and argued about sequencing. Rananda let the process play out, giving ownership to the participants. After a while, things settled down, and the sequencing took shape. They finished with a quick quality check to be sure that their project imperatives were represented in the deliverable's map.

We Can't Make It!

Once the team stepped back and looked at the wall, a heavy silence fell over the room. Even if they used their best-case estimate, they figured they would still miss their 5/15 target by nearly three months. The mood turned to gloom and doom. Both desire and confidence hit bottom. It looked as if they were facing a death march project.

Joshua then piped up: "I just attended a workshop on eXtreme project management. They told us about the ESP technique to compress a time line. Maybe that will help." Joshua explained that ESP stands for which deliverables can be eliminated, shortened, or done in parallel.

The team looked at every deliverable with a critical eye. Applying ESP with the help of their customers from Earthland's Marketing department, they were able to eliminate some of the nice-to-have requirements altogether. They also found they could save some time by designing and testing multiple Web pages in parallel and not waiting for the home page to be approved. And, finally, assuming they could get additional staff, some of the deliverables time could be shortened.

ESP helped, but they could still come up with only a savings of about one month, putting them at 7/15, still two months over.

At that point, Marsha spoke up: "Why don't we take a look at the PUP and see how much uncertainty we can iron out of the project? For instance, by co-locating the development team in the same room, we could possibly save 20 to 25 percent on the development component of the project. We did a comparison of projects similar to each other where I last worked. Face-to-face communication eliminated memos, e-mails, time lost in scheduling conference calls and meetings, unnecessary rework due to misunderstandings, and delays in feedback. The time saved really added up compared to when we used dispersed teams, even if they were in the same building or on the same floor."

Rananda liked what she was hearing. The team was taking ownership for the project. She was witnessing the impact of Accelerators 2 and 3: Build on people's desire to make a difference, and create ownership for results. Her job was to establish the environment for people to do good work, to create the circumstances for success.

After looking at all risk factors they felt they might be able to influence, they came up short again: the project would still be finished one month after the 5/15 target date.

What *Can* We Do in the Time Available?

Although the results of the wall exercise were depressing, it did have a cathartic effect. The team members weren't happy at all about their findings, but they did feel a great sense of relief by knowing the reality of their situation. The suspense was over.

Rananda could feel the sense of quiet relief. She thought to herself, "This gives new meaning to the old expression, 'The devil you know is better than the one you don't.' Maybe my job as eXtreme project manager is to be a sort of exorcist, allowing people to expel their fears and bring them

into the open where they have a better chance of taking corrective action."
A soothing calm energy permeated the room.

"We're dead in the water if we don't solve this problem. We have to schedule this project from right to left, from the end date backward," blurted Joshua.

Rananda looked at the sticky notes on the wall—not the individual notes but the overall pattern. Even after doing things in parallel, the project nonetheless looked like a waterfall. It started out with gathering requirements, then doing the design, followed by building, testing, and then releasing.

Due most likely to decades of social conditioning, the team had unconsciously scheduled the project using the Newtonian mind-set. Rananda thought to herself, "It's hard to think outside the box when you're in the box. But unless we do, they'll bury us in the same box. We need a different mental model if we are to survive."

She remembered having seen something about life cycles in the book Trinity had given her. During the meeting break, she looked it up, and there she began to get her answer.

She quickly made copies of the life cycle page and handed them out to team members when they got back from the break. She broke the group into subgroups of three to five members each. "In the next twenty minutes, I want each group to come up with a first- and second-choice life cycle and then present your recommendation and rationale to the entire group."

In making their selection, the team realized that picking a product development life cycle involves trade-offs among the 7 Win Conditions. In this case, quality had to be maximized (must-meet) and the schedule had to be optimized, two tough conditions when combined. Everything else had to take a back seat. Since the life cycle has a direct impact on the Win Conditions, it becomes the sponsor's decision, but with the project manager's recommendation taken into consideration.

Picking a Life Cycle

After a spirited debate, the team agreed on a hybrid of two life cycles. They would use concurrent development combined with fast track in what they referred to as their turbo life cycle. In version 1, they would develop all of the functionality that would be required before the catastrophic event took place. Version 2, which would contain all of the postevent requirements, would be developed in parallel.

Dedicated version teams with representatives from marketing would be set up in skunkworks in neighboring rooms. "Every two weeks," said Rananda, "we will have a formal meeting to reevaluate the entire project. At that time, we will reforecast the budget requirements."

Each team would work on a set of requirements prioritized by representatives of Earthland Security's Marketing department. Parallel development would put great demands on each team to synchronize their work closely. Here's how Rananda explained it: "We will be developing the Web site using short time boxes—one to two weeks in length to work on the top-priority requirements. At the end of each time box, we'll assess what's working and not. Then we'll plan the next time box based on what we learned. The project management approach we are using requires that each day, all the subteams attend the huddle to coordinate their efforts and identify barriers before they have an adverse impact on the project's quality, schedule, costs, and risks. We'll also look at the impact of the day's events on the time line and deplan and replan as needed." Not only would each team huddle each day, representatives of both teams would conduct a huddle of huddles on a daily basis for thirty minutes to synchronize their work.

In order to ensure system usability and integrity, focus groups would be conducted twice weekly with delegated Selected Ones and representatives of the animal community.

Of course, all of this would have to be approved by Dirk, the sponsor. It's the sponsor's job to approve the development life cycle.

Rescheduling the Project

Reinvigorated with a new sense of hope, the team rose out of their seats simultaneously as if someone had called a signal. They headed to the wall. They all knew exactly what to do without saying a word. Using concurrent versioning plus fast-track life cycles, they were able to lop off an estimated three to four months from the original schedule. That gave them an estimated completion date of 5/1 to 5/15, a buffer of roughly two weeks, allowing them to complete the project in the time available after all. They were by no means home free, but at last they could see the possibility of *getting* home.

By focusing her attention on the two-week buffer from 5/1 to 5/15, Rananda would considerably simplify her ability to manage the schedule. Taking a tip from critical chain scheduling, which she had read about in *Critical Chain* by Eli Goldradt (1997), the fifteen-day buffer would function like money in the bank—a sort of cash reserve that everybody was aware of but only she had access to. If a version team reported that they ran into a glitch and needed an extra day, Rananda could decide to take a day out of the savings account if there were no other way of making the time up. Some project managers like to keep a secret fund of extra days and not let anyone know about. However, by practicing the Shared Values of visibility and honest communication, Rananda would later learn that the version teams would take responsibility for managing and protecting the project buffer. And when one team needed a day, the other version team would try and help them out by looking to save a day on their schedule.

Having picked their life cycle, the team then identified a series of time boxes during which preagreed-upon requirements would be developed.

Assessing Team Requirements

Rananda was about to end the meeting when Sarah spoke up. "I think we are overlooking something here. We now know a lot more about the challenges and risks we face. The life cycle exercise was enlightening. But it tells me that we need to reexamine the makeup of the core team and the subteams."

Everyone in the room seemed puzzled. "I don't get your drift," said Francisco. All heads nodded up and down, echoing Francisco's puzzlement.

"Well," said Sarah, "the team makeup we started with might be okay if we were using our old sequential waterfall method that we are accustomed to, but now we need to have two separate teams working in parallel. That alone will require about twice as many people as we started out with."

It seemed so obvious now that Sarah explained it. Rananda thought to herself, "Yes, the old waterfall paradigm dies slowly."

Sarah continued: "Besides more people, we will need a different skill set. At my last company, it took two failures in a row to realize that the parallel-development, fast-track life cycle model requires highly experienced team members with proven skills in working on complex projects and coordinating their work with other teams under conditions of high speed and high stress. Moreover, we found that we needed technical team leaders who were adept at leading group problem-solving sessions since many unforeseen technical issues cropped up due to the intricacies of parallel development."

Rananda replied, "Now that this has come up, I will need ammunition tomorrow for my meeting with Dirk. It's my job to negotiate and close the gaps between what we have versus what we need in order to succeed. So let's brainstorm a list of skills we are going to need. Use the sticky notes you have."

Using sticky notes made the brainstorming go fast. Everybody could write at the same time, and the notes were easy to move around on flip charts.

The exercise proved they didn't have all the necessary talent on site. Certain team members would most likely be located in India and other remote sites, especially those whose work did not require ongoing coordination in real time.

It finally hit Rananda: "Even if I get everything else we need from Dirk, none of it will matter if I don't have enough of the right kind of talent to get the job done. And it's not likely I will be able to get everybody under the same roof, so I'm faced with virtual team members and contractors. But do we have in place the communications infrastructure we are going to need?"

Rananda thought she had seen something about real-time communication and how to get up and running fast in her new book, *eXtreme Project Management*. She'd look it up after lunch.

Hunger and impatience took over. After agreeing on the action items and quickly reviewing the work products completed against the original agenda, Rananda adjourned the meeting.

Ascertaining the Necessary Development Tools

A quick assessment revealed that much of the Web development work was done using primitive tools and aging software. Moreover, there weren't enough laptops to go around for all the developers, so the team made an inventory of what they would need. This was not time to scrimp.

Product Risk Management Grid

The planning meeting was nearing an end. People were tired after almost a day and a half of planning. Moreover, the thought of all the work to be done and the uncertainty associated with the project created a low-hanging cloud of FUD that blanketed the room.

Always sensitive to the emotional side of project management, Rananda was picking up on the prevailing dark energy. But rather than give a pep talk aimed at changing what people were feeling, she stayed with the prevailing emotions. She went around the room asking people to summarize how they were feeling: "exhausted," ". . .doomed,". . . "depressed," ". . . numb,". . . "encouraged,". . . "hopeful . . ."

That freed people up to vent their worst fears about the project: what they thought could go wrong. Using sticky notes, the group vented their fears, identifying possible adverse events that could hit the project. This became the basis for identifying risk events, the first step in compiling the Risk Management Grid.

Time was running out, and any more work would be pressing things beyond reason. So Rananda asked for volunteers to finish compiling the grid after the meeting.

The meeting ended with a review of the action items and a rundown of all the work completed in the past thirty-six hours.

We have seen how the Speculate cycle uses the planning meeting to address Business Question 2 head-on: What will it take to do it? The twelve-step planning meeting process provides a road map for going forward. But before embarking on that road, the results of the planning meeting need to be consolidated and put into context. This is the topic of the next chapter, in which we conclude Speculate, the second cycle in the Flexible Project Model.

eXtreme Project Management Model
Applying the Quantum Mind-Set

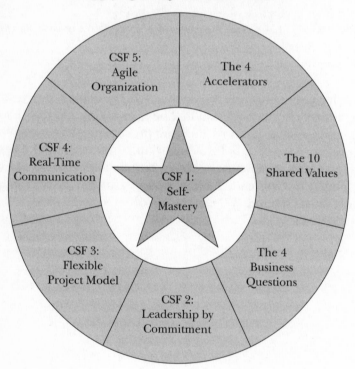

Chapter Eleven

Speculate: Postplanning Work

Don't just act. Stand there.
ELIA KAZAN

The planning meeting will have produced most of the answers to Business Question 2: What will it take to do it? The next step is to segue into the Innovate cycle, assuming the sponsor gives the go-ahead. That's where the postplanning activities come into play. They bridge the gap between the planning meeting and the Innovate cycle. Effectively, the postplanning work wraps up the Speculate Cycle, Critical Success Factor 3, of the Flexible Project Model.

Business Questions 3 and 4 now come to the forefront: Can we get what it takes? Is it worth it? Here, the work of the eXtreme project manager is to prepare information that the sponsor and other crucial stakeholders will need in order to make an informed decision about the future course of the project. A big trap in project management is to rush into doing the work before ensuring that the project is viable. Even if it is clear that the project can move ahead, the sponsor still needs to agree with the estimates for schedule and financial requirements.

Postplanning includes the following activities:

- Assessing the project management infrastructure
- Estimating financial requirements
- Updating the Project Prospectus

- Meeting with the sponsor to secure a go/no go decision
- Establishing partnering agreements
- Personal reflection

I'll elaborate on each of these points:

- Assessing the project management infrastructure. In its broadest sense, the project management infrastructure includes the appropriate project management method, tools, templates, and communications system to facilitate and manage the flow of information and communication. It includes the physical working environment as well.
- Estimating financial requirements. No project is free. Someone will eventually get the bill and be held responsible for the realization of the project benefits. Financial requirements include estimating the cost of the project as well as ascertaining the sponsor's expected ROI.

Someone will eventually get the bill and be held responsible for the realization of the project benefits.

- Updating the Project Prospectus. The Prospectus continues to be the focal point for essential information about the venture throughout the project.
- Meeting with the sponsor to secure a decision. Here, the project manager, perhaps with someone from finance, presents the financial implications to the sponsor. Negotiation is begun to close gaps between what it will take to succeed versus what is already allocated. The goal of the meeting is for the sponsor to answer Business Question 4: Is it worth it? It's also time to set the stage for turning benefits realization from a concept into a reality.
- Establishing partnering agreements. If the project is a go, partnering agreements with others need to be established to help ensure that the resources needed to get the job done are available. (These are covered in Chapter Seven.)
- Personal reflection. Just because the project is given the green light doesn't necessarily mean that you want to sign up for it.

It's important for you to make a conscious choice as to whether you want to continue in your role. Your own quality of life is at stake.

Assessing the Project Management Infrastructure

What project management approach will be used to run the project? Assuming yours is an eXtreme project, will you be saddled with a preexisting traditional method that can slow you down? Or perhaps your starting point is a culture that practices ad hoc project management, and now you see the need for adding some discipline. If there is a gap between what you need versus what's available, then you will have to make your case to the sponsor to close the gap.

The material I covered in Part Two, as well as how to establish a value proposition in the eXtreme Tools and Techniques section at the end of this book, can help you in making your case. Essentially, your argument centers around demonstrating what most sponsors want: a sense of control in the face of volatility.

> *Your argument centers around demonstrating*
> *what most sponsors want: a sense of control*
> *in the face of volatility.*

Beyond ensuring that you will be using an appropriate project management methodology, identify any organizational policies and procedures that can stifle progress. In order to succeed, you may need the sponsor's dispensation from bureaucratic sacred cows that can stymie the project. It's the sponsor's project, and it's within her self-interest to make life easier for you. This includes the physical working environment as well. As noted in Chapter Six, an important part of your job is to remove barriers to progress. On eXtreme projects, you lead people by standing behind them and lobbying hard for what they need.

> *On eXtreme projects, you lead people by standing*
> *behind them and lobbying hard for what they need.*

You will also want to assess your organization's current project management communications system. Chapter Fifteen will give you valuable information on how to assess your needs quickly and put in place what you need in a very short period of time with minimal cost.

If you can't get what you need to succeed, then you have some soul searching to do once again. All of this requires courage, and at times, even guts power to break the rules. The shaded area in Figure 11.1 shows you just where we are in the Flexible Project Model.

Estimating Financial Requirements

In the broadest sense of the term, financial requirements encompass the costs and revenues associated with the project before *and* after launch and the expected ROI.

Unless you are a financial expert, don't pretend to be one. And even if you are, you won't have the time on an eXtreme project. So make friends with someone in finance. Short of being a financial whiz, your job is to bring an ROI consciousness to the project. After all, that's the point of the 4 Business Questions. ROI comes home to roost in Business Question 4: Is it worth it?

I'm always surprised at the number of projects (upwards of half) that I run into that have no data on the expected financial return. Many of these are multimillion-dollar investments. And of those organizations that do look at changes in the ROI profile while the project is under development, only a small number of those actually follow up to see if the ultimate ROI was achieved. Yet few people would make a substantial investment in the stock market and then not follow up to see if it were paying off.

Among the organizations that do measure and track ROI, each seems to have a different approach. But whatever the approach, they invariably express ROI in present dollars, or as is commonly referred to, present value. Present value is a way of recognizing that future dollars are worth less than today's dollars. In calculating present value, all future benefits and costs are discounted back to today's dollars. This provides a common baseline for computing costs and returns over time.

For instance, if the profit expectation of a project were $2.5 million five years from now, the present value of that amount using

Figure 11.1. Critical Success Factor 3: The Flexible Project Model

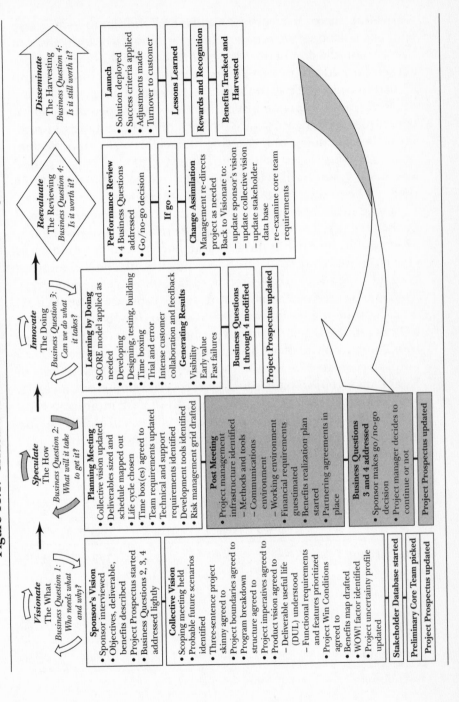

a discount rate of 8 percent would be $1.7 million in today's dollars. The discount rate is determined by the organization and can be based on the cost of borrowing or raising money or some other agreed-on value. The formula for calculating present value is included in the eXtreme Tools and Techniques section.

ROI can be expressed in a number of ways. Two of the more commonly used measures are payback period and time to profit. (For a full treatment of measuring financial returns on project investments, see Cooper, 2001, and Thomsett, 2002.) Payback period answers the question, "How long after release of the deliverable does it take to recover your prelaunch investment?"

Using the sample data in Table 11.1, the payback period would be the time that it took to get your $200 prelaunch investment back, which would be early in the first year since revenues would easily cover the up-front costs. To be exact, it would be 4.8 months: 200/500 or 0.4 years (0.4 years times 12 months equals 4.8 months).

Time to profit answers the question, "From the time the first dollar was spent, how long does it take to go from being in the red to being in the black?" Time to profit would take 7.2 months before going into the black, the time it would take for revenues to outpace costs to date. In the example, year 0 and year 1 costs of $300 (200 + 100) to date would be recovered sometime in year 1: 300/500 equals 0.6 years times 12 months, or 7.2 months.

The ROI after three years is 238 percent, calculated by the formula [Total revenues − total costs]/total costs × 100.

Table 11.1. Three-Year Cash Flow for Project XYZ

	Year 0	Year 1	Year 2	Year 3	Total
Total revenues	—	500	700	1,000	2,200
Costs					
Prelaunch costs	200	0	0	0	200
Postlaunch costs	0	100	150	200	450
Total costs	200	100	150	200	650
Net revenues	−200	400	550	800	1,550

Note: All dollars are in present value.

Rananda Prepares for Her Meeting with Dirk, 3/1 Y2K BC

Back in the parallel universe, Rananda has forty-eight hours to get ready for Dirk, who, among other things, wants to see the numbers.

She knows that Dirk's budget for her project was based on looking at figures from a prior Web site project. But this one is orders of magnitude larger and more complex. A more rigorous approach would be necessary to come up with a better fact-based estimate, however tentative the figures. Rananda's talents did not encompass finance, so she called in Feldon from finance who agreed to run the budget and do an ROI analysis.

In the meantime, she went ahead and updated the Project Prospectus. She was especially concerned about getting relief from organizational policies that could slow things to a crawl. Given that Dirk was holding all the cards, if for no other reason that he outranked her by ten levels, Rananda was understandably nervous. "On top of having to prove my case, I also have to contend with Ez, who wants us to run this project using M4. Based on what we know now, M4 would kill us. The documentation requirements alone would eat us alive."

She then remembered something she read earlier in her book: "You get what *you* want by showing someone how that will get them what *they* want." "And what does Dirk want?" she asked herself? "What do they all want?" She went into her alpha state for three minutes. She imagined the clouds forming words against a blue sky. Slowly the message was revealed: C O N T R O L. That would be the basis for her argument.

In preparation for the meeting, Rananda's strategy was now simple: "Dirk's Guardian temperament means he demands facts, not fluff. He also needs to feel that the project is under control, which is a major reason that he wants us to use M4. I'll let the facts do the talking." Rananda outlined her plan in the light of Dirk's control motivators:

- Bring quantitative data from the planning meeting (for example, the risk assessment, Project Uncertainty Profile (PUP,) and schedule, along with the rationale and metrics for the Win Conditions.
- Show why the waterfall approach espoused by M4 will cause the team to miss the target date by months.
- Explain how the turbo life cycle model will give Dirk and the team more control than the M4 method.

Show Me the Money

In the meantime, Feldon from finance was running the numbers. At the same time, finance was getting pressure from the Sponsor of All Sponsors, who had unkindly referred to the Information Systems Department as a "money-sucking black hole." The sponsor had a good point, thought Feldon. Information systems would typically track the development costs of a project, but the business sponsor was rarely held accountable for realizing the project benefits. In fact, nobody would mind the cash register. So all the Sponsor of All Sponsors would see was red ink from the initial IT investment plus the costs of follow-on system support. In that sense, IT was getting a bum wrap since the business owner and postproject stakeholders were let off the hook. The subject of benefits accountability was a missing link. Furthermore, ROI estimates, even if they were tracked, were typically calculated excluding ongoing systems support costs, giving an unrealistic picture of expected investment returns.

As a result of pressure from high above, Feldon's boss had given him a project whose mission was to put in place a financial model for measuring a project's business benefits: its added value and financial return. Having seen the benefits map presented in the just-completed Web site planning meeting, it hit Feldon that he had half of the puzzle solved already. The first half was to have in place the benefits map linking the project to its ultimate outcome. The next was to calculate the ROI.

Feldon did some fast figuring. His first step was to do a five-year best-case scenario. He started out using a best-case revenues/best-case costs scenario. Recognizing the time value of money, he calculated all benefits and costs in terms of present value using Earthland Security's customary discount factor of 8 percent. He summarized his figures in Exhibit 11.1.

The numbers looked good. "Too good to be true," thought Feldon. He took another look at the PUP included in his latest Project Prospectus. Given all the risk associated with this project, Feldon decided to perform a sensitivity analysis to see how the ROI fared under different scenarios. He referred to this as his risk-adjusted ROI, which he cogently summarized in Exhibit 11.2.

It occurred to him that this was a guess no matter what figures he used. In the final analysis, people were going to pick the approach that best justified their case. Furthermore, there were other considerations, such as strategic fit, to factor in.

Exhibit 11.1. SOS Web Site Project: Five-Year Cash Flow

All drachmas in present value (000s omitted)

	Year 0	Year 1	Year 2	Year 3	Year 4	Year 5	Total
Revenues	—	1,500	2,000	3,000	4,000	7,500	18,000
Costs							
Prelaunch costs	2,200	—	—	—	—	—	2,200
Postlaunch costs	—	800	1,000	1,200	1,600	2,400	7,000
Total costs	2,200	800	1,000	1,200	1,600	2,400	9,200
Net revenues	—	700	1,000	1,800	2,400	5,100	8,800

Payback period: 1 year, 4 months

Time to profit: 2 years, 2 months

Exhibit 11.2. SOS Web Site Project: Risk-Adjusted ROI from Best- Through Worst-Case Scenarios

All drachmas are in present value (000s omitted)

	Best-Case Revenues/ Best-Case Costs	Best-Case Revenues/ Worst-Case Costs	Worst-Case Revenues/ Best-Case Costs	Worst-Case Revenues/ Worst-Case Costs
Revenues	18,000	18,000	12,500	12,500
Costs				
Prelaunch costs	2,200	4,800	2,200	4,800
Postlaunch costs	7,000	10,400	7,000	10,400
Total costs	9,200	15,200	9,200	15,200
Net revenues	8,800	2,800	3,300	-2,700
Percentage ROI	96	18	36	-26
Payback period	1 year, 4 months	2 years, 5 months	1 year, 10 months	3 years, 1 month
Time to profit	2 years, 2 months	4 years, 1 month	3 years, 2 months	Over 5 years

Rananda came by to pick up the numbers. Feldon, who by now was reading his own copy of *eXtreme Project Management,* reminded Rananda of one of Noah's principles for stating estimates: "In talking with Dirk or any other sponsor, never give a point estimate. Always give a range." They both agreed. And when they were asked about the ROI projection, they would say: "The estimated ROI is between a negative 25 percent and plus 96 percent over a five-year period. Time to profit is estimated to be anywhere from two years to over five years."

Based on the financials alone, the Web site project was only marginally attractive. To be justified, it needed to be looked at in the light of its contribution to the entire program.

The Meeting with Dirk and Ez

Ez had shown up in Dirk's office just as Rananda had arrived. His M4 binder filled his entire briefcase. Over the past few days, he had added a number of new templates and project tracking procedures that he picked off the Web site ProjectConnections.com. What was three inches was now closer to five. Rananda thought, "M4 on steroids."

Not only that, Ez had just passed his PMP® exam and flashed his certificate to prove it. Ez knew enough to pass the exam, but he hadn't yet run his first project other than the one to create the M4 binder. That concerned Rananda, since he was now heading the project office and already had a lot to say about the SOS Web Site Project.

Rananda started the discussion by reviewing the 7 Win Conditions. Dirk quickly agreed with the conditions of success as stated since he was involved in shaping these early in the project. She then went over the PUP. That would give her the context and rationale for when Dirk and Ezekiel started questioning her estimates and the recommended turbo life cycle.

Dirk Sees the Logic

Dirk seemed to understand the logic behind using concurrent development and the need for the recommended turbo life cycle. Ez did not. In fact, it was as if someone had called his only child ugly: "This is not the tried-and-true waterfall model we prescribe in M4. All this prototyping stuff is nothing more than an excuse for developers to hack around and skip the requirements-gathering stage. We don't have time for experimenting. We have to get it right the *first* time. The project will be out of control from the start."

By this time, Rananda was very familiar with the Newtonian worldview. It was unlikely that she was going to change Ez's mental model or that of Dirk either. Instead, she simply pointed out that no one had ever built one of these Web sites before and that to keep the project under control, they would have to do things differently given the quality requirements and the tight time frame. "We want to substitute experiential learning for prolonged planning. If it's not working, we want to find out early," she said as she remembered the Shared Value of fast failures. "Nobody knows enough to get it right the first time. We want to get it right at the end, when it really counts."

Ez was dumbstruck, and Dirk was uneasy about what he was hearing. At one level, it felt right and made sense. It was just different from what he was used to.

The Downfall of the Waterfall

Having boned up on her negotiation approaches, Rananda knew she was not going to win by taking a quantum position versus a Newtonian position. Besides, Dirk held all the cards. Instead, she looked for the common denominator: "We all want this to succeed, and we all want to be sure the project is under control. Agreed?" Dirk gave a slight nod. Ez's look could be explained only as a stoned-faced squint.

"Our first draft project schedule was based on the waterfall," she pointed out. "See. Here's our original time line. We'd all be dead even after we pared it back to the bone using ESP. So we decided that our only chance would be to do a lot of work in parallel, because the scheduled end date of 5/15 must be optimized."

"But what about keeping the project under control? And how do you plan to keep this from being an endless experiment?" asked Dirk.

Time Boxing

Rananda explained the time boxing process they had decided on in the planning meeting. "At the end of each time box, we'll assess what's working and what's not. Then we'll plan the next time box based on what we learned. Each day, all subteams will meet to coordinate their efforts and identify barriers before they have an adverse impact on the project's quality, schedule, costs, risks, and team and stakeholder satisfaction.

"Every two weeks, we will have a formal meeting to reevaluate the entire project. At that time, we will reforecast the budget requirements." Dirk started to relax. And Rananda continued, "That way you will be in a position to make go/no go decisions and cut any losses before it's too late to recover. These frequent checkpoints will give you more control over the project.

"We will also put up a project Web site so that key stakeholders and the project office can keep up with everyday events. Not having to generate a lot of formal reports will save time and effort."

At that point, Dirk didn't care what life cycle methodology the project adopted. As for Ez, about all he could do was drum his fingers on the surface of his M4 binder. The concept of planning, deplanning, and replanning was anathema to everything he had been taught. Unfortunately, for Ez, PMP® came to mean, "Plan my project. Protect my plan."

"Whadaya think, Ez?" queried Dirk.

"You're the boss." Ez quipped, and left the room on his way to inflict M4 on the animal gathering project.

Rananda Shows Dirk the Money

Dirk was astonished by the estimated budget: the best-case revenues/best-case cost scenario was 50 percent more than he anticipated. After calming down, Dirk launched into nitpicking mode, questioning every figure. To her credit, Rananda had been smart enough to engage Feldon from finance, so her numbers were defensible.

Dirk ultimately gave the go-ahead.

Before she left the room, Rananda had one more piece of business: to come to an understanding of their working relationship, that is, what Dirk expected of her and what she needed from him. They agreed on what decisions she could make on her own and those that she had to consult on with Dirk. Dirk also agreed to get back to her within two hours on any decision that would delay the project.

Results After the Meeting

Things started to move faster than lightning after the meeting with Dirk. Most of Rananda's efforts were spent in recruiting qualified team members. This was her most difficult task. Dirk actually turned out to be a big help in recruiting. Not only did he have the necessary political and organizational clout, as sponsor he also had financial authority. Rananda got pretty much what she wanted to execute using the turbo life cycle model.

To be sure there was no misunderstanding with functional managers who were to supply team members to the SOS Web Site Project, Rananda drafted simple partnering agreements spelling out what was promised. The most important part of the agreement as far as she was concerned was that it got managers to identify backups in case the primary provider became unavailable.

We have seen how the Speculate cycle addresses Business Question 2 head-on: What will it take to do it? In this cycle, the eXtreme project manager promotes ownership of the project by those who will be doing the work, helps the core team and stakeholders produce a flexible road map, and fosters a sense of confidence and trust. In the next chapter, we will see how the Innovate cycle generates early wins—and early failures, which lead to learning. The Innovate cycle is the third in The Flexible Project Model, Critical Success Factor 3.

eXtreme Project Management Model
Applying the Quantum Mind-Set

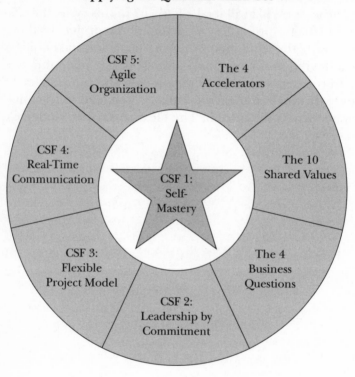

Chapter Twelve

Innovate: Learning by Doing

Demo or die.
Sign over the door of the MIT Media Lab

The Innovate cycle puts the emphasis on experimenting, rapid development, and generating timely and even real-time feedback from stakeholders, leading to, "Yes, that's what we really want!" or possibly, "Oh, no! We can't make it happen! Back to the drawing boards."

Innovate means learning by doing rather than by planning. It means generating early wins. And it means failing your way to success by finding the quickest route to failure. Unlike traditional project management, which may spend months in requirements gathering, eXtreme project management is impatient yet very focused. The focus comes from the team's shared understanding of the answers to Business Questions 1 and 2, which have been refined during the Visionate and Speculate cycles. Innovate is the third cycle of the Critical Success Factor 3, The Flexible Project Model.

In this chapter I will:

- Review time boxing.
- Outline the SCORE Model for creating innovative products and services.
- Discuss several good techniques for generating new ideas.

The Underlying Dynamics

Many unknowns, including evolving and even rapidly changing product requirements and technical feasibility, plague the Innovate cycle. Moreover, external factors can throw the project into turmoil: government regulations may cause additional work or rework, and competitors may beat you to market with new features or even introduce breakthrough ideas that leave your project in the dust. Enticing and untried new technologies may give you a potential edge and need to be tested. Vendors and other projects that your project depends on may default or be delayed.

As the team learns by doing and experiments with new and innovative concepts and begins to build the project deliverable, the answers to all 4 Business Questions start to change. This happens because the product vision (what the customer needs) will likely change as a result of the trial, error, and discovery of what is really needed, as well as the technical feasibility of producing it and the associated risks. As the product vision changes, the answers to Business Questions 2, 3, and 4 will also change. This is because new information will shed light on what it will now take to produce the deliverable, as well as whether the team can even get what it takes to do it. And this assumes that the project is still justifiable from the perspective of its intended business benefits. This vital information from the Innovate cycle provides the input for the Reevaluate cycle, a pause point for reviewing the latest findings and their impact on all 4 Business Questions.

Under pressure to get work done, team members may burn out, sacrificing their health and family lives. Creative thinking may stagnate, and the capacity to generate breakthrough ideas may evaporate. Moreover, rampant overtime may cause errors to be passed down the line, resulting in loss of valuable time due to rework.

In view of all this, it's only human to want to lock into a project deliverable and nail down the specifications as early as possible in the hope of reducing uncertainty, and then do it. Yet you are pulled in the direction of being fluid and flexible as long as possible so that the team can quickly respond to the unforeseen, make adjustments in what they are developing, and deliver a winning product. Figure 12.1 highlights just where we are in Critical Success Factor 3, the Flexible Project Model.

Figure 12.1. Critical Success Factor 3: The Flexible Project Model

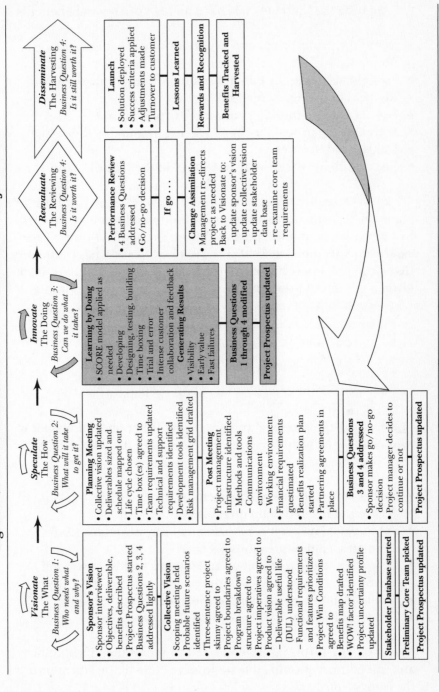

Applying the Innovate cycle has a number of important benefits:

- Keeps the project fluid and avoids locking into a solution prematurely
- Front-loads failure by experimenting with multiple options
- Reduces unnecessary rework
- Fosters creative thinking and breakthrough results
- Increases the probability of producing a valued end product
- Helps avoid burnout
- Enables the project to stay in control in the face of volatility

You are ready to start the Innovate cycle when you have in place the information and resources you need to move forward. Just because you got the go-ahead from the sponsor doesn't necessarily mean you have what you will need to succeed. I estimate that close to 75 percent of the projects I run into that have been given a green light do not have the requisite resources in place. Like a train without tracks, they are derailed.

> *You are ready to start the Innovate cycle*
> *when you have in place the information*
> *and resources you need to move forward.*

Here's the test to see if you are ready. Either on your own or in your negotiation with the sponsor at the end of the Speculate cycle, were you able to:

- Ensure that funds were allocated for the project?
- Secure the needed team members?
- Put in place the project management infrastructure (tools, templates, communications system)?
- Get access to the technology and systems that the team will need?
- Secure a conducive working environment?
- Get relief from policies that could slow you down?

As for the information you need to move ahead with clarity and speed, you should now be in excellent shape for meeting these prerequisites:

- Know your customer or intended audience
- Know the problem to be solved or the opportunity to be pursued
- Know what you are building or developing
- Know how success will be measured

The answers have all been accounted for in your Project Prospectus in the form of the project skinny, product vision, and Win Conditions. Not only that, by now you have been working hard to gain the buy-in and commitment of the project sponsor, crucial stakeholders, and core team. So you have that critical dynamic working for you.

The Innovate cycle is kicked off in a meeting attended by those who will be doing the work, as well as those who will be coordinating the work. This includes the core team and subteams. The purpose of the meeting is to focus everyone on the work to be done as well as how things will proceed during the Innovate cycle.

Time Boxing

The time box is the construct within which the Innovate cycle takes place (Figure 12.2). Rapid development, testing, and refinement of prototypes take place within the time box that was scheduled

Figure 12.2. Using the Time Box

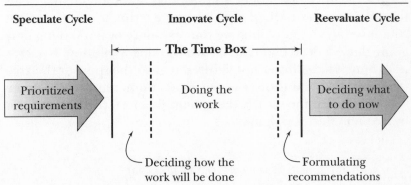

Note: The vertical solid lines represent the start and end of the time box. The vertical dotted lines represent the rough amount of time typically spent for the beginning and ending activities: deciding how the work will be done and formulating recommendations.

during the Speculate cycle. The time box can be anywhere from a few days to six weeks or so. If the work to be done is expected to take longer than six weeks, I recommend descoping it to whatever the team believes can be done in that amount of time. Then plan on a second time box for the remaining work.

The secret to success here is to set up multiple decision points so that the project can constantly be adjusted based on the latest findings. It's similar to sailing. A sailboat rarely makes a beeline to its destination. It's constantly off course, so the captain tacks, that is, makes frequent adjustments and changes in direction caused by the shifting of winds. The sailboat zigzags its way to port. Waiting too long to tack could be dangerous. The sailor may be so off course as not to be able to recover in time. Time boxing is the project management equivalent of tacking.

At the end of the series of time boxes, data are consolidated and used to help determine the future course of the project. This takes place in the next cycle of the flexible project model, Reevaluate. Since time is of the essence on eXtreme projects, open-ended experimenting on prototypes has to be restrained. Time boxing offers a way to do that.

The purpose of time boxing, then, is to force frequent decisions on the future course of the project. Time boxing gives an early answer to the question, Can we do it? At the end of the time box, the team assesses if it has been able to solve the problem or produce the intended work product.

If a prototype or model isn't working out, time boxing helps force a decision on whether to continue trying to fix it or to cut your losses. It's a way of limiting your exposure by not wasting time going down a dead-end road or overworking a solution. Not only does time boxing foster fast failures, it gives the sponsor the ability to decide to cut losses early or fund another approach. Sponsors usually like the idea of the greater financial control afforded by frequent decision points.

If a prototype or model isn't working out,
time boxing helps force a decision on whether
to continue trying to fix it or to cut your losses.

The basic rules of time boxing in the Innovate cycle are as follows:

- Start with a list of requirements to meet or a specific goal to achieve.
- Estimate how much time will be needed based on a forty-hour work week.
- Never extend the end date of the time box.
- Do not make any staffing increases during the time box.
- If the goal or requirements change materially, start a new time box.
- At the end of the time box, decide the next steps: abandon the prototype, begin a new time box to address specific problems, or declare victory and move on.

You can think of the Innovate cycle as a time box itself during which the SCORE Model is applied.

Applying the SCORE Model

In its essence, the Innovate cycle is a discovery process. The discovery model I like to use is the one that I have called SCORE. SCORE is a five-step approach for creating innovative products and services and parallels a model used by IDEO, a leading design firm (Kelley, 2001):

S—Scan the environment and available technology.

C—Comprehend how intended users function in real-life situations.

O—Originate by visualizing brand-new ideas.

R—Refine ideas by putting working models and prototypes into the hands of the intended population.

E—Execute by building the final version.

This commonsense SCORE model can be adapted to any kind of project that requires discovery and innovation. A strength of the model is that it raises more questions than it answers. Knowing the right questions to ask before rushing to a solution is the doorway to breakthrough ideas.

Once you are familiar with how SCORE works, you should be able to adapt it easily to your situation. For instance, if you are developing a new e-commerce capability and already have a good understanding of the market (the customer segments and the competition as well as the available technology), you will focus most of your initial attention on the second step: understanding customer needs and wants. Then proceed to brainstorming new solutions. Or your project may have started at a stage where the solution has already been proposed. The next step would be to develop models and prototypes to test and refine the idea or concept.

Once you are familiar with how SCORE works,
you should be able to adapt it easily to your situation.

Once the team has taken the SCORE process as far as it can and the Innovate cycle is over, the project moves on to Reevaluate, a major checkpoint in the project's life: a decision is made to continue the project (usually with changes being made to the deliverable or plan) or end it.

The decision to continue the project could send it back through another Innovate cycle. Or the decision could be to release the deliverable to customers because it is now good enough. In other words, the deliverable would move onto Disseminate, the last element of the Flexible Project Model.

In applying the SCORE Model, you can apply time boxing to each SCORE element by evaluating progress and deciding if what has been accomplished is good enough. By forcing frequent decision points, even every few days, time boxing helps to avoid gold-plating, a practice resulting in doing more than necessary to get the job done. A variation to going through the SCORE Model sequentially is to apply it in a spiral fashion. For instance, over a week, you quickly go through the entire SCORE cycle, doing a little in each element and ending up with a conceptual design or crude prototype. Then see what was learned and launch a more directed and expanded round by refining the prototype, involving more prospective users or inventing new prototypes. Here, the boundaries between each element may be a little fuzzy, but that is okay. Whether you are working sequentially or going around in circles, it is important to build in review points. This can take the form of the daily huddle or more formal lessons learned at the completion of each element. In practice, I prefer the spiral approach because each quick SCORE iteration feeds the next, adding progressive levels of sophistication and refinement while producing a stream of results (fast failures).

Now let's take a closer look at what goes on during the SCORE process of scanning, comprehending, originating, prototyping, and executing. First, a caution is needed: SCORE is not a rigid formula, prescription, or lockstep process for innovation. It's more like a jazz composition consisting of a basic structure and guidelines. The rest is improvisation. For instance, it is not uncommon that in scanning the environment (the first element), the team drifts into one of the other elements and comes up with an innovative idea, which is really slotted for the forth element, originate. Or the team may start talking about solution domains during the first element, before getting to originate. This is not a problem. Getting too Newtonian or complicated about the model puts people in a straitjacket and inhibits creativity. If a step inside one of the elements is skipped, then go back later to see if it makes sense to do it.

Because SCORE is really a set of guidelines, you'll need to adapt them to your situation. The principles apply whether you are coming out with a new hair mousse or working on a new process to reengineer your organization's procurement system.

Getting Ready

In setting the stage for brainstorming and idea generation that takes place throughout the SCORE Model, I recommend the twelve techniques outlined by Weinberg (1986):

1. *Create a conducive environment.* Ideas tend to flourish in a relaxed environment, free from everyday interruptions. Have everything you need handy, from food to flip charts.
2. *Encourage copying of useful ideas.* Borrow and build on ideas from anywhere. The hotel industry had much to learn from the airline industry about reservation systems.

3. *Elaborate on an idea that a teammate contributed.* This will give a better appreciation for an idea you might have initially ruled out.

4. *Drop your own idea in favor of an idea that the team wants to develop.* If your idea has little support, it's not going to go far. Capitalize on the group's enthusiasm.

5. *Refuse to let an idea drop until everyone understands it.* Studies have shown that people at first often react negatively to an idea at face value, especially if they think they might have to implement or live with it. Have people play back the idea in their own words to help ensure that they really understand what they are ruling out.

6. *Resist time pressure, and take time to listen when people explain their ideas.* We all want a fair hearing. You never know when a breakthrough is going to come.

7. *Test ideas contributed by outsiders.* People from different disciplines and industries bring new perspectives. They have not been blinded by the same mental models, assumptions, and perceived constraints as insiders.

8. *Withhold criticism in order to keep the flow going.* Criticism or premature evaluation of ideas severely limits the number of candidates. The idea is to diverge before you converge on a solution or start eliminating.

9. *When you must criticize an idea, make it clear that you are criticizing the idea, not the person.* Nothing stifles idea generation more than when people feel criticized.

10. *Test your own ideas before offering them.* Group leaders, because of their position, tend to think they are where they are because of their ability to generate ideas. They tend to spout a stream of ideas, stifling others who may defer to authority. So come to the table with something you can stand behind and avoid pontification.

11. *Encourage the team to drop ideas that had succeeded earlier but cannot be extended to the current situation.* At some point, you have to get down to doing the work.

12. *Revive a dropped idea later when its value becomes relevant.* Ideas are not perishable. They can live in hibernation, ready to blossom. Their time can come.

S—Scan the Environment and Available Technology

Scanning the environment means to look at what's out there, if anything, that addresses the need you are trying meet. It includes identifying customer segments, investigating existing products or services, and evaluating the competition. It also includes an understanding of constraints, such as government regulations that may restrict what you can do or by when.

Understanding the technology means to learn if the means already exist to bring your idea into reality. For instance, a hydrogen-propelled family car would be a breakthrough in the fuel industry. Hydrogen can be turned into fuel. But the technology and infrastructure to bring the idea to the consumer are expected to be at least fifteen years off. In this case, technology is a limiting factor.

At the other extreme, available computer and Internet technology is opening up myriad new product and service opportunities that weren't available five years ago. Know who the customer is, know the constraints, and know how you can leverage existing technology.

C—Comprehend How the Intended Users Function in Real Life

One of the problems that has plagued the development of software over the years is that developers have all too often had to build solutions in a vacuum, best-guessing what was needed. Either the customer wasn't available often enough for feedback, or the developer was handed a list of requirements but was not part of the process of understanding the true need. Most of the time, they miss the mark—not because they didn't meet the requirement but because what was asked for wasn't what was really wanted.

To vastly increase the odds of being successful, you can't beat firsthand experience of knowing what it's really like to live a day in the life of your intended customer. Rather than merely observing, use their systems and their work processes. Feel what they feel. Experience their frustrations firsthand. Experience what works. Even better is to do their job for a day or a week.

*You can't beat firsthand experience of
knowing what it's really like to live a day
in the life of your intended customer.*

O—Originate Brand-New Ideas

Once you have scanned the market, found out about available technology, and gathered some experience with the intended customer, you have laid the groundwork for brainstorming new ideas.

A related question comes up: Where do you look for new ideas? If you look only within your existing idea domain, you may miss opportunities to come up with a breakthrough as opposed to merely improving on something that already exists.

How do you come up with innovative ideas? Many books have been written about the subject. There is no one way, but there are some general principles that fit many situations.

Let's say that the project mission is to develop a revolutionary new running shoe with capabilities not currently available, and perhaps not even imagined. If I were to ask a group of people to start brainstorming revolutionary new running shoe ideas, most would tend to go into mind lock. The task in its present form is too daunting for most people to work with.

The secret is to break the problem down into tangible bites. The idea is based on the saying that every act of creation is first an act of destruction. Destruction in this sense means to decompose the idea or problem. The process of decomposing and inventing goes like this:

1. Understand the functionality.
2. Identify attributes.
3. Factor in the customer experience.
4. Explore solution domains.
5. Invent new solutions.
6. Select the most promising.

Understand Functionality

A function is the purpose for which the deliverable is to be used. The idea here is to become free of our existing mental picture or model of what a running shoe is. We are taking a first step in thinking outside the box by seeing the running shoe abstractly, without the limitations of its form. By this, I mean looking at the essence of what a shoe does or might do for a person. By distilling its functions from its form, we open the door to many new possibilities.

The group may come up with a list like this of running shoe functions:

- Provide protection from bruises
- Help protect from injuries
- Help you run faster
- Help you jump higher
- Make a social statement
- Let others see you in the dark
- Keep feet warm in cold winter
- Keep feet dry in rain

To trigger more brainstorming, the group can be asked to think of the ideal running shoe. At this stage, it is important to set aside any judgment as to feasibility. The crazier the idea, the better. This may prompt the following ideas about characteristics of the best running shoe:

- Glows in the dark
- Has a built-in odometer
- Has a navigation system that prevents the jogger from getting lost
- Can leap tall buildings in a single bound
- Contains a vibrator for giving a foot massage

Each of these functions becomes a candidate for possible development.

Identify Attributes

This involves breaking down the object of our investigation, the ideal running shoe, into its parts: laces, sole, eyelets, toe, tongue, heel, inside cushion, color, materials, style, and many other factors.

These attributes, like the functions brainstormed earlier, become candidates for exploration. For instance, the laces and eyelets might be made to glow in the dark. The heel might be made more functional by adding loops that can be used to hang the shoes.

Factor in the Customer Experience

Knowing what's it like to be a customer will help you come up with new ideas to improve the experience when you get to the point of inventing new solutions in the next step. For example, spending time with the community of running shoe customers should give you a pretty good understanding of what it's like to be a runner, from the time you purchase the running shoe until you discard it and everything in between. You may have even run a mile in their shoes and have firsthand experience of their frustrations, wishes, and *unarticulated* needs. Your group may have discovered:

- The shopping experience is too time-consuming and inconvenient.
- The body cloth wears out way before the sole does.
- The shoes should be lighter.
- Wearers run them into the ground before replacing them, causing foot injuries due to a too-thin sole.

Explore Solution Domains

A lot of this process is aimed at enabling the group to see things from a new perspective. We started out by encouraging everybody to step outside the box and live the customer experience. But our mental models die hard. So how else can we begin to see the problem with a fresh set of eyes? The answer lies in stepping out of our box, the domain of running shoes, and looking into how similar problems have been solved or solutions found in other domains.

Let's say a group is to work on one item: customers wait too long to buy replacement shoes, resulting in foot injuries and lost sales. Their task is to brainstorm possible options for solving the problem or exploiting the opportunity, identify other domains (that is, other specialized areas of expertise) that have been successful in a parallel situation and can teach them something, and indicate how the solution may be transferred to the new running shoe.

A domain is a specialized area of expertise—for example, medicine, computer technology, biology, nature, physics, the animal world, other industries than your own, psychology, religion. All you are looking to do is to harvest one potential workable idea. For instance, the group working on the problem of customers' waiting too long to buy replacement shoes brainstorms possible solutions that go from conservative to wild:

- Send customers a reminder by e-mail when the shoes are six months old.
- After running a thousand miles, runners can trade their running shoes in for a new pair.
- Install a treadometer in the shoe. When the tread is 75 percent used up, an audio chip turns on and signals that it is time for a new pair.

Although an idea may seem to be highly impractical, always probe into what aspect of that idea has merit. Let's say the group feels that their second idea—trading in their old pair after a thousand miles—is worth exploring. What domains can we go to in order to learn how to make a business out of trading things in? One might think of the auto industry, any kind of leasing business, and the tire industry (dealers give credit on new tires based on remaining tread). Should trading in prove to be a viable option in the revolutionized sneaker, the team would go on a field trip to learn practices and then adapt best practices.

Invent New Solutions

By now the subteams have produced a cornucopia of new ideas and places to look (domains) for bringing them into fruition. But which ideas should they pursue?

This is the point at which the group develops multiple running shoe concepts. And using the agreed-on selection criteria, they narrow the list of concepts to those that are the most viable. The selection criterion is any and all relevant Win Conditions, as well as other criteria, including marketability, technical feasibility, and competitive advantage. For instance, one Win Condition stipulated by the sponsor might be for the shoe to be ready in time for the Christmas selling season eighteen months down the road.

In our example, the group arrived at three concepts for a new running shoe:

Springstep: Springs are build into the sole, giving the runner an extra bounce and enabling him to take longer strides and effectively run faster. This shoe has the added advantage of being easier on the foot.

Tread bare: The shoes have a built-in audio chip (an idea borrowed from the greeting card domain) that goes off when the tread reaches a certain level of wear. The chip is programmed to sing, "Trade in time. Trade in time." The shoes are sold with a certificate that enables the runner to turn them in for a new pair and get credit for the unused portion of the old shoes.

Technofoot: When the tread gets low, the shoe has a built-in sensor that signals the built-in modem to transmit the shoe's status to a central computer. That activates an e-mail to the runner, offering a discount coupon and noting the nearest shoe outlet.

Select the Most Promising

Will it be Springstep? Tread bare? Or Technofoot? Selecting one of more concepts to pursue is accomplished by applying a set of criteria to each of the candidates. In the case of the sneaker example, criteria might include the size of target market, competitive advantage, technical feasibility, or likely profit margin. The next step is to build and test the prototypes for the most promising.

R—Refine Ideas by Using Models and Prototypes

Experimenting with prototypes brings into play the Shared Values of client collaboration, early value, fast failures and results orientation. It also leverages Accelerator 1: Make change your friend.

Rather than prototypes, the temptation for some project teams is to settle for blueprints, pictures, and documentation describing the new idea and how it will be designed and used. Descriptions do not provide a good basis for feedback from intended users, who cannot be expected to imagine how they might truly like or use the product in the real world. The menu is not the restaurant. You need to resist the pressure from typical Newtonian personality types to design the whole thing and then build it in compliance with the specs, which the production of blueprints and documentation can lead to. All too often, projects become reduced to designing blueprints and refining documentation, while the actual deliverable is lost sight of. Think of a prototype as an invitation to play and discover and get real-world feedback. Test results and feedback lead to redesigned prototypes, which are subjected to further testing in a series of short, dynamic iterations. The mental model here is one of cycles and curlicues rather than a waterfall sequence of straight lines.

In projects intended to produce physical products, scale models can often serve as useful prototypes. These can be handled and inspected by the intended users and can be tested in various ways, such as in wind tunnels.

Software developers tend to use different kinds of prototypes: business prototypes for determining all of the functions the software is intended to perform, usability prototypes to test the user experience, capability and design prototypes to try out particular design approaches, and performance and capacity prototypes to help ensure the hardware system can handle the demands placed on it.

Speaking of the pharmaceutical industry in his book, *Agile Project Management,* Jim Highsmith (2004) points out that "new technologies such as combinatorial chemistry and sophisticated computer simulation are fundamentally altering the innovation process itself." Instead of months to develop a single compound, hundreds and even thousands can be created and tested in a few days.

E—Execute the Final Version

At some point, all the experimenting has to stop and the final solution locked in. Execute takes place after the final Reevaluate cycle, when the go-ahead is given to finalize the production version of the deliverable. It then moves to Disseminate, where it is put in the hands of the customer.

At some point, all the experimenting has to stop and the final solution locked in.

The Goal of the Innovation Cycle

The Innovate cycle should provide a lot of information about your project and its associated risks. During this cycle, you experiment and innovate, encounter fast failures, and probably have some early successes. You now develop a better sense of the technical, schedule, and budget risks, as well as the project's ability to meet its Win Conditions. You will be able to use this information to look ahead and make critical decisions about the future of the project in the Reevaluate cycle.

With this overview of the Innovate cycle completed, let's look at how it plays out in the parallel universe.

It's an Ark. Or Almost, 4/1 Y2K BC

All the SOS project teams had gotten through Visionate and Speculate cycles. Trinity's quarantine and X-Virus antibiotic projects were well into the Innovate cycle, as was Rananda and her SOS Web Site Project.

Noah too had moved into the Innovate cycle. The latest meteorological forecasts put the probability of a flood of historic proportion at 95 percent. He found himself facing the daunting challenge of building a massive ark that would house the Selected Ones throughout the flood. No one had ever built a seafaring vessel even one-thousandth of the anticipated size. Moreover, Noah and his team also had the problem of not knowing the total head count for all the inhabitants. This had significant ramifications for the kind and quantity of food that would be needed, to say nothing of the housing and maintenance requirements. Even if the team wanted to lock into a final ark design, they didn't have enough information.

Moreover, the ark project was so politically sensitive that Noah was spending much of his time doing relationship management. He found himself consoling, cajoling, and trying to get the support of the many stakeholders who would be negatively affected by the SOS program and the events to come, as well as others on whom he was relying for resources and decision making.

The rest of his time was being devoted to coordinating with the human selection and animal-gathering teams. He barely had time to manage the actual development of the ark. The coordination details of these interdependent projects were enormous. How many Selected Ones would be delivered? How much would they all weigh? How much food would be needed? When would they arrive? How would they be cared for between when they arrived and when the flood arrived? Who would be responsible for loading the Selected Ones? What about quality control, that is sex-checking animals and humans to ensure each couple was properly paired? What about same-sex couples? Moreover, Gabriel was constantly asking him for updated progress reports. Although managing and facilitating these interactions was a vital part of Noah's job, they were taking him away from overseeing the design and building of the ark itself.

Fortunately, before the project got out of hand, Noah remembered the important context versus content distinction from Chapter Four in his favorite book on project management about the eXtreme project manager's leadership role. On an eXtreme project, the project manager needs to focus on managing the context: the relationships and everything else surrounding the project's content, that is, the thing that is being built. Noah was trying to be both the technical expert and relationship manager, and it wasn't working.

Once he explained the situation and gave the facts to his sponsor, he was able to make a solid case for getting relief. The sponsor agreed to let Noah hire a technical expert to oversee the design, building, and testing of the ark. Noah was relieved and hired Enoch, an experienced nautical engineer to serve as chief arkitech.

Getting Ready to Innovate

With Enoch on board, the Noah team got together to begin to innovate in earnest. The meeting started by revisiting the current version of the project skinny, which was prominently displayed on a flip chart in the meeting room, in order to anchor the team. They also reviewed other important information that would be needed to move ahead with clarity and speed: the product vision, project boundaries, and Win Conditions.

The team decided to use the SCORE Model to generate new ideas. They wanted to learn by doing rather than by planning.

S—Scan the Environment and Available Technology

Noah facilitated the discussion about the market: "Just who does the ark need to accommodate? What animal species? How many? How many pairs of humans? What about their food, shelter, and medical needs? What about . . . ?" The list seemed endless.

Enoch wasted no time in weighing in: "What about building the ark? Where will we go for ideas to build a boat of such magnitude? Let's stop and ask ourselves what the purpose of the ark is in the first place."

Zoey, the team's subject matter expert on zoology, replied, "To house the Selected Ones and keep them safe throughout the flood."

"If that's the case," said Enoch, "then where can we look for ideas and technology for keeping large numbers of people and animals safe for long periods of time?"

Joanna was quick to jump on it. "We also need to look at our Win Conditions for more clues as to where we should be looking. Our must-meet condition is delivering on time before the flood comes.

Enoch's question about where to look for ideas, along with keeping the Win Conditions in mind, was the spark that the team needed to begin to think out of the box as they planned the ark. Using sticky notes, the team was quick to brainstorm a list of potential solution domains where they could go for fresh ideas to help answer the questions that had been raised early in the meeting:

Being on time
- Crisis management centers
- Theater preparations for opening night
- Emergency rooms

Housing issues
- Hotel management
- Hospitals
- Shipbuilding
- Hotel and zoo design

Loading and coordination issues
- Subways during rush hour
- Observing an ant colony
- Mob control procedures
- Loading dock management
- Queuing theory
- Sheep herding

Life-sustaining issues

- Diet and nutrition Web sites
- Supermarkets for storing food
- Neutraceuticals
- Animal and human psychology
- Zookeeping

C—Comprehend How the Intended Users Function in Real Life

Next, the team decided to learn what actually went on in the real world. Since loading the ark was a big concern, one subteam went to cattle ranches and observed how cattle were herded and eventually loaded into cattle cars. Several brave souls wanted to feel what a cow felt and lined up with the herd to experience the experience. (Talking about a moooving experience.)

One team went on a field trip to a subway stop during rush hour and learned the dangers and challenges of too many people squeezing through too small a space. On their way back, they took the freeway during rush hour and liked the idea of stoplights at the end of on-ramps that regulated the flow of merging traffic in a timed-release pattern.

Another team learned that animals left to roam in their natural habitat were healthier than those kept in cages. Other expeditions were made to hotels and hospitals.

O—Originate Brand-New Ideas

To guide them in their brainstorming to visualize new ideas, the team adopted Weinberg's twelve techniques for generating new ideas (1986).

Having done their homework, the team collaborated effectively in generating and discussing new ideas and then zeroed in on a breakthrough idea for housing the animals: use barges that were designed to simulate the native habitat of certain animals. The barges could be towed behind the ark and partitioned so that selected animals had the freedom to roam but would not be able to destroy each other. Not only would this produce a healthier animal population, but the barges would provide the needed flexibility to expand capacity late into the development cycle. This would help solve the problem of not knowing the head count and makeup of the final animal or human populations. Moreover, barges were already plentiful, and if more were needed, barge building was a proven technology and offered little risk. The idea to go with barges drove home the value of Accelerator 4: Simplicity wins. They decided to change the name to arkobarge.

R—Refine Ideas by Using Models and Prototypes

The temptation of some team members was to settle for blueprints, pictures, and documentation describing the arkobarge and how it would be designed and used. The prevailing philosophy was to design the whole thing and then build it in compliance with the specs. This was typical of Newtonian personalities. But it was Nadia, a quantum thinker, who made a poignant comment: "The blueprint is not the arkobarge anymore than a travel brochure is the vacation." She then asked a loaded question: "Are we interested in compliance to spec, or are we interested in whether what we build actually works?" She continued, "If a picture is worth a thousand words, then a prototype is worth a thousand pictures."

After a heated discussion, the team decided to do a minimal design of the arkobarge and then turn its attention to building a prototype of the arkobarge and its fleet of tethered barges. The prototype would then be tested. The test results would lead to a redesign, which would be subjected to further testing in a series of short, dynamic iterations.

It became clear to Noah that his job was to get people thinking, talking, and interacting. He reminded the team of the operative Shared Values that were now in play: results orientation, fast failures, early value, and visibility.

The team started out by building a scale model of the ark and doing a simulation of the entire loading process in a local swimming pool. They used off-the-shelf toys from the local Toys 4 Tots toy store. The simulation was cheap and quick.

They were now ready to scale up their prototyping and simulation before beginning to build in earnest. A major concern of the Noah team was how to time and integrate their work with the animal- and people-gathering teams, so the Noah team, along with the animal- and people-gathering teams, arranged a real-life simulation at the Mesopotamia shipyard. Twelve barges were tethered to the *Gigantic*, a renowned ocean liner that was on tour. The animal-gathering team made arrangements with the local zoo to borrow its animals for a couple of days. The people-gathering team worked closely with Earthland Census to recruit an ethnically balanced profile of the arkobarge's human population. They also took the opportunity to identify ethnic food requirements.

On the day of the simulation, the arkobarge team brought camcorders so that they could review real-life experiences rather than attempt to draw conclusions from lifeless, second-hand after-action reports and slide presentations. The real-life simulations had bolstered the team's confidence and trust. They were ready to start designing and building the combination ark and barge flotation model. In order to ensure clarity of purpose and results orientation, two of the Shared Values that had gotten them this far, the team redrafted the first sentence of their project skinny to synchronize it with the current direction of their project: "The Noah team will build an arkobarge for the Selected Ones." And realizing that eXtreme project management is an iterative process, they updated their in-scope work to include, "Provide a sufficient number of barges."

As for how the arkobarge was to be powered, the team came up with three options: wind, turbo power, and animal power. The thought was that certain animals, especially the four-legged ones, would benefit by the exercise if they could be mounted on treadmills. Once these options had been investigated and tested, they would pick the best one for their final build.

Enoch pointed out that since time was of the essence, they couldn't afford open-ended experimenting to decide which of the three options would be used to power the arkobarge into the new world. The team decided to run all three time boxes in parallel to test the feasibility of wind, animal, and turbo power. While part of the team was working on how the arkobarge would be powered, another team was using computer simulations and time boxing for stress testing and floatability by testing various arkobarge designs.

Recognizing the need for all the pieces to fit together at the end, the leaders of different teams conducted a daily huddle of huddles to synchronize their work.

At the end of the series of time boxes, data were consolidated and used for deciding on the future course of the project. This would take place in the next cycle of the Flexible Project Model, Reevaluate.

E—Execute the Final Version

The team wanted to know what the "E" was for in the SCORE model. Noah pointed out to the team that during the Reevaluate cycle, a decision would be made on the future course of the project. "If the project is still a go, we'll begin to develop the final version of the arkobarge, but always keeping our options open as late into the development cycle as possible. The E stands for Execute."

Noah and team were now ready to go the Reevaluate cycle.

Catching Up with Rananda

In the meantime, Rananda and the SOS Web Site Project team were well into the Innovate cycle doing their own brand of prototyping to model and build the Web site.

The daily interaction with a cross section of eventual Web site users led to a major modification of the site's front page. Performance and capacity testing led to a significant hardware upgrade, which was approved by the steering committee within eight hours. Having seen the role models of Rananda, Trinity, and Noah and having experienced tangible benefits, management too was starting to get the hang of eXtreme project management. It gave them a sense of control in the face of volatility.

Having reached their first milestone, a fully functioning prototype, the SOS Web site project was now ready to go on to Reevaluate.

Now that you've gone through an iteration of the Innovate cycle, you are a lot smarter about your project and its associated risks. During the Innovate cycle, you experimented and practiced fast failures, and you may have had some early success stories. You have a better idea of the technical, schedule, and budget risks, as well as the project's ability to meet its Win Conditions.

You may have had a favorable event that will boost the project's WOW! factor. Perhaps a long-awaited piece of legislation was passed that will give your project a new kick and change the entire financial equation; for example, Congress passed a new clean air bill that will spark sales of the new advanced air quality technology system you are working on. Or your project may be less attractive now that two competitors beat you to market and with a technology superior to yours. Or perhaps your firm changed its strategy, making your project a misfit. Any of these events (call them POW! factors) could significantly alter the viability of the project's business proposition and cause it to be stopped.

Unlike traditional project management, which is preoccupied with measuring conformance to the original plan, eXtreme project management benchmarks against future possibilities based on the latest results and events. Whereas traditional project management takes a retrospective look and asks, "How do we bring the project back in line with the plan?" eXtreme project management takes a forward look and asks, "How do we move forward in the light of current realities and in view of what we now see in front of us?" This is subject of the next chapter, where we look at Reevaluate, the fourth cycle in the Flexible Project Model, Critical Success Factor 3.

eXtreme Project Management Model
Applying the Quantum Mind-Set

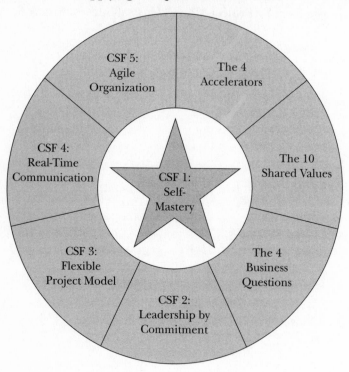

Chapter Thirteen

Reevaluate: Deciding the Project's Future

I'm not afraid to die. I just don't want to be there when it happens.
WOODY ALLEN

The Reevaluate cycle revolves around Business Question 4: Is it worth it? The purpose of this cycle, then, is for management to step back and make a decision on the future course of the project. Is this still the right project? Can we win? Should we change direction? Put it on hold? The decision is ultimately based on the likelihood of obtaining the project's postdelivery business benefits as well as its relative attractiveness with respect to other projects in the portfolio. Although the project manager, the team, and the sponsor have been taking the project's pulse on a daily and weekly basis, reevaluation is a full-fledged physical examine and takes place at several formal check points during the project's life time.

Is this still the right project?

Said another way, whereas time boxes are very short checkpoints, the Reevaluate cycle is a major point where a holistic view is taken of the project and its future prospects. The reevaluate pause point is typically triggered by agreed-on milestones, junctures in a project that represent the completion of significant work. Some milestones are also major decision points where the next round of funding would take place. Examples are technical feasibility confirmed, customer testing completed, and ready to go into production.

For short-duration projects, say three to six months in length, reevaluate sessions may occur every three to four weeks. For longer projects, the Reevaluate cycle may take place at two- to three-month intervals. They are typically scheduled ahead of time at the expected completion of an Innovate cycle.

As noted in the previous chapter, during the first run-through of the Innovate cycle, you experimented, practiced fast failures, and may have had some early success stories. You should have developed a better understanding of the technical, schedule, and budget risks, as well as the project's ability to meet its Win Conditions. The purpose of the Reevaluate cycle is to use this new knowledge to make decisions about the way ahead. When incorporated into the project management process, the Reevaluate cycle minimizes financial risk by funding the project in increments. It also ensures that funding and sponsorship continue, if warranted. And it can lead to freeing up resources for other projects, when it turns out that it does not make sense to continue the project, either because the project is not likely to succeed as a business proposition or because other projects in the portfolio are now considered to be more strategically important. I'll say more about the portfolio part of the decision later.

The shaded area in Figure 13.1 illustrates where we are in Critical Success Factor 3, the Flexible Project Model.

The focal point of the Reevaluate cycle is the reevaluate meeting, the event during which crucial stakeholders review results and make a go/no go decision. The decision to move ahead has several variations. A conditional go-ahead can be given pending a piece of missing information—for instance, if the team can demonstrate that they can bring down the unit cost of the new high-tech sneaker to $18.50 per pair. In some cases, the plan forward is approved as is, with no conditions. This outcome is more typical of early Reevaluate cycles when the project is still in the research and development stage and concrete data are lacking regarding the project's Win Conditions.

In later cycles, the stakes become higher, as when the project moves from small-scale prototyping to extended testing or is about

Figure 13.1. Critical Success Factor 3: The Flexible Project Model

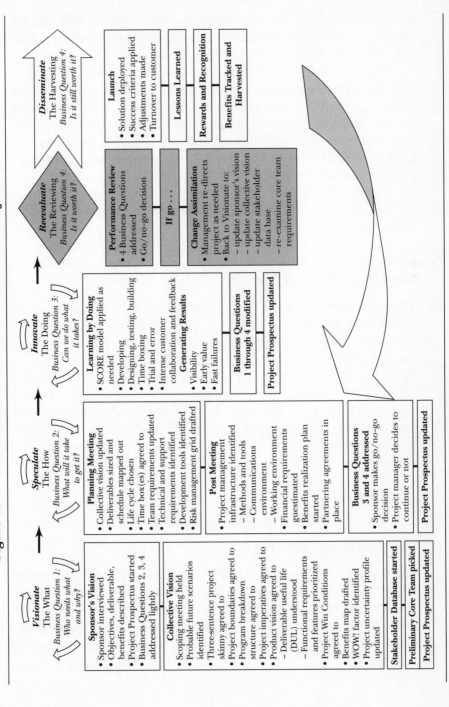

to move into production and go public. Millions of dollars may be on the line. In these situations, management may become more involved in shaping the plan for the next round of financing.

The eXtreme project manager is the catalyst whose job is to lead the team in gathering and presenting information needed for the reevaluate meeting, which is attended by the project sponsor and members of the steering committee, managers who are typically sponsors of other related projects, as well as the bosses of sponsors. (The role of the steering committee was covered in Chapter Seven.)

In this chapter, I'll provide an overview of the reevaluate process. But first, a few words on what the reevaluate meeting is not are necessary.

What Reevaluate Is Not

The reevaluate meeting is not the place for conducting project retrospectives. These are conducted in preparation for the reevaluate meeting. Nor is the reevaluate meeting a platform for asking management for routine approvals or changes in, or dispensation from, burdensome corporate policies, approval processes, or oppressive methodologies. Why? If you've been applying eXtreme project management as it is intended, these troublesome matters would already have surfaced through the daily huddle and should have been eliminated by the project manager and project sponsor. You don't have the luxury of waiting for the reevaluate meeting to come along in order to resolve interim problems on complex, fast-paced projects.

The Reevaluate Process

The 4 Business Questions are the scaffolding of the reevaluate process. Using the 4 Business Questions as the framework ensures that all stakeholders continue to calibrate the project against its ability to deliver the intended business benefit. Each business question is addressed from the perspective of what management wants to know.

*Each business question is addressed from the
perspective of what management wants to know.*

Three distinct assessments are implicit throughout the process:

- Performance to date is reviewed against deliverables and Win Conditions.
- The business attractiveness of the project is reevaluated with respect to the project itself, as well as its alignment with current business strategy.
- The proposed plan for moving forward is evaluated.

Business Question 1: Who Needs What and Why?

The intent here is to provide management with a quick refresher on what the project is intending to accomplish. Use your updated Project Prospectus to quickly reorient everyone as to the latest version of the three-sentence project skinny, product vision, Ins and Outs, Win Conditions matrix, and importantly, the Project Uncertainty Profile (PUP).

Business Question 3: Did We Do What It Takes?

If Business Question 1 relates to what you set out to do, the next question management wants answers to the question, Were you able to do it?

For purposes of logical information flow, Business Question 3 is asked out of sequence at this point, which can really drive the Newtonian personalities in the room crazy. If that weren't enough, there is a slight twist on the usual way of asking Business Question 3 (Can we get what it takes?). It is now phrased to convey that an assessment is being made of the team's prior accomplishments: Did we do what it takes?

Here, the crucial stakeholders evaluate the team's progress against what you set out to do in the just-completed Innovate cycle. These are the questions you should be prepared to answer.

Context-related questions

- How have the project's purpose and product vision changed since the last review?
- How have the Win Conditions changed in terms of priority or success measures?
- What major obstacles have you encountered, and how successful were you in overcoming them?
- What, if any, new opportunities presented themselves that might change the attractiveness of the project? Examples might be access to a new technology, a favorable government regulation, or a discovery.

Accomplishments

- What major deliverables were you shooting for?
- How are you doing against the Win Conditions?
- Specifically, how are you doing in achieving the must-meet and optimize conditions?
- Is the project still expected to be within the acceptable limits of the other Win Conditions?
- What's working? What's not working?

Outlook

- What do you foresee to be the greatest risks in the latest intended business benefit and ROI? Specifically, what business risks are there? Market and competitive risks? Technology risks? Development risks? (By now you'll recognize these as coming from your PUP analysis.)

Business Question 2: What Will It Now Take to Do It?

Given what has been learned to date, where do we go from here? What's the new plan?

Management will want answers to questions like these:

- How do you want to change the project parameters in order to meet or beat the ROI proposition? That is, what changes do

you want to make to the product vision or the Win Conditions
(for example, extend the deadline or tighten or loosen the
quality parameters)?
- What can be done to reduce the level of uncertainty?
- What is the expected impact of all this on the budget for the
  next project cycle? The impact on the ultimate business outcome and ROI?
- All considered, what is your plan for the next cycle? Go back
  to the drawing boards (meaning Visionate)? Go directly to the
  next Innovate cycle?

The work products listed in the Speculate cycle are your blueprint for preparing your path forward.

Business Question 4: Is It Worth It?

By this point, management should have the information needed
to make an informed decision on the viability of the project. It
is recommended that they look at the project from two distinct
perspectives:

Strategic fit: In the light of our current or expected shift in busi-
    ness strategy, is this still the right project for us to be doing? In
    other words, does it still have a place within our larger portfo-
    lio of projects?
Project viability: How likely is it that we can succeed?

The first question relates to how the project fits within the overall project portfolio. Assuming there is still a strategic fit, the second relates to the probability of achieving that project's expected
business benefits. Guidelines for addressing both questions are offered below.

These decisions are squarely in the court of the sponsor and
steering committee. Up to now, you've been taking the lead in presenting the background information. As the project champion, it's
your sponsor's turn to be in the forefront and argue in favor of the
project.

Scoring the Project for Strategic Fit

Looking at the project from this perspective requires looking at the must-meet criteria and the should-meet criteria. Here, must-meet and should-meet refer to the organization's criteria for evaluating projects.

Must-Meet Criteria. Must-meet criteria are just that: a set of do-or-die requirements that the project must meet to continue to have a place in the organization's overall portfolio of projects. Must-meet criteria depend on the type of project. Here are some examples of typical criteria for IT projects and new product introductions:

IT projects

- Alignment with strategic plan
- Meets compliance standards (for example, Freedom of Information Act)
- Significant competitive advantage
- Demonstrable cost reduction
- Demonstrable cost avoidance
- Generates incremental revenues
- Improves customer service
- Significant impact on operations
- Technically feasible
- Resources available
- Critical feed: other projects depend on this one

New product introductions

- Alignment with strategic plan
- Sufficient market size and need
- Superior competitive advantage
- Leverages existing competencies
- Provides quick market entry
- Satisfactory (risk-adjusted) financial return
- Technically feasible
- Resources available
- Critical feed: other projects depend on this one

Because the world of eXtreme projects is dynamic, the answers to any single must-meet criterion can change from cycle to cycle depending on how the project evolves, as well as external (contextual) circumstances. For instance, I led a project to relaunch a computer industry newspaper. The project was meeting its agreed-on value proposition, but the organization decided that for strategic purposes, it would no longer publish computer-related periodicals.

Failure of the project to achieve any single must-meet criterion is by itself reason enough to kill the project. If the project passes on all must-meet criteria, it is then subjected to a second screen: should-meet attributes.

Obviously, selection criteria will differ from organization to organization. A should-meet criterion for one may be a must-meet criterion for another. The criteria listed above could be either must or should meet depending on the organization.

Should-Meet Criteria. If a project has already passed the must-meet hurdle, why bother to look at less critical criteria? The answer is that not all worthy projects are created equal. Some are more equal than others. Most organizations have more projects in the funnel than they can undertake with the people and funds available. As a result, all projects get jammed up and slowed down as people play project hopscotch, jumping from one to the other. Addressing the should-meet criteria offers a way out because it takes into consideration other criteria for assessing projects in a way that allows different projects to be considered on their overall contribution to the portfolio. This approach provides a rationale for eliminating projects that rate poorly relative to others on the should-meet criteria, even if they meet all of the must-meet criteria. It's similar to managing an investment portfolio. You put some stocks on hold, invest more in others, and sell those that are underperforming in relative terms.

Exhibit 13.1 is a sample scoring sheet. Since some criteria are more important than others, a weighted assessment can be made. This is done by assigning high or lesser point values to each criterion.

Scoring the Project on Its Own Merits

It's possible to have a project that enjoys a tight strategic fit but has little chance of succeeding. The purpose here is to score the project

**Exhibit 13.1. Portfolio-Level Scoring Sheet:
Should-Meet Criteria Using Weighted Scoring**

The sponsor and each steering committee member score the project against the agreed-on criteria.

Criteria	Weight	Your Score: 1 = very unattractive, 10 = very attractive	Total Points (Weight × Score)
Competitive advantage	10		
Meets compliance standards	10		
Improves customer service	10		
Demonstrable cost reduction	5		
Makes good use of resources	5		
Total points			

on the perceived likelihood of being successful (Exhibit 13.2). The four risk elements come from the four categories of the PUP.

The advantage of the scoring process is that it facilitates comparisons with other projects across the portfolio based on accumulated points earned. The risk is that the go/no go decision is reduced to a sterile numbers exercise, not uncommon when management is reviewing project after project. Ultimately, the numbers are based on opinions and not scientific certainty, which numbers can imply. What's important is that a discussion around the numbers takes place so that people are given an opportunity to explain and defend their thinking. If necessary, a rescoring should follow.

The advantage of the scoring process is that it facilitates comparisons with other projects across the portfolio.

Exhibit 13.2. Project-Level Scoring

	Likelihood Score: 1 point = low, 10 points = high
Win Conditions: Ability to meet	
Must-meet condition	
Optimize condition	
Satisfactory ROI	
Risks: Ability to overcome	
Business risks	
Technical or development risks	
Project risks	
Environmental risks	
TOTAL POINTS	

When a project is given the go-ahead, especially in the later stages when the stakes become higher, it is common for management to call for changes in the proposed new plan or outline conditions that need to be met for continued funding. For instance, a team may still be trying to solve a technical problem that would enable the project to move forward. Management may then give a limited green light and time frame for the problem to be solved before the project is resumed in full.

If a competitor has upstaged you, making your project less attractive, management may give you time to assess the situation and come up with a new strategy. You may be able to beat the competition on price, range of features, or some other variable. Or you may have particularly strong distribution in Europe and be able to steal the show in that market.

Checking the Project's ROI

The next test for the project is to see how it fairs financially. Exhibit 13.3 was originally generated during the Speculate cycle after the planning and updated periodically thereafter. Since eXtreme projects have a high uncertainty factor, even the most carefully thought out numbers need to be viewed skeptically. In the early

Exhibit 13.3.   Risk-Adjusted ROI from Best- Through Worst-Case Scenarios: Present Value at the End of the Fifth Year (000)

	Best-Case Revenues/ Best-Case Costs	Best-Case Revenues/ Worst-Case Costs	Worst-Case Revenues/ Best-Case Costs	Worst-Case Revenues/ Worst-Case Costs
Revenues	18,000	18,000	12,500	12,500
Costs				
Prelaunch costs	2,200	4,800	2,200	4,800
Postlaunch costs	7,000	10,400	7,000	10,400
Total costs	9,200	15,200	9,200	15,200
Net revenues	8,800	2,800	3,300	–2,700
Percentage ROI	96	18	36	–26
Payback period	1 year, 4 months	2 years, 5 months	1 year, 10 months	3 years, 1 month
Time to Profit	2 years, 2 months	4 years, 1 month	3 years, 2 months	Over 5 years

stages of the project, more emphasis is placed on the strategic fit criteria and the numbers are given less credibility due to the high uncertainty. In his book *Winning at New Products* (2001), Robert Cooper cautions that financial analysis alone can do much damage if it is used too soon and with the wrong projects and that qualitative and nonfinancial considerations must also enter into the decision.

Reevaluating the Web Site Project, 4/7 Y2K BC

Although Rananda had been keeping the crucial stakeholders up to date, it was still initially intimidating to see them all in one room at the same time. At that moment, the title of a book she had read on public speaking flashed through her mind: *I Can See You Naked* (Hoff, 1992). The thought of everybody sitting there without their clothes on gave her the levity she needed to calm down. Not even Ez bothered her. He was in attendance to double-check that any proposed project management methodology was acceptable for the next project cycle. Although he did not have voting power in the meeting, he could easily muddy the waters and cast doubt on any proposed project plan.

In attendance were all the decision makers, including the heads of the GIA and SBI as well as the Earthland Security's vice president of marketing, the chief information officer, and Feldon from Finance.

Business Question 1: Who Wants What and Why?

Since things had been going so well on the SOS Web Site Project, Dirk decided that he would kick off the meeting and give an overview of the project as it now stood. He had become a real fan of the Project Prospectus. He used it to quickly reorient everyone as to the latest versions of the project skinny, product vision, Ins and Outs, Win Conditions matrix, and, importantly, the PUP.

Business Question 3: Did We Do What It Takes?

He also reviewed the major changes that occurred during the just-completed Innovate cycle. These included adding a dating service module to the Web site in order to accelerate the new world repopulation program, which would increase the size of the tax base. Another major scope change was to provide wireless technology for the new world population since there would be no dependable infrastructure in place. Moreover, system reliability, which was flagged as one of the Win Conditions, was upgraded to 99 percent. And finally, stress testing of the system revealed the need for two redundant backup systems, which were added to the budget.

Rananda was up next. She was really catching on to eXtreme project management as being relationship management. As part of her job, she had been keeping crucial stakeholders up to date all along. That had two payoffs at the reevaluate meeting: there were no surprises (because managers hate surprises) and there was less micromanagement (when people feel they are informed, they don't feel the need to control as much). These two benefits came from putting into action three of the ten Shared Values: client collaboration, honest communication, and visibility, all of which served to build trust and confidence in the project's ability to succeed.

Rananda quickly went down a list of major deliverables and noted where each stood versus the plan. Several were not completed according to plan and would be carried over to the upcoming Innovate cycle: the e-commerce capability that would allow the Selected Ones to shop over the Web for new world supplies and the software program that would be used to qualify those who would be chosen. Both were plagued by technical difficulties.

Business Question 2: What Will It Now Take to Do It?

In developing their new plan, Rananda had told the team to "think of the next Innovate cycle as the start of a new project, because it is, and plan it accordingly." By this time, everyone on the team had their own copy of *eXtreme Project Management*. Chapter Eleven, "Speculate," was their guide.

Ez just couldn't wait for the discussion of the proposed project methodology and life cycle. He was loaded for bear having brought with him the latest M4 binder, which now was six inches thick. Part of the reason for the increased heft was his infatuation with 6 Stigma, the quality assurance method that had come out of the closet after a well-deserved dormant period. Before he could take a pot-shot at Rananda's methodology, Dirk stole Ez's thunder. He proudly proclaimed, "6 Stigma is our new program du jour." What he thought he was saying was, "new program to save the day."

To prevent any further embarrassment to Dirk, Warren Windbreaker, Earthland Security's CIO, quickly changed the subject. He looked at his watch and said, "It's getting to that time. We need to look at the numbers."

Business Question 4: Is It Worth It?

This was the moment everybody had been waiting for. Feldon from finance and Yolanda, chief spin doctor and director of public information for Earthland Security, would co-lead the session to score the project in terms of its portfolio fit and chances for success.

Originally, Dirk had wanted Rananda to take the group through this exercise. However, Rananda used her speak-up power and pushed back, making the case that Earthland Security's management, the project customer, would ultimately be responsible for realizing the project's business benefits and needed to take ownership for them. Her role was to collaborate with them in getting the numbers together and to defend the project management cost figures that she would come up with.

Because not everybody had been through the scoring process, Yolanda did a quick orientation. She scribbled the two key questions to be addressed on one of the four flip charts:

- Is it still aligned with Earthland's core strategy?
- How likely is it that the project will succeed?

"The first question," she said, "relates to the business worthiness of the project: the business benefit in terms of added value and ROI. The second relates to the probability of ever achieving the expected business benefits in the first place." She emphasized, "If the project passes this first screen, a set of do-or-die criteria, it will then be subjected to a second screen comprising should-meet attributes."

The criteria had been set at the beginning of the project. In fact, Earthland Security had developed different must-meet criteria for different kinds of projects. The must-meet criteria to be used for the SOS Web Site Project were:

- Alignment with strategic plan
- Technically feasible
- Significant impact on SOS operations

"By definition, a score of no on any one of the must-meet criteria is reason to stop the project," stressed Yolanda. "Now, go ahead and mark your ballot." After a pregnant pause, she asked, "Any no's?" There were none.

"Next, we'll take a look at the should-meet criteria. Use your ballot to score each of the factors on a scale of 1 to 10," Yolanda directed. At that point, Victor Voyeur, secretary of the Global Intelligence Agency (GIA), asked, "If the project already passed the must-meet hurdle, why are we bothering to score it further?"

Ez, whose job responsibilities included keeping tabs on Earthland Security's entire project portfolio, was quick to jump in: "We have more projects in the SOS program portfolio than we can undertake with the people and funds available. At some point . . . " And Dirk weighed in to finish Ez sentence, "We're going to have to eliminate the lower-scoring projects." Apparently, Dirk had been given a copy of *eXtreme Project Management* and read the last chapter on agile organization. It had hit home.

The assembled executives looked at each other quizzically. Until now, any project that breathed was implemented. As a result, all projects slowed as people played project hopscotch, jumping from one to the other—sometimes as many as three or four projects in a day. Like Humpty Dumpty, projects had broken into so many pieces that no one could get the whole picture on any one venture. Instead of fixing the core problem (indiscriminate project selection by management), executives mandated more tracking reports, which tied up resources even more as everybody filled out status reports, most of which were exercises in Nobel-quality fiction writing. On top of that, most projects failed to meet expectations since in the press of time, people had to cut corners, which caused rework, diverting people from working on new projects.

"Okay, everybody," Yolanda said. "Score the project against the should-meet list." The total points on each ballot were consolidated, and the project was given a single total score of 1,260 points. Later, the point score would be used to see how the project stacked up against others.

The next test for the SOS Web Site Project was to see how it faired financially. It was Feldon's turn. So that people had a reality-based understanding for why the numbers were the way they were, Feldon referred everyone to the PUP. He pointed to three high-risk areas that had a heavy influence on his budget numbers:

- No experience meeting the e-commerce needs of a global community
- The fact that the schedule was short compounded by a due date that had little latitude
- The high dependency on other projects that would feed into the Web Site Project

He also noted that the project was still high risk, having scored 3.3 on the PUP, down from 3.7 during the first Speculate cycle.

With that background in mind, he turned to the flip chart page he had prepared ahead of time to summarize the latest ROI estimate (Exhibit 13.4). Nobody liked the numbers. "Let's face it," bellowed Caldwell, "if it

Exhibit 13.4. SOS Web Site Project: ROI Expressed in Revenues in Present Value at the Five-Year Point (000)

	Best-Case Revenues/ Best-Case Costs	Worst-Case Revenues/ Worst-Case Costs
Net revenues	8,000 drachmas	2,000 drachmas
Percentage ROI	75	−20
Time to profit	2 years, 6 months	7 years, 8 months

weren't for the dependence of the entire SOS program on the Web site project, it would not have been an attractive investment at all."

The Newtonians in the room did love the quantitative approach. But Feldon, who was a whole brain thinker, recognized it for what it was: "Let's realize that all this is highly subjective. The main thing is that it gets us talking and focusing on business value. Early estimates for eXtreme projects can be off by magnitudes of four."

Portfolio Review

Although the SOS Web Site Project would go on the next Innovate cycle after tightening up its plan by making a quick stop at Speculate, it was another story for the antibiotic project.

Having made his point about the need for portfolio management, the following week Dirk rounded up Earthland Security's SOS steering committee to do a review of the entire project portfolio. There were simply too many projects chasing too few resources. In preparation for the meeting, Feldon from finance consolidated the scores of all projects in the SOS program.

Trinity's X-Virus antibiotic team had been struggling to come up with an antidote to the virus. The combination of applying time boxing and taking the Shared Value of fast failures seriously boiled down to this: there was less than a 10 percent chance of technical success. Moreover, the project was bleeding resources from other projects for which failure was not an option.

Dirk announced that the antibiotic project would be stopped. Some of the scientists were emotionally attached to the project and would go on to lobby that it not be put to sleep. In its place, Trinity's quarantine project would now be expected to carry the day and protect the Selected Ones from contracting the virus in the first place.

As time went on, Dirk had become more people sensitive. He had also been reading his project management book where it covered emotional intelligence, and he was able to comprehend the Feelings → Facts → Solutions model. So when it came time to eliminate Trinity's X-Virus antibiotic project, he called the entire team into the room and told them firsthand rather than his usual practice of sending out an e-mail or posting a notice on the bulletin board. He went to lengths to praise them for the work they had done. He commended them for having produced early evidence that the project was a long shot. As a result of their work, critical resources would be freed up to work on other projects that had a higher chance of success.

This would benefit everybody. "You didn't fail," he assured them. "You succeeded in proving it wouldn't work within the time frame."

Although the team was not happy about the end of their project, they were relieved that management recognized their feelings. That would begin to free them up emotionally and mentally to move on to other projects. Dirk had also learned that his role was similar to that of the project managers he had been working with: to manage the emotional well-being of those whom he would lead.

Noah's Project Moves Ahead

Just the previous week, Noah and the arkobarge team had concluded their reevaluate meeting and were given the green light for the next Innovate cycle: to frame the arkobarge and subcontract all components. The meeting was not easy. Gazelle, who heads GAAR, the Global Association for Animal Rights, was not happy with the arkobarge's blueprint for housing the animals and refused to sign off on the arkitech's plan. However, Gabriel prevailed, and the blueprint was accepted over Gazelle's objections. But this would not make it easier in the future for Noah, who would have to bear the brunt of her ire.

Noah's latest budget was nearly 30 percent more than the organization had initially budgeted. The increase was due largely to expensive navigational and waste management equipment, as well as the unanticipated requirement to house the SOS Web site infrastructure since a fully functioning system would be needed once the arkobarge hit dry land and the new world began.

Moreover, other projects in the SOS portfolio were now requiring more funds than available, putting some projects at risk of being terminated. The pressure was being felt up and down the organization.

Time Marches On

Once the first round of reevaluate meetings had been conducted, things seemed to move at warp speed. The SOS Web Site Project went live on 6/1, two weeks after its target date. This was not a show stopper since the schedule was an optimize Win Condition and not a must-meet. Schedule would have been a show stopper if it had gotten out of hand and extended beyond 6/15 according to the latest estimate. At that point, there would not be sufficient time to survey and screen the Selected Ones and make travel plans and other accommodations in time for 11/9.

Cyberterrorism was a big problem for the SOS Web Site Project, which was continually under attack by ingenious hackers who managed to wreak havoc with the site's database and had brought the system to its knees on three occasions. The two redundant backups, a must-meet quality Win Condition, saved the day.

Two Weeks to Go

With just weeks to go, the animals and humans began to converge at the staging ground, about 2 kilometers from the site of the arkobarge. The animal-gathering team had been at serious risk of not meeting its schedule. They were the only team following Ez's M4 method. That, combined with the mandated 6 Stigma program, nearly sank the project even before the flood came. The methodologies had taken on a life of their own and were now feeding on the project. To make things worse, when M4 and 6 Stigma were not working, the team thought *they* were doing it all wrong, so they redoubled their efforts to apply the practices in what amounted to a bizarre Newtonian lunacy loop. Fortunately, the second Reevaluate cycle caught the problem when the team's upcoming action plan called for more M4 and 6 Stigma training. The Sponsor of All Sponsors had to intervene and told Dirk to have Ez lighten up. He reminded Dirk that even if they did have time for it, project management is a contact sport and classroom training doesn't work anymore than you can train a football team to win by giving them a lecture and then putting them on the playing field.

Noah was pulled off the arkobarge project for a few days and sent to coach Praja Pati, the project manager for animal gathering, on the basics of eXtreme project management. To reboot the project, Noah showed Praja Pati how to generate a new sense of clarity and purpose quickly. This was accomplished by having the team produce the basic work products of eXtreme project management and logging them into the Project Prospectus in under four hours. Noah realized that not only is eXtreme project management useful to start off a project, it is equally valuable for turning around a project that has gotten out of control.

As the Selected Ones began to enter the hermetically sealed quarantine tents to protect them from the anticipated X-Virus, health examiners and sex checkers from the repopulation team validated that pairs were healthy and properly matched for repopulating the earth after the events of 11/9. Same-sex couples were permitted providing arrangements had been made for them to adopt the offspring of others.

Seaworthiness was a Win Condition for the arkobarge project, which was now having its problems. Arcademies, who had been hired to conduct stress tests and floatability simulations, determined that the arkobarge's hull would not tolerate impacts of 15 kilometers per hour and greater, which made the arkobarge vulnerable to icebergs. As a result, the arkobarge team was now working around the clock to reinforce the hull.

The flood team, which had been experimenting in the rain forest of South America, was having success in making it rain. The combination of drumming circles plus rain dances seemed to be working in producing sustained precipitation at will. It didn't hurt that the team was sponsored by the Sponsor of All Sponsors who would augment their efforts with a wink and the occasional cloudburst.

At noon on the afternoon of 11/8, the first drops were felt and the first claps of thunder heard, as if to applaud the start of a new world.

====

In the final chapter on the Flexible Project Model, we'll cover Disseminate, the fifth and last cycle.

eXtreme Project Management Model
Applying the Quantum Mind-Set

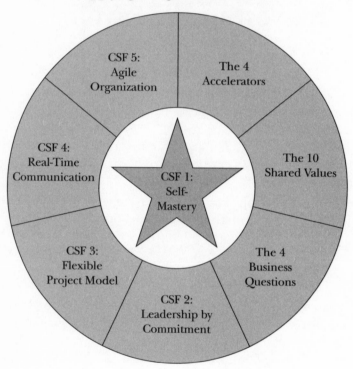

Chapter Fourteen

Disseminate: Harvesting the Payoff

It's not over until it's over.
YOGI BERRA

Disseminate is the final element of The Flexible Project Model, Critical Success Factor 3 in the overall eXtreme Project Management Model.

The Flexible Project Model is an iterative process. An eXtreme project may cycle through the Visionate, Speculate, Innovate, and Reevaluate cycles numerous times with the objective of getting it right the *last* time. Each round through the process should bring you closer and closer to getting it right, and when that happy day finally comes, you will be tempted to declare victory and go home. But it is premature to declare victory until you have released the project deliverable to the customer and kicked off the benefits realization process. This is the focus of the Disseminate cycle. The benefits of conducting this cycle are bringing the project to closure, ensuring the organization is prepared to reap the payoff from the project, and capturing lessons learned.

The deliverable can be a new process, a new consumer product, a new information systems application, a component or subsystem that will be incorporated into another system, or it can be a feasibility study or a training program. It is whatever your project was about. The customer can be the final customer (end user) or an interim customer such as marketing, manufacturing, or distribution.

The transition process can take an hour to days, to weeks or even months, depending on the project. At the very least, the customer will want to know that everything agreed on has been included in the deliverable. For projects where there is a prolonged transition and stabilization period (as with a new manufacturing system or information system), the role of the eXtreme project manager is that of catalyst and process leader. In this case, you are responsible for building the bridge from project delivery through the shakedown period up to the point where the customer is in a position to harvest the financial reward. Figure 14.1 shows the major elements of the Disseminate cycle.

The transition process can take an
hour to days, to weeks or even months.

There are two major components of the transition process, or postimplementation, phase:

1. Ensuring that the project deliverable does what it is supposed to and the sponsoring organization is satisfied
2. Ensuring that the sponsoring organization is ready and able to reap the outcome: the business benefits to be derived from the deliverable

Traditional project management calls it a day when the first component is completed. eXtreme project management keeps the lights on until both components 1 and 2 are completed.

The elements covered in this chapter will apply more or less to you depending on the kind of project you are working on. If your project was to reengineer the order processing system, what you turn over to the customer will look a lot different than if your project was to reengineer the printing mechanism for your company's new laser printer. Whereas the performance of the printing mechanism might be easily measurable by those in product development, the performance and the expected benefits of the new order processing system are quite a bit fuzzier and much more difficult to quantify. Although one might be able to measure how well the system is performing (speed, error rate, usability, and other characteristics), less tangible benefits, such as dollar impact on

Figure 14.1. Critical Success Factor 3: The Flexible Project Model

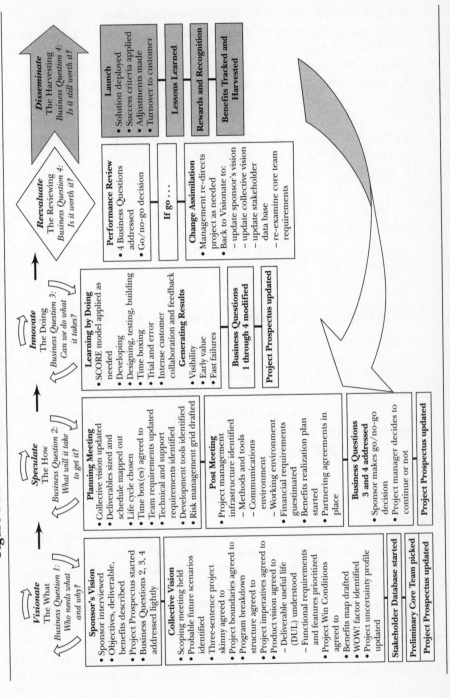

sales, improved customer loyalty, fewer employees required in the future, and measuring ROI in general, can be difficult to calibrate. Nonetheless, many of the principles discussed here apply to most projects. You'll need to adapt them to fit your situation.

In this chapter, I'll cover the postimplementation process:

- The turnover point
- The activities that comprise the stabilization period
- The key elements of the project review meeting
- Kicking off the benefits realization process

Before covering these points, let me take a reality check. Most people will agree that following up to see if a project investment is paying off is a good thing to do. But it often doesn't happen. Business Question 4 seems to have been forgotten.

What Happened to Business Question 4: Is It Worth It?

Once the project has been delivered, Business Question 4 doesn't go away. It just changes slightly and reads, Is the project paying off? Traditional project management leaves the ball in the sponsor's court and goes home. And the ball usually doesn't get picked up. Experience has demonstrated that sponsors tend to duck the ROI question in the first place.

> *Experience has demonstrated that*
> *sponsors tend to duck the ROI question.*

One reason is that, unlike eXtreme project management, the financials might not have been baked into the project from the onset or were ill defined and not traceable. Who can be held accountable for something that can't be measured? In other cases, the internal accounting systems may not be in place to isolate costs. Or what if the project were measurable but loses money? Why stick your head out if you're not being pressed?

In addition, sponsors are not customarily measured on benefits realization. Traditional project managers and project sponsors have struck a tacit deal: don't ask, and don't tell. Ultimately the problem and the solution lay in the organization's reward system. What gets measured gets managed. What gets rewarded gets done. Both measurements and rewards are needed. (See Chapter Sixteen.) In the meantime, we can't wait for the organization to become enlightened.

So if everybody around you is dropping the ball, what should you as a project manager do? I had this discussion with colleague and author Gary Heerkens, who summed it up cogently: "The project manager is the conscience of the project."

eXtreme project management strives to form a partnership with the customer organization in pursuit of benefits realization. Because eXtreme project management is fiscally responsible (notice our preoccupation with the 4 Business Questions), it goes the distance. It takes the project from the point of turning over the deliverable through the point of putting in place a process to realize the deliverable's intended payoff. And the process, as we have seen from the Visionate chapter, continues from the start when the project manager first interviews the sponsor and starts to identify expected business outcomes.

> *eXtreme project management strives to form*
> *a partnership with the customer organization*
> *in pursuit of benefits realization.*

In contrasting traditional project management with the new project management, John Thorp, author of *The Information Paradox* (1998), observes that traditional project management reaches from "design to delivery" rather than from "concept to cash."

But, you ask, "If the sponsor is not measured on, and not rewarded for, extracting profitability from projects, what's the motivation for the project manager to carry the flag?" The answer is *integrity*. And in the absence of a supporting reward system, what's the motivation for integrity? My answer again is *integrity*. Integrity is its own reward.

The postimplementation process extends from the time the deliverable is turned over to the customer and continues through its useful life. It has these components (Figure 14.2):

- The turnover point
- The stabilization period
- The project review meeting
- Maintenance and support
- Benefits realization

The Turnover Point

Typically, the customer thinks the project is over when he can answer yes to each of these questions:

- Did I get everything I was supposed to?
- Is it being used as intended?
- Does it work as expected?

Figure 14.2. The Postimplementation Process

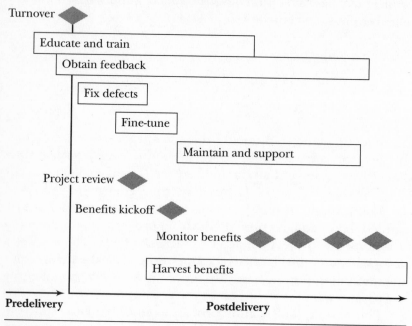

Note: The diamonds are the points in time when the activity takes place. The bars indicate ongoing activity.

At the point that the deliverable goes into service, an inventory is taken of what was delivered, installed, or deployed and compared against the agreed-on deliverables. The documentation is turned over (for example, user manuals, specifications), and the service and support agreement is reviewed.

For systems and other complex projects, it will be too early to tell how well the deliverable is performing until after stabilization.

The Stabilization Period

Even when teams follow eXtreme project management principles and practice evolutionary development and get the customer involved and do testing each step of the way, when the system or product goes live and rolls out to the customer population, "stuff happens," as they say. Inevitable bugs need to be fixed, things need to be tweaked, and ultimately, the system or product needs to be maintained. So for many projects, you can't simply leave them on the customer's doorstep and walk away. Be sure to consider including activities such as the following (or ensuring that they get done by others) as being in scope for your project:

- Training and education
- Following up on utilization rates
- Capturing systems or product performance data and comparing them to the project Win Conditions
- Capturing and analyzing customer feedback data
- Correcting defects

The Project Review Meeting

The project review meeting is timed to take place once the system or product has stabilized and there is enough information to conduct a fact-based review. This is why for many projects, conducting the so-called postmortem right after the handoff makes little sense. The verdict is still out.

The purpose of the project review meeting is to:

- Assess the utilization and performance of the deliverable.
- Agree on what still needs to be fine-tuned.

- Conduct a lessons-learned session.
- Review how the deliverable will be supported and maintained.

The review meeting is attended by the project manager, core team, and representatives of the customer organization. It can take a full day, depending on the project.

Assess Utilization and Performance of the Deliverable

You've collected performance, utilization, and customer feedback data from the time the system or deliverable went live. Flaws have been corrected. The performance assessment involves comparing the data to the project Win Conditions and any other agreed-on metrics. If needed, an action plan is put together to close any gaps.

Agree on What Still Needs to Be Fine-Tuned

By this point, the deliverable should have stabilized, meaning all the components have been put in place and adjustments made. If not, then you will need to finalize the turnover and do further fine-tuning. Once that is completed, the deliverable moves into the maintenance and support stage. Granted, the lines between the two stages may be fuzzy, and there is likely to be overlap. The point is that they are separate operations, usually staffed with separate people who come under a different budget. To use a slightly exaggerated example here, when I have a problem or want to upgrade my computer printer, I call the customer and technical support people. I don't call the engineering department or product development group. They've already (I hope) worked out any final bugs and turned printer support over to the support staff.

For the purposes of benefits realization, being able to track maintenance and support costs is necessary to get an accurate measure of ROI.

Lessons Learned

Few projects ever take the time to capture lessons learned. People are too busy starting on the next venture. Besides, lessons-learned sessions can be notorious for dispensing blame. However, if you factor the activity into the project plan, there is a better chance that the session will be scheduled. And if a few simple guidelines are followed, the meeting will not become a finger-pointing session.

Few projects ever take the time to capture lessons learned.

I once attended a so-called postmortem run by a delegate of the project sponsor. He opened up the meeting by saying, "We're all grown-ups. Let's admit our mistakes and move on. So who screwed up?" No one said a word.

These are the guidelines that I've used many times:

- Ask three questions: What went well? What didn't work? If you were going to do it over again, what would you do differently the next time?
- Focus the discussion on the development life cycle and the project management process used. If you used eXtreme project management, how did you do against the 10 Shared Values? The 4 Accelerators? The 4 Business Questions? In reviewing the elements of the project management process, go through each Shared Value, Accelerator, and so on, one element at a time. These, combined with the 5 Critical Success Factors, form a powerful framework for conducting a project assessment.
- Set a few basic norms for the session: no personal attacks, and follow the rules of good brainstorming.

Review How the Deliverable Will Be Supported and Maintained

This should not be the first time you've addressed this topic. Back in the Visionate cycle, one of the elements to address as part of the product vision was the DUL factor, that is, the deliverable's useful life. Is the project merely a one-time fix and to be discarded with little or no follow-on support required? In a database conversion project I am familiar with, a software program was written to consolidate three separate databases into one. This specialized one-of-a-kind data conversion program had no further value and was junked. Support and maintenance was not an issue. But when the system or other deliverable has an extended life, resources and support systems need to be allocated, budgeted, and implemented. The level of support and service needs to be understood and agreed to by the customer.

Importantly, a mechanism needs to be put in place to ensure that maintenance and support costs are in fact tracked. Otherwise, there is no accurate way of measuring the business payoff or ROI.

Benefits Realization

During the Visionate and Speculate cycles, crucial stakeholders were given responsibility for realizing expected benefits. The purpose of the benefits kickoff meeting is to formalize the accountability for benefits realization among the stakeholders in the customer organization. The meeting is attended by the project manager as well as the sponsor, and those stakeholders who will be held accountable for harvesting the benefits afforded by the project deliverable. (For an in-depth discussion of the benefits realization process and how it is used in information systems projects, I recommend Rob Thomsett's *Radical Project Management* [2002] and John Thorp's *The Information Paradox* [1998]).

The purpose of the benefits kickoff meeting is to formalize the accountability for benefits realization.

The fundamental question this meeting addresses is how to ensure that the intended organizational outcome is achieved. Ideally, there is a traceable link between the project objectives, the objectives associated with the deliverable, and the ultimate business outcome. Otherwise, we should likely not have undertaken the project. That's why we built in the Benefits Map at the start of the project.

In our eXtreme project management model, the project's objectives were defined by the in-scope work that was identified and updated starting with the scoping meeting. The product vision and related metrics were used to define the objectives for the deliverable. The organizational outcomes were captured in the third sentence of the project skinny. For the SOS program, the organizational outcomes were to establish a 100 percent increase in world peace within four generations, to increase per capita income from 18,000 to 24,000 drachmas, and to reduce overhead costs to maintain from 18,000 to 16,000 drachmas.

Figure 14.3 pictures a highly generalized Benefits Map. The map shows the interdependencies of multiple projects in pursuit of the intended business outcome. The challenge is that there is not necessarily a clean, one-to-one cause-and-effect relationship between a project and the intended organizational benefit. A web-like program of projects may be required to achieve the final outcome, and the contribution of any one project might not be clear. For example, to achieve the organization's desired outcomes in the SOS program, required multiple projects, including the arkobarge project, Web site project, quarantine project, animal-gathering project, and others. Beyond these, a whole new set of projects would need to be launched to achieve the ultimate business outcome in the era that followed the virus and flood. These would include infrastructure, housing, agriculture, commerce, government, and repopulation to name just a few.

Ensuring that all the pieces fit and that they are contributing to the program can be a challenging task. Nonetheless, we still have to mind the cash register.

During the benefits kickoff meeting, the Benefits Map is updated, cost data are analyzed, and estimates are made of expected benefits in terms of revenues, cost savings, or improved service. An action plan is put in place, with individual stakeholders assigned the responsibility for realizing and reporting benefits at agreed-on checkpoints. More specifically, the meeting game plan is to:

Figure 14.3. Generalized Benefits Map

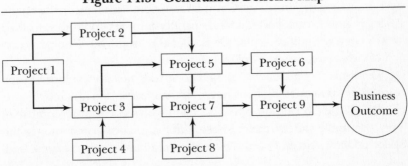

- Review the project objectives, deliverable objectives, and organizational outcomes.
- Confirm the link between the project, deliverable, and the intended business outcome in relation to other projects.
- Assign accountability for objectives to individual stakeholders.
- Estimate the financial benefits associated with those objectives (revenues, cost savings, improved service).
- Estimate the associated operational costs.
- Estimate the timing for when benefits are expected to be realized.
- Agree on checkpoints to review progress.
- If it is discovered that other projects are needed to ensure the ultimate outcome, appoint someone to start the ball rolling.

Once again, we can see the role of the project sponsor surfacing as paramount. Without overall accountability for benefits realization, it's unlikely to happen. The interdependency of projects requires a coordinated effort to ensure that sponsors and crucial stakeholders of other projects are holding up their end of the benefits realization process. Hence, it is important for the steering committee to be made up of sponsors of interrelated projects as well as senior management as needed.

On Board the Arkobarge, 11/29 Y2K BC

Twenty days had passed since the flood and the X-Virus hit. As the SOS Web team walked down from the poop deck and headed to their project review meeting, the stench on board the arkobarge was overwhelming. "Are we passing by Jersey City?" asked Ez. Apparently, in the process of installing the advanced waste management system, the contractor realized he was not among the Selected Ones. Out of revenge, the ventilation portion of system was never installed.

The loading of the arkobarge had gone fairly well, except that the unicorns and two-headed dragons never made it to the staging area.

The SOS Web site, despite a problem with the customer interface, managed to get the job done. Phase II of the project kicked in once the Selected Ones were on board. The mission of Phase II was to provide vital new world orientation information and e-commerce capability to help the Selected Ones make the transition.

The core team had been busy collecting customer feedback and system performance data once Phase II went live on 11/9. Although they had a limited crew, they managed to correct all major defects. They were very grateful for including Sally and Linda, a pair of Java programmers, among the Selected Ones.

The SOS Web Site Project review meeting would be facilitated by Noah. That would free up Rananda to fully participate from her perspective as project manager. The core team and crucial stakeholders all entered the meeting room.

Ten minutes before the meeting started, Noah realized he had left his Project Prospectus in the mess hall. No problem. He plugged in his wireless laptop and downloaded it from the SOS Web site. He breathed a sigh and gave thanks that Rananda had taken seriously the idea of real-time communication and had established a virtual workspace.

The Meeting Begins

After the usual warm-up exercise to get everyone focused, Noah reviewed the meeting purpose, which he had outlined on one of the four flip charts. He also handed out a detailed agenda and asked for volunteers to act as scribe, timekeeper, and recorder, now standard practice for SOS meetings. Ez volunteered to record. He had all but given up on his M4 and 6 Stigma methodologies, but nonetheless continued to tote his six-inch binder, which had become his transitional object from the preflood days. Other than that, he found a second use for the binder: to prop up his laptop so he could capture the meeting work products.

Assessing the Deliverable

Noah asked two basic questions: "How well is the system being used?" and "How is it performing against the Win Conditions?"

In answer to the first question, the product vision was used as baseline against which to compare the usage data that had been collected for the past eighteen days. All of the SOS Web site functions had higher-than-expected utilization rates. Underused functions had to do with selecting candidates who were running for office (it seems that the new world inhabitants had their fill of politics).

The SOS Web site did well in meeting its functional requirements, but when it came to the quality metric of being multiuser friendly, it didn't fare well at all (Exhibit 14.1). Although it filled the bill to prepare the Selected Ones to get safely to the arkobarge and on-board, the help desk had to work three shifts to answer questions about how to log on and navigate the system. Nearly one hundred translators had to be hired because there was not enough time to configure the site to speak all languages. The problem persisted after 11/9. In a tribute to Rananda's process and people-centric leadership style, one of the Win Conditions, team satisfaction, came in at 6.6 out of 10, close to the minimum acceptable metric of 6.5.

Lessons Learned

Noah was now ready to help the group learn from experience. To tee up the session, Noah went to his favorite book of quotes and read one from George Santayana: "Those who do not remember the past are condemned to repeat it." It's so rare that anyone takes the time to do a lessons-learned session that Noah had to copy a page out of his favorite book on project management to remind himself and the group just how to conduct the session.

Looking back at the project since inception and using sticky notes, the group addressed the three lessons-learned questions:

What went well?

- We were able to complete the project in half the normal time.
- The sponsor was available when needed.

Exhibit 14.1. SOS Web Site Project: Performance Against Win Conditions

1	Quality	Problems with languages and navigation
2	Schedule	Okay
3	Budget	Okay
4	Stakeholder satisfaction	Complaints above average
5	Functions and features	Back-end integration with suppliers incomplete
6	ROI	Too early to tell
7	Team satisfaction	Okay

- The project management methodology didn't get in our way.
- We succeeded in doing a good enough job on the Win Conditions to be here now.

What didn't work?

- The instant messaging function didn't work.
- We got too bogged down in trying to get consensus when we didn't need it.
- The system is not sufficiently user friendly.
- There was too much overtime, causing poor work and extra rework.

What would you do differently?

- Not spread the same people over so many projects
- Take more time for partying
- Mandated time off
- Spend more effort getting feedback from users

Supporting the Deliverable

Feldon from Finance had a sharp eye. He scanned the pro forma budget for upgrading the SOS Web site over the next five years. Conspicuously absent were any funds for maintenance.

Apparently Dirk didn't take the project's DUL factor seriously enough. All agreed that it was a level 2 long-term commitment: fix flaws and upgrade the system. But this implied that funds would be made available to maintain the system. In the past, it was assumed that maintenance was free since people were already paid for. (In the IT world, studies by the Thomsett Company [2002] indicate that the original development of the system is only 20 to 30 percent of the organization's total investment. The balance is spent after implementation.)

Under the new world accounting rules and at the behest of the Sponsor of All Sponsors, maintenance and support budgets would be required. Having to pay for support and maintenance hit Yolanda in the pocketbook since the SOS Web site would be under her management. She began to turn crimson and blow off steam.

After logging the action items, the review meeting was adjourned, Finally, it was time to celebrate. Rananda and Noah, who had become close friends, knew that one of the best ways to get people to attend meetings is to advertise food will be served. Noah managed to bring on board a couple

Learning from History

The best time to learn from history is while it's happening. eXtreme project management by nature is a process of continuous learning and adjustment. The project is constantly in a state of self-correction. What's working and not working is dealt with on a daily basis through the mechanism of the huddle. And teams are given the latitude on the spot to adjust how they will work. For eXtreme project management, then, the formal project assessment is more a summation than a revelation of what was learned.

In contrast, traditional project managers like to save up the lessons learned until the end of the project or conduct—and this is rare—interim assessments. But why postpone learning? This would be like waiting for the autopsy to diagnose the patient.

I've been involved with projects for nearly thirty-five years. Today I sit in astonishment when I see, day after day, the same mistakes that happened in 1969. Who's learning from experience? Who's passing it on? Very few. If they were, I'd be out of a job.

We've been given a binary choice to make: either grow or die. There is no in-between. Even if you decide not to conduct a formal lessons-learned session, you owe it to yourself to do it by yourself and for yourself. This is the call of self-mastery, the art of being self-directed. Personal growth requires feedback. Take fifteen minutes of quiet time and ask yourself the three key lessons-learned questions outlined earlier in this chapter.

The next time you kick off a project, use self-disclosure power. Start by telling the group what you learned on your last project and what you will be doing differently on this one. Then ask others to do the same.

---

of cases of microbrew from the old family business. As the sun slowly set in the west the team feasted on fried calamari and filet of unborn octopus.

Benefits Realization Kickoff Meeting, 12/14 Y2K BC

Feldon from finance was in front of the room. Not only was Feldon a whole brain manager, with solid business planning and interpersonal skills, he was also a clear and concise thinker. To get the group focused, he said,

"We are here to answer two questions." And he unveiled one of the four flip charts and said, "Here they are":

1. How to ensure that the SOS Web site achieves the intended financial outcome?
2. Who will be held accountable?

He then unveiled a second flip chart: it contained the meeting agenda that started out by focusing on an examination of the Benefits Map from the Project Prospectus (Exhibit 14.2). Ez volunteered again to record the session. This time his chair was too low, so he propped himself up by sitting on his M4 binder.

Benefits Map Updated

The first topic was the pivotal one, and Feldon was prepared. He brought with him the latest Benefits Map (Figure 14.4), which was first developed by crucial stakeholders during the Speculate cycle at the planning meeting and then updated regularly. The map showed the expected link between each project in the program and the intended ultimate outcome: increased revenues from Earthlanders. Other projects would be expected to decrease per capita costs of maintaining the Planet Earth.

Exhibit 14.2. SOS Projects Benefits Planning Kickoff Meeting Agenda

Start	End	Topic
9:00	10:00	Confirm and refine the link between the project's deliverables and the intended benefits
10:00	11:00	Determine responsibilities for ensuring the deliverable performs and is used as intended and for ensuring the financial benefits are siphoned off
11:00	11:15	Break
11:15	12:00	Establish a plan and set time frames for the estimated benefits and costs to be realized
12:00	12:30	Lunch
12:30	1:30	Agree on a method and schedule to track results
1:30	2:00	Unplanned topics
2:00	2:20	Action items
2:20	2:30	Meeting review and close

Figure 14.4. SOS Program Benefits Map

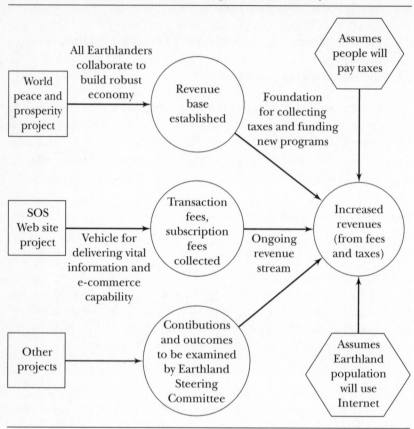

"After all these months had gone by," Feldon said to himself, "can you imagine, some projects get to this point only to discover that there was no strong link? Now I really understand the saying, 'Projects don't fail at the end, they fail at the beginning.'" Then he reassured himself: failure at this point would be an unlikely outcome since Rananda had validated and updated the Benefits Map right after the last reevaluate meeting.

As the group went through and updated the map, they began to see the value of looking at the contribution of all projects. It became apparent that projects could no longer be viewed in isolation and that there is an intricate network of projects required to achieve the ultimate outcome.

In looking at the Benefits Map, it became clear that other new world projects would be necessary to achieve the ultimate outcome of increased revenues from Earthland population. It seems that Throckmorton, Earthland's chairman and his staff, had put so much effort focusing on preflood projects that the aftermath programs were not well thought out. As a result, at least 87 billion drachmas more would need to be allocated to other new world projects, including infrastructure projects and others yet to be determined.

The Assumptions Call for More Projects

It also became clear that the assumptions behind the ultimate outcome would require other projects to ensure that the ultimate outcome of increased revenue was achieved. Trinity, who was at the meeting, piped up: "What project will supply the mechanism to actually collect the taxes from the population?"

Ez jumped in: "Yes we need a collection . . ." And Dirk finished his sentence, "agency." "Right," said Yolanda. "Let's call it the ERS." "ERS?" asked Dirk. "Yes," agreed Yolanda. "Earthland Revenue Service."

Accountabilities Assigned

Although nobody particularly liked it, specific assignments were made. Yolanda would be responsible for realizing the income benefits. Feldon would be on the line for monitoring the cost side of the benefits realization equation. Windbreaker, the CIO, would be responsible for ensuring that an IT accounting system was in place so that costs were accurately tracked. Benefits review meetings were scheduled to take place quarterly starting on February 1.

The meeting came to a close, and so did the SOS Web site project. It was now in the hands of Yolanda and Feldon.

And the Sun Sets

Noah and Rananda headed back to the poop deck to watch the sun set.

"So, your project is over," said Noah. He went into his wallet and pulled out a fortune cookie saying he had been carrying around. He had found it crumpled up in the ashtray of the Wok and Roll restaurant. He read it to Rananda. "Begin at the end and end at the beginning."

"Yes," she nodded knowingly.

| Managing the Project Environment

The two chapters in this part provide guidance on managing the project environment. They cover the final two Critical Success Factors in the eXtreme Project Management Model: Real-Time Communication and Agile Organization.

Communication is critical on eXtreme projects, which require that information be available at any time to anyone who needs it. eXtreme projects also require an agile organization, that is, a change-tolerant, project-friendly culture—one that recognizes and supports the special needs of different projects from traditional to extreme.

Things happen fast on eXtreme projects. As Chapter Fifteen explains, people need a forum for discussion and debate so that the best options are surfaced and addressed. They need to share documents and have ready access to project management tools. Stakeholders need to be kept up to date. *Real-time communication* means to put in place the project management infrastructure to ensure that information is available at any time to anyone who needs it in order to speed the flow of thoughts and, ultimately, decisions.

Projects are like flowers. If the soil is toxic, one or two flowers may make it, but sooner or later the rest will die. Chapter Sixteen explains the management practices that support a change-tolerant, project-friendly culture that recognizes and supports the special needs of different projects, from traditional to eXtreme. This chapter offers project managers useful talking points in explaining to senior management how they can unintentionally undermine eXtreme projects and the organizational practices that senior management can promote to support eXtreme projects. The chapter also provides a compendium of best practices.

eXtreme Project Management Model
Applying the Quantum Mind-Set

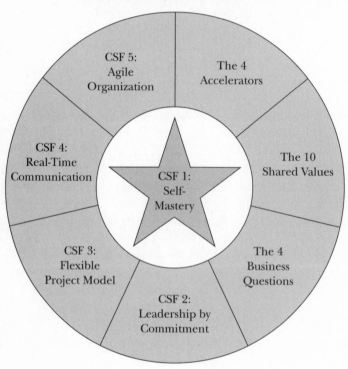

Chapter Fifteen

Real-Time Communication

A project is only as sick as its secrets.
MIGNON LAWLESS

Real-Time Communication is the fourth Critical Success Factor in eXtreme project management. With little time to waste, eXtreme teams need to get up and running fast and keep up the pace. Everyone both internal and external to the organization needs to stay on the same page, especially under fast-moving conditions when everything on the page keeps changing.

Because eXtreme projects live in turbulent, fast-changing environments, these ultrademanding ventures require the timely exchange of information among both co-located and geographically dispersed team members, as well as among the members of the extended stakeholder community: management, business partners, and other project teams, both internal and external to the organization.

The timely distribution and exchange of information makes it possible for the stakeholder community to self-organize and self-correct in order to solve problems and respond to sudden threats and opportunities. In this sense, no single person is in control because everyone is in control.

Yet given the size and complexity of even a small stakeholder web, the volume of information and associated discussions and interactions can create a monumental body of knowledge. Timely and easy access are essential. Add to this the need for distant groups of stakeholders to interact in real time in order to discuss, brainstorm, do joint work, problem-solve, and reach consensus, and the communications infrastructure for eXtreme projects takes on a critical role.

If information and collaboration are the lifeblood of an eXtreme project, then keeping the arteries clear is essential for success. Moreover, the absence of a robust Real-Time Communications capability will relegate the eXtreme project manager to being the project's administrative assistant: a highly paid information traffic coordinator who sits at the hub facing a computer monitor instead of facing people, hopelessly bogged down in overhead tasks that could be better handled by a more distributed system.

Not only do eXtreme project teams need a virtual workspace for ongoing information sharing, they also need the capability to run virtual meetings: forums where problem solving and decision making take place, rather than passive events where information is merely presented and exchanged.

Not only do eXtreme project teams need a virtual workspace for ongoing information sharing, they also need the capability to run virtual meetings.

In the absence of a flexible and easy-to-use communication infrastructure, the flow of thoughts, emotions, and interactions becomes blocked, starving the project of its vital energy. Moreover, no one will know what anyone else is doing. Worse yet, the project will suffer from paresthesia, a breakdown in the neurological network that cuts off sensations. Imagine finding your hand roasting on a hot burner because you couldn't sense the pain.

Both information sharing and collaboration are essential capabilities for eXtreme teams if they are to respond to change and work cohesively to uncover innovative solutions. Ensuring a viable project management communication infrastructure is a top responsibility of the eXtreme project manager.

But how? Existing internal project management and other communication systems may not be the answer: internal legacy systems can be cumbersome and difficult to use, with steep learning curves. Others have tightly prescribed methods, templates to file, forms to fill out, and policies to adhere to, all of which may be out of step with the requirement that eXtreme projects be nimble.

Even the newer Web-based project management systems may not be the answer: disparate hardware and software environments can make it technically impossible for the have-nots, that is, remote team members and outside suppliers, to participate. Nor is it practical to go out and shop for a complete, unified system for $250 to $500 per user to get a project off and running. You've got a project to get off the ground next week.

And what do you do when the sponsoring organization (and this is very common) has little or no project management communications capability in house at all?

It is no wonder that eXtreme project managers are looking for quick-start, low-cost ways to jump-start the team and even bypass internal systems, while ensuring timely, secure, and equal access for sharing information and collaboration across time zones and hardware and software platforms.

The central question addressed in this chapter is how to get up and running quickly with the Real-Time Communications capabilities you need. We'll address these questions:

- What are the basic communication needs of stakeholders?
- What are the hallmarks of a viable Real-Time Communications system?
- What specific real-time features do you need?
- Where do you find affordable, quick-start solutions?
- What are the technical considerations for planning and running virtual meetings?
- What do you need to know in planning and running Web conferences?
- What's the big trap to watch out for in all of this?

A viable Real-Time Communications system energizes the Shared Values not only of client collaboration but those of visibility and results orientation as well. Visibility avoids mushroom management that keeps people in the dark. Instead, project documents and vital information are available for those who need to know, anytime and anywhere. Performance against goals is easily tracked by all. Results orientation helps keep people focused on doing real work, minimizing time on project administrative tasks and information chasing.

Real-Time Communication makes a direct contribution to all 4 Accelerators for unleashing motivation and innovation:

1. *Make change your friend.* New information and changes to the project are quickly accessible to all stakeholders.
2. *Build on people's desire to make a difference.* When people have up-to-the minute information, they have the ingredients to come up with timely and innovative solutions.
3. *Create ownership for results.* By facilitating collaboration, Real-Time Communications helps keep customers involved in shaping the product deliverable and building acceptance for the end result.
4. *Keep it simple.* If the system is easy to learn and useful, people will seek it out, just as thousands rushed to the Palm Pilot when it was introduced.

What Are the Basic Communications Needs of Stakeholders?

When all the dust settles, adaptability means using information to respond to environmental uncertainty. A good communication system creates an information and collaboration environment that enables stakeholders to answer three fundamental questions about the project's environment:

Adaptability means using information to respond to environmental uncertainty.

1. What's happening right now?
2. What do we anticipate happening?
3. What needs to change?

Table 15.1 takes a deeper look into stakeholder communications needs. In this view of the world, information provides the raw material for changing and adapting. But just how are we going to adapt? That's where collaboration comes in. It entails the processing of information in order to solve problems and reach decisions.

Here are some observations from Table 15.1, based on my experience:

Table 15.1. Information and Collaboration Needs of Various Stakeholders

	Needs of Those Doing the Work			Needs of Interested Parties		
	Project Manager	Team Members	Suppliers and Other Project Teams	Customers	Sponsor and Senior Management	Project Office
Type of information						
Project Prospectus	••	••	•••	••	•	•••
Technical documents	•••	•••	••	•••	•	••
Project management tools and techniques	••	••	•	•		••
Performance	••	••	•••	••	•••	•••
Links to other Web sites	•	•	••	•••	•	••
Project news, high impact	••	•••	••	•••	••	•••
Project news, general	••	•••	••	••	••	••
Project portfolio	••	•	•	•	•	••
Collaboration mode						
Discussions and debates, real time and asynchronous	••	••	••	••	•	•
Idea generation	••	••	••	••	•	•
Organizing and displaying data	••	••	••	••	•	•
Joint work, decision making, problem solving	••	••	••	•	•	•

Note: Relative importance of information access and collaboration needs among different stakeholders: ••• = high; •• = medium; • = low.

- Be prepared to meet stakeholders' information and collaboration needs.
- Everyone wants to get project performance information (although it will differ in detail among different stakeholder groups); everyone is interested in current events or possible future events that have a high impact on the course of the project. Use a portion of your project Web site for news.
- Suppliers and other project teams, often left out of the mainstream communications loop, have substantial information and collaboration needs. Ensure they have access.
- Not all information is equally important to everyone. Those doing the work will want more detail and different slices than interested parties. Be prepared to meet a range of needs.

What Are the Hallmarks of a Viable Real-Time Communications System?

Here I'll describe the big-picture attributes to look for in a viable Real-Time Communications system—one that meets the information and collaboration needs across the spectrum of stakeholder groups outlined in Table 15.1.

The overarching distinguishing feature of a viable Real-Time Communications system is that it resembles a web rather than a wheel. Its main function is to coordinate change. In the web model, we see stakeholders as different nodes of the same project body linked together in a neural network, a complex web in which everything and everyone is connected to everything and everyone. Any event that happens in one part of the web has reverberations throughout. And although an event may not be felt by everybody all at once, they are nonetheless affected.

Events can create unforeseen consequences that can be adverse or fortuitous. Software developers experience adverse reactions all the time. A developer adds or modifies a program feature, which causes a tried-and-true feature to malfunction. Or you get a toothache, and it has impacts on your entire sense of physical well-being and even your attitude. Each part has an impact on the whole, and the whole has an impact on the part. Feedback leads to change. Change and adaptability go hand and hand.

This means that all cells in the project body need to have access to what's going on in other parts. No one can be cut off, that is, deprived of information, because they are affected. If your brain didn't know that your hand was on the hot stove, you'd be in trouble.

All cells in the project body need to have access to what's going on in other parts.

The web model is compatible with the quantum worldview: it recognizes the inherent unpredictability of systems, while building in flexibility so that each of the parts can adjust to unforeseen events. In contrast, the Newtonian, hub-based bicycle wheel model of the world is incompatible with the world of eXtreme projects. In the bicycle wheel model, communications is centered at the hub, a command-and-control post and clearinghouse situated far from the action. In the eXtreme world, not only does the hub model cause bottlenecks and delays, it runs the risk of making decisions without sufficient stakeholder input.

Following are ten major attributes to look for in a Real-Time Communications system. You may want to use this as a checklist to assess how your existing in-house system matches up. When you add these together, they spell web-based communication:

1. *Distributed.* The web or quantum model distributes rather than centralizes intelligence and decision making. Any node in the web has complete access to all vital information. Moreover, the system is organic. Through the use of simple guidelines, the information and its organization requires little central administration. People will adapt the system to meet their needs.
2. *Inclusive.* The system works with a web browser over low bandwidth. It's universally available to all authorized stakeholders, internal and external to the organization.
3. *Intuitive.* The system is user friendly and has a low learning curve. First-time participants can get up and running in an hour or two.
4. *Holistic.* Both information and collaboration needs are found in a single system.

5. *Good enough.* Some systems have so many bells and whistles that you get lost in all the functionality, distracting participants from the essential functions and features. A good system does a great job at meeting minimum requirements.
6. *Self-sufficient.* Unlike many legacy systems, it is virtually glitch free, requiring minimal technical support.
7. *Subservient.* Some project management systems have so many built-in methods and must-do templates to fill out that participants become a slave to the system instead of the other way around. It becomes a handcuff instead of a tool.
8. *Vibrant.* It is easy to update with breaking, high-impact news to all constituencies.
9. *Customizable.* It is easily tailored to meet the needs of different stakeholder groups.
10. *Contagious.* Utilization snowballs. The more you use it, the more you want to use it.

What Specific Real-Time Features Do You Need?

Ultimately you are looking for a virtual workspace, one that embodies the attributes I've just described and also has a set of features that are especially useful for eXtreme projects.

Michael Kaplan, founder of Effective Link and a leading expert in Real-Time Communications infrastructure for project management, defines a virtual workspace as "a secure, dynamic web-based environment designed to support processes that help people work together."

Here I'll look at specific hands-on features to consider in selecting a Real-Time Communications system, the backbone of your virtual workspace. Not surprisingly, the features break down into two broad categories: (1) information sharing and management and (2) collaboration management.

Information Sharing and Management

Information sharing includes quick access to essential documents, as well as the ability to create and manage documents.

A good communication system has a repository for essential project and technical (product-related) documents as well as on-tap tools and techniques. These include project planning templates (such as those for the project skinny and PUP) and templates and techniques for running meetings, estimating, and a host of other aids. But much more than a passive repository, the system needs to provide basic document management capabilities. These document management capabilities include:

A good communication system has a repository
for essential project and technical (product-related)
documents as well as on-tap tools and techniques.

- Version control, which enables stakeholders to check out and check in documents without fear of overwriting or deleting documents that have been updated. Users are also able to roll back to previous versions of the document.
- Work flow, which is the ability to depict and coordinate the flow of a document throughout its life cycle. This feature is useful for technical and other documents that need to be progressively passed on to others to work on.
- Full text search and retrieval, which includes the ability to search across different file types.
- Document import, which allows the user to easily migrate documents stored in other systems into the project's virtual workspace.
- Application sharing, which is ability to share commonly used programs such as project scheduling software and a database management package.

Collaboration Management

Collaboration capabilities facilitate the ability of stakeholders to tap into the collective intelligence of the project community by collecting data and brainstorming in order to solve complex problems, make decisions and reach consensus. Among the capabilities are these:

- *Contact lists management.* As the name implies, this is the ability to have on tap contact information for all stakeholders using the virtual workspace as well as other key people and organizations.

- *Database sharing.* Beyond contact lists, a project can have any number of databases that might be of interest to participants; examples are a catalogue of parts, a glossary of terms, and a customer database searchable by demographics.
- *Instant messaging.* This increasingly popular method allows two people to have a text-based conversation in real time. It comes in handy for problem-solving sessions when the telephone is not practical.
- *Multithreaded discussions.* The system permits discussions to be organized by topic, enabling participants to track the entire conversation easily.
- *Polling—the ability to vote and tally.* This increasingly popular capability allows quick feedback against a set of options. For instance, stakeholders may be asked to assess a potential vendor against a set of criteria.
- *Computer-based white boarding.* This capability allows team members to create, display, and manipulate graphic elements on a shared white board on their computer screen. It's the electronic version of what you normally do on a flip chart or with an in-room white board. It is good for sharing and modifying diagrams or doing mockups of a new product or service, such as a quick layout of pages for a new Web site.

Where Do You Find Affordable, Quick-Start Solutions?

Basically there are three alternatives: stay with the in-house system, go for a hosted solution, or home brew (make it yourself)—or some combination of these three.

In-House

If your organization already has the Real-Time Communications capabilities I've been describing and these meet your basic requirements and are affordable, then you already have what you need.

Hosted Solution

Over the past few years, there has been a proliferation of hosted solutions that provide some or most of the capabilities I've been covering. Moreover, these Web-based workspaces tend to be user friendly and inexpensive, ranging from ten to fifty dollars per month per user; sometimes they are even cheaper. Time is money on eXtreme projects, and the cost of many hosted services is small in proportion to the entire project cost. Shaving a week off an eXtreme project (or any other project, for that matter) can result in thousands of dollars per day in realizing project benefits in revenues or cost savings. In addition, you can get up and running fast. And when the project is over, you simply stop the service: most require no cancellation notice.

Some services have tools and templates that are project management specific and can also be customized, or you can upload your own. In addition to finding a vendor that meets your top capabilities, there are several other important considerations:

- Check out how secure the third-party system is.
- Select one that has in-person technical support.
- Ask for references, and interview several customers.
- Check out the service's viability. You don't want it to go out of business in the middle of your project.

Following is a list of vendors that supply hosted solutions at the time of this writing (since there is turnover among vendors, no list can be up-to-date for long):

www.bfcollaboration.com/features/

www.e-project.com

www.groove.net

www.intranets.com/Home.asp

www.mediachase.com

www.online.4team.biz/registration/default.asp

www.projectlounge.com/home.nsf/index.html

www.projectconfig.com

www.ramius.net/solutions-features.cfm

www.Sitescape

www.teamspace.com

www.yahoogroups.com

Home Brew

Sometimes what you need is right in your own back yard. Guest author and project management bon vivant and guru Carl Pritchard of Pritchard Management Associates offers these tips and techniques when you want to brew your own.

All too often, we feel compelled to rely on the organization and its infrastructure to support us on our projects. Hours, even days, are spent with the IT office, attempting to establish project Web sites, get approvals for applications, or jump through administrative hoops in hopes of following corporate protocol. While there is still every reason to advocate consistency and chain of command, there are also times when efficacy demands that we forge ahead and find means outside the conventional corporate space to get things accomplished. Rather than wait for approval or for a few additional organizational dollars, there are inexpensive and effective ways to "brew your own" while the organization's processes ferment around you.

The most ubiquitous component of any information-sharing methodology today is the Internet. With the advent of the Internet, many project organizations now commonly apply project Web sites, white boards, and instant messaging as components of their information-sharing strategies. Unfortunately, some organizations still see these components as technologically advanced or unwieldy and have not yet adopted them. What do you do? Project managers sometimes need to strike out on their own to find reasonably priced alternatives to their organization's infrastructure.

Web Sites

A project Web site is not necessarily an elaborate affair. What it needs to be is a repository for information and somewhere that team members can post and retrieve data. In some organizations, the notion of adding Web pages on a project-by-project basis can involve approvals at the highest levels. Instead, project managers may wish to consider the simpler approach of buying Web space from a publicly available vendor. Through some sites, domain registration can be less than twenty-five dollars per year and actual hosting less than ten dollars a month. With that minor investment, the team can have a repository for (nonsensitive) project information. With the addition of Web-logging software (blogging), it's possible for anyone to post information (and files) to the site for use and retrieval.

A project Web site is not necessarily an elaborate affair.

The major downside to this approach is security. Since much project information is secure by necessity, open Web site access may not be appropriate for all projects. But since communications are the currency of project management, it's worth considering.

Instant Messaging

Instant messaging (IM) is another technology that some project managers have adopted with zeal. In one major telecommunications organization, project team members are required to have their IM boxes open through the day, and if they're away from their desks, they must log an automated response to let people know when they'll return. Instant messaging is not a high-end technology. Microsoft, Yahoo, and AOL all have their own forms of the tool. The beauty of it is the universal availability of much of the software and the ability to integrate team members outside the organization into the project communications loop with the addition of a new name on the messaging list.

The only caveat on IM applications is that the project manager may wish to identify some protocols for appropriate use, as some individuals may abuse the open door policy that IMs invite.

Web Conferencing

Internet conferencing, supported by telephone and not, is another readily available tool for even most low-end Internet users. Basic Windows software comes loaded with Microsoft's NetMeeting, and other Web-based tools like WebEx are available on a fee-per-use basis. With Web conferencing, information can be shared in a meeting setting with virtual users working from the same applications, white board, and other data sources at the same time.

Particularly for projects with geographically dispersed teams (with some team members with limited access to the organization's infrastructure), such team settings can be invaluable for real-time sharing of information.

What Are the Technical Considerations for Planning and Running Virtual Meetings?

eXtreme teams, virtual or co-located, need to synchronize their work continuously. Daily synchronization meetings (the huddle) are not uncommon and often are necessary, if not wise. Weekly overall project coordination meetings are a necessity, as are meetings held at major decision points during the Reevaluate cycle.

Virtual meetings represent yet another challenging opportunity for eXtreme project managers to facilitate and manage the flow of thoughts, emotions, and interactions. And there's a lot more to it than picking the right technology. Duarte and Snyder (1999) point out that technology cannot make up for poor planning or ill-conceived meetings.

In addition to the meeting planning and management techniques covered in Chapter Six, here are two important planning guidelines from Duarte and Snyder (1999):

- The purpose of the meeting will determine the level of interaction required among participants.
- The level of interaction will determine the most appropriate technology.

A general rule of thumb is the greater the level of interaction required, the greater is the need for an experienced facilitator (Table 15.2). For instance, if the purpose is merely to exchange and clarify information, then putting on a full-fledged interactive videoconference would be a waste of time and money. As you move from information sharing to joint problem solving and decision reaching, the technology will need to be more sophisticated.

The greater the level of interaction required, the greater is the need for an experienced facilitator.

Avon D'Cunha, president of Net Solutions and an expert in virtual meeting technology and facilitation, offers his ten best practices for preparing and facilitating a virtual meeting:

Table 15.2. Meeting Interaction Continuum

Information Sharing (Low Interaction)	Brainstorming and Decision Making (Moderate Interaction)	Collaborative Work (High Interaction)[a]
Voice	Electronic bulletin board	Real-time data conference with audio/video and text and graphic support[b]
E-mail	Chatrooms	White boards with audio/video link
	Videoconference	Electronic meeting system with audio/video and text and graphic support[c]
	Audio conference	Collaborative writing tools with audio/video links[d]
	Real-time data conference[b]	

[a]Examples are agreeing on the project boundaries, the 7 Win Conditions, and other elements of the Project Prospectus or joint work on product design or some other aspect of the project.

[b]Synchronous interaction with one or more participants using a computer plus video and audio capability.

[c]These are sophisticated computer-aided systems. They generally require professional facilitation.

[d]The ability to jointly author documents serially or synchronously.

Source: Adapted from Duarte and Snyder (1999).

1. Meeting participants do not receive body language feedback when working in a virtual meeting. Ensure that you have checkpoints often during the meeting, and encourage the use of channels that the technology offers for feedback. A channel is a mechanism that participants can use during a presentation to send messages to each other or to the presenter. For instance, by the touch of an icon, a participant can turn on a red light on the presenter's computer screen, telling him to slow down, or someone could send the presenter a text message with a question.

2. It is very easy to forget who is at a virtual meeting. Remember to take the time to have participants introduce each other. Consider

distributing photos and short bios, especially for intact teams that will be together for an extended period.

3. It is harder to follow a meeting process from a distance. Plan the meeting in a much more rigorous way than you would an in-person meeting. There are many variables to deal with and possible glitches.

4. Recognize that you cannot build a team purely by virtual meetings. Have initial meetings face-to-face. Remember to include an icebreaker, and allow ample time for participants to chat during meeting breaks. One of the purposes of an icebreaker is to enable participants to begin to connect. There's a lot of value in having each participant give his or her name, job title, department, and country location. This encourages people to strike up a chat either during scheduled breaks in the on-line conference or later.

5. Stuff happens. Network connectivity cannot always be available during a virtual meeting. Have a fallback plan and have technical support teams on call.

6. It is not very easy to figure out multiple channels of communications (for example, web, audio, video). Use technology channels only when absolutely required.

7. Remember that the use of audio and video channels in a virtual meeting is an art that is intended to foster interaction. Engage in a dialogue rather than give a briefing during the meeting.

8. Some people find it hard to voice opinions during virtual meetings. Conduct frequent checks during the meeting to ensure that everyone is being heard.

9. It is easy to forget that you are geographically dispersed. Remember and respect time zones and cultures, especially when conducting a virtual meeting with participants in a number of nations. Avoid slang and localisms that may not be understood across multiple cultures.

10. Remember that it is not about the technology but about people who happen to be using technology to facilitate information sharing and collaboration. Take care not to let the technology dominate the meeting and become a distraction to the meeting purpose and agenda. All the bells and whistles can be tempting, but they can also distract people. For instance, some systems allow the speaker to put on a Web tour by having participants visit one or more satellite Web sites during his presentation. Once at the

satellite Web site, any curious participant can go his merry way, off on his own. In the meantime, the presenter has lost her audience.

What Do You Need to Know in Planning and Running Web Conferences?

The Internet combined with a standard Web browser makes it far easier to collaborate than ever before and without leaving one's desk. Web conferencing is the ability to use a browser-based communications service for live, interactive meetings and presentations conducted over the Intranet or Internet with voice as well as data and graphics. It has these typical features, according to Avon D'Cunha of Net Solutions:

- Conduct secure on-line presentations.
- Perform instant polling and secure voting.
- Present PowerPoint slides.
- Work on documents simultaneously.
- Transmit screen shots.
- Perform shared white-boarding sessions with real-time annotations.
- Conduct Web tours.
- Record and play back e-meetings with the ability to archive voice and audio.
- Share any desktop application.
- Engage in audience chat and instant messaging.
- Have a question-and-answer session on-line.

Many of the tools and technologies noted in Table 15.2 are packaged into services sold by Web conference vendors.

Web conferencing helps streamline the decision-making process: more diverse viewpoints can be considered in less time than is feasible for meetings that are limited to those who are near enough to attend. It enables participants to collaborate with colleagues whether they are at their office desk, their residence, or while traveling. All you need is an Internet connection. And the level of interactivity permitted by the technology helps to make decisions in shorter periods of time. Moreover, significant costs savings can be achieved by eliminating travel-related costs as well as unproductive time spent on the road.

At the time of this writing, these are some of the better-known providers of Web conferencing, according to Avon D'Cunha of Net Solutions:

Centra Software (http://www.centra.com)

Eroom Technology (http://www.eroom.com)

Genesys Meeting Center (http://www.genesys.com)

Interwise (http://www.interwise.com)

Latitude Communication (http://www.latitude.com)

Microsoft Live Meeting (formerly Placeware) (http://main.place ware.com/index.cfm)

Raindance Communication (http://www.raindance.com)

Spartacom Technologies (http://www.spartacom.com)

Webex Communications (http://www.webex.com)

What's the Big Trap to Watch Out For?

The siren's call of technology can be tempting. It can also be fatal if one key point is forgotten: connectivity does not equal communication. Communication is most effectively achieved in person, through eye contact, rather than Icontact. Too many project managers strap themselves to their chairs, endlessly tweaking the project plan, even assigning tasks and giving orders via e-mail. They take themselves out of the project.

As vital as Real-Time Communications technology is on an eXtreme project, it is no substitute for walking around and even traveling around.

The Shared Value of people first is a good reminder. In this case, it's people before technology.

In the next chapter, we move on to Agile Organization, eXtreme project management's fifth Critical Success Factor.

eXtreme Project Management Model
Applying the Quantum Mind-Set

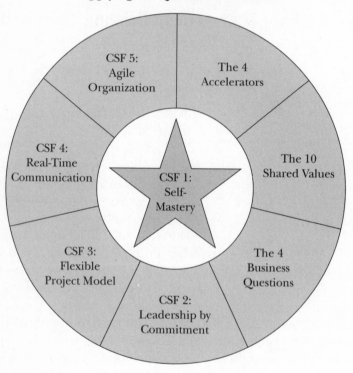

Chapter Sixteen

Agile Organization
A Senior Management Briefing

You don't manage the unknown the same way
that you manage the known.
DOUG DECARLO

Traditional project management is about managing the known. eXtreme project management is about managing the unknown. By comparison, traditional projects are slow and stable and lend themselves to orderly planning. eXtreme projects are change-ridden ventures. They are chaotic and messy, and speed and innovation are at a premium. They are also quite manageable, if you know how. It takes an agile organization. Being an agile organization is the fifth Critical Success Factor in eXtreme project management.

When the stakes are high and failure is not an option, when speed innovation and profitability count, eXtreme project management excels and traditional project management bogs down. Traditional projects follow the classic model of the *ready, aim, fire* waterfall model. In contrast, on eXtreme projects, we shoot the gun and then attempt to redirect the bullet. It's not for lack of a plan; rather, reality doesn't care about our plan, rendering it obsolete from the start.

On eXtreme projects, we shoot the gun
and then attempt to redirect the bullet.

This is the reality that business managers, project managers, and their teams of professionals face. The bureaucracy, rules, and mechanistic Newtonian practices that work on traditional projects backfire on eXtreme projects, where uncertainty, improvisation, and spontaneity replace predictability, command, and control.

eXtreme projects require a new mind-set and management model, one that enables project managers and business managers to stay in control in the face of volatility. It must insist on profitability and not neglect quality of life in the process.

eXtreme projects are like jazz. Traditional projects fit the mold of classical music. eXtreme projects pose a special challenge to management. These high-change, high-risk ventures are fraught with unknowns and uncertainty. They defy management's attempts to impose the rigor and rules typical of construction industry projects, the birthplace of traditional management.

Yet at the same time, management requires a reasonable degree of predictability to run the business. The tension between the need for predictability and the reality of rampant change poses a dilemma: Can predictability and high change coexist? Yes. Yet with all good intentions, senior management typically undermines itself in its quest for predictability and profitability from its investment in projects. Because of unwitting and counterproductive practices, each month a typical organization routinely forecloses on hundreds of thousands of dollars in project benefits and doesn't even realize it.

With all good intentions, senior management typically undermines itself in its quest for predictability and profitability.

Over the past ten years, I have collected a set of worst and best practices as they apply to most project environments, but especially to eXtreme project settings. I cover both in this chapter after first addressing these questions:

- What are the realities, that is, the dynamics, that surround eXtreme projects?
- What does management do, however inadvertently, to foreclose on expected business benefits from their project investments?

The New Dynamics of Projects

The pressures and opportunities posed by today's dynamic business environment have caused businesses to reinvent themselves. Missing a critical market window can result in millions of dollars in lost sales, to say nothing of the greater cost of relinquishing a market position that may never be recouped. Succeeding can bring enormous strategic and financial benefits. The Internet alone has reshaped the world of commerce and has raised fundamental questions. How do we now compete? With whom do we compete? For what customers? How do we change our internal systems and reengineer our vital processes? How do we synchronize our organizational values and culture and hiring and retention practices to match the demands of today's and tomorrow's global markets?

It's all up for grabs, and it all spells "projects." We live in an age of management by projects. An increasing number of today's projects fall into the eXtreme category. These are complex, high-speed ventures that feature high change and high uncertainty. Many are mission critical.

We live in an age of management by projects.

Many organizations are still in the dark ages when it comes to having adapted to the new economy. "Most of our assumptions about business, about technology and organizations are at least 50 years old" (Drucker, 1998).

The same is true for project management. Most of the assumptions about traditional project management are outmoded when it comes to today's eXtreme projects. eXtreme projects are surrounded by unpredictability and require a change-tolerant model and agile organization to succeed. The traditional project management model focuses on the mechanics of project management and works well in the linear, cause-and-effect Newtonian world of construction and engineering. And even this is being questioned. In their landmark paper, "Reforming Project Management: The Role of Lean Construction" (2000), authors Gregory Howell and Lauri Koskela point out, "Project management as taught by professional societies and applied in current practice must be reformed because it is inadequate today and its performance will continue to decline as projects [including construction] become more uncertain, complex and pressed for speed." As if the external dynamics were not enough, compounding the challenge, eXtreme projects are typically marinated in internal politics and are routinely sabotaged overtly, covertly, and by just plain management naiveté and default. These are soft-side dynamics that rule the world of projects. Why? Because:

- eXtreme projects can create winners and losers when they cut across silos, eliminate old jobs and create new ones, and shift the power structure.
- eXtreme projects compete with other projects and rely on the good graces of functional managers to loan scarce staff members to populate projects. eXtreme team members are routinely yanked from one project to another, causing serious delays.
- eXtreme projects depend on other projects. When senior managers reprioritize in a vacuum, they harm other projects.
- eXtreme projects require swift, local (team-based) decision making in order to respond to change. Yet functional managers can be reluctant to release control, causing serious and mysterious delays due to elongated approval cycles.
- eXtreme projects put stakeholders in conflict. Marketing wants to maximize the schedule, the project team wants to optimize quality, finance wants to optimize the budget, and sales wants to maximize the number of functions and features offered.

In talking with senior managers, I find that they rarely see these soft-side dynamics as even part of the project management process, not to mention even recognizing the management of these dynamics as being the top priority for improving project performance. Instead, and in response to their dissatisfaction with project results, the fix is routinely placed on improving the mechanics of managing projects in the hopes of gaining more control and predictability. By mechanics, I am referring to the techniques and tools for planning, scheduling, estimating, and controlling projects. These traditional hard-core solutions are not only naive; they are ineffective in the face of today's eXtreme project dynamics. It turns out that the soft side is the hard side, and the mechanics are the easy stuff.

> *In talking with senior managers, I find that*
> *they rarely see these soft-side dynamics as even*
> *part of the project management process.*

How Top Managers Can Undermine Effective Project Management

The management mind-set that stresses the mechanics of project management misses the point. I have referred to this syndrome earlier in the book as Newtonian neurosis. The preoccupation by management with the hard-side mechanics over the soft-side dynamics of project management comes with little surprise in the light of the statistics compiled by Kroeger and Thuesen (1992) and adapted by Lewis (2003). Sixty-two percent of corporate executives are Guardians, who place heavy emphasis on logistics and organization. They want to nail down a plan and stick with it. Yet in the world of eXtreme projects, which is subject to the volatilities of competition, government regulations, changes in consumer preferences, and new technologies, yesterday's plan is as useful as last month's newspaper.

Newtonian neurosis nearly always escalates into the institutionalization of more policies and practices, along with a prescribed methodology and associated templates in the hopes of taming the tiger. But little good is accomplished. The reason is that eXtreme projects succeed first and foremost by managing the dynamics much more so than the mechanics. And when the prescribed methodology doesn't work, and often in desperation, additional funds are approved to start a project support group, often called the project office. The role of the project office (sometimes referred to as the project police) is to bake in a set of project management best practices that invariably enshrine the mechanics of project management.

Eventually this turns into the wide-scale introduction of mandated policies and practices along with a prescribed and usually monumental methodologies. When all this ceremony shows little improvement, the next move is to embed everything into a sophisticated project management software scheduling, time management, and reporting tool. I have named this practice totoolitarianism. Here, the de facto motto has become, "Since it's not working, let's do more of it."

The de facto motto has become,
"Since it's not working, let's do more of it."

The dysfunction is further institutionalized by sending people off, sometimes en masse, to project management training and certification programs that teach traditional project management techniques, which are counterproductive in the face of high-change, complex eXtreme projects. The impact is wasted money and lost time. The real benefits of good project management fail to materialize in any appreciable way.

In the meantime, the root cause of all of this is invisible to management. They keep pointing the figure outward. Hint: When one finger points outward, three point inward.

The combination of Newtonian thinking, totoolitarianism, and project management bureaucracy is the formula for putting projects in a straitjacket. These practices stifle motivation and innovation, the lifeblood of eXtreme projects. Instead of responding with ability, the organization now responds with disability, as people work to comply with the system instead of the system working for people.

And there is more. Exacerbating these realities, organizations typically do a mediocre job at best of prioritizing projects based on resource availability and return on investment. More projects are launched than can be effectively managed. The impact is that people are spread so thin that the majority of projects are delayed, shortcuts are taken, and quality suffers. Institutionalized overtime and chronic crunch time become rampant, along with burnout. People go into a zombie state. And so do projects. No wonder. "Projects *are* people," as my colleague and project management author Jim Lewis is fond of saying.

Too many projects chasing too few resources buried in burdensome project management bureaucracy and infused with management-imposed deadlines is deadly. And it leads to the ubiquitous vicious cycle.

The vicious cycle has been described by Timm Esque (1999):

- Project managers and teams perceive schedules as unreasonable.
- Covert trade-offs are made in features and quality to meet the schedule.
- Finger pointing takes place as needed inputs from related projects fail to show up on time.
- Milestones are missed.
- The acceptable lie is told: "We're still going to make it."
- Schedule pressure intensifies.
- Institutional overtime becomes the norm.
- A faulty project is delivered to the customer.
- Resources from the next project are diverted to fix the problems.
- Management tightens the screws: the next deadline is more aggressive.

Actually, this cycle is close to the ideal scenario. It assumes that new projects are not introduced into the system, further diluting scarce people resources and escalating the lunacy.

In the middle of all of this stand the project manager and project team. The project manager has significant responsibility yet little authority in a cross-functional setting. Even experienced project managers are at a disadvantage: they are invariably outranked by those on whom they rely for decisions, resources, and conflict resolution when another project bumps theirs. And since their job is usually perceived as overseeing the development of the project deliverable (the new product, service, or process), they do not have the time to manage the relationship and organizational dynamics I described earlier, even if they did have the clout.

The Role of the Project Sponsor

The prevailing model of the project sponsor is a manager who sets the objective, funds the project, turns it over to a project manager, and signs off at the end. It amounts to absentee management disguised as management by objectives and delegation. This is a poor role model for today's eXtreme projects. Not only does it leave the project manager and the team in the lurch and at the mercy of the external and internal organizational dynamics I've been describing, it also leaves no one accountable for ensuring that the business benefits of the project are realized after the project is delivered. There's no such thing as a drug development project, IT project, reengineering project, or consumer electronics project; there are only business projects.

The role of the project manager is to deliver the project. In the new world of projects, the role of the project sponsor is to deliver the project's business outcome: the ROI and other expected strategic and tactical benefits. Given the prevailing organizational dynamics, today's project sponsor needs to be proactive throughout the project life cycle. She needs to have substantial organizational clout to be able to influence high-ranking project adversaries and resolve conflicts over priorities. She needs financial clout to be able to allocate resources to the project team. After all, the project *is* her business. eXtreme projects also call for swift barrier busting and decision making even when those decisions might be unpopular. The project sponsor is the single most important factor in the success or failure of today's volatile business projects.

The role of the project sponsor is to deliver the project's business outcome.

Measuring Success

In the traditional world of projects, success is defined by the old rules of on time, on budget, and with all the features as specified up front. In the world of eXtreme projects, these success measures don't make sense. What good is it to meet all the criteria if the project ultimately loses money after it's deployed? eXtreme project managers do worry about schedule, budget, scope and quality, but they also recognize that these do not define success.

Instead, eXtreme project management takes a holistic view of the project. Rather than merely ensuring the project stays on budget and schedule, we focus on ensuring that it will turn a profit. As volatile circumstances reveal themselves, the business proposition changes, as might the schedule, budget, and quality expectations.

It's all fluid, yet it's all managed. When circumstances reveal that the risk of delivering the intended business benefits is unacceptable, the project is killed from the project portfolio, and resources are freed up for a more worthwhile venture.

Yet it's all too common to hear management (and project managers) parrot the old shortsighted textbook phrase; "Bring it in on time, on scope, and on budget." Most of the tools available to project managers today help institutionalize this approach by generating data in support of these traditional metrics. What you really want to know is what is the likely impact of a requirement change, new opportunity, or risk event on the business value of the project? How does it affect time to profitability? What's the dollar impact of each week the project is delayed?

Put all of this together, and it spells insanity. Effectively, no one is running the asylum. The inmates just think they are. It's denial of reality at its best.

No One's to Blame

Despite the challenges that project managers face, I have pointed out in this book that there are no victims, just volunteers. The organizational dysfunction they may experience is not an excuse to fail. They need to be able to navigate the system. They're not off the hook.

Starting with the chapter on self-mastery, I have provided eXtreme project managers with the principles, values, and tools, along with insight into the appropriate management worldview and management mind-set, that they need to succeed. I have emphasized that despite their best efforts, if they feel they can't succeed, it's time to look elsewhere for a different profession or different organization.

Blaming management or the organization is a waste of time. Management is doing the best it can with the best intentions. So where is the common ground? I've pointed to what project managers can do in this book. Now I look at what senior management can do.

Is there a way out of the asylum? The answer is yes: by adopting the best practices of agile organizations.

Becoming an Agile Organization: Best and Worst Practices

To succeed in today's volatile world of eXtreme projects, the critical ability is agility: being able to respond to the external dynamics that hit the project from any and all directions: competitive moves, shifts in customer needs, new government regulations, political changes, economic fluctuations, and new technologies.

Being able to respond to change is not enough to be considered an Agile Organization. My favorite definition of agility comes from Jim Highsmith (2002): "Agility is the ability to both create and respond to change in order to profit in a turbulent business environment (p. 29). Jim goes on to say, "Agile projects are not controlled by conformance to plan, but by conformance to business value" (p. 32).

Becoming an Agile Organization by adopting the eXtreme project management approach described in this book brings a number of benefits. It enables the organization to respond to and create change and to respond more rapidly to external demands and new opportunities. It reduces risk by improving the odds of extracting the intended business value of projects. And it improves management's ability to predict and control when confronted with volatility.

Organizational practices, mind-sets, systems, and approaches can help or hinder organizational agility. In the following section, I describe how best practices promote agility while the worst stifle agility—and the effective management of eXtreme projects.

Over the past ten years, I've compiled a growing list of the hallmarks of Agile Organizations along with set of best and worst practices for each. Here are the latest. For each hallmark of an Agile Organization. I describe the associated best and worst practices.

Agile Worldview

Your mind-set is your core belief—call it internal programming about reality: how the world works. Agile Organizations clearly require that people have a mind-set that embraces change, that is not paralyzed by uncertainty.

Best Practice: Adopt a Quantum Mind-Set

Think of a project as a squiggly line. This is reality. The quantum mind-set is congruent with reality. It's a change-tolerant view of the world. It believes that the world is uncertain and that change is the norm. As a result, it recognizes that accurate plans are not possible; there is a need to be fluid, and methods must be flexible. Rather than make a vain attempt to prevent change, the quantum manager dances with it and gives people the latitude to self-correct. She changes the plan to fit reality. Here the motto is, "Get it right the last time." For the quantum personality, effectiveness (project profitability) is more important than efficiency. The quantum manager asks, "Is the project going to make a profit?"

The quantum-style manager has a mental model of projects that looks like this:

The secret to keeping an eXtreme project in control is to *not* attempt to turn it into a straight line. This is futile, wishful thinking. Instead, put upper and lower boundaries around the project, and add many checkpoints along the way. The boundaries permit variance within acceptable limits. The frequent checkpoints permit greater control and predictability from one point to the next.

Worst Practice: Adopt a Newtonian Mind-Set

Think of a project as a straight line. The Newtonian style manager has a mental model that all projects should look like this:

This mental model represents a break with reality and is at odds with reality. The Newtonian mind-set strives for accurate plans at all costs and imposes elaborate systems and policies to prevent and minimize change. The Newtonian manager seeks to change reality to fit the plan and manages people by compliance. But reality rules. For the Newtonian personality, efficiency takes precedence over effectiveness (read, profitability). She asks, "Is the project on schedule and budget?"

Some managers talk a quantum mind-set but practice a Newtonian management style. This is the management equivalent of cross-dressing. You are what you do, not what you espouse. The quantum and Newtonian mind-sets are discussed in depth in Chapter One.

Market Alignment

To succeed, an organization's culture—the way it does things—needs to be compatible with the dynamics of its external customer groups. Do you tailor the customer to fit the suit—or tailor the suit?

Best Practice: Align Your Project Management Methods to Your Customers and Organizational Culture

It's futile to change the market to fit your way of doing business. So, too, the chosen project management approach needs to fit the existing organizational culture and be responsive to the exigencies of the marketplace. Adapt the project management approach to work within your existing organizational norms. As Tom Tarnow (2000), former head of the project management organization for Morgan Stanley Dean Witter, acutely observed, "Standardized project management practices will likely fail in an individually oriented setting like a Wall Street investment firm."

Worst Practice: Install a Prepackaged Project Management Methodology

Superimposing a project management infrastructure that's not compatible with how your organization gets work done—or with how your customers and vendors do business—is a recipe for disaster. Employees, who are ultimately driven by customer and other demands, will find ways not to comply. They will defeat processes that don't work for them.

Unleash Motivation and Innovation

Motivation and innovation are the lifeblood of eXtreme projects and the agile organization.

Best Practice: Be a Relationship Manager

Unleashing motivation and innovation happens only when people can take ownership of and responsibility for their work and collaborate freely. Live by the 4 Accelerators. These times of rapid change, high uncertainty, and mind-boggling complexity call for collaboration. No one is smart enough to figure it all out with no help. In our project management consulting practice, we have identified four principles that foster motivation and innovation and ultimately speed. These are the 4 Accelerators to live by:

1. Make change your friend.
2. Build on people's desire to make a difference.
3. Create ownership for results.
4. Keep it simple.

The 4 Accelerators are covered in depth in Chapter Five.

Worst Practice: Be a Taskmaster

The Newtonian-minded manager will rule by directing rather than guiding people. Power wielding, as opposed to empowerment building, in a high-speed, high-change world runs the risk of making poor decisions and with little buy-in for their implementation.

Establish the Trust and Confidence to Succeed

Trust, a mutual feeling that people can be depended on to keep their commitments and deliver the goods, is the bedrock of teamwork and collaboration. Confidence keeps people going, even in the face of volatility and adversity.

Best Practice: Promote to a Set of Shared Values

A mutually shared set of values builds confidence and trust. In our practice, we have identified 10 Shared Values that bind people together when faced with an eXtreme project:

People values: people first, honest communication, quality of life, and courage

Process values: client collaboration, fast failures, and visibility

Business values: clarity of purpose, results orientation, and early value

The Shared Values are summarized in Chapter Two.

Worst Practice: Place Expediency Above People

Managers who care only about reaching the objective by any means necessary destroy confidence and trust. Those around them sense that winning is the only thing that counts, and they cannot be confident that what the manager says today will mean anything tomorrow.

Bottom-Line Focus

A project is first and foremost a business venture. In Agile Organizations, project teams, stakeholders, and top management keep their minds eye trained on the intended business outcome that lies on the horizon beyond the project deliverable.

Best Practice: Focus on Business Value-Added

The project team, the project manager, sponsor, key stakeholders, the steering committee, and senior management all need to keep an eye on the end game each step of the way. In the thick of battle, people may become locked in to a fixed outcome and lose sight of what's really important. To keep people focused on business value, I have identified 4 Business Questions that are addressed constantly throughout the eXtreme project—and the answers can change weekly:

1. Who needs what and why?
2. What will it take to do it?
3. Can we get what it takes?
4. Is it worth it?

At any point, the answer to Business Question 4 can turn to no, at which time the project is cancelled. The frequent go/no go decision points called for in eXtreme project management add another layer of control in the face of changing conditions.

The 4 Business Questions are covered throughout the book and are summarized in Chapter Two.

Worst Practice: Focus on Conforming to Schedule, Budget, and Scope

Measuring success based on conformance to schedule, budget, and scope takes a narrow view of projects. Like the old joke—that the operation was a success but the patient died, projects that are a success based on conformance to plan can be business failures, and vice versa.

Define Success

The 7 Win Conditions of eXtreme project management, in no particular order, are:

1. Schedule
2. Budget
3. Requirements
4. Quality
5. Stakeholder satisfaction
6. Team satisfaction
7. ROI

These Win Conditions are owned and prioritized by the project sponsor and other crucial stakeholders. Each of the seven has a set of metrics that define success. Of the seven, only one of the conditions is designated a "must meet" at any one time. One other is designated as "optimize." The remainder are expected to come in within an acceptable range as defined by the metrics. The project manager's job is to facilitate the resolution of the inevitable and healthy conflict among stakeholders as they debate conflicting priorities for the project at hand. The project sponsor has the final word.

Best Practice: Establish Metrics

Establish metrics for each of the 7 Win Conditions, and continually monitor the project against those metrics.

Worst Practice: Have No Metrics or Traditional Metrics

Traditional metrics fall short because they are mainly concerned with conformance to schedule, budget, requirements, and quality rather than conformance to business value. If a project is brought in on time and on budget but doesn't turn a profit and meet the quality requirements, it has no redeeming value.

Set Strategic Priorities

It's not enough to focus on project profitability. Not all projects that are profitable are worth doing. Agile Organizations have a clear sense of their strategic direction, make sure that people across the organization understand that direction, and prioritize projects accordingly.

Best Practice: Manage Projects as You Would Your Own Investment Portfolio

Select those based on business strategy, launching only those that can be properly resourced. The impact is that people are not diluted and can focus on the highest-payoff projects, resulting in shorter time to profitability and higher-quality deliverables.

The secret to investing is diversification. The same goes for project selection. Choose from high-risk projects that blaze new trails to bread-and-butter projects that keep the lights on. Kill those that no longer fit. Kill early and often. As Ken Orr, a computer industry consultant, says, "If there's a dead whale on the beach, beating it with a stick won't make the smell go away."

Worst Practice: Practice Project du Jour

Don't look at the strategic fit and how the project contributes to the overall mix. Make decisions before looking at the capacity to deliver. Treat all projects as top priority. Overwhelm the organization with projects. Then impose mandated deadlines. And when projects fall behind, tighten the deadlines for the subsequent projects.

Think Cross-Organizationally

eXtreme projects do not live in isolation. They connect up with multiple projects and overall business objectives. Managing the project portfolio requires a holistic approach.

Best Practice: Appoint a Cross-Functional Steering Committee

Appoint a cross-functional steering committee to identify the right projects in the service of overall business goals rather than just departmental interests. Empower the committee to resolve interproject conflicts.

Worst Practice: Keep People in Their Silos

Allowing fiefdom thinking and vested interests to prevail is a sure way to make change as difficult as possible.

Sponsors Who Really Are Champions

eXtreme projects step on toes. They cause conflicts. Project managers cannot go it alone as much as they will try. They will work miracles on one or two projects, but this is not sustainable. Projects and fish have something in common: both rot from the head. eXtreme projects need strong management support.

Best Practice: Ensure That Each eXtreme Project Has a Bona-Fide Sponsor

A bona-fide sponsor is someone who has a vested interest in the project and will be held responsible for extracting profitability from the venture. Ensure that project sponsors have the organizational and financial clout to go along with their responsibility. A job description for the project sponsor is included in Chapter Four.

Worst Practice: Assume the Project Manager Can Do It Alone

Ignore the impact of organizational dynamics on project success, and put the whole burden on the project manager. Take the role of project sponsor for granted.

Develop Excellent Process Leaders

Projects don't suffer from lack of subject matter experts nearly as much as they suffer from lack of the requisite process skills to turn experts into a functioning unit that can move toward a commonly understood goal with clarity and speed.

Best Practice: Hire Project Managers Who Are First and Foremost Excellent Facilitators

As catalyst and process leader, the role of the eXtreme project manager is to facilitate and manage the flow of emotions, thoughts, and interactions in a way that delivers business value. Smart people plus solid process skills—project management, negotiation, conflict resolution, meeting management, problem-solving, decision-reaching—create winning projects.

Senior leaders must offer project managers the support they need to ensure they have the talent and skills to:

- Be politically astute (can align conflicting stakeholder interests)
- Practice emotional intelligence (help keep the project in a an upbeat mood)
- Put in place a project management and reporting system suitable for the project at hand
- Ensure business value (in conjunction with the project sponsor)

Chapter Four sets out a complete job description of the eXtreme project manager.

Worst Practice: Appoint Project Managers Who Lack People Skills

Appoint eXtreme project managers who are Newtonian thinkers and see themselves as project mechanics: they practice project management by template, tools, and conformance to plans and rules. To make matters worse, qualify them based on their ability to pass project management certification exams.

Distribute Power and Authority

Things move fast on eXtreme projects. There's no time to run every new situation up the chain of command, wasting weeks and adding months in time-to-profit. Those who are closest to the action are in the best position to make decisions. eXtreme teams need room to self-correct, and they can do this with amazing effectiveness when they understand the overall purpose of the venture and the expected business value.

Best Practice: Empower Those Closest to the Action to Make Decisions

Adapt, promulgate, and role-model the 4 Accelerators, 10 Shared Values, 4 Business Questions, and 5 Critical Success Factors for eXtreme project management. These are summarized in Chapter Two.

Worst Practice: Insist on Retaining Decision-Making Authority

eXtreme projects by their very nature cannot be forced into the Newtonian straitjacket of project schedules and command-and-control management models. Senior managers who insist on retaining control sacrifice the speed, collaboration, creativity, and constant self-correction that eXtreme projects demand.

Close the Knowing-Doing Gap in Project Management

You have to decide if you want to improve knowledge about eXtreme project management, or any other kind of project management, or if you want to improve performance. Knowledge doesn't necessarily translate into action. For instance, everybody knows how to lose weight: eat less. Yet most people fail to shed pounds, and those who do typically don't keep them off for long. Knowing does not equal doing. The challenge is to close the knowing-doing gap.

Best Practice: Promote Learning by Doing

Expect immediate results from project management—not in months but in weeks and days by insisting on just-in-time project management. If you want measurable results in real time, dispense with traditional classroom training. Instead, pick a set of compelling projects, appoint the right sponsor and project manager, and bring in an experienced project management consultant-coach. Under his or her direction, have the project team apply eXtreme project management to this actual project right on the spot. Then have the consultant-coach train the project manager to train other project managers in the just-in-time approach. That way you become self-sufficient.

Worst Practice: Send People Off for Project Management Training

Classroom training generates knowledge but not behavior change. If you believe you can learn how to ride a bike by reading a book or watching a movie about it, then by all means, send everyone off to classroom or Internet training.

Create Lasting Change One Project at a Time

Massive organization-wide change programs suffocate under their own weight. They're too big. There's not enough energy or time to boil the ocean. In the press of everyday business, the initial enthusiasm and good intentions of widescale programs to install a project management discipline die on the vine.

Best Practice: Start a Grassroots Movement

Pick a handful of breakthrough projects—those that will set the standard for the future of project management. Start a grassroots movement by applying just-in-time project management. Spread project management by building on real successes rather than building plans to succeed. Create project management envy.

Worst Practice: Initiate a Top-Down Change Initiative

Assemble a team and develop a charter to study the situation and develop a plan and set of standards, policies, and methods for project management. Then attempt to roll out the plan and get everyone to change their ways.

Build in the Right Rewards

The old saying is still true: "What gets rewarded gets done." Agile organizations require reward systems that reinforce the values and behavior needed in an eXtreme world.

Best Practice: Design Rewards Systems
That Reinforce Flexible Behavior

Agile organizations view project management as a career path. They reward sponsors for harvesting measurable business value from their projects and team members for both individual and collective efforts. They train and reward functional managers to be coaches, not quarterbacks. Quarterbacks call the shots; coaches make it possible for others to call the shots and to be self-sufficient. This is similar to the parenting model.

Worst Practice: Design Rewards Systems
That Reinforce Bureaucratic Behavior

Reward functional managers for loyalty to silo thinking and for being *the* subject matter experts. Reward heroic efforts, which can lead to sanctioning individualism and encouraging coercion at the expense of teamwork. The impacts are chronic overtime increases, quality of life decreases, and accelerated turnover of key people. And although the occasional project succeeds, the organization is put at risk for projects at large.

Do Projects the Right Way

More than doing the right projects is needed. These have to be done the right way. Applying a Newtonian mind-set to an eXtreme project will wreak havoc. Applying a quantum mind-set to a traditional project will ensure failure.

Best Practice: Select a Flexible Project Management Approach

Agile Organizations avoid one-size-fits-all project management. They avoid project management consultants and software vendors with solutions that are panaceas. Recognize that you don't manage a highly regulated project to shut down a nuclear power plant for maintenance the same way you manage an exploratory project to develop new products. One requires high rigor and the other high creativity. Ensure that a variety of approaches are sanctioned to fit the customer and project domain.

Insist on a plain-English project management framework. The impact is that project management is not perceived as a foreign language that sends stakeholders into what veteran project manager Andrew Gerson refers to as "project management shock."

Worst Practice: Insist on a Monolithic Project Management Methodology

Pretend that all projects are created equal. Base your decision to adopt a uniform project management methodology on the need to standardize reporting for management purposes. Then force-fit all projects to conform to the methodology. The impacts are bad information and bad project management.

The chapters in Part Three cover the Flexible Project Model, a powerful project management framework that is adaptable to all eXtreme projects.

Institutionalize Success

At the beginning of this chapter, I painted a grim but nonetheless starkly realistic picture of how well-intentioned senior management can inadvertently institutionalize failure. The same power that can make failure the norm can make success the standard. To whom does it fall to institutionalize success? Management and its emissaries. A chief project management emissary can be the project support group, an agent that can kill the project or cure it depending on how it is commissioned.

Best Practice: Tailor the Project Support Group to Fit the Organization's Culture

The role of the project support group is to provide a combination of the following components, which will vary by organization and situation:

- Direct project management support (a bullpen of experienced project managers who are deployed to manage and facilitate projects)
- Methodology (supporting a wide variety of approaches to meet the unique needs of different project domains and projects)
- Coaching (mentoring and developing project managers)
- Administration (handling the mechanics and reporting for individual projects)
- Portfolio management (providing management with a cross-organizational view of project status)
- Tools (ensuring that project managers, teams, and other stakeholders have adequate project management and collaboration technology, templates, and techniques at their disposal)

Worst Practice: Make the Project Support Group an Enforcement Agency

Use the project support group to force the organization to comply with a standardized methodology and set of practices without regard to the project landscape.

Landing on Common Ground

The focus of this chapter has been on how Agile Organizations stay in control and deliver bottom-line results in the face of volatility. I started out by posing the question, "How do we accommodate the need for predictability *and* the need to respond to high change at the same time? I stated earlier that both can coexist. How so? What is the common ground?

The 5 Critical Success Factors and related senior management practices covered in this chapter are the common ground on which change and predictability dance together. These practices detoxify the soil of the unwitting dysfunctional organizational management I described at the beginning of the chapter, and they provide the infrastructure that allows high change and predictability to coexist.

The squiggly line depicted in Figure 16.1 depicts the mental model that holds the secret to success in an eXtreme world. It shows the path of an eXtreme project when looking back from the finish line. The mental model recognizes that eXtreme projects look like vacillating squiggly lines. And the path that the project takes is not unlike that of a heat-seeking missile in pursuit of its target, constantly self-correcting based on the latest information. Figure 16.1 is a visual description of how to stay in control and deliver value in the face of volatility.

Figure 16.1. eXtreme Project Management Model for Accommodating Predictability and Change

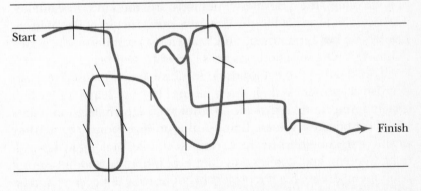

Time boxes (short lines) are the basis for frequent checkpoints along the way.
The outer limits (parallel lines) are governed by the metrics for the 7 Win Conditions.

Note: The vertical lines represent review and recalibration points, and the space between the top and bottom parallel lines represents a set of metrics or tolerances based on the 7 Win Conditions.

eXtreme project management recognizes this reality. Rather than attempt to change reality to fit the plan, we instead go with the flow—the volatility—yet stay in control. How? By establishing frequent recalibration points (the vertical lines in Figure 16.1) and by establishing a set of metrics or tolerances based on the 7 Win Conditions (the space between the top and bottom parallel lines) and allow the project to fluctuate within these limits.

Making the Transition

If your organization has a rigid and bureaucratic approach to project management—or no approach at all—how do you make the transition to eXtreme project management? There are two essential steps,

Step 1: Adopt a Flexible Project Model

If projects are squiggly lines, then we need a compatible project management model that enables project managers and stakeholders to navigate through uncertainty.

The Flexible Project Model described in this book is the vehicle and the process that pulls together the 4 Project Accelerators, the 10 Shared Values, the 4 Business Questions, and the 7 Win Conditions. The model is propelled by the Critical Success Factors of Self-Mastery, Leadership by Commitment, and Real-Time Communication, as well as the Agile Organization practices I've addressed here.

The Flexible Project Model is intuitive and explained in plain English so project stakeholders do not have to learn a new language. Importantly, it provides continual go/no go decision points based on business value—that put the project sponsor and other business stakeholders in the driver's seat. Like tacking with a sailboat, frequent checkpoints and daily twenty-minute huddles among team members enable the project to continually self-correct and be adjusted to unforeseen risks and new opportunities in real time.

The Flexible Project Model has four iterative cycles plus Disseminate:

1. Visionate—understanding who wants what and why
2. Speculate—understanding what it will take to do it

3. Innovate—generating early wins and fast failures
4. Reevaluate—deciding the future of the project based on business value
5. Disseminate—reaping the business benefits

Step 2: Apply Just-in-Time Project Management

Now that you know what you know, this will come more as reinforcement than as a surprise. To make project management work and to create project management envy is 10 percent education and 90 percent perspiration, so do not start with classroom training. Start with real projects and just-in-time project management, and create early and successful experiences rather than dwell on creating a plan to be successful. Here is how to do it:

1. Apply eXtreme project management to two to six current projects and do so in real time with the real team, sponsor, and crucial stakeholders.
2. Mentor the sponsors.
3. Extend success by coaching project managers to train others using live projects.

In other words, heed the words of David Schnarch, author of *Passionate Marriage* (1998): "It's easier to act your way into a new way of thinking than to think your way into a new way of acting."

The World Is Only Going to Become More eXtreme

I don't think anyone would bet against me that the world will become more eXtreme. So what can we do about it? Nothing and everything. I'll explain.

But first, let me tell you a secret. I have a confession to make, or maybe you already found me out. This book is not really about project management. It is about making a difference in an eXtreme world. Project management was merely the excuse for writing this book.

This has really been about changing the world around you . . . disguised as a book on eXtreme project management. And that is what project management is first and foremost about: changing the world one project at a time.

When it comes to change, whether you are a project manager, a project sponsor, or the CEO of an organization who wants to facilitate change, eXtreme project management levels the playing field. When it comes to change, reality doesn't care what your job title is, where you live or how much money you have in the bank. Change is the great equalizer.

There is no bad news here. It's all good news. That's because in the face of change, we are all equally powerful. The only thing that ever has to change is not something out there but rather in here. We just have to change our mind about what's out there, and that change begins with you and me and no one else. The world we live in is eXtreme by past standards for one reason: it's supposed to be. Nobody can change this reality.

Our hope is that in an eXtreme world, the most important thing we can do for ourselves and for others is to change our mind and adopt a new worldview, to put on a quantum mind-set. I had to change my mind about project management. Changing our mind is where our power lies. That's how we succeed in the face of volatility. Change *your* mind; change *your* world.

Afterword

And so there you have it: our journey through eXtreme project-land. By now you have come to realize that there is a vast landscape of projects between what we comfortably know as traditional project management and what we uncomfortably know as eXtreme project management. Furthermore, across that landscape, we can expect to encounter any number of untold adventures, land mines, peaceful valleys, and turbulent storms. If we wish to be successful contemporary project managers, we must learn to be proactive. We must anticipate and act accordingly. We must equip ourselves with approaches to project management that are responsive and adaptive to the characteristics of the project at hand. And so in this book, Doug DeCarlo has presented a view of project management that works for a very special class of projects—those that look like squiggly lines rather than neat waterfalls. These are projects whose goals are not clearly defined and may even be changing. Their solutions remain to be discovered and done so while working under conditions of high complexity (both technical and organizational), high volatility, and high stress.

eXtreme project management exactly fits the needs of that special class of projects:

- It doesn't waste time planning for the future. It does limited just-in-time planning for the next iteration.
- It fully engages the client in a journey to find a solution to an elusive goal.
- It places a premium on managing the project's dynamics over its mechanics.
- It is change embracing rather than change intolerant.
- It transforms the project manager into an empowering relationship manager rather than a hands-on taskmaster.

- It shifts the emphasis from conformance to plan to conformance to business value.
- It gets results.

We could say that the process of discovery characterizes the heart of the eXtreme project management approach. For this approach to be effective, there must be a sense of a true team between the client and the project team. That means that there is constant openness and dialogue between the two parties. Ideas, learning, and discovery are what fuel an eXtreme project to go forward toward an emerging goal and its solution. Contrast that with the traditional project management environment, where the client and the project team often have very little interaction with one another, and even then it may be only a cursory exchange or sign-off at the next stage gate or milestone.

To succeed on eXtreme projects, DeCarlo gives us a people- and business-centric *project* model, one that begins by shifting our mental model of the world from the Newtonian view to the change-embracing quantum view of the world. To turn the quantum worldview into a down-to-earth solution, we are given, for the first time, a holistic and integrated project management model built on a set of Accelerators for unleashing motivation and innovation, a set of Shared Values for establishing trust and confidence, and a set of fundamental Business Questions for ensuring the customer receives value each step of the way. And we are provided with a set of Critical Success Factors—the skills and tools for self-mastery and project management mastery as well as the organizational practices that get the job done under eXtreme conditions.

As project management matures into a recognized discipline and professional career, I often wonder where it's all headed. If I could come back in fifty years, would I recognize the profession? Probably not. But at least I can conjecture where it is headed and what it might look like when it gets there. I guess that is just another eXtreme project underway, isn't it?

First, we are entering a completely new paradigm of how businesses operate. We no longer have to physically be in the same place. We can get data, information, and even knowledge immediately from the Internet, no matter where we are physically located. Technology continues to be pervasive in every aspect of our lives and will continue to do so for as long as anyone would care to conjecture. If project management is going to continue to be a value-added part of our business lives, it must adapt to that environment. What does that mean in terms of the processes, tools, and templates in the project manager's tool kit? Let's look inside and see what we can find.

Before we can look inside the tool kit, we have to find it. My sense is that project management is going to be embedded in other disciplines, and it is in those other disciplines that we will find the tool kits we are looking for. An example may help. New product development models will have project management embedded within them. The manager of a new product development project will have the tool kit we are looking for. It will contain several low-tech and high-tech tools designed specifically for the needs of the new product development project. For a second example, consider the vast array of software development models in use today. For project management to be used effectively with any of those models, it must be fully integrated into those models. The principles of project management will persist in their new software development home but will not otherwise be distinguishable as project management.

Now that we have found a tool kit, it is fair to ask about its use. The virtual workspace brings with it a level of individual responsibility heretofore not part of the game plan. People work more independently because they are not under the watchful eye of a peer or their manager. New responsibilities come with that independence. People are accountable for their actions. Once they know what is expected, by when, and under what conditions, they will deliver without the need for vigilance, worry, and constant reminders from the project manager. If the team member encounters a problem or an unexpected delay, the project manager will be promptly informed. It would seem, then, that my project manager of the future will have a much easier time of it. All of the technology needed to make this happen already exists. It just needs to have the behavioral components added.

I'm encouraged about the future of project management as a vital component of successful organizations. While I don't see the project manager as a wandering professional with tool kit looking for a project to manage, I do see project management becoming fully integrated into the tool kit of every professional. They will do it as part of their job but not as a job in its own right.

These are obviously my own opinions, and I will be held accountable someday for their having come true or ridiculed for having been so far off the mark. But that's the risk you take whenever you step out into the great unknown.

Worcester, Massachusetts
June 2004

Robert K. Wysocki
President
Enterprise Information
Insights, Inc.

eXtreme Tools and Techniques

Self-Mastery Tools and Techniques

Discovering Your Temperament

The information that follows has been synthesized from Keirsey's book, *Please Understand Me II* (1984), as well as Jim Lewis's book, *Project Leadership* (2003). It will help you interpret your results and better understand why people around you are the way they are.

Keirsey associated each temperament with the individual's use of "words" and "tools." Here are a few basic definitions:

- *Communication.* This refers to how people use words to communicate. Keirsey's two dimensions for using words are *abstract* and *concrete*. Someone who expresses himself through concrete communication uses words that appeal to the five senses; that is, this person speaks in terms of things you can see, feel, touch, or smell. Abstract communication is symbolic. Abstract communicators speak in terms of truth, fairness, love, and values, for example.

- *Tools.* Tools refer to how a person uses resources of any kind, including policies, physical objects, and other people. *Cooperative* use of tools means they are used for their intended purpose, that is, their "approved" or accepted use. *Utilitarian* refers to using the tool in a situation or to solve a problem in a way it was not originally intended, for example, using a toaster as a doorstop.

- *Role intelligences.* Role intelligences refer to observable, skilled actions that can be objectively defined. They have to do with how well we act in a given situation, not how well we think. Although a person may have a predisposition toward a certain role, he may need to learn new skills to be effective in putting the role into practice. Keirsey has identified four managerial intelligences:

Diplomacy. "The ability to deal with people is a skillful, tactful manner" (Keirsey, 1998). Those who have diplomacy as their primary managerial intelligence focus on people, human relations, reconciliation, and facilitating progress.

Strategy. Here the focus is on the grand plan: the masterminding of what has to be done, including the ways and means necessary to achieve the goal.

Logistics. Logistics in Keirsey's definition (1998) is "procurement, distribution, service and replacement of material goods." It's the ability to ensure that everybody has the right thing at the right time and making it all come together. It involves working out the interrelationships and integrating all of the components.

Tactics. "Tactics is the art of making moves to better one's position, here and now" (Keirsey, 1998). Those who are strong on tactics have the ability to focus in and come up with the right move at the right time.

Understanding how different people communicate and how they go about getting things done enables you to get your message across better, appreciate what motivates them, and reduce conflict. For me, it was quite humbling to learn that my own temperament was not the only legitimate way of being. The table on page 469 highlights the characteristics of Keirsey's 4 major temperaments. Start here:

- *Idealist.* Idealists, who make up about 10 percent of the population (see the table), are cooperative in their use of tools and abstract in communication. They are big-picture people and lead followers to pursue great dreams. They thrive on people issues and gravitate toward the soft skills: conflict resolution, negotiation, team building, and facilitating.

- *Artisan.* Artisans make up about 40 percent of the population. The opposite of the Idealist, the Artisan communicates in concrete terms and is utilitarian (uncooperative) in the use of tools. Artisans dislike bureaucracy and abhor rules. As a result, very few are found in corporations. Their natural forte is tactics, turning strategy into action and with little regard for whose toes they step on. Their concrete, meaning direct, communication approach puts them in conflict with Idealists, who tend to tip-toe around the issue.

- *Guardian.* Guardians (45 percent of the population) are concrete in communication and cooperate with tools, preferring to use them for their intended purpose. Compliance with rules, policies, and procedures is of utmost importance to Guardians, along with meeting deadlines and budgets. Guardians are the stabilizers of the corporate world. Their strongest managerial intelligence is logistics, getting all the pieces to work together.

- *Rational.* Rationals, only 5 percent of the population, are the opposite of Guardians. They are abstract in their communication and utilitarian (uncooperative) in their use of tools, doing whatever works, including violating the rules, which puts them in direct conflict with the Guardian preservationist. Scientists, who tend to be Rationals, can't understand why management expects them to "come up with breakthroughs on a schedule." Rationals are the strategists who have a natural ability to come up with the game plan.

What Does This Mean to You?

It's important to understand that these are general patterns and that it's a mistake to use this or any other assessment to stereotype or pigeon-hole yourself or others. Nevertheless, we can make some general observations:

- Different temperaments are better suited to different aspects and different phases of a project. Idealists, with their people skills, are natural motivators, inspiring the team to pursue the great dream and managing the people side of the project. Rationals are good at setting strategy. Guardians are well suited to ensure that everything integrates, that people conform to the plan, and that all the documentation is in order. Artisans excel at getting the job done.
- There are inherent conflicts among the different temperaments, implying a need for the Idealist's talents for facilitating conflicts.
- Projects require a mix of all temperaments.
- The dominant temperament on a particular project will vary with the type of project. For instance, a construction project, where a building is being built to spec and adherence to the architect's design is of primary importance, might do best with a project manager who has strong Guardian skills. A project that requires a lot of creativity and discovery work might do better with the skills that the Rational project manager brings to the endeavor. These are the inventors, scientists, and engineers who are utilitarian (in this case, flexible) when it comes to adherence to plans. If a project is organizationally complex, meaning it cuts across multiple departments and may be politically sensitive, then a project manager with the Idealist's diplomatic skills will be important.

eXtreme projects are typically organizationally complex, requiring strong diplomatic skills, because the eXtreme project manager's work is relationship management. If I were picking an

Major Characteristics of the Four Temperaments

	Idealist (10%)	Artisan (40%)	Guardian (45%)	Rational (5%)
Famous people	Gandhi	Barbara Streisand	Mother Teresa	Bill Gates
Communication	Abstract	Concrete	Concrete	Abstract
Use of tools	Cooperative	Utilitarian	Cooperative	Utilitarian
Managerial intelligences: Strongest suits	Diplomacy, strategy	Tactics, logistics	Logistics, tactics	Strategy, diplomacy
Lesser suits	Logistics, tactics	Strategy, diplomacy	Diplomacy, strategy	Tactics, logistics
General orientation	Pursuit of great dreams	Master techniques, develop skills	Planning, structure	Science, experimentation, "bend nature"
Job role	Mentor, advocate, champion, healer	Promoter, crafter, entertainer	Administrator, conservator, protector	Coordinator, master-mind, engineer, inventor
Interest	Humanities, morale, personnel, communicating	Artcraft, technique, equipment	Commerce, morality, policy	Science, technology, systems, organisms
Focus	Morale, self-worth, self-image, respect, esteem, confidence, feelings	Perfection, quality	Budgets, deadlines, scheduling, record keeping, smooth operations	Economic, technical issues, logic

Note: Percentages refer to the total population.

Sources: Percentages come from Wysocki and Lewis (2001). Contents of the table derived from several sources, including www.keirsey.com, Kiersey (1984) and Lewis (2003).

eXtreme project manager, I'd lean toward the Idealist. I would want a good Rational to oversee the technical development side of the project, even if I were highly competent technically. I'd also like to have an Artisan to cut to the chase and get the job done when the going gets tough.

The person least suited for leading the eXtreme project (high change and politically sensitive) in my experience would be the Guardian. The Guardian's conformance to rules, policies, and procedures would put a discovery-oriented project in a straitjacket. But once the discovery had been made (or the problem solved) and all the major unknowns were ironed out, I'd look for a Guardian with good people skills to pull it off.

A project manager cannot be all things and do them sufficiently well. It's important that your strongest suit be congruent with the dominant temperament required by the project. That doesn't mean that if there is a mismatch, you will not succeed. Many do. But if the mismatch continues project after project, a malaise will set in, and the formula for self-misery will take over. And the project will be at risk.

Discovering Your Motivated Abilities

We may have numerous abilities, but not necessarily be motivated to use them. For instance, I can do a good job in putting together spreadsheets and crunching numbers, but I dislike doing it. For me, this is an unmotivated ability, something I do when I have little choice. We grow by building on our strengths and using our motivated abilities.

The Lewis Method
The process that Jim Lewis (2003) uses is simple and it works. You can use it to identify someone else's motivators, which is essential for influencing others or for identifying your own. (Good influencing skills are required for eXtreme project managers and are covered in Chapter Five.) The idea here is to uncover your pattern of activity, that is, the repetitive patterns that are woven throughout your life experiences. Here's how to do it:

1. Begin with a past job, Think of a past job or work experience within the past two years that you really enjoyed. Perhaps it's

one that you think back on from time to time. Ask yourself, "What role did I play?" "What activities did it involve that I liked doing?" Write them down. If you can't find something in the past two years (and I'm sorry to hear that), then go back in time until you hit on some job or aspect of a job that you really enjoyed. Include volunteer work if you'd like.

2. Think about a hobby or sport that you engage in—something active that you would do more of if you had the time. (Sedentary activities like lying on the beach or watching TV don't count.) For instance, I exercise, but it doesn't count because I wouldn't do more of it if I had the time.

I like playing tennis. When I ask myself what I like about this activity, I realize that I enjoy rallying: just hitting the ball back and forth. I can do this for hours for the sheer challenge and pleasure of perfecting my strokes. I also like teaching others what I've learned about how to hit the ball. I don't ever play matches because I don't like to compete (when it comes to tennis). Playing tennis reveals two of my key activity patterns: fine-tuning my skills and teaching. Notice that what's important is not the content of the activity (tennis) but the patterns associated with tennis.

3. Think about a fantasy. What's something that you always wanted to do but never got to it—perhaps working with kids, starting a food co-op, being a belly dancer, or hang gliding. Then probe. Probing is the key. Ask yourself, "What about it turns me on?" "At the outset, during, after?" Take hang gliding. The turn-ons might be taking risks, being on my own, minutely inspecting the apparatus for safety, being outdoors, telling other people about the experience. By cross-checking these turn-ons with others from the first two questions, a clear pattern will emerge.

4. Write down the recurring themes or patterns that run through you motivated abilities. When I did this for myself, I came up with this list:

- Working on very difficult projects
- Looking for groundbreaking ideas
- Making it possible for people to bring out the best in themselves
- Teaching
- Delivering unique presentations
- Writing

You can find out someone else's motivators by asking these same questions of them. You can do it formally or informally by asking the questions as part of a friendly conversation over coffee. Knowing what motivates enables you to link project work with what really excites people on the team. This is a big step in gaining and sustaining commitment to the mission of the eXtreme project and can give you a strong competitive advantage over projects that compete for the same people. (When asking these questions of others, refrain asking what the person likes about her current job. She may hate it.)

The SIMA Method

SIMA stands for System for Identifying Motivated Abilities. In the Lewis method, you ask yourself open-ended questions and do your own analysis. The SIMA method by People Management does all the work for you. You go on-line to www.sima-pmi.com and answer a series of multiple-choice questions. For twelve dollars, a report is e-mailed to you. If you want to go further, you can sign up for the full-blown MAP (Motivated Ability Pattern). I did this in 1983, and the results were so powerful that this information enabled me to reshape the job I had and later redirected my entire career.

The on-line report will give you insight into your motivated strengths and how these match up with your current job. You can use the results for your own edification as well as a basis to have a discussion with your boss about more closely aligning your job with your talents. Or perhaps you may be able to adjust your job to be a closer fit with who you really are.

The Power of Meditation

If there is one thing that is common to all eXtreme projects, it's stress. Even ten to twenty minutes of meditation can significantly reduce anxiety.

This is nothing new. Meditation has been practiced for thousands of years. The Vedic tradition alone of meditation has been traced back to 2000–3000 B.C. when it was described in Hindu texts. Previously left to faith, a substantial body of scientific evidence has been amassed to document the benefits of meditation—for example:

- Ability to manage pain
- Lower blood pressure
- Relief from depression
- Less stress in the face of common everyday disturbances, such as traffic jams and annoying people
- Less oxygen required
- Lowered heart rate
- Increased contentment
- Increased focus in the moment, leading to a better ability to respond

We are not our best when we are under constant stress. When that happens, our breathing gets shallow, and less oxygen reaches the brain. We end up operating on fewer cylinders, which impairs our ability to respond intelligently and creatively. This is in addition to the negative impact that continued stress can have on physical health.

Although there are many schools of meditation, you don't need to learn esoteric techniques to get the benefits. Find a quiet place, and relax by taking several deep breaths. Find a soothing word (*om* has worked for many) that you focus on, and repeat it over and over on your out breath. When your mind wanders, be gentle with yourself and simply return to your soothing word.

Alpha is a state of relaxation where your brain waves are slowed to about 10 cycles per second. You experience the alpha state when you are waking up from a deep sleep, having been in delta (unconscious sleep with brain waves from 0.5 to 4 cycles per second) or in theta (the zone of deep comfortable sleep with brain waves from 5 to 7 cycles per second).

When you are in the alpha state, you are relaxed and alert. You have the ability to concentrate and think clearly and are free from the anxiety characteristic of the beta state of heightened activity, where the mind is restless and flighty.

Here is the technique adapted from *Silva Mind Control* (Silva and Goldman, 1988). To get to your alpha state, where you do you best thinking, do the following. Go to a quiet place, and take several deep breaths to relax. Exhale slowly, counting 1, 2, 3 on each out breath. Visualize the numbers as you count them. Do this a few more times saying, "relax," slowly on each out breath. Then count down slowly from 10 to 1, visualizing each number. Feel yourself getting more relaxed.

Once you are in the alpha state, there are many possibilities. You can simply relax there and let stress dissipate, or pose a question and wait for the answer, or ponder a problem. Taking a few alpha breaks during the day will improve your performance.

Neutralizing Your Self-Defeating Beliefs

The Work is a process developed by Byron Katie for achieving a sense of inner peace. It enables the individual to investigate a disturbing thought and effectively diffuse of the power it holds over us. Doing The Work (Katie, 2002) consists of these steps:

1. Describe and write down the situation: descriptions of people, circumstances, events, or behavior patterns that cause you stress or frustration.
2. Identify the underlying beliefs.
3. Investigate each belief by asking the Four Questions: (1) Is it true? (2) Can you absolutely know that it is true? (3) How do you react when you think this thought? and (4) Who would you be without that thought?
4. Write turnaround sentences.

For the process to work, the exercise must first be done in writing. I'll use Jeff (not his real name) to give an example of how The Work works.

I was teaching a workshop in project team leadership at a client organization where a pervasive victim mentality prevailed. During the workshop, Jeff, a project manager in marketing, was particularly outspoken about not having what he needed from management to be successful: "We don't get the budget, the authority, the time frame, or the team members we need to get the job done."

I asked Jeff, "What if you were given a project and the CEO walked into your office and said this was an important undertaking. He then went on to ask you how much time you need." And you told him. Then he asked you, "How much budget will you need?" And then, "How many team members do you want, and who?" And you told him that as well. And then the CEO said, "You got it, and if you need more, just let me know." I then asked Jeff, "How would you feel about being in this situation?"

Jeff, without a pause, said, "I'd be scared."

When I asked him why, he replied, "I'd be exposed. I wouldn't have any excuses."

There is a built-in payoff for us when we believe, complain, or perpetuate the thought pattern that we do not have what we need to get the job done. Many project managers, including myself, have fallen into this trap. It's self-sabotage, resulting in a rationale for not making a commitment and ultimately for not being successful.

When this exchange took place, I asked Jeff's permission to work with him to investigate his underlying belief: "To lead a project, I need to have excuses to point to just in case I fail." This represented Jeff's uninvestigated belief.

When I asked Jeff to identify and describe the situation, he said, "If I'm given all the support I need, I will not have any excuse except to succeed."

Then Jeff identified a number of underlying beliefs:

"Management expects me to succeed when they give me everything I ask for."

"It's not possible to fail if you have all the people, the time, and the money."

"To lead a project, I need to have excuses to point to just in case I fail."

We decided to work with the last belief. When doing this exercise by yourself, it's very important to write down your answers. I did it verbally with Jeff, asking him each of the 4 Questions. Each question always refers to the one belief that is being investigated and not to any subsequent ones that come up in the process of asking the questions.

• Question 1. Is it true? "Yes," said Jeff. "I don't think it's possible to succeed 100 percent of the time. And when you don't, you need to be able to give a reason."

• Question 2: Can you *absolutely* know that it is true (meaning that to lead a project, you need to have an excuse in case it fails)? "Yes. I think so."

I asked, "Can you find an example of having failed at something and not having had to come up with an excuse?"

Jeff replied, "I once headed a project to launch a new snack food. The market test showed it wouldn't meet the volume requirements. My boss killed the project."

I asked, "Did you have to make any excuses?"

Jeff responded, "No. The market is the market."

• Question 3: How do you react when you think this thought? "I keep looking for reasons why we might fail. But that might also be good if I can eliminate the risk," said Jeff.

"Yes," I agreed. "How else do you react?"

Jeff explained, "I keep on top of people and tend to micromanage. I may also not ask for what I need to succeed, like more time or money."

"And what does that buy you?" I asked.

Jeff answered, "I guess it buys me the excuse I've been looking for. I could always say we didn't have the necessary time or funds."

• Question 4: Who would you be without that thought (and I am not asking you to drop that the thought)?

Jeff continued, "I wouldn't be acting defensively. I wouldn't be so worried all the time."

"And what else?" I probed.

Jeff continued, "I'd be more proactive in asking for what I need. I'd be more inclined to bring up and resolve all matters that need attention. Not save any, just in case I needed an out."

The turnarounds are essential. You do the turnarounds by rewriting your original belief statement. You can turn around the belief 180 degrees, as illustrated in the first sentence below. Another way of doing a turnaround is to substitute someone else's name for yours, as in sentence 2. When doing The Work on a particular person who is irritating you, come up with variations that substitute your name for his name. Also try varying the sentences by playing with the key words as illustrated, in the third and fourth examples. Try coming up with at least two turnarounds.

1. I don't need to have excuses if my project fails.
2. My boss needs to come up with excuses why my project failed.
3. In leading a project, I can find reasons to succeed.
4. My project can fail even if there are good reasons for it to succeed.

Having written out your turnarounds, ask yourself which of the statements is at least as true as or truer than your original belief statement.

When I asked Jeff, he replied that all four turnarounds were at least as true as or truer than the original belief. This was unusual. All it takes is one to begin to get out of the vise of the defeating belief.

To do this yourself, sit quietly and ask yourself which of the statements is at least as true as or truer than the original belief. Listen for the slightest twinges in your body or opening in your mind. Sometimes the internal reaction is delayed for a day or two, as when you finally get a joke someone told you. Doing The Work will never leave you worse off, and chances are you will be better off.

In transforming your belief, the goal is not necessarily to try to eliminate the thought itself. That is, Jeff may still have the thought that he needs to identify excuses, but the thought may no longer hold any power over him. It exists but is weakened or completely detoxified. The charge is gone. If it comes back, then what? Keep doing The Work on it.

"Yes We Can't": How to Say No

Rarely a day goes by on most projects when our ability to act assertively is not challenged. This is especially true when it comes to handling change requests that affect the project schedule, resources, scope, or risk.

Take this example. The sponsor of FasTrak, the new high-tech sneaker project, is a manager who outranks you by three levels. She invites you into her office and asks that your team incorporate a new feature into the sneaker, one that's sure to leave the competition (and you) in the dust. It's a ThickOmeter, a digital communication device that will tell the runner how much tread remains on the sole of the running shoe while simultaneously launching an e-mail that alerts the runner to the address of the nearest FasTrak shoe outlet.

The Price of Nice: Accepting the Insurmountable Opportunity

A can-do attitude can do you in. When the project sponsor says, "Jump!" the good soldier says, "How high?" on the way up. After all, we want to be team players, and get ahead in the organization. We want to be known as a "can-do" person and not get fired.

Call it the Good Soldier Syndrome. It's one of the biggest silent killers of projects. It means being a people pleaser, that is, satisfying someone else's needs at your own expense, being an order taker who is ready and willing to follow instructions or make commitments and set aside personal feelings, thoughts, or needs—in a word, self-sacrifice.

When you commit to something you (or the team) cannot handle, even if you succeed by heroic efforts to accomplish the feat, the expectation is now set that you can be counted on to keep pulling off small miracles, so more work is handed to you. This is a downward spiral. The pattern of escalating self-sacrifice leads to loss of self-esteem. As you take on more work, you eventually do a poor job, which makes you want to work that much harder, leading to burnout and even poorer results, which reinforces your lowered self-esteem. You may even get fired for lack of performance, which, paradoxically, is just what you wanted to avoid in the first place.

As a business proposition, saying yes when you need to say no puts the organization and profits at risk.

How to Be Assertive: Get "Nohow"

You can be a certified project management professional (PMP®) and hold a Ph.D. in project management, but unless you know how to say no, it doesn't mean anything. Jim Haggarty, a senior IT director, once told me, "Sometimes you just have to be able to say, 'Yes we can't.'"

Here are the steps followed by the most effective project leaders and team members:

1. Confirm the request by playing it back in your words.
2. Always take the time to analyze the impact.
3. Return with fact-based information—for example: "Yes, it can be done. It will add $500,000 to the project cost, take about four more months longer to complete, and add twelve dollars to the retail price of the running shoe. We won't be able to tell if the ThickOmeter really works until after the testing is completed, about two months from now. We run the risk of missing the Christmas selling season. We'll have to shift two people from the new Fleetfoot project, which could delay its start by up by two months."

4. Have alternatives and make a recommendation:

"An option would be to do minimal testing and save two months. That would raise the risk factor to about 50 percent where at least one out of ten pairs sold will be returned for malfunction."

"We could add the ThickOmeter to the next release of the shoe when we can do it more justice. That's our recommendation."

"This is your decision. If you believe the business case justifies this, we can move ahead."

5. Affirm your commitment: "We want the FasTrak Project to be a success. The team looks forward to working on the next release."

6. Accept the request (if all else fails): "Okay. We'll add the ThickOmeter with your understanding of its impact on the project schedule, cost, risk, retail pricing of the shoe, and the delayed start on the Fleetfoot project."

The table shows possible responses to the ThickOmeter request.

Possible Responses to the ThickOmeter Request

Passive Behavior	Aggressive Behavior	Assertive Behavior
Self-abuse (You win, I lose): "Yes, sir. Great idea. Wow. Let's go with it."	Abuse of others (I win, you lose): "Shove it. We've been barraged constantly with your change requests throughout the entire project." "Your committee continues to change direction and to be insensitive to the negative impacts these last-minute requests are creating."	Mutual respect for yourself and others: "Interesting idea. Right now, we're spread thin and other projects are at risk. Once I know the impact this will have on our schedule and budget, I'll get back to you with options and a recommendation for your final decision. I'll need forty-eight hours to do this."

Interpersonal Tools and Techniques

Developing Your Listening Skills

When people think of communication skills, they usually think of speaking and presentation skills and pay little attention to listening skills. We need both.

Practice Full Attention Listening

Are you taking in the whole story? This can be a real challenge because you have to turn off your own chatter to let in information. You know what I mean if you've ever listened to someone tell you a joke and your mind is going through its database and rehearsing in order to respond with a joke of your own. And you miss his punch line and laugh anyway.

Here is a comprehensive list of communications blocks to active listening adapted from *Messages: The Communications Skills Book* (1983), an excellent book on the essentials of communication by McKay, Davis, and Fanning. Read through the list below and pick out one or two that you need to work on the most. Then just concentrate on those few:

- Mind reading (trying to figure out what they are really saying because you distrust them)
- Comparing (them to you)
- Rehearsing (planning your comeback)
- Filtering (you listen for some things and not others to get just what you want to hear)
- Judging (prejudging the competence of the person based on appearances, ethnicity, or some other characteristic)
- Dreaming (mentally going off on your own agenda)
- Matching (continually referring to similar situations in your life)
- Advising (solving their problems on the fly)
- Sparring (debating and taking stands)
- Being right (going to lengths to discount anything that will make you look wrong)
- Derailing (shifting the subject)
- Placating (agreeing with everything they say).

The point is that if you are practicing these blocks, you are cutting yourself off from understanding what's important to them.

Practice Whole Person Listening

On an eXtreme project, since you are managing a complex web of relationships and information in a fast-paced setting, it's crucial to be able to know what people are really telling you. You have to listen for both the verbal and nonverbal cues. Don't limit your listening to the content, that is, just the words being said. Try to listen to the whole person. What other messages are coming through in the form of facial expressions, tone of voice, personal appearance, and general demeanor?

In citing the research of Albert Mehrabain, authors McKay, Davis, and Fanning (1983) point out that 93 percent of the total impact of a message comes from nonverbal cues; that is, cues other than the words themselves that are being used: 7 percent verbal (the words), 38 percent vocal (volume, pitch, pace, inflection), and 55 percent body movements (mostly facial expressions).

Body language is more important than the other two cues because it is often more believable. You ask the chief scientist on a project if the stability tests are proceeding according to schedule. Rather than look at you, he casts his eyes to the left, says, "Yes," and then puts his tongue between his nearly closed lips and moves it to the left corner of his mouth. What would you believe? What you are looking for is congruence between verbal and nonverbal cues.

Look for congruence in your own messages. If you have a burning idea that will save money, does your nonverbal communication lend credibility to what you say? For instance, if you timidly express your idea with your arms folded and glance downward while slouching in your chair, you've lost credibility.

If your project sponsor is telling you how important the project is but it's not reflected in his nonverbals, that's a big clue that you are will be hard-pressed to get his attention when you need his clout and answers to get things done. He'll have other priorities.

Know How to Match and Pace

"If you would win a man to your cause, first convince him that you are his friend," said Abraham Lincoln.

One of the most effective ways of establishing rapport and to influence people is to match and pace. People like people who are like themselves. Matching and pacing involves duplicating the person's body language and verbal expression. This puts you both on the same wavelength.

Body language includes facial expression, weight shifts, posture, breathing, gestures, pupil size, voice tone, pace, and pitch. If he is standing, you stand. If he is sitting with his legs crossed, you do the same. If he speaks slowly and softly, you match that. When he gets animated, so do you.

When you get accomplished at this, you can also learn if the person is auditory, visual, kinesthetic, or generic. By understanding the other person's modality, you can respond in like terms, enabling you to establish rapport. Listen for the other person's choice of words—for example:

Auditory: "I hear you." "Sounds good." "It rings a bell." "That resonates." "I'm all ears."

Visual: "I see what you mean." "I get the picture." "I envision it this way." "I don't like that image." "That's still foggy to me."

Kinesthetic: "I feel good about it." "I'm touched by what you have said." "That smells fishy to me." "What does your gut tell you?" "Hot idea." "Solid idea."

Generic: "My experience is . . ." "I understand." "I find that this is true." "I get it."

None of this is intended to be manipulation or patronization. It's relationship management and is the basis for getting the job done.

How to Motivate Someone

In the Discovering Your Motivated Abilities tool, I reviewed the Lewis process for uncovering your own motivators. The same process works to discover what motivates others.

It probably wouldn't be a good idea to stop a colleague in the hall and say, "Hey. Let's get together. I'd like to find out what your motivators are." More likely, you will broach the person in an informal, conversational way so as not to appear intrusive or patronizing. This is not about manipulation. It's a genuine attempt to unleash an individual's desire and commitment.

Here's how to go about this:

1. Pick a casual setting, perhaps lunch.

2. Come up with your own words and speak from your heart rather than your head or mind. This way you will come across in a genuine and sincere say. Here's how I'd say it: "Since you'll be playing an important role on this project, I want to be sure I do everything I can as the project manager to make it an enjoyable experience for you. Where possible, I'd like to incorporate those things into your work that give you the greatest satisfaction in the past. Is it okay that I ask you a couple of questions?"

If she says no, that's okay. At the very least, you're earned her respect just because you asked. Very few managers care enough to do this. The asking alone is likely to raise her level of motivation to want to be on the project and to go the extra mile. This is known as the Hawthorne effect, which was based on studies conducted in the 1920s by Elton Mayo, a Harvard University researcher. Mayo discovered that a worker's behavior changes and his productivity increases when people who are important to him take an interest in him.

If she says yes, you can ask her some questions and then ask the three key questions (which follow). In asking the questions, do so from your heart center rather than your head or mind so you will come across in a genuine and sincere way.

3. Ask the questions (these are virtually the same questions and guidelines as covered earlier in this section):

- Think of a job you had in the past that you really enjoyed. What role did you play? What activities did it involve that you like doing?
- What about a hobby that you enjoy? What is it that you like about it?
- What's something that you've always wanted to do but never got around to it?

4. Summarize the patterns. Go over what you learned. Review the patterns with your colleague and clarify your findings.

5. Collaborate to make it happen. This involves applying Accelerator 3: Create ownership for results. Brainstorm together, and identify ways in which her motivated strengths can be put to work. Let her have the lead role in deciding how what she enjoys can be used (with your help if necessary) to exploit her motivated strengths.

Using Winning Value Propositions in Negotiations

A great sales pitch that doesn't hit people where they live and breathe is a futile exercise. Crafting targeted value propositions is your doorway to successful negotiations.

As the name implies, a value proposition is a compelling benefit statement. It's built on the principle that you get what you want by showing the other person how that will get him what he wants. It's important that your value propositions not be idle, sound-great slogans. This is about your wanting to make a difference (Accelerator 3). You will back up your propositions with facts and rationale. The Shared Values that come into play when building value propositions are the people values of people first (you're walking in their shoes) and honest communication and the business values of results orientation and early value. The operative accelerator is, "Simplicity wins."

The more you know about the motivators of your audience, the more powerfully you can develop your value proposition. Once you know who the decision makers are, then:

- Identify their business motivators.
- Identify their personal motivators.
- Understand their temperaments.
- Build a powerful value proposition.

Here are the steps, spelled out.

Step 1: Identify Their Business Motivators

You're looking for this person's top one to three motivators. It could even be the one or two hot buttons that just came out of last week's management off-site meeting. Which of these are the motivators for the person you would like to influence? How can you show that what you want will help to satisfy one of her motivators?

Business motivators typically fall into these areas:

- Competition (market share, customer satisfaction)
- Financial viability
- Human development
- Risk mitigation

- Quality (price-performance, product benefits)
- Schedule (time to market, time to profit)
- Shareholder value
- Legal (regulatory compliance, lawsuit avoidance)

Step 2: Identify Personal Motivators

Personal motivators reflect an individual's management style and temperament. These include:

- Job (security, advancement, rewards)
- Looking good (recognition, peer acceptance, industry leadership)
- Risk tolerance (conservative, aggressive, early adopter)
- Efficiency (quick, easy, cost effective)
- Effectiveness (reliability, performance)
- Management style (controlling, consensus builder, delegator)
- Focus (short term, long term)

Step 3: Understand Their Temperaments

This takes us back to the Keirsey temperament styles I covered in Self-Mastery Tools and Techniques. Use your observational powers to understand what managerial intelligences to appeal to: diplomatic (big picture), strategic, logistical, or tactical. An excellent way of walking a mile in the shoes of your sponsor is to imagine you were to play his role in the annual company skit. What would you say and do as you lived out your experience of him?

Step 4: Build a Powerful Value Proposition

Constructing a value proposition involves linking what you want to the other person's motivators. For example, if you need more staff, then show how that can help your sponsor satisfy one of her motivators. Although you need only one good value proposition, if you can string together both a business and a personal value proposition, all the better. Say that you're heading the project to launch a new over-the-counter liquid to cure head lice. In order to meet the deadline, you calculate that you will need more staff. You figure it will take the addition of three full-time-equivalents for eight months for a total cost of $240,000. The table on page 486 shows examples of value propositions that you might build if your project sponsor were any one of the managers in the table.

Value Propositions Based on Business and Personal Motivators

Project Sponsor	Vice President, Drug Development	Director, Global Delivery	CEO
Business motivator	Minimize adverse reaction to the drug	Penetrate multiple markets	Improve profitability
Value proposition	The additional staff will enable us to produce a more fully tested product	The increased staff will improve the odds that we can launch in all three developing countries	Every week that we are not in the market costs us an estimated $250,000 in profits. The increased staff will pay for itself if we save just one week.
Personal motivators	Low tolerance for risk, Tight controls	Peer recognition	Short-term focus
Temperament	Detail oriented	Big picture	Strategy
Value proposition	We will have a better chance of passing FDA scrutiny	This will put us in contention to receive one of the coveted global achievement awards for humanitarianism in 2006 at the Drug Information Association Conference	This supports our strategy of being an early bird in our key targeted markets

Facilitation Skills

The Do's and Don'ts of Leading the Virtual Team

*Debbie Duarte**

Being the project manager of a virtual team has its own special challenges and success factors: there's more to it than being good at running virtual team meetings.

The leader of a virtual team requires taking an active role in the team's formation and its ongoing development. This is particularly critical during the team start-up phase, when it is the leader who is responsible for forming the team, establishing its communication protocol, team norms and presenting its success criteria. One of the greatest myths around leading a virtual project team is that because the team is virtual, team members don't need attention, coaching and guidance. The challenge of the virtual team leader is to actively balance the advantages of leveraging remote resources and the autonomy of virtual team members with ensuring that team members feel connected to the project, included in decision making, valued and "in sync" with the rest of the team.

Throughout the lifecycle of a virtual team, the leader plays many important roles. Below are listed some of the vital activities and dos and don'ts for virtual team leaders.

1. Team Start-Up

Do focus on defining the direction, objectives and roles for team members as well as development of team norms for working across time and distance. Do not assume because the team is virtual that they do not need direction and guidance. Do not email team objectives, project plans and norms or just send people to a web site to read about the project. Don't kick off the team over a teleconference or a video conference. Do ask for a face-to-face kick off session to define objectives, roles and team norms. This might be the most important thing you do as a virtual team leader. During team start-up do:

- Provide definition and direction of team tasks and objectives.
- Provide clarity and focus for team objectives.

---

*Duarte is the coauthor (with N. T. Snyder) of *Mastering Virtual Teams* (1999).

- Solicit input from the team regarding objectives and roles.
- Share information regarding team's purpose, politics, challenges, etc.
- Define team output measures and critical success factors: outputs as well as team process measures.
- Define how teams will operate across time and distance including team norms for working together and using technology including norms for availability, acknowledgement, use of technology, email etiquette, and norms for conflict management.

2. Development

Do focus on development of team skills and adequate resources for team performance. Do not assume that team members will have the skills and resources to do their job or to use technology appropriately. Do conduct an "audit" of team skills that focuses on team members' ability to communicate and work remotely, use technology as well as their access to important information sources related to the project. Do:

- Provide process recommendations that help the team define the ways to accomplish its tasks that assure full team involvement. This might include norms for keeping others informed, norms for reviewing others' work and norms for communicating progress and problems.
- Emphasize developing team capability in remote decision-making, problem solving and effectiveness. After team sessions review how well the team did in making decisions, sharing information and solving problems.
- Provide a direct linkage to information sources that the team needs.
- Provide a direct linkage to sources of power and resources in the organization such as access to senior management, etc.
- Provide a direct linkage to expertise that team members might need.
- Set logistics and team meeting agendas. Make sure that all team meetings have agendas and that minutes are distributed within 24 hours.
- Provide training for team members if they need it in areas related to project management, using technology and virtual teaming.

- Do pay attention to team members' career development. Project team members need your attention even if you do not see them every day.

3. Performance

Effective virtual team leaders focus on ensuring that there are ongoing information exchanges and resources among team members. Working virtually can lead to working too autonomously. The virtual team leader needs to pay strict attention to making it a requirement that team members share information. Make sharing and access to resources a key part of your role. Do:

- Provide resources the team needs to further its performance. This could be information, access to management and access to customers. You are often the broker of this type of resource exchange.
- Emphasize challenging the team to stretch itself.
- Receive and act on information from the team. Do act on information once you receive it from team members. You lose your credibility if you do not respond to team input, even if you choose not to use it. Time and distance make this worse rather than better.

4. Conclusion

Do focus on celebrating achievement and transitioning team members when appropriate. Do:

- Provide a review and celebration of achievements, even if you have to conduct these remotely over video conference.
- Help team members make the transition off the team to their next assignment.
- Emphasize what the team learned from the experience. Conduct lessons learned sessions with the team on a regular basis.
- Seek to share learning with other teams.

Six Essential Facilitation Techniques

Two of the simplest yet most powerful but misused and underused facilitation techniques are brainstorming and the T. Both go a long way in coming up with new ideas and reaching a decision.

Brainstorming

The purpose of brainstorming is to get as many ideas out in the open as possible. Only then does the group narrow the list. The problem is that people tend to be critical and interrupt the free flow of ideas before all of them get out in the open. This stifles creativity and frustrates group members. As a reminder, here are the rules of brainstorming, which I suggest you announce each time:

- No idea is a bad idea.
- Get as many ideas out as possible.
- Don't stop to assess until all ideas are out.

To capture the ideas, hand out large sticky notes and markers. Let everyone do the writing and then have them post the notes on flip charts.

Reverse Brainstorming

One of my favorite brainstorming techniques is reverse barnstorming. Let's say you have a project to improve customer service for telephone sales. You can generate a lot of ideas by starting the session as follows: "Let's say we wanted to create the worst possible customer experience when they call in—an experience so bad that they would never want to do business with us again and also tell their friends how lousy we are. What could we do to make this possible?"

When you do this, the group is likely to be amazed at how many worst practices are already going on. This is also a very cathartic exercise in that it makes it safe for people to say things they may normally keep to themselves.

Once you complete your reverse brainstorming, remember to reverse all the negative ideas. These become your potential solutions to improve the customer experience.

The T

This is a focusing technique that ends endless debates and produces a better-quality decision. Set up a T for each item under debate. Then have the group brainstorm the pros and cons, and list them on either side of the T. I'm always amazed how the preferred choice becomes obvious with little need for further discussion.

Weighted Voting Technique

The purpose is to rank-order a list of options based on the number of points each option receives.

Each voter is given a certain number of votes and points that they can allocate to the items being considered. For instance, in voting on a list of eight items, have each voter pick his or her top three choices. Tell the voters that when it comes time to vote, to give a value of three points to their favorite item, two points to their second choice, and just one point to their third choice. Go down the list of items. Have each voter hold up one to three fingers to indicate the number of points they decided to give to their top choices.

If you have a list of ten or more items, give voters a proportional number of more votes and points to use. For a list of eighteen items, for example, give them six votes for their first choice down to one point for their last choice.

Tally the vote (the points) for each of the items.

Gate Opening

For any number of reasons, certain group members will say little or remain silent, yet they may have information and ideas that can move decisions ahead. To encourage full participation and buy-in for ideas, be aware of the quiet ones. A gentle gate-opening phrase I use often is, "Francisco, we haven't heard from you on this one . . ." Or, "Tamara, what data might marketing have that could shed light on the subject?"

Gate Closing

Sometimes it's tempting to want to say, "Shut up, will you?" Since that is likely to backfire, a more gentle approach is to say, "Yes, we've heard from you on that one. I'd like to hear from others as well." Or, "I'm getting a little lost here. Would you please summarize your key points for us?"

The 4A Model for Dealing with Feelings

Having been a professional facilitator for fourteen years, I can tell you that the most important skill I have is to be able to deal openly and effectively with feelings in a group situation. On eXtreme projects, your team is almost guaranteed to encounter situations that stir strong emotions. In these situations, saying, "Let's put our feelings aside," is almost always the wrong thing. When feelings prevail, it's fruitless and counterproductive to attempt to move forward and expect the group to bang out meeting work products in the interest of keeping to task and schedule.

Here's the approach I use in dealing with a group or several members who have moved into the feelings domain. I call it the 4A model (for attitude, awareness, acknowledgment, and adjustment).

Attitude

First and foremost, I maintain an attitude that feelings expressed are one of the most valuable gifts to the project. Understanding what's behind someone's anger, fear, frustration, or doubts can reveal risks that can be addressed and barriers that need to be broken for progress to take place. I don't look at the facilitation of a group's feelings as a defensive but rather a proactive skill that can unearth opportunities.

Awareness

Be continually on the lookout to detect if the group or one or more members has moved into the feelings stage around a particular issue. Here, you need to make a judgment and decide if the issue is such that it requires processing. Awareness also means to tune into your own feelings and biases about the topic.

Acknowledgment

When the strong feelings surface, use your reflective listening skills (see Chapter Five) as a way of letting the group or individual know that you recognize he has strong feelings about the subject.

Ask each member to express his or her feelings on the topic. Your role is to reflect but not to evaluate the feelings. Use the whole person listening technique, tuning into both verbal and body language, reflecting back key words as well as an appropriate level of the emotional content: "I hear that you are continually held back by our policy to get three approvals before you can select a vendor." Capture the concern on a flip chart so that it is visibly acknowledged.

If you are the person with a strong feeling on the subject, it's okay to share it. But in doing so, you want to state publicly, "I am stepping out of my role as facilitator for a moment, . . ." and then state your view on the subject. Unless you take off your facilitator's hat momentarily, you will lose your objectivity and credibility. Having stated your own feeling or opinion, go back into the facilitator role. The key point here is that as facilitator, you want to preserve the integrity of your role by standing on the side of the pool and not get drowned in the turbulent emotional waters.

At times you may find that the issues polarize people into two or more subgroups. In that case, have each group prepare a page or two on the flip chart listing their concerns and providing summary statement.

In situations where individuals may feel at risk by stating their feelings (perhaps fear of reprisal by a senior manager in the meeting), break the group into small subgroups, instructing them to prepare a statement and list of concerns on a flip chart.

Adjustment

The last step is to come to resolution. Take sixty seconds of silence for people to calm down by asking them to reflect on their feelings and how strongly they hold their views on the topic. Here, I have found that in about half of the situations, there is no further need for processing the feelings. That is, people are satisfied that they have been heard and to know that they have been understood and are not alone in their concerns. When further processing is necessary, your job is to have the group identify the priority items and identify action items to resolve the issues.

Project Management Tools

Creating a Compelling Value Proposition for Being a Dedicated Project Manager

If you find that you are headed to be both the project manager and the technical-development manager on the same project, then your most important task is to make the case for being a dedicated project manager. Timing is important. The best time to do this at the end of the Visionate cycle or, at the latest, at the end of Speculate. At that point, the project is further defined; that is, you'll be able to answer Business Question 2: What will it take? giving you the information and facts that you will need to build your case.

The guiding principle here is to demonstrate how what you want will give the person you want to influence what she wants.

Here are the steps:

1. Know your outcome. "I want to be freed up to be the dedicated project manager" and "I want a technical-development manager assigned to the project."

2. Describe the realities. Establish that "we" have an eXtreme project on our hands. Do this by using the facts from the scoping and planning meetings in order to summarize why the project is eXtreme: the degree to which it is high speed, high change, highly complex (technically or organizationally), high risk, or high stakes (in terms of business outcome).

Point out the other projects that your project depends on and the need for you to coordinate these interdependencies. Point out that the pace of the project will require that you spend time securing decisions and feedback from crucial stakeholders in order to keep the momentum going.

3. Draw conclusions. Given these realities, a dedicated project manager is needed in order to:

- Focus on continually interfacing with key stakeholders
- Keep on top of dependencies of other projects
- Prevent and contain risks
- Provide project management oversight including the management and tracking of scope, budget, and business benefits and risks
- Coordinate with remote teams

4. Create the value proposition. Now that you have amassed compelling evidence, the next step is to turn it into a compelling value proposition by understanding your sponsor's motivators and incorporating these in the four-step model covered earlier in this chapter. This involves showing how having a development or technical manager on board will enable you to concentrate on doing things that will make it more possible for you to achieve your sponsor's Win Conditions.

You can also supplement your case by using referential power: Cite this book as a third-party source and point to the job description of the eXtreme project manager that I already gave you.

Calculating Present Value

Present value (PV) is a way of recognizing that future dollars are worth less than today's dollars. In calculating PV, all future benefits and costs are discounted back to today's dollars. This provides a common baseline for comparing costs and returns over time. The formula for computing PV is:

$$PV = FV/(1 + r)^n,$$

where FV = future value, r = discount rate, and n = the future year. The discount rate is the percentage amount that is used to reduce future dollars back to today's dollars. It recognizes that \$2,500 five years from now is worth less than the same amount today. For example, PV = \$2,500/$(1 + .08)^5$ = 2,500/1.469 = 1,700 (net revenues in present value).

The discount rate, determined by the organization, can be based on the cost of borrowing or raising money or some other agreed-on value of reference.

Here is the formula for calculating the percentage return on investment (ROI):

[Total revenues – total costs]/Total costs × 100.

References

Brooks, F. P. Jr. *The Mythical Man Month*. Reading, Mass.: Addison-Wesley, 1995.

Buckingham, M., and Clifton, D. *Now, Discover Your Strengths*. New York: Free Press, 2001.

Cooper, R. G. *Winning at New Products*. Cambridge, Mass.: Perseus, 2001.

Covey, S. R. *The Seven Habits of Highly Effective People*. New York: Simon & Schuster, 1989.

DeMarco, T., and Lister, T. *Peopleware*. New York: Dorset House, 1999.

Drucker, P. "Management's New Paradigms." *Forbes*, Oct. 5, 1998.

Duarte, D. L., and Snyder, N. T. *Mastering Virtual Teams*. San Francisco: Jossey-Bass, 1999.

Esque, T. J. *No Surprises Project Management*. Mill Valley, Calif.: Act Publishing, 1999.

Fisher, R., Ury, W., and Patton, B. *Getting to Yes*. New York: Penguin Books, 1983.

Frankel, V. *Man's Search for Meaning*. New York: Touchstone, 1984.

Gioia, L., Milleman, M., and Pascale, R. *Surfacing the Edge of Chaos*. New York: Three Rivers Press, 2001.

Goldradt, E. *Critical Chain*. Great Barrington, Mass.: North River Press, 1997.

Goleman, D., Boyatzis, R., and McKee A. *Primal Leadership*. Boston: Harvard Business School Press, 2002.

Greenhouse, S. "Americans' International Lead in Hours Worked Grew in the 90s, Report Shows." *New York Times*, Sept. 1, 2001.

Grey, J. *Men Are from Mars. Women Are from Venus*. New York: HarperCollins, 1997.

Highsmith, J. A. *Adaptive Software Development*. New York: Dorset House, 2000.

Highsmith, J. A. *Agile Software Development Ecosystems*. Reading, Mass.: Addison-Wesley, 2002.

Highsmith, J. *Agile Project Management*. Reading, Mass.: Addison-Wesley, 2004.

Hock, D. "Institutions in the Age of Mindcrafting." Paper presented at the 1994 Bionomics Annual Conference, San Francisco, 1994.

Hoff, R. *I Can See You Naked.* Kansas City, Mo.: Andrews and McMee, 1992.

Howell, G., and Koskela, L. "Reforming Project Management: The Role of Lean Construction." Paper presented at the Eighth Annual Conference of the International Group for Lean Construction, Brighton, England, July 17-19, 2000.

Huse, E. F. *The Modern Manager.* St. Paul, Minn.: West Publishing, 1979.

Katie, B. *Loving What Is.* New York: Harmony Books, 2002.

Katzenbach, J. R., and Smith, D. K. *The Wisdom of Teams: Creating the High-Performance Organization.* Boston: Harvard Business School Press, 1993.

Kayser, T. A. *Mining Group Gold.* El Segundo, Calif.: Serif Publishing, 1990.

Keirsey, D. *Please Understand Me II.* Del Mar, Calif: Prometheus Nemesis Book Company, 1998.

Keirsey, D., and Bates, M. *Please Understand Me: Character and Temperament Styles.* Del Mar, Calif: Prometheus Nemesis, 1984.

Kelley, T. *The Art of Innovation.* New York: Doubleday, 2001.

Kroeger, O., and Thuesen, J. *Type Talk at Work.* New York: Delacorte Press, 1992

Kuhn, T. *The Structure of Scientific Revolutions.* Chicago: University of Chicago Press, 1996.

Levine, H. *Practical Project Management: Tactics, Tips, and Tools.* New York: Wiley, 2002.

Lewis, J. P. *Team-Based Project Management.* New York: AMACOM, 1997.

Lewis, J. P. *Project Leadership.* New York: McGraw-Hill, 2003.

McConnell, S. *Rapid Development.* Redmond, Wash.: Microsoft Press, 1996.

McGregor, D. *The Human Side of Enterprise.* New York: McGraw-Hill, 1985.

McKay, M., Davis, M., and Fanning, P. *Messages: The Communications Skills.* Oakland, Calif.: New Harbinger Publications, 1983.

Packard, V. *The Pyramid Climbers.* New York: McGraw-Hill, 1962.

Peters, T. *The Project 50.* New York: Knopf, 1999.

Prigogine, I. *The End of Certainty.* New York: Free Press, 1997.

Schnarch, D. *Passionate Marriage: Keeping Love and Intimacy Alive in Committed Relationships.* New York: Holt, 1998.

Schrage, M. *Serious Play.* Boston: Harvard Business School Press, 2000.

Sher, B. *Wishcraft.* New York: Ballantine Books, 1979.

Silva, J., and Goldman, B. *The Silva Mind Control Method of Mental Dynamics.* New York: Pocket Books, 1988.

Sisgold, S. *Consciously Creating Your Life the Way You Want It.* Corte Madera, Calif.: On Dream Publications, 1993.

Stacey, R. D. *Managing the Unknowable.* San Francisco: Jossey-Bass, 1992.

Tarnow, T. *Thirteen Easy Steps to Implement Project Management into a Financial Firm.* Proceedings of the Project Management Institute Annual Seminars and Symposium, Austin, Tex., Sept. 7-16, 2000.

Thomsett, R. *Radical Project Management.* Upper Saddle River, N.J.: Prentice Hall, 2002.

Thorp, J., and DMR Center for Strategic Leadership. *The Information Paradox.* New York: McGraw-Hill, 1998.

Weinberg, G. M. *The Secrets of Consulting.* New York: Dorset House, 1985.

Weinberg, G. M. *On Becoming a Technical Leader.* New York: Dorset House, 1986.

Weinberg, G. M. *Quality Software Management,* Vol. 4: *Anticipating Change.* New York: Dorset House, 1997.

Wheatley, M. J. *Leadership and the New Science.* San Francisco: Barrett-Koehler, 1992.

Williamson, M. *A Return to Love.* New York: HarperCollins, 1992.

Wolf, A. *Mind into Matter: A New Alchemy of Science and Spirit.* Portsmouth, N.H.: Moment Point Press, 2000.

Wysocki, R. K., and Lewis, J. P. *The World Class Project Manager.* Cambridge, Mass.: Perseus, 2001.

Yourdon, E. *Death March.* Upper Saddle River, N.J.: Prentice Hall, 1997.

Zukav, G. *The Dancing Wu Li Masters: An Overview of the New Physics.* New York: Bantam Books, 1979.

Index